450

THE ITALIAN ECONOMY

Donald C. Templeman

PRAEGER

PRAEGER SPECIAL STUDIES • PRAEGER SCIENTIFIC

Library of Congress Cataloging in Publication Data

Templeman, Donald C
    The Italian Economy

    Bibliography: p.
    Includes index.
    1. Italy--Economic conditions--1976-
2. Italy--Economic policy. I. Title.
HC305.T357   330.945'0927   80-23478
ISBN 0-03-057612-1

Published in 1981 by Praeger Publishers
CBS Educational and Professional Publishing
A Division of CBS, Inc.
521 Fifth Avenue, New York, New York 10017 U.S.A.

© 1981 by Praeger Publishers

123456789   145   987654321

Printed in the United States of America

To my mother, whose support and encouragement
followed me to Italy and home again.

FOREWORD

Each national economy differs in numerous important respects
from every other. This is true even among the so-called large,
Western, mixed economies. Such differences reflect, of course,
each nation's peculiar endowment of natural resources, along with
the quantity, nature, and quality of its labor supply and accumulated
capital. They also reflect each country's particular governmental
structure, historical evolution, dominant political ideology, and economic and social institutions. Relevant institutions surely include
each country's educational, political, and legal systems; the existence, cohesion, and attitudes of its social classes; the structure of
its labor organizations and its traditional labor practices; the attitudes of its public toward risk taking, work and leisure, consumption
and saving, foreign ideas, the nature and content of a "good life";
and the many, many, other economic, social, and political institutions and patterns of behavior that make countries different.

Economists who wish to understand economic events abroad—
if only in order better to evaluate the impact of the other economies
on their own—will often reach mistaken judgments unless they appre-
ciate the sometimes subtle but always important ways in which the
foreign society and economy differ from their own, and the implica-
tions of these differences for the economic outcomes in which they
are interested.

There are other important reasons, however, for studying
foreign economies. I regard as perhaps the most important contribution of my own study of foreign economies (the two that I know best
being the Italian and the Japanese) the improved understanding that I
think this has given me of my own economy. Most economic ideas,
arguments, and principles are framed by U.S. economists in terms
that imply their universal applicability, under a wide variety of
American situations. Yet when one studies another economy carefully enough, it is quite often discovered that one or another such
principle does not hold there, or holds with significant variation or
exception. In seeking to understand the reasons, one is led to think
more critically about the application of that principle to one's own
economy, and may better understand why and how—and to what
extent—the principle really applies at home.

For twenty-five years I have regarded the Italian economy as
one of the most interesting for an economist to study. Many of the
problems experienced by other Western mixed economies turn up in

exaggerated form in Italy. For example, one can learn much about the nature and variety of inflationary problems (and about public policies and private practices to use or to avoid) by studying Italian inflation. One can learn much about the contribution of money and capital markets and the requirements for their success by studying that country where capital markets are very much less developed (in many respects) than our own, and where the central bank has therefore been forced to use a variety of unconventional instruments to deal with emerging problems. One can learn much about the dynamics of enterprise by studying the small firms of Prato or the rural Veneto, the merchants of fourteenth-century Florence or Venice, a moribund current giant like Montedison, or any or all of the nationalized firms that make up the IRI collection. One can learn a lot about exchange rates by watching the Banca d'Italia and the Treasury manipulate the foreign operations of Italian banks and the foreign borrowings of state enterprises. One can learn a great deal about regional economic development by studying the Italian Mezzogiorno and the effects of the policies designed to temper or to eliminate its gross underdevelopment. One can learn a lot about retail banking simply by maintaining an account in an Italian bank. And so on.

With so much to learn, it seems a pity that language problems have closed off most U.S. economists from a careful study of so interestingly different an economy as Italy's. To be sure, several Italian journals are published in English—of which the best is the Banca Nazionale del Lavoro Quarterly Review. Few of its articles, however, deal with the Italian economy. Only a handful of English-speaking economists have learned enough Italian to read national sources, or have gone there to study the Italian economy and to write about it in English. This limited group includes Vera Lutz, Hollis Chenery, George Hildebrand, Charles Kindleberger, Franco Modigliani (a special case), Robert Stern, and in a modest way, myself. Only the British Allen and Stevenson have attempted to write a recent organized and rounded treatment.

Now Donald Templeman has added greatly to our store of detailed knowledge—and particularly to our up-to-date, quantitative, and institutional knowledge—of the recent and current situation. The Italians produce reams of statistics, but great care is required in using them (as with any statistical series) unless one is very clear about the concepts the data purport to measure. Official or literal translations are often highly misleading. Templeman knows the Italian economy as well as any American; he here tells us what he knows, and he gives us an abundance of relevant and well-annotated data to support it.

Donald Templeman is a member of a small and specialized elite corps of civil servants that is not well known even to many who are quite expert in governmental affairs. Its members are responsible for analyzing and reporting on economic and financial developments in foreign economies, and for maintaining close contacts with ministries of treasury or finance, central banks, and other important official and private economic institutions. Like Foreign Service officers, members of this corps rotate between home assignments in the Department of Treasury's Washington Office of International Affairs, and service as Treasury attachés abroad, where they are housed in U.S. Embassies, working closely with the economic affairs officers of the embassy and, on important economic and financial problems, with the office of the ambassador. Donald Templeman was not Treasury attaché while I was U.S. ambassador to Italy (although I knew two of his predecessors very well). I became acquainted with him during a year of private residence in Italy in 1976–77, and learned from him many things that I did not know about the Italian economy.

Mr. Templeman has here assembled an enormous volume of relevant facts and figures, along with explanations of institutional arrangements and analyses of policy implementation in Italy, which provide a basic background for understanding the Italian economy and assessing its future prospects. I am delighted to have the opportunity to recommend his book to my fellow economists.

Gardner Ackley

Henry Carter Adams University
Professor of Political Economy
The University of Michigan

PREFACE

This book presents a case history of Italian economic problems in the 1970s and the policy response to those problems. It has two main parts: a discussion of the evolution of economic institutions, economic policy tools, and economic trends in the 1970s, and an assessment of the management of economic policy by the Italian authorities. The book progresses logically to discuss the rising labor costs and growing budget deficits that were the main domestic sources of economic problems; to include reference to exogenous factors, especially the commodity boom and the oil price rises of the middle and late 1970s; to outline the effect of these factors on growth, income, employment, inflation, and the balance of payments; to review monetary developments, especially monetary policy accommodation to domestic and foreign cost-push factors and the key role played by the public sector deficit in monetary expansion; and to analyze the specific ways in which the authorities responded to economic problems through the use of fiscal, monetary, exchange control, exchange rate, and wage and price policies.

The book is not a theoretical or econometric work. Rather, it attempts to present the way in which policy makers responded to real-world problems within a set of institutional constraints. Of particular interest to an outside observer are Italian economic developments in some areas where experimentation has gone farther than in most other industrial economies and where foreigners may be able to learn something from the Italian experience. Specific examples include wage indexation, the growth of social insurance expenditures, the transformation of the budget into a vehicle for redistributing income through transfer payments, the financing difficulties encountered by local governments and other state bodies and the expanding role of the central government as a financial intermediary, the relative decline in business profits and in productivity growth, the rise of youth unemployment, the growth of job security and labor immobility, the existence of a dual labor market (open and underground), the erosion of current income and accumulated savings due to rapid inflation, the question of periodic balance-of-payments problems due in part to repeated oil price increases by the Organization of Petroleum Exporting Countries (OPEC) cartel, and the difficulty of making the traditional, and even innovative, economic policy tools work in such an environment.

ACKNOWLEDGMENTS

I would like to express my gratitude to my colleagues at the Treasury Department, C. Fred Bergsten, F. Lisle Widman, and Donald E. Syvrud, who made it possible for me to write this book by supporting my request for a Federal Executive Fellowship at the Brookings Institution. Also at the Treasury, Robert L. Harlow and William W. Nye provided comments on several chapters of the book, which were very welcome. At Brookings, Robert W. Hartman and Walter S. Salant were kind enough to review several chapters and provide helpful suggestions. Hans Schmitt and Teresa Ter-Minassian of the International Monetary Fund and Raymond Lubitz of the Federal Reserve Board also made very useful comments.

I am particularly grateful to a large number of officials of Italian institutions, especially Franco Diotallevi of the Central Statistical Institute (ISTAT), Paolo Savona of Confindustria, and former Governor Paolo Baffi of the Bank of Italy and Director Antonio Fazio of the Research Office for help both on matters of fact and on understanding various aspects of Italian economic developments. Finally, I would like to thank Ciro De Falco and his colleagues in the Office of the Treasury Attaché in the American Embassy in Rome and Erik Floyd in the Treasury in Washington for their assistance in providing me with current data and for acting as liaison with Italian institutions. Carolyn Barbour, my former secretary, provided her usual patient and efficient services in helping to prepare the manuscript.

Any errors in the text of the book are, of course, the responsibility of the author. Also, all the views expressed in this book are those of the author and do not represent the views of the U.S. Treasury Department or of the U.S. government.

CONTENTS

PART I: ECONOMIC INSTITUTIONS
AND ECONOMIC TRENDS

Chapter

PART II: THE USE OF ECONOMIC POLICIES

LIST OF TABLES

LIST OF FIGURES

LIST OF ACRONYMS

ANAS	Azienda Nazionale Autonoma delle Strade Statali (state superhighway agency)
BOT	Buoni ordinari del tesoro (treasury bills)
BTP	Buoni del Tesoro poliennali (multiyear treasury bonds)
CAP	Common Agricultural Policy (of the EC)
Cassa	Cassa per il Mezzogiorno (Fund for the South)
Cassa DD.PP.	Cassa Depositi e Prestiti (Postal Savings Fund)
Cassa Integrazione	Cass Integrazione dei Guadagni (Wage Supplement Fund)
CCT	Certificati di credito del Tesoro (variable interest rate treasury certificates)
CGIL	Confederazione Generale Italiana del Lavoro (Communist/Socialist-led labor confederation)
CICR	Comitato Interministeriale per il Credito e il Risparmio (Interministerial Credit and Savings Committee)
CIP	Comitato Interministeriale Prezzi (Interministerial Price Committee)
CIPE	Comitato Interministeriale per la Programmazione Economica (Interministerial Committee for Economic Planning)
CIPI	Comitato Interministeriale per il Coordinamento della Politica Industriale (Interministerial Committee for Coordination of Industrial Policy)
CIS	Credito Industriale Sardo (Sardinian Industrial Credit Fund)
CISL	Confederazione Italiana dei Sindacati dei Lavoratori (Christian-Democrat-led labor confederation)
Confagricultura	Confederazione Generale del Agricultura Italiana (General Confederation of Italian Agriculture)
Confcommercio	Confederazione Generale Italiana del Commercio e del Turismo (General Confederation of Italian Commerce and Tourism)
Confindustria	Confederazione Generale dell' Industria Italiana (General Confederation of Italian Industry)
COL	Cost of living
CONSOB	Commissione Nazionale per le Società e la Borsa (National Commission for Corporations and the Stock Exchange)
CNR	Consiglio Nazionale di Ricerche (National Research Council)

CPP	Comitati Provinciali di Prezzi (Provincial Price Committees)
CREDIOP	Consorzio di Credito per le Opere Pubbliche (Credit Consortium for Public Works)
EC	European Community
EFIM	Ente di Partecipazioni e Finanziamento Industria Manifatturiera (state holding and finance company for the manufacturing industry)
EGAM	Ente Autonomo di Gestione per le Aziende Minerarie Metallurgiche (metallic minerals holding company)
EIB	European Investment Bank (of the EC)
EMS	European Monetary System (of the EC)
ENEL	Ente Nazionale di Energia Elettrica (national electric company)
ENI	Ente Nazionale di Idrocarburi (national petroleum company)
FEOGA	Fondo Europeo di Orientamento e di Garanzia Agricola (European agricultural fund)
FINSIDER	Finanziara Siderugica (financial holding company for steel industry)
FS	Ferrovie dello Stato (state railways)
GDP	Gross domestic product
GEPI	Società per la Gestione e Partecipazioni Industriali (state industrial management and holding company)
GFI	Gross fixed investment
ICE	Istituto di Commercio Estero (Foreign Trade Institute)
ICIPU	Istituto di Credito per le Imprese di Pubblica Utilità (Credit Institute for Public Utility Projects)
ICS	Istituti di credito speciale (special credit institutes)
IGE	Imposta generale sulle entrate (sales tax)
ILOR	Imposta locale sui redditi (local income tax)
IMF	International Monetary Fund
IMI	Istituto Mobiliare Italiano (industrial credit institute owned by Postal Savings Fund, commercial and savings banks, holding companies, and social security and insurance agencies)
INA	Istituto Nazionale delle Assicurazioni (National Insurance Institute)
INAM	Istituto Nazionale per l'Assicurazione contro le Malattie (National Health Insurance Institute)

INPS	Istituto Nazionale della Previdenza Sociale (National Social Security Institute)
INVIM	Imposta sull' incremento di valore degli immobili (local tax on capital gains on real estate)
IRFIS	Istituto Regionale per il Finanziamento delle Industrie in Sicilia (Regional Institute for the Financing of Industry in Sicily)
IRI	Istituto per la Riscostruzione Industriale (state industrial holding company)
IRPEF	Imposta sul reddito delle persone fisiche (personal income tax)
IRPEG	Imposta sul reddito delle persone giuridiche (corporate income tax)
ISCO	Istituto Nazionale per lo Studio della Congiuntura (National Institute for the Study of Economic Trends)
ISFOL	Istituto per lo Sviluppo del' Addestramento della Formazione Professionale e Dei Lavoratori
ISTAT	Istituto Centrale di Statistica (Central Statistical Institute)
Isveimer	Istituto per lo Sviluppo Economico dell' Italia Meridionale (Institute for the Economic Development of Southern Italy)
IVA	Imposta sul valore aggiunto (value added tax)
Mediobanca	Banca di Credito Finanziario (industrial special credit institute owned by three IRI-owned commercial banks)
Mediocredito	Istituto centrale per il credito a medio termine a favore delle medie e piccole industrie (medium-term industrial and export credit discount institute)
NATO	North Atlantic Treaty Organization
OECD	Organization for Economic Cooperation and Development
OPEC	Organization of Petroleum Exporting Countries
SACE	Sezione Speciale per l'Assicurazione del Credito all' Esportazione (special section for export credit)
SDR	Special Drawing Right (of the IMF)
SIP	Società Italiana per l'Esercizio Telefonico (telephone company)
STET	Società Finanziaria Telefonica per Azioni (state telephone holding company)

TDC	Total domestic credit
UIC	Ufficio Italiano dei Cambi (Italian Exchange Office)
UIL	Unione Italiana del Lavoro (Socialist/Social Democrat/Republican-led labor confederation)

I
ECONOMIC INSTITUTIONS
AND
ECONOMIC TRENDS

1

BACKGROUND: ECONOMIC PERFORMANCE IN THE 1960s

> During the 1961-70 period, the economy's development
> process was bolstered . . . by the decisive contribution
> of the industrial sector. . . . This was achieved both
> by reorganizing the companies' internal structure and
> by making the production process more capital-intensive
> and finally by the improved skills of the labour force.
> Stepped up productivity had its toll, particularly in
> heavier workloads. This, plus a lag in the development
> of social infrastructure, produced strains in the phys-
> ical and mental well-being of workers.
>
> Guido Carli
> Governor, Bank of Italy
> Annual Meeting, Rome, May 1972

The serious economic problems that Italy faced in the 1970s take on an added dimension when contrasted with the good years of the 1960s. While some problems could be identified even then, economic performance in nearly all areas was favorable for the decade as a whole. True, some of the problems of slow growth, high rates of inflation, and balance-of-payments deficits were foreshadowed in the period 1963-65. The crisis was overcome, however, and the apparent return to a stable growth path was reassuring.

GROWTH AND EMPLOYMENT

Real economic growth averaged 5.8 percent in the period 1961-69 (Table 1.1). (Comparable data are not available for 1960.) Both the labor force and the number of employed declined quite

TABLE 1.1

Comparative Economic Performance, 1960s and 1970s
(average annual percent change, unless otherwise indicated)

	1960s[a]	1970s[b]
Growth and employment		
GDP (real)	5.8	3.1
GFI/GDP ratio (real)	22.2	19.0
Productivity (per worker in industry)	6.1	3.1
Employment growth	-0.6	0.5
Percent of total employment, by sector, 1960 and 1979		
Primary	32	15
Secondary	34	37
Tertiary	34	48
Prices and wages		
Cost of living	3.7	12.2
GDP deflator	4.3	13.1
Wage rate (blue-collar in industry)	8.1	19.7
Unit labor costs (in industry)	3.9	15.4
Balance of payments (cumulative total in billions of dollars)		
Current account	11.9	-0.1
Overall balance	2.3	-0.1
Monetary growth		
Monetary base	9.4	17.5
Money supply (M = 3)	13.2	20.2
Treasury cash deficit (ratio to GDP)	2.8	8.6

[a]1960-69 (1961-69: For real growth, GDP deflator, productivity, and unit labor costs).

[b]1970-78.

Source: Compiled by the author; data from Relazione Generale, ISTAT, Bank of Italy (various bulletins and annual reports).

steadily during the decade, however, as Italy underwent a structural shift in employment. On average, more than a quarter of a million workers left the (low productivity) agricultural sector each year in the 1960s and agricultural employment fell from 32 percent of total employment in 1960 to 22 percent in 1969. Some farm workers withdrew from the labor force, while others found work in industry and the services sector. Net migration showed a rather steady outflow, averaging over 100,000 per year. Productivity in the expanding industrial sector was rising rapidly (6.1 percent per year), which contributed strongly to real growth.

The average ratio of real gross fixed investment (GFI) to gross domestic product (GDP) in the 1960s was over 22 percent, comparing favorably with that in the major European countries. GFI registered average annual increases of over 5 percent during the 1960s (1961-69), despite substantial drops in investment during the 1964-65 economic slowdown.

Private domestic consumption and exports (GDP concept) were growth leaders, averaging real growth rates of over 6 percent and nearly 13 percent, respectively. Imports also rose (by 11 percent) as the Italian economy substantially increased its economic integration into the world economy, and particularly into the European Community (EC). The growth of private consumption followed a pattern of expanding consumption of consumer durables (especially automobiles) and services, commensurate with Italy's growing per capita income and more in line with Italy's wealthier neighbors. Public consumption grew rather modestly in real terms during the period at an average annual rate of 4 percent.

INFLATIONARY PERFORMANCE

The average rise in the cost of living (COL) in the 1960s was less than 4 percent, with the range of annual price increases from 1 to 8 percent. The highest annual rise occurred in 1963, when food prices rose by 8 percent and housing costs increased by more than 10 percent (although the latter was a lower rate of increase than in the preceding three years). In that year the economy approached full capacity utilization and there were important three-year wage contract negotiations. Price increases during the decade were greatest for housing and miscellaneous goods and services. Political resistance to increases in fuel prices and in electricity rates (following the nationalization of the electric utility industry in 1962) held down the average annual rise in these prices to only a little over 1 percent during the 1960s. While the annual rise in housing costs decelerated significantly later in the decade, such costs regularly exceeded the average rise in the COL itself. In particular, the sharp annual increases in housing costs in 1960-63 contributed to a decision in 1963 to extend rent controls to postwar housing.

Nominal wage rates grew on average by 8 percent per year during the 1960s. (In real terms, deflated by the COL index, the average rise was a little over 3 percent.)

Unit labor costs in industry rose on average by about 4 percent during the period 1961-69. Nominal wage rates in the entire industrial sector (including construction) rose quite rapidly in 1963-64, following the 1963 wage contract negotiations. This boosted unit labor costs by 15 percent in 1963 and 8 percent in 1964. During the remainder of the 1960s, however (including the 1966 round of wage negotiations), the rise in unit labor costs was very modest. Indeed, unit labor costs fell in three years of the decade: 1965, 1966, and 1968.

THE BALANCE OF PAYMENTS

The balance of payments was in persistent surplus during the 1960s both on current account and overall (as measured by monetary movements—that is, changes in net official reserves and in the short-term net foreign position of the commercial banks). The typical pattern was a modest deficit on trade, a large surplus on services and unilateral transfers, and substantial deficits on capital account.

The lira value of exports rose on average by 15 percent annually during the 1960s (customs basis), while imports also rose by nearly 15 percent. In both cases virtually all the increase was in real terms, as both export and import unit values (in lire) were remarkably stable, in each case rising on average by only about 0.5 percent per year. In the case of export unit values, there were actually annual declines in four years of the decade: 1961, 1965, 1966, and 1968. The composition of exports did not change dramatically, although food exports declined in relative importance and consumer durable goods and final investment goods increased their share of the total to some extent, as might be expected as the economy continued to industrialize.

On the import side, the composition of imports also remained quite stable. More than half of imports consisted of the primary and intermediary goods needed for Italy's transformation economy, of which energy imports alone accounted for about 15 percent of the total. The income elasticity of imports (ratio to GDP) averaged about 1.6 during the period (1961-69).*

---

*The ratio is measured as the annual percentage change in

Services and transfers played a critical role in maintaining equilibrium in Italy's balance of payments, especially tourism, worker remittances, and emigrant remittances. On average, Italy had a surplus on net tourist transactions of nearly $1 billion per year. This surplus ceased to grow after 1965, however, in large part because the rise in Italy's per capita income began to generate an offsetting outflow of tourist expenditures. Worker remittances, too, which had risen rapidly in the early part of the decade, tended to level off in the last half of the period, as Italians were better able to find employment at home. Net income from private remittances grew fairly steadily during the period, mainly reflecting the effects of earlier permanent migration from Italy.

The capital account was in persistent deficit, especially in the later years of the decade. The deficits reflected a number of factors: political uncertainty, tax evasion, interest rate differentials, and exchange rate speculation. Although there were small surpluses in 1960, 1961, and 1964, deficits became quite large in the latter half of the decade—reaching a peak of $3.6 billion in 1969.

Italy's first balance-of-payments crisis in 1963 (overall deficit of $1.3 billion) reflected both an overheated economy leading to a deficit on current account, and capital flight ($1.5 billion in recorded repatriation of exported Italian banknotes) triggered by political uncertainties in connection with the political "opening to the Left" involving the formation of Italy's first Center-Left government that year. In addition, the introduction of dividend withholding at the source at the end of 1962 had an adverse effect on investor confidence.

During Italy's second balance-of-payments crisis in 1969 there was actually a surplus of $2.3 billion on current account, but this was insufficient to offset the massive capital outflow stimulated by political and economic uncertainty arising from the "hot autumn" of labor agitation that year. Unlike the 1963 crisis, resort was not made to foreign official financing. To some extent official reserves were protected by the central bank's requiring the commercial banks to reduce their net foreign assets and, in the following year, the authorities obtained foreign balance-of-payments financing indirectly through Euromarket borrowing by public enterprises, such as the national electric company (ENEL) and a state-owned steel company (FINSIDER).

---

imports divided by the percentage change in GDP. In this period, the average annual ratio was virtually the same for imports of merchandise (customs data), alone, as for imports of goods and services (GDP concept).

USE OF DEMAND MANAGEMENT TOOLS

The principal policy tool used to manage the economy in the 1960s was monetary. The treasury deficit was not large and the tax and expenditure systems were not well designed for use as demand management tools. Monetary policy was aimed at assuring a sufficiently low and stable level of long-term interest rates to encourage investment, compatible with balance-of-payments equilibrium. The persistent tendency toward large capital outflows required that balance-of-payments considerations, at times, override domestic considerations.

The average annual increase in the monetary base in the 1960s was about 9 percent. Money supply (M-3) registered an annual increase of 13 percent, compared with growth of real GDP of 6 percent (1961-69). During the decade, financing of the treasury deficit through creation of monetary base accounted for almost two-thirds of the total monetary base creation, with central-bank lending to the banks accounting for more than one-quarter. The foreign sector contributed 11 percent and other small transactions were negative.

While on average 70 percent of the treasury cash deficit was financed from the creation of monetary base in the decade, the deficits themselves were not large. This treasury cash deficit definition includes the central government budget plus a number of off-budget cash operations by the Treasury (see Chapter 4). These treasury deficits averaged less than 3 percent of GDP during the decade. Also, much of the creation of monetary base by the Treasury was financed from postal savings deposits, rather than lending from the central bank to the Treasury.

Variation in the discount rate was not a tool of monetary management in the 1960s. There was no change in the rate between June 1958 and August 1969, when the rate was raised by 0.5 percentage points from 3.5 to 4.0 percent. Control over the access of commercial banks to the Bank of Italy discount window, however, was an important tool of credit control. The use of interest rate policy was somewhat limited by the extensive use of a system of subsidized interest rates, particularly designed to provide incentives for investment in the south. Bank reserve requirements were changed twice, once by a reduction of 2.5 percentage points in 1962, and in 1965, when banks were first allowed under certain conditions to substitute some long-term securities for more liquid assets as reserves against savings deposits. Little use was made of open-market operations because of the absence of a developed money market. In particular, the Bank of Italy's policy of selling treasury bills "on tap" (that is, on demand) limited the use of open-market operations in treasury bills as a tool of liquidity control. The main form of money market operations involved interbank deposits, consisting of the collection of deposits by the large banks through their national networks of branches for relending in the major money markets.

The tax system was widely recognized as needing reform and became, in fact, an area of comprehensive reform early in the 1970s. A great number of specific taxes had accumulated over the years and tax evasion was widespread. The fact that the income tax system did not provide for comprehensive current withholding nor self-assessment and payment at the time of filing limited its usefulness for managing the economy. (Under the prevailing system taxpayers submitted tax declarations, the tax authorities subsequently assessed the tax, and the two parties then reconciled their differences, usually over a two-to-three-year period.)

On the expenditure side, the public administration was slow to use appropriated funds, partly due to complex preaudit and postaudit requirements. The accumulation of residui passivi (appropriated but unspent funds) became a subject of constant debate. Much of the delay was in the expenditure of multiyear investment programs, which made any attempts to use public works as a method of cyclical "pump priming" inefficient and sometimes pernicious in the timing of their final effect.

Until the "hot autumn" of 1969, the three principal labor confederations were not unified and were not the powerful force in wage bargaining and even in management of the economy that they were later to become. The rise of nominal wages in industry of 8 percent per year compared to the good growth of productivity (over 6 percent in industry, 1961-69) did not seem excessive, price inflation was moderate, and there was no apparent need for resort to an incomes policy.

The Italian authorities did employ changes in exchange control regulations, including control over the net foreign position of the commercial banks, with some regularity during the 1960s as means of achieving both domestic liquidity and balance-of-payments goals. The exchange rate itself was kept exceptionally stable around its International Monetary Fund (IMF) par value, which was not changed during the decade.

CONCLUSIONS

Assessments of Italian economic performance in the 1960s have tended to attribute good economic growth to a combination of such factors as the availability of labor, the weakness of the trade unions, good productivity growth, the evolution of the state holding companies, the discovery of natural gas, the importation of foreign technologies, EC integration measures (reduced tariffs, exchange convertibility, and capital movement liberalization), and an under-valued currency. These factors then contributed to a pattern of growth led by investment and exports. At the end of the decade, however, there remained some important problem areas: a backward agricul-tural sector, a depressed south, a low level of productivity by indus-trial country standards, a modest technological base, reduced labor availabilities, inadequate social infrastructure, an underdeveloped capital market, inadequate tools of demand management, and an inefficient public administration.[1]

While the existence of these weaknesses in the Italian economy at the beginning of the 1970s is undeniable (some of the problems will be examined in later chapters), Italy's economic record in the 1960s provided rather little forewarning of the difficulties to come.

NOTE

1. See Pierluigi Ciocca, R. Filosa, and Guido Maria Rey, "Integration and Development of the Italian Economy, 1951-1971: A Re-examination," Banca Nazionale del Lavoro Quarterly Review (September 1975): 284-320; also Kevin J. Allen and Andrew A. Stevenson, An Introduction to the Italian Economy (London: Martin Robertson, 1974), pp. 1-42.

2

THE HOT AUTUMN OF 1969 AND
ITS AFTERMATH

The events of last autumn caused very serious losses in
production and their effects are still being felt . . . and
the failure of labour relations to return to normal is
giving rise to new uncertainties. . . . The recent wage
increases . . . confront the monetary authorities with
complex problems from the dual angle of curbing inflation and safeguarding the economic equilibrium of enterprises as prerequisites of growth.

> Guido Carli
> Governor, Bank of Italy
> Annual Meeting, Rome, May 1970

THE ECONOMIC SETTING

The wage explosion of 1969 can be attributed in part to the
effect of a tightening labor market, but also to some powerful social
pressures. Following an economic slowdown in 1964-65, Italy had
once again returned to high rates of growth. In the four-year period,
1966-69, preceding the end-1969 labor negotiations, real economic
growth (GDP in 1970 lire) averaged 6.4 percent. Unemployment fell
from 5.9 percent in 1966 to 5.7 in 1969. (Excluding marginal workers, who tended to inflate the figures during this period of rapid
growth, unemployment fell from 4.2 percent to 3.8 percent between
1966 and 1969.) Also, reflecting stronger demand for labor at home,
net emigration dropped substantially between the two years. Per
capita domestic wage and salary income had increased at an average
annual rate of nearly 8 percent compared to an average rise in the

cost of living of 2 percent. The share of wage and salary income in total income (net national income at factor cost) was quite stable at 57.1 in 1966 and 56.7 in 1969. New jobs created in industry and services exceeded 600,000. This rate of job creation, however, was still insufficient to offset the continuing exodus from agriculture of nearly 900,000 people during the period. The decline in the labor force was slowing down and total employment in 1969 was virtually identical with that in 1966.

In view of such generally good economic performance one might ask why there was labor discontent when a new round of labor negotiations began late in 1969. There were two main reasons: a feeling that labor had not obtained its fair share of the benefits of economic growth, and a belief that much of the economic gain had been offset by the failure of the public administration to provide social services in line with Italy's growing wealth. While wage and salary income had risen significantly (over 9 percent per year), nonwage income had been rising even more, by nearly 11 percent in 1966-69. Although the wage and salary share of total income had fallen very little, when adjusted for the increase in the number of wage and salary earners there had actually been a decline in the wage and salary share of the total from 60 percent in 1966 to 57 percent in 1969. Admittedly, inflation had been moderate, but during the course of 1969 there had been some acceleration in the rise in the cost of living, so that the increase from December 1968 to December 1969 amounted to 4.3 percent, a disturbing rate compared to that in the previous extended period of considerable price stability.

While unemployment had fallen, the proportion of the unemployed accounted for by young first-job seekers had risen considerably, from 31 percent in 1966 to 40 in 1969. Finally, the mostly young workers who migrated from the depressed south to the large cities of the north encountered an environment of rising urban problems. Wives found it less easy to supplement income than had been possible in agriculture, and the extended family of the south was no longer available to help in time of trouble. Finally, there was growing dissatisfaction with the quality of education, health care, pensions, and other social services. The public administration seemed to dissipate what funds were allocated for these purposes, with little to show in the way of a larger quantity and better quality of such services.

THE WAGE NEGOTIATIONS AND THEIR OUTCOME

The economic slowdown of 1964-65 and the growing feeling that the worker had not got his share of the benefits of postwar growth

were incentives for a greater effort toward unity of action by the
labor confederations in 1969.

During the previous major round of wage negotiations in 1966,
the economy had not yet recovered sufficiently to provide a good
environment for strong wage pressures, so that wage rate increases
were moderate and achieved without a great deal of strike activity.
Contractual wage rates in the metalmechanical sector (metallurgy
and engineering) were up only 6 percent in 1967 over 1966 and for
industry as a whole the increase was only 5 percent. Lost time due
to labor disputes amounted to 116 million hours compared to 182
million hours in the previous peak year of 1962.

In the spring of 1966 there began a series of talks that stretched
into 1968 among the three major confederations—CGIL, CISL, and
UIL—aimed at greater unity of action.* Already toward the end of
1968, partly in sympathy with student and worker agitation elsewhere
(for example, Paris), there were strikes and disorders in agriculture, industry, and the universities.

In 1969 an unusually large number of labor contracts came up
for renewal, involving some 5 million workers, notably in the metalmechanical, construction, chemical, pharmaceutical, agricultural,
banking, and public services (restaurants, bars, hotels) sectors.
The metalworkers, in particular, were in the forefront of labor agitation. Concentrated in the large cities of the north, workers in this
industry were more affected than most by the social problems created by migration from the south to the northern urban areas. Dissatisfaction with the lack of militancy on the part of union leadership
led to the formation by the rank and file of factory committees elected
from both union and nonunion workers. Urged on by rank-and-file
pressures, union leaders took strong positions during the talks,
leading to particularly bitter labor conflicts. A record number of
hours were lost from strikes (almost 303 million), nearly equal to
time lost in the previous four years combined, and still a record.

---

*The three major labor confederations are the Communist-
Socialist CGIL, Confederazione Generale Italiana del Lavoro, with
about 4.3 million members; the Christian Democratic CISL, Confederazione Italiana dei Sindacati dei Lavoratori, with about 2.8 million;
and the Socialist/Republican/Social Democratic UIL, Unione Italiana
del Lavoro, with about 1.1 million. In addition, there are about one
million "autonomous" labor union members outside the three major
confederations. Thus, the 9.2 million union members (in 1978) represented 64 percent of employed wage and salary workers or 42 percent of the labor force.

Nearly half the lost time was in the metalmechanical sector. The nature of the "articulated" (that is, selective) strikes was such as to cause a more than proportional decline in production. Because unions did not have large strike funds, strike action generally took the form of short work stoppages aimed at maximum disruption of the production process. (The industrial production index fell 11 percent between October and November.) Even after national contracts had been settled, labor agitation continued as negotiations moved to the plant level.

When final agreement was reached the unions had made very substantial gains—both in money terms and work conditions, and also toward achieving some broader goals. There was a provision for gradual reduction in the work week to 40 hours. The metal-mechanical contract provided that all contractual wage increases would be front-end loaded in the first year of the three-year contract. The increase in contractual wage rates in 1970 over 1969 was 21 percent for industry as a whole (including construction). Metalmechanical workers, alone, gained an increase of 28 percent and construction workers 19 percent (blue-collar worker rates excluding family allowances). White-collar workers in industry experienced a much smaller rise in contractual wages of 14 percent, beginning a pattern of compression of wage-rate differentials between blue-collar and white-collar workers that reflected the increasingly egalitarian emphasis of the unions. (Monthly pay increases under the new contracts were often a flat amount, representing a larger percentage increase for lower-paid workers than for higher-paid workers.)

In addition to these monetary benefits, union pressures in late 1969 and early 1970 resulted in accelerated passage of a new "Workers' Statute." Also, the new-found power of the unions became increasingly directed toward social as well as economic goals.

The Workers' Statute, which became law in May 1970, provided certain guarantees of the right to form unions, some rights to assembly in the plant without loss of pay, paid leave for union leaders to conduct union business, the right to voluntary check-off of union dues, the provision of union facilities on the premises of the larger firms, protection against unjust dismissals, and the prohibition of management's verification of the certificates issued by health insurance doctors, attesting to the health of employees who claim sick benefits.

Interest on the part of the unions in social reforms had already been demonstrated in a general nationwide strike in November 1969 in support of housing reform. Increasingly the unions came to take a more active interest in reforms in the areas of education, health, pensions, and housing. They pushed for accelerated southern development, and sought a role in determining industrial policy concerning criteria for new capital investment, location of new plants, and re-organization and rationalization of industry.

AFTERMATH

There was both an immediate aftermath of the hot autumn with consequences for growth, employment, inflation, and the balance of payments, and a more important longer-term effect on the respective roles of unions, business, and government in the management of the Italian economy.

Statistics for 1970 show a sharp rise in wage and salary income and a corresponding decline in the rate of growth of other factor income (see Table 2.1). Unit labor costs rose by over 14 percent. Private consumption rose by nearly 13 percent, reflecting both real growth and a rise in the price of consumer goods. The decline in nonwage income (for example, profits) contributed to a sharp drop in the growth of real gross fixed investment from nearly 8 percent in 1969 to only 3 percent in 1970. Although GDP rose by more than 5 percent, the rate of growth decelerated during the course of the year. The unemployment rate actually declined slightly, reflecting the lagging nature of this indicator. The balance of payments showed

TABLE 2.1

Aftereffects of the Hot Autumn
(annual percent change, unless otherwise indicated)

	1969	1970
Wage/salary income (GDP concept)	10.2	16.9
Nonwage income (GDP concept)	11.7	6.1
Unit labor costs (industry)	2.8	14.4
Private consumption (real)	6.5	7.3
Gross fixed investment (real)	7.8	3.0
GDP (real)	6.1	5.3
GDP deflator	4.1	6.8
Unemployment rate (percent)	5.7	5.4
Balance of payments (billions of dollars)	-1.4	0.3

Source: Compiled by the author; data from ISTAT and Bank of Italy.

a small recorded surplus, but this was only made possible by large-scale compensatory borrowing in the Euromarket by public enterprise at the behest of the central bank. Without this capital inflow, the balance of payments would have been in deficit by $1.2 billion. (Labor agitation in the autumn of 1969 had already triggered large-scale capital flight, leading to a massive deficit on capital account of $3.6 billion that year and an overall balance-of-payments deficit of $1.4 billion in 1969.)

CONCLUSIONS

The hot autumn of 1969 was a watershed in Italy's economic history. It had far-reaching effects on Italy's economic performance and prospects and it changed the manner in which Italy's economy is managed. Although there were immediate adverse aftereffects, the events of 1969 are interesting mainly because they became typical of what was to follow. A pattern was set of periodic three-year rounds of nominal wage rate increases far in excess of productivity, which sharply raised unit labor costs and squeezed profits. Rising labor costs contributed directly to price increases, which, in turn, led to further rounds of price rises due to an increasingly effective system of indexing to changes in the cost of living wages. Self-financed business investment became more difficult. Although household saving continued strong, Italy's financial markets were deficient in providing a system of intermediation and the public sector was unable to boost total real demand to offset weakness in the private sector. Rapid price inflation became endemic and put pressure on the balance of payments in the form of official reserve losses during the period of fixed exchange rates, and afterward, on either rates or reserves, or both.

The relatively high cost of labor compared to capital and a strong system of job security and labor immobility favored capital-intensive modes of production and hurt employment, especially for new job seekers, including the youth and women who had benefited from increased educational and social opportunities fostered by the labor unions.

Because of the inadequacies of the fiscal system, the authorities were periodically forced to rely heavily on tight monetary policies to shock the economy back into equilibrium through a slowdown in investment and in overall economic activity. At the same time, some of a laudable efforts to improve social welfare, financed by increased transfer payments from the central government to lower levels of the public administration, raised the treasury deficit, whose financing tended to preempt credit that might otherwise have gone to the private sector for productive investment and job creation. The worsened financial position of business, in turn, put further pressure on the budget in the form of transfers to alleviate the financial problems of business.

The hot autumn of 1969 also changed the pattern of labor relationships and the way in which economic policy was made in Italy. The Workers' Statute firmly established the presence of unions inside the plant. Labor negotiations increasingly involved the government at the bargaining table, partly because the unions' wage demands were so great as to threaten the health of the economy, and also because union demands, more and more, were not limited to salary and fringe benefits that could be conceded by management, but involved social reforms that were the responsibility of government. The continuing ties of the three labor confederations with the political parties also inevitably linked economic issues with broader political party strategies.

The behavior of the unions in 1969 and subsequently can be explained in large part by justified dissatisfaction with the apparent inability of the public administration to provide the higher level of social welfare that Italy's expanding economy made possible. Pressure from the labor movement in 1969 was important in alerting the government to the need for stronger efforts to achieve social goals. The labor movement, then and subsequently, filled a vacuum created by a political system so balanced between opposing forces as to be unable to act forcefully and a public administration inadequate to carrying out the reforms that could be agreed upon at the political level. The continued union pressure for inflationary wage settlements, however, the obsession with "equality" in the distribution of income, and pressures to insure job security at all costs ended up by improving the welfare of already employed workers, but jeopardized the employment growth and social welfare goals of the society at large.

3

RISING UNIT LABOR COSTS

Negotiated increases in nominal wages larger than the
growth in productivity lead to a rise in real earnings
but reduce the advantage to the firm of expanding production and employment, thus laying the basis for
further inflationary pressures. As a result of this
process, the immediate benefits obtained by individuals
and groups become harmful through their secondary
effects on the conditions of the working class as a
whole and on that of the younger generation.

Paolo Baffi
Governor, Bank of Italy
Annual Meeting, Rome, May 1979

This chapter addresses one of two problems (labor costs and
budget deficits) that are at the heart of Italy's growth, employment,
inflation, and balance-of-payments difficulties. The subjects to be
covered include the rapid rise in contractual wage rates and actual
hourly earnings, the growing importance of automatic cost-of-living
adjustments (the scala mobile), the size of other (social insurance)
components of labor costs, the high degree of job security and low
level of labor mobility, Italy's dual labor market (including the
question of illegal "black" labor), productivity performance, and
the rapid growth of unit labor costs in Italy compared with Italy's
major trading partners.

CONTRACTUAL WAGE GAINS

Gross minimum contractual hourly wage increases grew very rapidly in the 1970s. Contractual wage rates include basic pay and other forms of pay that are general and continuous. Specifically, they include automatic wage adjustments under the scala mobile (wage indexation system). The irregular pattern of increases in contractual rates reflects the effect of the three-year labor contracts that are common in Italy. While some contracts fall due each year, there was (as in 1969) a considerable concentration of certain important industrial contracts (headed by the metalmechanical workers contract) at three-year intervals that fell due late in 1972, 1975, and 1978. In each of those years the national negotiations carried forward into the following year and were often followed by plant-level negotiations, especially in large and medium-size companies. Thus the statistical recording of the effects of this group of important contracts appears mainly in the years 1970, 1973, 1976, and 1979. As in the case of the 1969 contracts, contractual wage rate increases in the 1970s were typically front-end loaded, although somewhat less so in 1976 and 1979 than earlier. On the other hand, because of the growing importance of automatic quarterly cost-of-living adjustments following the 1975 revision of the scala mobile, clear three-year peaks of wage rate increases in industry became somewhat less striking later in the decade than previously (Figure 3.1).

The average annual percentage increase in contractual wage rates per hour for blue-collar workers in agriculture and industry grew in the 1970s (1970-78) at a rate about two and one-half times as fast as in the 1960s, and in commerce and public services (restaurants, bars, hotels) the growth rate was triple that of the 1960s (see Table 3.1). For white-collar workers the acceleration was somewhat less rapid—a little more than double the rate of the 1960s for industry and commerce. In the public administration (general government) wage rates rose less than one and one-half times as fast in the 1970s as in the 1960s.

Increases in agricultural wages were surprisingly rapid, with an average rise of 22 percent, compared to 9 percent on average in the 1960s. In fact, in the later years (1974-78) the average was almost 28 percent per year. In industry, commerce, and transport, average annual blue-collar wage increases were somewhat lower. In the major sectors that employ large numbers of both blue-collar and white-collar workers (industry and commerce) a considerable compression of wage rate differentials between white- and blue-collar workers occurred.

The closing of the gap between white-collar and blue-collar wage compensation during the 1970s was the result of a deliberate

FIGURE 3.1

Minimum Hourly Contractual Wage Rates in Industry for Blue–Collar Workers, 1970–79
(excluding family allowances; percent change over previous month)

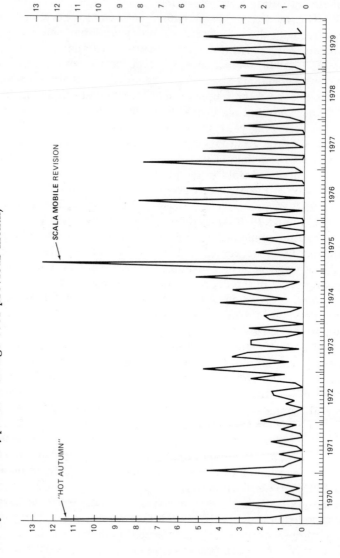

Source: Constructed by the author; data from ISTAT bulletins.

TABLE 3.1

Minimum Contractual Wage Rates per Hour, 1960s and 1970s
(excluding family allowance; average annual percent change)

	1960-69	1970-78
Blue-collar		
Agriculture	9.2	22.5
Industry	8.1	19.7
Commerce/public services	6.7	20.5
Transport/communications	6.4	17.0
Average (unweighted)	7.6	19.9
White-collar		
Industry	7.5	16.1
Commerce/public services	7.4	17.9
Transport/communications	n.a.*	13.5
Public administration	7.5	10.2
Average (unweighted)	7.5	14.4

*Not available.
Source: Compiled by the author; data from ISTAT bulletins.

policy of egalitarianism practiced by the labor confederations. For
example, new wage contracts frequently provided for fixed monthly
increases in pay without regard to absolute levels of pay. The scala
mobile mechanism also had a leveling effect. Late in the period,
however, there developed some concern about the effect on work
incentives of the pattern of narrowing wage differentials. In fact, the
1979 wage contracts typically provided for equal pay increases in the
first year, but higher increases for higher-paid workers in the second
and third years of the contracts. Still, according to Confindustria
estimates, this would offset only approximately the expected leveling
effect of the scala mobile during that period.

Following the 1969 round of major wage contracts, the negotiation of additional wage benefits at the plant level became more common and contributed to "wage drift" in actual average hourly earnings.
Data for actual gross hourly earnings in industry (including overtime
but excluding fringe benefits and family allowances), based on

Ministry of Labor surveys, show that these earnings grew on average by about 24 percent per year (1970-77) compared to a 20 percent rise in contractual rates in the same period. Since there are rather stringent limits on overtime in Italy, much of the greater increase in earnings than in wage rates was due to benefits negotiated at the plant level. To some extent plant-level negotiations may have counteracted the leveling effect of the national contracts, as local pressures were exerted to reestablish geographic, sectoral, or blue-collar/white-collar differentials.

There was a rather rapid rise in real per worker wage and salary income* in the 1970s, as shown in the table below. The rise

Year	Annual Increase (percent)
1970	9.8
1971	7.4
1972	4.1
1973	6.2
1974	0.8
1975	2.7
1976	2.5
1977	2.6
1978	2.0

was particularly rapid in the first four years of the decade, when the average annual increase in real wages was 6.9 percent. With the acceleration of inflation later in the decade, however, the annual real increase for 1974-78 fell to 2.1 percent. For the entire nine-year period the average rise was 4.2 percent, against an average increase of less than 3 percent in productivity. (The average real rise for 1961-69 had been 6.4 percent.)

INDEXATION OF WAGES (THE SCALA MOBILE)

Contractual wage rates include the effects of automatic cost-of-living adjustments both on base pay and on some other components of contractual rates. (In the latter case, the extent of indexation varies from industry to industry.) Italy has employed wage indexation

---

*Net domestic wage and salary income per worker deflated by personal consumption deflator.

since 1945, but the present system dates from a labor-management agreement in 1975. The wage indexation system or scala mobile (literally "escalator") covers all dependent workers—that is, wage and salary workers. As of 1978 (yearly average) this meant that 14.4 million out of 20.1 million employed workers were so covered— 72 percent of the total. In addition, retired workers with pensions also benefit from indexation of their pension payments. In fact, pensions above the minimum are doubly indexed to provide not only for protection against increases in the cost of living but also to allow for an increase in the real value of the pension.

Scala mobile wage adjustments are calculated on the basis of movements in a special price index. Although the percentage changes in the various goods and services components of the index are taken from the regular cost-of-living index, the scala mobile "market basket" is rather different from the ordinary COL market basket (see Table 3.2). Whereas the present cost-of-living index is on a 1976 base and the market basket has been subjected to occasional revision (latest in 1976), the scala mobile index still uses a market basket dating from 1956. This results in a much higher weight being given to basic necessities such as food and clothing in the latter index (71 percent) than in the regular COL index (51 percent). Conversely, other goods and services are understated in the scala mobile basket. For example, the latter does not assume car ownership by workers (gasoline is not in the index) and it does assume that the worker lives in rental property subject to rent controls. (Despite the difference in the composition of the two baskets, over the decade price increases for the two series were very similar.)

Both the COL index and the scala mobile index are based on price surveys carried out by the Central Statistical Institute (ISTAT), although the COL survey uses data from 20 provincial capitals and the scala mobile from only 16 provincial capitals. The results of the latter survey are then submitted to a labor-employer committee made up of the labor confederations (CGIL, CISL, UIL) and the employer associations for industry, agriculture, and trade (Confindustria, Confagricultura, Confcommercio) for final determination of the number of "points" of wage adjustment to be made in the next quarter. (For government employees adjustments were made only annually until July 1975 and semiannually through 1979. Quarterly adjustments began in February 1980.) Each point increase in the index is worth a fixed lira amount per monthly paycheck. Adjustments are made quarterly at the beginning of February, May, August, and November and are based on three-month survey periods ending on the fifteenth day of the previous month.

The current basic scala mobile agreement between labor and management, which originally covered industry, commerce, and

TABLE 3.2

Relative Weights of Two Cost-of-Living Indexes

	Cost of Living	Scala Mobile
Food	40.82	57.33
Clothing	10.19	13.77
Heat and light	3.45	3.39
Rent	6.04	7.58
Other	39.50	17.93
Total	100.00	100.00

Source: Compiled by the author; data from ISTAT.

transportation, dates from January 1975. Later in 1975 the agreement was extended to agriculture, and a similar arrangement was made to cover public employees and state pensioners. (The three-year agreement is renewable automatically in the absence of contrary action by either party.) Prior to 1975, the lira value of each point rise in the scala mobile index varied considerably from sector to sector. The new agreement provided for gradual unification (generally upward) of the lira value per point so that, effective on February 1, 1977, each point became worth 2,389 lire for all wage and salary workers, regardless of their level of income. (This was the maximum value then paid in the industrial sector.) In some sectors outside industry, especially the financial sector, each point was worth more than the standard 2,389 lire. It was later agreed, however, to eliminate this "anomaly" at the time of final unification in February 1977.

As the effectiveness of the scala mobile adjustment increased after 1975, and with the high rate of price inflation that prevailed, the proportion of wage rate increases accounted for by this automatic mechanism increased in comparison with "volitional" wage increases directly negotiated between labor and management. For example, according to Bank of Italy calculations, the scala mobile accounted, on average, for about 25 percent of the increases in nominal hourly wage rates in manufacturing in the five-year period (1970-74)—that is, prior to reform of the scala mobile in 1975. In the subsequent period 1975-78, the scala mobile accounted for about 55 percent of such nominal wage rate increases.

Various estimates have been made of the extent to which workers are protected against future price increases through wage indexation adjustments. In a 1979 study Ignazio Visco calculated the theoretical extent of such coverage among different economic sectors and subsectors for both blue-collar and white-collar workers (see Table 3.3).[1] Visco defined coverage as the ratio of wage adjustments to changes in the cost of living in the succeeding 12 months, using prevailing gross contractual wage rates and the actual scala mobile payment arrangements applicable in each sector. He also calculated actual coverage over a period of years in industry, using national income accounting data (see Table 3.4). Visco identified six main scala mobile payment systems in effect, the least generous being that applicable to public sector employees and the most generous applying to full-time agricultural workers. (The degree of generosity

TABLE 3.3

Theoretical Scala Mobile Coverage by Sector, 1979

	Blue-collar	White-collar	Total
Agriculture	1.22	—	1.22
Industry	1.09	0.76	1.04
Services for sale	n.a.[a]	n.a.	0.90[b]
Services not for sale (including public administration)	—	0.85	0.85
Economy	n.a.	n.a.	0.98[b]

[a]Not available.

[b]Calculated by the author by weighting sectoral figures by the share of total employment accounted for by each sector.

Note: Coverage is defined as the ratio of wage adjustments to changes in the cost of living in the succeeding 12 months (assumed at 14.1 percent) that would be applicable to average gross contractual wage rates (that is, before taxes and employee social insurance payments) in 1978 (actually February 1978 to January 1979, the 1978 scala mobile year).

Source: Extract by the author from Ignazio Visco, "L'indicizzazione delle retribuzioni in Italia: analisi settoriale e stime per il 1978-1979," Rivista di Politica Economica (Vol. III, July 1979): 820-21.

TABLE 3.4

De Facto Scala Mobile Coverage
in Industry, 1976-79

1976	0.66
1977	0.96
1978	0.79
1979	0.78
Average	0.80

Note: Coverage is defined as the
ratio between the percentage change in
average gross income based on national
income accounts between one year and
the next and the contemporaneous percentage change in the cost of living. The
figure given for each of the years refers
to average of cost-of-living increases in
that year based on the previous year's
income levels.
Source: Extract from Ignazio Visco,
"L'indicizzazione delle retribuzioni in
Italia: analisi settoriale e stime per il
1978-1979," Rivista di Politica Economica
Vol. III (July 1979): 829.

depends mainly on the number of bonus months paid and the extent to
which various components of labor costs are linked to the scala
mobile.)

Visco's estimates of theoretical coverage show a greater degree
of protection against price increases in agriculture than in industry,
and in industry than in the services sector, with blue-collar workers
better protected against inflation than white-collar workers. To a
large extent this pattern is explained by the fact that scala mobile
adjustments are equal for each one-point increase in the index, without regard to the income level of individual workers. This means
that lower-paid workers receive a higher percentage degree of compensation than higher-paid workers. (The differences in specific
scala mobile payments systems by sector account for other inter-
sectoral differences.) Thus in the most favored sector (agriculture)
a worker could expect to receive a wage indexation adjustment in his

pay of 1.2 percent for each 1 percent increase in prices. A blue-collar worker in industry would receive 1.1 percent, a white-collar industrial worker 0.8 percent, a bank employee (in the least favored sector) 0.5 percent, a government employee 0.8 percent, and so on. For the economy as a whole the coverage was about 1.0 percent (based on the author's weighting of sectoral ratios). On the basis of national income account calculations for the industrial sector, however, Visco calculated the actual coverage to be somewhat lower, reaching about 1 percent in 1977, but falling to 0.8 percent in 1979.

The consequences of the scale mobile system for inflation, income distribution, collective bargaining, and management of economic policy after its unification in February 1977 have been widely debated.[2] Because wage adjustments now cover a large portion of employed workers, are made very promptly (quarterly), and provide very considerable coverage to offset price rises, there is much concern that the system has rendered Italy's economy more inflation-prone than before the reform. Not only do domestically generated price rises cause prompt upward wage adjustments, but the impact of foreign events, such as crude oil and other commodity price increases, may also feed a wage-price spiral. The fact that some workers may actually receive more than one-for-one compensation for price increases tends to undercut resistance to inflation. At the same time, those workers who are relatively less favored by the scala mobile system may try to recoup by seeking more generous (and differential) wage increases through plant-level bargaining, thus contributing to wage drift. Since the fixed lira value per point of adjustment tends toward a general leveling in wage rates across the economy, without regard to differences in productivity, this may cause undesirable changes in work incentives and relative profitability among economic sectors and among individual firms, and lead to a misallocation of resources. The rather effective protection of real wages by automatic wage adjustments reduces the role of union leaders and may put pressure on them to negotiate additional wage increases to justify their existence. In addition, the relative decline in the importance of volitional rather than automatic increases in wages makes it less easy to effect any deliberate shift in economic priorities (for example, wages versus employment) in response to changed economic conditions. Finally, the inclusion in the scala mobile market basket of price increases, due to changes in most indirect taxes and public service rates, seriously restricts the ability of economic policy officials in manipulating tax rates and public service rates as tools of fiscal policy, since such increases in taxes and rates are promptly offset to a large extent by automatic wage rate adjustments.

OTHER LABOR COSTS

Social Insurance Contributions

Various forms of social insurance contributions make up a substantial portion of total labor costs in Italy. National income data show that, on average, in the 1970s (1970-78) 28 percent of total net domestic wage and salary income at factor cost was accounted for by social insurance contributions paid by employers, with 72 percent accounted for by gross pay. (Gross pay includes base pay, cost-of-living adjustments, seniority pay, bonuses, and other forms of direct or indirect compensation, which vary from industry to industry. Employee social insurance contributions are subtracted from gross pay to arrive at net pay.) Looked at another way, social insurance contributions added an additional 38 percent to employers' gross pay costs during that period. This percentage did not change much during the 1970s, although a partial "fiscalization" of employer health insurance costs by the Treasury in 1977 and 1978 reduced the figure to only 36 percent in each of those years compared to a range of 38-41 percent in the previous years of the decade. (There had also been some fiscalization in earlier years, but on a smaller scale.)

The major social insurance contributions made by employers are for pensions, family allowances, unemployment insurance, health and tuberculosis insurance and maternity allowances, wage supplements (to compensate for short-time work), and workmen's disability compensation. Employees make some contributions—to pensions and health insurance but not to unemployment, family allowance, wage supplement, and workmen's disability programs (see Table 3.5). By far the larger share of social insurance contributions falls on employers. In 1978, of total contributions made for social insurance and social assistance programs, employer contributions accounted for 63 percent of the total, employee contributions less than 18 percent, and other regular sources 19 percent (including government, but not including treasury coverage of social insurance fund deficits).

Annual ISTAT surveys of the composition of labor costs in selected economic sectors show that the relative share of contributions of employers and employees differs quite substantially from sector to sector. (Rates are set by law.) For example, in agriculture employee contributions actually exceed those of employers. In industry, construction, and commerce the relative burden is much higher for employers than for employees (see Table 3.6).

The pattern over time of relative employer and employee contributions as a share of total labor costs shows some shift toward an increase in the employee share, particularly in agriculture. The large share of total social insurance fund deficits accounted for

TABLE 3.5

Social Insurance Contribution Rates in Industry in 1979
(as of February 1979)

	Blue-Collar	White-collar
Employer		
Pension	16.61	16.61
Unemployment	1.91	1.91
Family allowance	6.20	6.20
Wage supplements	1.30	—
Disability	5.18	—
Health/tuberculosis	14.86	12.86
Other[a]	1.97	1.97
Subtotal	48.03	39.55
Employee		
Pension	7.15	7.15
Health	0.30	0.30
Other[b]	0.35	0.35
Subtotal	7.80	7.80
Total	55.83	47.35

[a]Includes programs for orphans, assistance to agricultural workers, maternity care, and worker housing.

[b]Worker housing.

Note: Rates are applied to average daily wages for blue-collar workers and average monthly salaries of white-collar workers.

Source: Extract by the author; data from Confindustria, Rassegna di Statistiche del Lavoro, No. 2-3 (1979), p. 64.

by deficits in the agricultural pension fund is explained in no small part by the low level of contributions to social insurance made by employers in this sector. In 1977 and 1978 the deficits of the pension fund for agricultural workers (1,458 and 1,815 billion lire, respectively) accounted for 89 percent and 44 percent, respectively, of the total deficits of all social insurance and social assistance funds.

TABLE 3.6

Composition of Blue-Collar Labor Costs in 1978
(percent of total)

	Net Pay	Employee Social Insurance	Employer Social Insurance	Total Labor Cost
Agriculture	88.1	11.1	0.8	100.0
Industry	59.2	11.7	29.1	100.0
Construction	52.6	10.2	37.2	100.0
Commerce	60.3	12.8	26.9	100.0

Source: Extract by the author; data from ISTAT, Compendio
Statistico (Rome: 1979), p. 323. Data are based on selected subsectors.

Social Insurance Programs

With the exception of unemployment pay, Italian social insurance
programs are generous. The main features of these programs are
outlined below. (Certain benefits may differ in some respects from
sector to sector.)

Pensions

Italy has the lowest retirement age in Europe, 60 years for men
and 55 years for women. In by far the largest pension program,
Istituto Nazionale della Previdenza Sociale (INPS), all wage and salary
workers with at least 15 years of contributions are eligible for an old-
age pension. The pension is calculated at 2 percent for each year of
work of the workers' best three years' earnings in the last ten years
of work, with a maximum of 80 percent. A minimum pension is established, however, that applies in the event that the standard calculation produces a lower figure. Annual adjustments in pensions are
made, differing according to the level of the pension. Adjustments to
minimum pensions are made at a percentage equal to the change in a
special index of wages of blue-collar workers in industry. (The adjustment applies in all economic sectors and not just in industry.)
For pensions above the minimum (122,300 lire per month in 1979),
two adjustments are made: one based on changes in the scala mobile
index and a second based on the difference between the change in the

special index of blue-collar-worker minimum contractual wages in industry and the ordinary cost-of-living index. For the whole economy, average contributions amount to about 24 percent of basic salary, of which about 7 percent is contributed by employees and 17 percent by employers. (These contributions also cover disability insurance.)

In 1969 a "social" pension was established for all citizens over 65 years of age who have little or no other income. The permissible income is fixed periodically by law. The pension (72,250 lire per month in 1979) is financed entirely by the state and is adjusted annually on the basis of changes in the ordinary cost-of-living index.

Disability pensions are available to wage and salary workers if contributions have been paid for at least five years and at least one of those years falls in the five-year period immediately preceding a work-related accident. Disability is ascertained through a complex set of rules that take into account socioeconomic factors as well as physical factors. A generous interpretation of the socioeconomic factors (such as living in a depressed area) has permitted the mushrooming of disability pensions.

Survivor benefit pensions of up to 60 percent of the pension owed to an insured or pensioned worker may be paid to the spouse and up to 20 percent to minor or university-aged children, up to 100 percent of the pension.

Health Insurance

Active workers and their families and most pensioners are covered for the main costs of medicines, doctors' fees, and hospitalization. Blue-collar workers under the largest health program, Istituto Nazionale per l'Assicurazione Contro le Malattie (INAM), receive their normal wage for the first three days of sickness and then cash sickness benefits equal to one-half of earnings for the fourth to twentieth days of sickness and two-thirds from then on, up to a maximum of 180 days in any one year. White-collar workers receive their normal salary up to a maximum established in individual labor contracts.

Workmen's Disability Compensation

For work-related injuries 60 percent of the previous earnings of the worker are paid for 90 days and 75 percent of earnings thereafter until recovery, or until a permanent disability settlement has been reached.

Maternity Allowances

In industry 80 percent of earnings are paid for two months before birth and three months afterward (during which time workers are forbidden to work). In the year after birth, workers may be absent for up to six months at 30 percent of their wage. Also, during the year after birth the worker may be absent from work for two hours per day at full pay. Specific contracts may provide for additional benefits.

Family Allowances

For industrial workers (including pensioners with families) allowances are paid for dependent children and for spouses, provided that neither have an income above a certain maximum level fixed by law (159,000 lire per month in 1979). In 1979 the allowance amounted to 9,880 lire per month per dependent.

Unemployment Pay

The basic payment is 800 lire per day for a maximum of 180 days per year. Wage and salary workers for whom contributions have been made for at least two years, one of which immediately preceded separation, are eligible. Although basic unemployment pay is low (about 30 percent of average daily gross pay in 1978), it can be substantially supplemented under certain conditions; for example, the unemployed worker may also collect family allowances and wage supplement payments for short time work.

Wage Supplements

Under the ordinary wage supplement program for blue-collar industrial workers temporarily laid off or put on short-time (less than 40 hours per week), wage supplement payments amounting to 80 percent of gross salary for lost hours (up to 40 hours per week) are payable for up to 52 weeks, The maximum period may be extended by the government in special cases. The Wage Supplement Fund (Cassa Integrazione dei Guadagni) is financed by an employer contribution of 1 percent of the employee's gross salary if the firm has no more than 50 employees and by an employer contribution of 1.3 percent if the firm has more than 50 employees. Contributions of 4 to 8 percent of amounts compensated (4 percent for employers with no more than 50 employees, and 8 percent for employers with more than 50 employees) are required of firms with workers temporarily laid off or put on short time, both under the ordinary and the extraordinary programs.

The extraordinary program, which covers both blue- and white-collar workers, makes up 80 percent of lost wages or salaries for any time period. It is dependent, however, upon issuance of an authorization contained in an interministerial decree, which specifies a sectoral or local crisis, or which is based on industrial conversion or restructuring programs. This program is partially financed with state funds.

Redundancy Pay

Industrial workers laid off because they are superfluous, but who have been employed for more than 13 consecutive weeks, receive two-thirds of normal wages (less any unemployment benefits) for six months. Men aged 57, or women aged 52, who have made pension contributions for 15 years or more become eligible for the pension that would have been due if they were of pensionable age (60 for men and 55 for women).

Severance Pay

Redundant workers and workers terminating service are eligible for severance pay. This is based on contractual arrangements and varies among industries and sectors, but generally both blue-collar and white-collar workers receive one month's income for every year of service.

JOB SECURITY AND LABOR MOBILITY

Italian law, supplemented by labor agreements, envisages the possibility of discharging an employee only under carefully prescribed conditions. In practice, discharging a worker is extremely difficult. Unions frequently bring heavy pressure to bear through agitation and work stoppages. Magistrates (the pretori) regularly interpret the law in favor of the worker. Discharge attempts are frequently rejected and employers are ordered to restore the workers to the payroll. The final appeal procedure usually takes a minimum of three to four years. The net result of the difficulty in discharging workers is that employers fear that, in hiring a worker, they will have acquired a lifetime dependent.

The principal legislation concerning dismissals is Law No. 604 of July 15, 1966 and Law No. 300 of May 30, 1970 (the Workers' Statute). Under the latter law no worker may be dismissed without "just cause" or "justified reasons." Law 604 classifies the two types of reasons for which dismissals are permissible as subjective and

TABLE 3.7

Labor Turnover Rate in Industry, 1960s and 1970s
(departures per 1,000 workers)

	Dismissals	Resignations	Other*	Total
Average				
1961–69	35.44	34.74	10.04	80.22
1970–77	22.98	30.56	8.56	62.10
Annual				
1970	26.65	41.46	8.03	76.14
1977	10.65	21.04	9.37	41.06

*Incapacity, old age, death, and intracompany transfers.
Source: Compiled by the author; data from Bank of Italy annual reports (MinLabor data).

objective. The first involves dismissal of an individual worker because of an infraction or a failure to fulfill contractual obligations. The second involves dismissal related to the company's economic activity and use of its work force and has no relevance to the behavior of the individual worker. Objective reasons have been further broken down in court cases between individual dismissals due, for example, to abolition of a job deriving from technological change, and multiple dismissals owing to, say, the need to implement work force reductions due to lessened competitiveness. Although Law 604 states that "collective dismissals due to reduction in force shall not be subject to the provisions of this law," in fact, no other law applies to such dismissals. This seeming void is filled in several ways, notably through collective bargaining. Although in Italy collective bargaining agreements in the private sector are not legal documents enforceable in court, in practice, when suit is brought on matters involving them, magistrates typically take into account the terms of contracts and almost invariably render judgments in accordance with their provisions.

In cases of collective dismissals where no contractual agreement applies (or even in many cases where collective agreements specifically provide for the possibility of such dismissals), the affected workers routinely sue. In the absence of direct legal foundation for dealing with collective dismissals, magistrates have frequently treated reductions in force as a series of individual dismissals, requiring employers to justify the dismissal of each individual involved, in accordance with the provisions of Law 604.

Given the extreme difficulty of dismissing workers and the contractual and practical limits on labor mobility, even within the plant, employers in recent years have had good reason to pause before taking on new workers.

Available Ministry of Labor statistics on labor turnover in industrial firms show a marked slowing down in total departures and entries into industrial firms in the 1970s compared to the 1960s (see Table 3.7). The turnover rate declined sharply after 1973. In the period 1961-69 total departures averaged 80 per 1,000 workers. In the 1970s (1970-77) departures averaged only 62 per 1,000 workers. (Entries were correspondingly reduced between the two periods, averaging 84 and 60 per 1,000 workers, respectively.) Since 1974 the decline in the rate of dismissals and of total departures is even more striking, with dismissals per 1,000 workers (1974-77) falling to only 12 and total departures to only 43. In short, the pattern is one of sharply decreased labor mobility in the firms surveyed.

DUAL LABOR MARKETS

Considerable attention has been given to the problem of dual labor markets in Italy.[3] The differences are regional (north versus south), public versus private sector, and white-collar versus blue-collar. In more recent years priority attention has been given to the illegal ("black") labor market and to continued absolute differences in economic treatment (even legal treatment) between different bodies of workers, particularly within the public sector. (The latter pattern of differences and anomalies in wage compensation for similar jobs became known as the "wage jungle.") Much of the de jure dualism of the 1950s has been eliminated. What remains is largely the direct consequence of attempts to circumvent the existing laws and contractual arrangements that are designed to raise and equalize wage compensation, protect jobs, and insure more generous social insurance benefits.

Organized labor has had considerable success in obtaining uniformity of wage rates within and industry and in narrowing wage differentials among economic sectors (see Chapter 5). This tendency toward equalization of wage compensation does not necessarily reflect a corresponding leveling out of productivity among industries and sectors. Although labor contracts are contracts under private law and legally apply only to members of the employer associations and labor unions that are parties to the agreement, in practice other employers usually apply the same contract terms, and courts, in practice, often enforce these terms. Some limited measures were taken in the late 1950s to impose uniformity of contract terms throughout the economy through legislation. Also, under a 1969 agreement effective from July 1972, interarea contractual wage differences were abolished, making contract rates applicable without distinction throughout the entire country.

Because of the tendency toward nearly uniform extension of wage and social insurance benefits across the board, without regard to the ability of some firms to pay such wages and benefits, it is widely believed that a perceptible part of the Italian work force does not work under the conditions the law and labor contracts provide. This means that contractual wage rates are not being paid, social insurance contributions and income taxes are not being withheld, and job protection rules are not being respected in this illegal, or black labor area.

The exact size of the black labor sector of the economy is difficult to determine. In 1975 the number of unrecorded members of the labor force employed in this area was estimated by Luigi Frey and ISFOL-Doxa at as high as 2.2 to 2.8 million.[4] More recently (since 1977) the Central Statistical Institute (ISTAT) has included questions regarding second jobs in its labor surveys. In 1977 and 1978, respectively, 1.4 and 1.2 million respondents (6.9 and 5.7 percent of total employed persons) admitted to having second jobs. These figures, however, may underestimate the number of second jobs, due to reluctance on the part of those surveyed to admit their participation in possibly illegal work arrangements. On average for the two years, 40 percent of the principal jobs of workers with second jobs were in the services sector, 37 percent were in industry, and 23 percent were in agriculture. All of these second jobs were not necessarily illegal or black labor positions. Whatever the exact size of the black labor market may be, it is important enough to have been implicitly recognized in the revision of the national income accounts introduced in 1979 (see Chapter 5).

There is a variety of incentives for both worker and employer to engage in illegal work arrangements. For example, if a pensioner officially takes a job, his pension is reduced. A housewife can accept a part-time job and may have no need of social insurance coverage because she is already covered as the wife of an insured worker. An employer saves financially on taxes, wage rates, and social insurance contributions, while escaping legal constraints on recruitment, dismissal, advancement, severance pay, and other obligations concerning working conditions.

The problem of black labor is concentrated in smaller firms, of which there are many in Italy—for example, the last industrial and commercial census (1971) showed that 22 percent of workers in manufacturing, 31 percent in construction, 80 percent in trade, and 67 percent in services were employed in firms with no more than nine employees—a structure that offers great scope for black labor activities.

The existence of black labor undercuts the law and has become a subject of political contention. On the other hand, rightly or wrongly, the existence of black labor has been a source of flexibility in the Italian economy in time of stress, as has been the continued existence of a large block of small and medium-size firms in which black labor activity is most prevalent. In an economy in which it has become virtually impossible to dismiss workers it is not surprising that there should develop escape mechanisms whereby small business is able to survive and prosper by obtaining labor for a temporary period of time, without having to assume the burden of virtually permanent employees. Given that contractual wage rates in industry have increased on average by nearly 23 percent per year (1973-78) and far in excess of productivity, it is natural that ways should have been found to avoid the full burden of such increases. Where social insurance contributions rise at a similar rate and add almost 40 percent to the cost of gross pay, some employers will seek to avoid making such contributions. They will also acquiesce in the desire of many workers to avoid withholding of income tax on wages.

A distinction should be made between the exploitation of workers with no other employment and cooperative arrangements between an employer and a worker who already has another (legal) job. For example, it is widely believed that, particularly in boom times, much of black labor consists of moonlighting and accounts for the high level of absenteeism in industry that also prevails at such times. Given the great difficulty of dismissing workers, even for cause, and the inability of employers to check on the legitimacy of sick-leave claims, a full-time employee in an industry with strong labor demands is quite easily able to continue to draw nearly full benefits (wage, social insurance, and job protection) at his principal place of employment, while also earning tax-free income on the side.

Apart from the flexibility these arrangements provide in good times, they also may provide a source of employment in bad times. Since unemployment insurance is poor, a slowdown in production typically leads to short-time work. In such circumstances workers are able to use their free time productively by being reabsorbed into small and family-run operations. Indeed, this form of employment is akin to that formerly available in agriculture in the south, before a large part of the work force migrated to the industrial areas of the north.

It is regrettable that such illegal activities must be depended upon to provide a necessary degree of flexibility in the economy. It would be better if wage rate, social insurance, and job protection laws and agreements were sufficiently realistic in terms of Italy's economic resources to allow laws and contracts to be universally enforced without damage to the economy. So long as unrealistic requirements persist in these areas, however, it will be difficult to deal with the black labor problem. It is worth noting that the increasing financial difficulties of large firms, especially the state holding companies, can be partially attributed to the fact that such companies are simply too large successfully to evade compliance with overly generous wage rate agreements and sharply restricted labor mobility.

PRODUCTIVITY PERFORMANCE

Productivity performance in Italy in the 1970s became a cause for serious concern. For the economy as a whole the average rate of growth in output per worker in the period was only 2.7 percent, less than half the average annual increase in the 1960s (see Table 3.8). Growth of productivity in agriculture exceeded that in industry, which exceeded that in the services sector. The relatively good performance in agriculture no doubt reflected the continuing exodus of marginally productive workers in Italy's still large agricultural sector.

The prevalence of sharp cyclical fluctuations in economic activity in the 1970s was reflected in considerable volatility of productivity changes from year to year. Productivity per worker in industry in the recession or slow growth years 1971, 1975, and 1977 grew only very slowly or actually fell, pointing up the difficulty of dismissing excess workers in times of slack demand. Other reasons cited for slow productivity growth in Italy are low levels of research and development expenditures, the slowdown of capital formation, limits placed on overtime work, restrictions on labor mobility among firms and even within a firm, and high levels of lost time due to absenteeism and strike activity.

The prevalence of retaining workers on short time since it is difficult to dismiss them, can be seen in the three recession or slow growth years 1971, 1975, and 1977. In 1971, average recorded unemployment for the year actually remained unchanged from 1970, at 5.4 percent of the labor force. The number of workers on short time rose, however, from 250,000 to 311,000 (old labor survey).*

---

*Unless otherwise indicated, labor force data cited are consistent with the new labor force survey begun in 1977 and are based

TABLE 3.8

Productivity Growth, 1970–78
(output per worker, annual percent change)

	Agriculture	Industry	Total Services	Total Economy
1970	9.0	4.1	2.6	5.2
1971	0.7	1.6	2.4	1.9
1972	-0.2	5.5	1.9	4.2
1973	10.2	8.5	2.4	6.2
1974	4.1	3.0	1.2	2.5
1975	7.6	-8.7	-1.6	-3.9
1976	-3.2	10.2	1.7	5.1
1977	1.9	1.6	1.0	1.5
1978	4.5	2.4	0.9	1.9
Average 1970–78	3.8	3.1	1.4	2.7
Average 1961–69	8.8	6.1	3.8	6.3

Source: Compiled by the author; data from ISTAT, Conti
Economici Nazionali 1960–1978 (Nuova serie), Dati Analitici No. 7
(1979), p. 52.

Similarly in 1975 (the only postwar year in which real growth was
actually negative), unemployment rose by only 0.5 percentage point
(from 5.4 to 5.9 percent), while the number of laborers on short time
rose from 303,000 to 446,000 (old labor survey). In 1977 the corresponding figures were a 0.5 percentage-point rise in unemployment
and a rise in the number of short-time workers from 379,000 to
436,000. The effect of the system of short-time work as an alternative
to layoffs during periods of slow growth is that employers are not
relieved, even temporarily, of excess work force. At the same time,
employer contributions to the Wage Supplement Fund increase for
firms that must resort to the use of short-time work.

on ISTAT recalculations of old labor force survey data (see ISTAT,
Note e Relazioni, No. 56, 1979).

A 1975 study by the Organization for Economic Cooperation and Development (OECD) showed that among ten major OECD countries Italy was in last place in terms of the ratio of research and development expenditures to GNP.[5] For example, in 1971 the ratio of such expenditures to GNP was only 0.9 percent in Italy (unchanged through 1977), compared to 1.8 percent in France, 2.1 percent in Germany, and 2.3 percent in the United Kingdom. The United States, at the top of the list, had a ratio of 2.5 percent. Of course, in the past, the relatively less developed Italian economy did not have to depend upon generating new technologies in order to grow, since it was able to purchase such technology from the more advanced countries. In the long run, however, Italy cannot depend solely on imported technology to help assure an adequate rate of productivity growth.

It is generally recognized in Italy that the level of spending on research and development is insufficient. In 1977 there were about 70,000 workers in the scientific and technological sector and total expenditures were about 1.6 trillion lire, or slightly less than 1 percent of GDP. Of total expenditures about 54 percent were made by the public sector and 46 percent by business (including public enterprises).[6]

Apart from the low level of spending, there is room for improvement in the use of funds already being spent. In 1977 Ernesto Quagliariello, the head of the National Research Council (CNR), identified as problem areas the failure to create a new generation of practical researchers because of the crisis in the universities, the lack of mobility within the economic system, and an inadequate system for transferring information between science and business. Quagliariello found some cause for encouragement in the high quality of basic research in some fields and the shift in CNR's own priorities toward more applied research in such areas as energy, protein sources, land use and the environment, containers, and mechanization of agriculture. He urged the modernization of libraries and the establishment of document centers and data banks.

Another critical factor in maintaining an acceptable rate of productivity growth is the level of real capital formation (see Chapter 5). Real investment in Italy decelerated in the 1970s. Gross fixed capital investment in real terms, which had grown at an average annual rate of 5.5 percent in the period 1961-69, grew by only 0.1 percent annually in the years 1970-78. Similarly, the average GFI/GDP ratio fell from 22.2 percent (1960-69) to 19.0 percent (1970-78). By 1978 the ratio had reached a low point for the 1960s and 1970s—only 16.6 percent. (The ratio fell further in 1979.)

Productivity per worker is also related to the extent to which overtime work is possible. It has long been a goal of the Italian labor movement to restrict overtime work in order to spread around the employment opportunities. Most contracts limit overtime to about 150-200 hours per year per worker. Since 1923 the law has limited the workweek to 48 hours and the workday to 8 hours. Under 1955 legislation, industrial workers may exceed the 48-hour limit only in emergency situations when a factory's problems cannot be resolved by taking on additional workers. Permission must be sought from the Labor Inspectorate of the Ministry of Labor. Also, employers must pay 15 percent of the wages paid for hours worked over the 48-hour limit into the national unemployment insurance fund. (There is probably considerable evasion of the overtime rules.)

Data on overtime worked in large industry in the period 1972-78 show both a general decline in overtime worked and relatively little evidence that use of overtime responded to cyclical fluctuations in economic activity. In the period 1972-74 average overtime work was about 4-4.5 percent of total monthly hours worked, fluctuating from a maximum of 5.6 percent in June 1973 to a low of 3.1 percent in December 1974 (not seasonally adjusted). In the later years of the period, 1975-78, general economic stagnation limited overtime work. The annual average was 2.8 percent and the range of minimum and maximum monthly rates was 2.1 to 4.1 percent.

Italy is famous for hours lost due to strikes, which necessarily hurt labor productivity. According to the U.S. Department of Labor, in the period 1970-77 Italy led 14 major OECD countries in the number of days lost in industrial disputes, at an average of 1,374 days lost per thousand workers per year (see Table 3.9).[7]

Italy's strike record worsened during the 1970s, although there was some moderation in 1977-78 (see Table 3.10). In the 1960s, through 1968, average hours lost to labor disputes amounted to 91 million per year. In the hot autumn year of 1969, 303 million hours were lost—an all-time record for Italy. Moreover, that year was just the beginning of a consistently high level of hours lost, both in peak years of labor contract negotiations and in nonpeak years. Average hours lost in the period 1970-78 amounted to 125 million, compared to an average of 112 million in the 1960s (including the hot autumn of 1969). Of the average of 125 million hours of lost time per year in 1970-78, 52 percent was in the manufacturing sector (28 percent in the metalmechanical industry alone), far in excess of its share of the labor force.

In addition to hours lost due to labor disputes, Italian statistics since 1975 also show hours lost due to other causes—for example, in connection with protests concerning economic policy measures, social reform goals, and national and international events. In 1975-78 additional hours lost due to these causes amount to 114 million hours, compared to the 441 million hours lost in those years due to

TABLE 3.9

Strikes: Days Lost in Seven Countries, 1970–78
(per thousand wage and salary earners
in nonagricultural industries)

	Annual Average	
	1970–77	1970–78
Italy	1,374	1,291
Canada	919	909
United States	545	536
United Kingdom	509	499
France	230	n.a.*
Japan	149	n.a.
Germany	40	n.a.

*Not available.
Source: Compiled by the author; data from
U.S. Department of Labor.

labor disputes. Thus, lost time due to strikes not related to labor
disputes accounted for 21 percent of all hours lost from strikes.

Strikes are typically of short duration in Italy. In 1976, average
hours lost per worker participating in all kinds of strikes were only
15. In 1977 and 1978 the figure fell to about 8 hours. The reason is
that workers normally do not receive strike pay from the union because of scarcity of funds, and strikers are not eligible for social
insurance assistance. Also, strikes for reasons other than labor
disputes typically take the form of short demonstrations or very brief
work stoppages in the plant. Nonetheless, the unions have become
masters at effective disruption of the productive process through
selective strikes in small but crucial areas, frequently making it
impossible for workers remaining on the job to accomplish their
tasks. Furthermore, the constant pressure of strike activity has a
debilitating effect on efficient management of the work force and on
business confidence in general.

Hours lost due to strikes, however, need to be put in perspective. In the peak strike year of 1969, for the whole economy only
about five days were lost per dependent worker. In the 1970s the
average for the economy was a little more than one day (nine hours)
per worker per year for labor disputes. This is considerably less

than time lost from absenteeism. For example, among the 856 firms covered by an annual Mediobanca business survey for the period 1968-78, the average number of hours lost from strikes in the 1970s represented only 14.9 percent of total hours lost, as against 85.1 percent from absenteeism. As a percentage of total hours worked, lost time because of strikes was 2.4 percent and because of absenteeism 13.4 percent.

The high level of strike activity has engendered periodic debate about the need for enacting legislation that would lay down limits on strike actions. The principle of the right to strike is set forth in Article 40 of the Italian Constitution. The article reads: "The right to strike is exercised within the limits of the laws which regulate it." No such regulatory laws have ever been passed, however. In the absence of governing legislation, the courts have set certain limits on an ad hoc basis. At the same time, however, court decisions have also helped to widen the legitimate scope of strikes, inasmuch as political strikes have been ruled legal unless aimed at overthrowing the democratic order. All the unions—both the major

TABLE 3.10

Lost Time Due to Strikes, 1960-78
(millions of hours)

	Labor Disputes	Other	Total
1970	146.2	n.a.	n.a.
1971	103.6	n.a.	n.a.
1972	136.5	n.a.	n.a.
1973	163.9	n.a.	n.a.
1974	136.3	n.a.	n.a.
1975	181.4	8.9	190.3
1976	131.7	45.9	177.6
1977	78.8	37.2	116.0
1978	49.0	22.2	71.2
Average 1960-69	112.0	n.a.	n.a.
Average 1970-78	125.3	n.a.	n.a.

Note: n.a.—not available.
Source: Compiled by the author; data from ISTAT bulletins.

confederations and a number of smaller autonomous unions—strongly oppose regulatory legislation.

Despite the absence of legislation regulating the right to strike, a body of legal precedents has developed, setting some parameters within which that right is exercised. There have been various court decisions, but only those of the Constitutional Court have force of law, so that the legal situation remains murky. Some limits on strike activity exist: the right to strike may not with impunity violate other rights, especially the rights of personal freedom and property rights; a strike is not legal when it transgresses other rights covered by the Constitution; strikers may abandon their work only after having taken necessary steps to avoid possible damage or destruction to machinery and equipment, and strikers are not to cause damage to persons and property of the employer, and especially of third parties; the Penal Code places some restrictions on strikes involving public services and services of public necessity, coercion of the public authorities by means of a lockout or strike, and a lockout or strike for the purpose of solidarity or protest. (The Constitutional Court has ruled that possibly some of the latter "atypical" strikes do not cause greater damage than the conventional strike—suggesting that they may be, in principle, permissible.)

UNIT LABOR COSTS IN ITALY AND ABROAD

Given the slow rate of growth of productivity in Italy in the 1970s and the very high rate of increase in wages and social benefits, Italian unit labor costs rose at an exceptionally rapid rate in the decade. For the entire economy unit labor costs (based on output per worker) rose on average (1970-78) by 15 percent per year (see Table 3.11). This compared with an average increase of less than 4 percent in the 1960s. In the worst year (1975) unit labor costs for the economy rose by nearly 26 percent. The rise in unit labor costs was highest in agriculture, next highest in industry, and lowest in the services sector.

With these high absolute figures, it is also not surprising that Italian unit labor costs in manufacturing, in local currency terms, rose faster from 1970 to 1978 than in six other major industrial countries with which Italy must compete—United States, Japan, France, Germany, Canada, and the United Kingdom (see Table 3.12). According to U.S. Department of Labor data, Italian unit labor costs (calculated on the basis of productivity per hour, rather than per worker) rose on average by 16.3 percent per year from 1970 to 1978.[8] Only the United Kingdom experienced average rates of increase even approaching that (a rise of 15.8 percent). The average

TABLE 3.11

Change in Italian Unit Labor Costs, by Sector, 1970-78
(annual percent)

	Agriculture	Industry	Total Services	Total Economy
1970	10.9	14.4	7.3	9.6
1971	11.9	9.8	11.9	11.2
1972	17.3	5.4	7.5	6.3
1973	9.3	13.3	13.1	12.5
1974	28.3	19.9	17.2	18.8
1975	22.7	34.2	19.5	25.7
1976	27.3	11.9	16.5	15.1
1977	26.4	19.1	19.6	19.5
1978	13.5	10.9	14.8	12.9
Average 1970-78	18.6	15.4	14.2	14.6
Average 1961-69	3.2	3.9	5.4	3.8

Source: Compiled by the author; data from ISTAT, Conti Nazionali 1960-1978 (Nuova serie), Dati Analitici No. 7 (1979), p. 52.

increase for the other five countries ranged from 6 to 12 percent. The relatively faster rise in Italian unit labor costs was due more to the rise in hourly compensation—22 percent per year, on average— than to a low rate of productivity increase. The next highest increases were registered in the United Kingdom (18 percent) and Japan (17 percent). In the area of relative productivity growth Italy ranked third among the seven countries and Italian average annual productivity growth (4.6 percent) was only a little less than that of the first two countries in the ranking—Germany (5.4 percent) and France (5.0 percent).

Italy's very rapid increase in unit labor costs was an important contributing factor in forcing a sharp depreciation of the lira in the mid-1970s. The effect of the decline of the lira against the dollar was to reduce considerably the rise in Italian unit labor costs in dollar terms, to an average annual increase from 1970 to 1978 of 10.4 percent. This was higher than for the United States (6.1 percent) and Canada (7.5 percent), but less than for the other four countries.

TABLE 3.12

Unit Labor Costs (Per Hour) in Manufacturing
in Seven Countries, 1970-78
(average percent annual change)

	Output per Hour	Hourly Compensation	Unit Labor Costs National Currency	Dollars
Italy	4.6	21.6	16.3	10.4
United Kingdom	1.8	17.9	15.8	10.8
Japan	4.5	16.6	11.5	17.1
France	5.0	15.7	10.2	12.6
Canada	3.1	11.7	8.4	7.5
United States	2.4	8.6	6.1	6.1
Germany	5.4	11.7	5.9	13.5

Source: Compiled by the author; data from U.S. Department
of Labor.

CONCLUSIONS

Nominal wage rate increases in Italy grew at an exceptionally
rapid rate in the 1970s, particularly for blue-collar workers and
especially in agriculture and the manufacturing sector of industry.
They far exceeded productivity growth and generally more than offset price rises. Nominal wage rate hikes increasingly reflected the
effects of a comprehensive and generous system of wage indexation.
The nonwage (social insurance contributions) component of labor
costs grew apace with base pay. Much the largest share of the cost
of social insurance contributions was borne by the employer, although
the Treasury bore the burden of residual financing of social insurance
institute deficits. Productivity growth appreciably decelerated. A
variety of factors played a part: the difficulty of dismissing workers,
low research and development expenditures, stagnation in fixed capital investment, limitations on overtime work, a decline in labor
mobility, and a considerable amount of lost time due to labor disputes, political strikes, and absenteeism. The result of all these
developments was an exceptionally rapid rate of growth in unit labor
costs. Only by virtue of a large depreciation of the exchange rate
did Italy manage to remain competitive at home and abroad. Yet,

for an open and highly wage-indexed economy, dependence on exchange rate depreciation to offset too fast a rise in unit labor costs carries serious risks.

During the decade there was considerable growth in real wages (especially early in the period), coupled with increasing unemployment. [9] This growth reflected strong upward pressures on nominal wage rates, along with constraints on price rises due to the need to remain competitive internationally. It also reflected the action of an increasingly effective wage indexation system and the weakening threat of unemployment for workers already employed. Fear of unemployment became a less credible deterrent to excessive wage demands because of restrictions on dismissals and the common practice of placing workers on short-time work for which they were rather generously compensated. Evidence of the degree of job security obtained can be seen in the fact that by 1979 only 13 percent of the unemployed consisted of workers who had previously been employed and then lost their jobs. Instead, the burden of rising unemployment was falling on new job seekers and marginal workers, especially women.

The faster rise in unit labor costs than in prices caused a squeeze on profits (see Table 3.13). This, in turn, was an important cause of stagnation in fixed investment and poor employment growth (see Chapter 5). At the same time, rising unit labor costs were an important cost-push factor behind the rapid rate of inflation (see Chapter 6) and the weakness in Italy's competitive position when the energy crisis struck the balance of payments in 1974 (see Chapter 7).

The adverse effects on the employment of wage and salary workers due to poor profitability could be seen both in the economy as a whole and in the industrial sector during the 1970s. In both cases, prices (value added deflators) rose less rapidly than unit labor costs in six out of nine years and in both cases some recovery in profit margins after the 1975 recession (1976-78) failed to generate a corresponding recovery in employment growth. (Preliminary estimates for 1979 suggest a continuation of this pattern.) Developments for the total economy largely reflected conditions in the industrial sector. Poor profitability in agriculture, however, brought down the average for the total economy and rapid employment growth in government raised that average. (Prices rose less than unit labor costs in eight out of nine years in agriculture, while employment in the public sector averaged 4 percent per year in 1971-75.)

In industry, profit margins worsened in six out of nine years, especially in the early part of the decade, and employment of dependent workers fell in six out of nine years, especially in the latter part of the decade (Figure 3.2). For example, the erosion of profit margins in 1970-71 was followed by substantial employment declines in

TABLE 3.13

Relative Changes in Prices and Unit Labor Costs, 1970–78
(percent)

| | Economy | | | Industry | | |
	Value Added Deflator	Unit Labor Cost	Difference	Value Added Deflator	Unit Labor Cost	Difference
1970	7.0	9.6	-2.6	8.9	14.4	-5.5
1971	7.4	11.2	-3.8	6.7	9.8	-3.1
1972	6.5	6.3	0.2	4.8	5.4	-0.6
1973	10.8	12.5	-1.7	11.2	13.3	-2.1
1974	17.7	18.8	-1.1	21.6	19.9	1.7
1975	17.8	25.7	-7.9	21.3	34.2	-12.9
1976	17.5	15.1	2.4	16.8	11.9	4.9
1977	18.6	19.5	-0.9	18.6	19.1	-0.5
1978	13.7	12.9	0.8	12.8	10.9	1.9
Average 1970–78	13.0	14.6	-1.6	13.6	15.4	-1.8

Source: Compiled by the author; data from ISTAT, Conti Economici Nazionali 1960–78 (Nuova serie), Rome, 1979.

48

FIGURE 3.2

Changes in Profitability and Employment in Industry, 1961-78
(percent annual change)

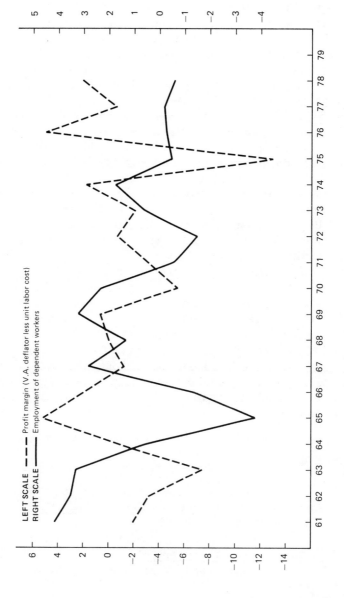

LEFT SCALE ▬ ▬ ▬ Profit margin (V.A. deflator less unit labor cost)
RIGHT SCALE ▬▬▬ Employment of dependent workers

Source: Constructed by the author; calculated from ISTAT data.

1971-72. There was a recovery in employment growth in 1973-74, following the relative improvement in profit margins in 1972-74. Employment in industry, however, continued to decline in 1975-78, despite the relatively better profit picture in 1976-78. The discouraging industrial employment picture late in the decade no doubt reflected the reluctance of employers to hire new workers in the face of continued strong wage pressures and rigidities in use of the labor force that accumulated during the course of the decade.

Toward the end of the decade flexible exchange rates and a slight moderation in the rate of increase in unit labor costs helped to improve the profit picture and the prospects for some revival of investment. Nonetheless, the years of poor profits seriously worsened the financial structure of parts of the business sector, especially large business and public enterprise. This, in turn, began to exert new pressures on the budget through the granting of subsidies to business in the form of fiscalization of part of employers' social insurance costs, capital endowment fund contributions to the state holding companies, and other forms of assistance to encourage industrial and financial restructuring of business. These government transfers, although smaller than transfers to public sector bodies, began to become a new burden on the Treasury (see Chapter 4).

In the early years of the decade there was little attempt by the government to exert restraint on labor costs (see Chapter 12). Indeed, for political reasons, the government tended to side with the unions. At the same time, new social benefits were being introduced, with much of the cost borne by employers. The one major attempt to restrict the growth of labor costs, during the 1976-77 stabilization effort, had very limited success. In sum, the rapid growth of unit labor costs adversely affected growth, employment, inflation, and the balance of payments.

NOTES

1. Ignazio Visco, "L'indicizzazione delle retribuzioni in Italia: analisi settoriale e stime per il 1978-79," Rivista di Politica Economica Vol. III (July 1979): 807-37.

2. Gino Faustini, "Wage Indexing and Inflation in Italy," Banca Nazionale del Lavoro Quarterly Review No. 119 (December 1976): 364-77; Renato Filosa and Ignazio Visco, "L'unificazione del valore del punto di contingenza e il grado di indicizzazione delle retribuzioni," Banca Nazionale del Lavoro, Moneta e Credito Vol. XXX No. 117 (March 1977): 55-83; Luigi Spaventa, "Ancora sul grado di copertura del salario: Un' estensione dell' analisi," Banca Nazionale del Lavoro, Moneta e Credito Vol. XXX No. 118 (June 1977): 217-27;

Renato Filosa and Ignazio Visco, "Copertura delle retribuzioni e inflazione a tasso variable," Banca Nazionale del Lavoro, Moneta e Credito Vol. XXX No. 119 (September 1977): 327-37. Franco Modigliani and Tomaso Papoa-Schioppa, "The Management of an Open Economy with '100% Plus' Wage Indexation," Essays in International Finance No. 130 (Princeton, N.J.: 1978).

3. See Kevin J. Allen and Andrew A. Stevenson, An Introduction to the Italian Economy (London: Martin Robertson, 1974), pp. 126-30; Vera Lutz, Italy: A Study in Economic Development (Oxford: Oxford University Press, 1962), pp. 13-54, 224-42; Giorgio Fua, "Employment and Productive Capacity in Italy," Banca Nazionale del Lavoro Quarterly Review No. 122 (September 1977): 215-44; Giorgio Fua, "Lagged Development and Economic Dualism," Banca Nazionale del Lavoro Quarterly Review No. 125 (June 1978): 123-34; Bruno Contini, "The Labour Market in Italy," Banco di Roma, Review of Economic Conditions in Italy 1 (1979): 93-114.

4. Luigi Frey, "Il potenziale del lavoro in Italia." Documenti ISVET No. 50 (1975); ISFOL-Doxa, "Forme e caratteristiche della participazione al lavoro," Osservatorio ISFOL, No. 5 (September 1975).

5. OECD, Patterns of Resources Devoted to Research and Experimental Development in the OECD Areas, 1963-71 (Paris: OECD, 1975).

6. Ernesto Quagliariello, "The State of Scientific Research in Italy," Banco di Roma, Review of Economic Conditions in Italy Vol. XXXI No. 1 (November 1977): 357-73.

7. U.S. Department of Labor, Bureau of Labor Statistics, Industrial Disputes, Workers Involved and Worktime Lost, Fourteen Countries, 1955-1978 (Washington, D.C.: June 1979).

8. U.S. Department of Labor, Bureau of Labor Statistics, Output Per Hour, Hourly Compensation, and Unit Labor Costs in Manufacturing, Eleven Countries, 1950-1978 (Washington, D.C.: July 1979).

9. See Jeffrey D. Sachs, "Wages, Profits and Macroeconomic Adjustment: A Comparative Study," Brookings Papers on Economic Activity 2 (1979): 269-332. Sachs presents a comparison of the role of real wages in the macroeconomic performance of seven industrial economies (including Italy).

4

GROWING PUBLIC SECTOR DEFICITS

The most subtle instruments of monetary policy cannot
protect the economy from the inflationary pressures that
derive from public expenditure which, at all levels, tends
to expand. . . . If the national and local communities . . .
refuse to coordinate their demands for social services
with the volume of available resources, and if the provision of these services continues to be characterized by
inefficiency and waste, the harsh necessity will arise of
enduring that most iniquitous of all taxes, that is,
inflation.

> Guido Carli
> Governor, Bank of Italy
> Annual Meeting, Rome, May 1970

STRUCTURE OF THE PUBLIC SECTOR

The public sector in Italy is large and financial interrelation-
ships are complex. Careful analysis of the statistics has become
particularly necessary with the growth of current and capital transfer
payments, mainly from the central government to lower levels of
government and to other public bodies, and with some recent consolidation by the central government of past debts accumulated by the
municipal and provincial governments, the hospitals, and the health
insurance institutes.

The "Public Sector" consists of

1. The state (Treasury)
2. The Postal Savings Fund (Cassa Depositi e Prestiti)

3. Autonomous entities of the central government (state railways, state highways, state monopolies, post and telecommunications, state telephone system, and state forests)
4. Other central government bodies
5. Local bodies (regions, provinces, municipalities, hospitals, and other minor bodies)
6. Social insurance institutes

This definition of the public sector notably does <u>not</u> include the state holding companies: the state industrial holding company, Istituto per la Ricostruzione Industriale (IRI); the national petroleum company, Ente Nazionale di Idrocarburi (ENI); the state holding and finance company for the manufacturing industry, Ente di Partecipazione e Finanziamento Industria Manufatturiera (EFIM); and the metallic minerals holding company (in liquidation), Ente Autonomo di Gestione per le Aziende Minerarie Metallurgiche (EGAM). Also not included in the "public sector" is the national electric company, Ente Nazionale di Energia Elettrica (ENEL).

For analytical purposes, some of these bodies are grouped into a category called "public enterprises," which includes the state holding companies, ENEL, and some minor central government enterprises. (The Bank of Italy's Credit risk Center data also include as public enterprise the central government's autonomous entities, local government autonomous entities, the hospitals, and a few other minor bodies.)

For national income accounting purposes another definition is used, covering most of the public sector—the "public administration." This includes the central administration (items 1 and 4 in the list of the components of the public sector, plus the state highways and state forests); local administrations (item 5); and social insurance institutes (item 6).

In this chapter major attention will be given to fiscal operations of still another part of the public sector, the "state sector," or treasury cash budget. This includes the Treasury's central government cash budget operations, plus certain off-budget treasury cash transactions. The Treasury is first of all responsible for providing financing for ordinary budgeted central government expenditures. It must also, however, provide financing for a considerable amount of off-budget operations. These consist mainly of "minor treasury operations," residual financing of local government deficits, and financing of deficits of the autonomous entities. While it is not directly responsible for financing the deficits of the state holding companies and ENEL, it does make periodic "endowment fund" contributions that are largely used for this purpose.

To further complicate matters, there may be shifts over time between budget and off-budget items. For example, the Treasury may effect an expenditure in off-budget accounts on a temporary basis until the item can be provided for later through the budget; or the Treasury may initially provide residual financing for deficits on an off-budget basis but eventually arrange for a permanent source of budgeted transfers to meet future financing needs; or a budget transfer may be made to a lower level of government (especially the regions) but then be recorded as an off-budget receipt in a holding account maintained with the Treasury. Finally, in recent years especially, treasury debt consolidation operations in favor of the local governments, hospitals, and health institutions have complicated the accounts.

The state sector (or treasury cash deficit) concept is the one traditionally employed in Italy for analyzing both fiscal developments and monetary developments, since it is integrated with the monetary base statistics. More recently, however, a broader definition of the "enlarged public sector" has also been employed in connection with fiscal targets established under lending agreements with the International Monetary Fund (IMF) and the EC. This enlarged public sector consists mainly of the public sector plus ENEL.

Each of these public bodies has its own sources of income and spending responsibilities. The main source of treasury income is, of course, tax revenues, although there are modest amounts of non-tax current income and capital income. Also, the Treasury's Postal Savings Fund receives postal savings of the public. These are used by the Treasury mainly to provide off-budget financing for local government deficits (through 1977, after which such financing was mainly included in budget transfers). Local governments, which provide the usual municipal services and some recently decentralized types of services formerly provided by the central government, now receive their principal income in the form of revenue sharing with the central government, but they also retain very modest sources of local tax revenues and have income from the sales of goods and services. The social insurance institutes cover most of the cost of their services from social insurance contributions from employers and employees, but residual deficits must be financed by the Treasury, either through periodic budget transfers or through off-budget financing. The autonomous entities, which are mainly in the transport and communication fields, also receive substantial transfers from government, but depend more importantly on the sale of their goods and services (for example, the state monopolies' sales of salt and tobacco, state railroad fares, postal and telegraphic fees, telephone charges, highway tolls, and the like). The state holding companies operate much like private companies—that is, through the sale of goods and services. In addition the Treasury, autonomous entities, and state holding companies may borrow from the banking system and issue public securities.

An important decentralization of government is taking place as a result of the long-delayed creation of the "ordinary" regional governments. (Previously there were "special" regional governments, created immediately after World War II for several regions.) In mid-1971 laws were passed concerning the regional electoral system, system of finance, and basic statutes. The actual transfer of responsibility, however, devolved only gradually upon the regions in succeeding years. The main areas of regional responsibility are health and public welfare, regional transport and other infrastructure, some economic activities (for example, agriculture, tourism, inland fishing, minerals, thermal waters, quarries, and peat bogs), and fairs and markets. Responsibility for industry and education were not included in the powers assigned to the regions (except in the older special regions). In addition to transferring certain taxes, a "common fund" corresponding to the yield from various taxes and a "fund for development programs" were created to provide channels for financial assistance to the regions.

A major responsibility in the health field was transferred to the regions, effective from January 1, 1975 when they became responsible for hospitalization services. As of July 1, 1977 the former health insurance institutes were placed in liquidation, but they continue to carry out some functions, pending implementation of a planned health reform.

THE TAX SYSTEM

Tax System, Tax Reform

Italy's present tax system is in large part the result of a comprehensive tax reform first authorized by enabling Law No. 825 of October 9, 1971. A new indirect tax, a value added tax, went into effect at the beginning of 1973 and new income taxes at the beginning of 1974.* The tax reform, aimed at greater efficiency and greater

---

*The basic tax laws provided for a personal income tax, by Presidential Decree 597 of September 29, 1973; for a corporate income tax, by Presidential Decree 598 of September 29, 1973; for a local income tax, by Presidential Decree 599 of September 29, 1973; and for a value-added tax, by Delegated Decree 633 of October 26, 1972. Various revisions have subsequently been made in these laws.

equity, simplified, centralized, and modernized the tax system. The simplification involved the elimination of a large number of indirect taxes that had accumulated over the years, and substitution of separate personal and corporate income taxes for an income tax that formerly had applied to both types of income recipient (but which had varied according to type of income). Centralization involved the termination of most local taxing authority and substitution of a form of revenue sharing with the central government. The modernization consisted mainly of the extension of withholding at the source. After 1974 additional improvements were added, mainly concerning more current methods of payment of tax on income not subject to withholding.

In the field of indirect taxes, the old principal sales tax, the imposta generale sulle entrate (IGE), and a number of minor indirect taxes were replaced by a new value added tax, the imposta sul valore aggiunto (IVA). Adoption of a value-added tax was in part a response to EC tax harmonization efforts and to the belief that tax evasion could be reduced by the adoption of a more self-enforcing type of tax. The IVA applies at different rates to nearly all domestic and imported goods and services with the principal exemptions applying to rents, some public service charges, banking, insurance and stock brokerage services, health and welfare services, educational, cultural, and research services, and games of chance.

Second in importance in terms of revenue among Italy's indirect taxes is a group of excise or manufacturing taxes on such items as petroleum products, spirits, beer, sugars, edible fats and oils, gas, electric energy, and methane. There is a third group of taxes on business transactions, mainly consisting of a registration tax, stamp tax, mortgage tax, a tax on advertising, and a government concessions tax. In addition, tax revenue comes from consumption taxes (coffee, cacao, and bananas) and other minor taxes. (Customs duties are transferred to the EC.)

Direct taxes consist of a personal income tax (imposta sul reddito delle persone fisiche—IRPEF), a corporate income tax (imposta sul reddito delle persone giurdiche—IRPEG), a "local" income tax (collected by the Treasury) from persons and corporations on nonwage incomes (imposta locale sui redditi—ILOR), a (definitive) withholding tax on interest income, a withholding tax (on account) on dividends, an inheritance and gift tax, and some other minor taxes. There is also a local tax on capital gains on real estate (imposta sull' incremento di valore degli immobili—INVIM). In addition, for several years after the reform, revenue was still being received from the delayed collection of income taxes abolished under the reform. Table 4.1 shows principal direct and indirect tax rates.

While the income tax laws originally did not provide for self-assessment and current payment of the tax on income not subject to

TABLE 4.1

Principal Tax Rates
(percent)

Income taxes	
Personal (IRPEF)	10-72[a]
Corporate (IRPEG)	35
Local (ILOR)	15
Withholding taxes[b]	
Interest	
Public debt bonds[c]	Exempt
Special credit institute bonds	10
Private/public enterprise bonds	20
Bank and postal deposits	20
Dividends	10
Gift tax	3-29[d]
Inheritance tax	3-60[d]
Value added tax (IVA)	
Standard	14
Intermediate	18
Luxury	35
Reduced	
Food necessities	1
Other food	3
Housing	6
Textiles/clothing	9

[a]10 percent on taxable income up to 3 million lire;
72 percent on taxable income above 550 million lire.

[b]Taxes on interest are definitive taxes; tax on dividends is on account against overall tax liability.

[c]Includes issues by Treasury, Postal Savings Fund, local governments, and autonomous entities.

[d]Inheritance tax rates include both tax on estate and tax on inheritance. Applicable rates depend on amount of gift or inheritance and relationship of beneficiary to gift giver or deceased.

Source: Compiled by the author from Ministry of Finance data.

withholding by individuals and corporations at the time of filing annual declarations, this shortcoming was subsequently corrected with the Visentini minireform of 1975.* In addition, advance payments of tax on income not subject to withholding were introduced by subsequent laws of 1977-78.[†] Thus, on income subject to IRPEF and IRPEG, individuals and corporations were required (effective in 1977) to make advance payments on current-year income amounting to 75 percent of the estimated personal or corporate income tax due, calculated on the basis of the prior year's income, whenever such tax exceeded 250,000 lire (personal income) or 40,000 lire (corporate income). Effective in 1978, the same obligation was applied to income subject to ILOR, whenever the tax exceeded 40,000 lire. (Also in 1978 the minimum personal income tax subject to advance payment was reduced from 250,000 lire to 100,000 lire.) In all cases, the advance payment is due by the end of November of the year in which the income is earned.

Tax Evasion

Prior to the tax reforms Italy suffered from a particularly high rate of income tax evasion. Such evasion was possible for rich and poor alike, because withholding at the source (even on wages and salaries) was not comprehensive and because the "negotiation" between the taxpayer and the tax collector of the tax to be assessed left much room for uncertainty. Furthermore, the longer the eventual payment of the tax could be delayed, the more depreciated would be the lire in which payment was made. Evasion was always easiest for nonwage income than for earned income. With the introduction of more comprehensive withholding at the source, not only on wages and salaries but also on interest earnings, dividends, and professional services extended to corporations, and with the adoption of nearly pay-as-you-go taxes on nonwage income, most of the income received by the bulk of the population became subject to prompt payment requirements.

Also, when the value-added tax was instituted at the beginning of 1973, it was widely believed that the tax would be largely self-enforcing, since at each stage of sale the purchaser would have a self-interest in assuring that the previous seller had recorded the

---

*Law 576 of December 2, 1975, applicable to 1975 and subsequent income.

[†]Personal income and corporate income tax, Law 749 of October 17, 1977; local income tax, Law 38 of February 23, 1978.

amount of tax owed at that stage, so that the buyer could deduct that amount from the calculation of his own tax liability. Especially in the beginning, and as regards sales of domestically produced goods and services, the revenue generated from IVA was disappointing. It is still believed that IVA tax evasion is widespread.* For example, if the initial seller of the goods and services does not begin the tax calculation process, then all the succeeding processors may also escape the tax. Moreover, given the large number of small producers and distributors in Italy, enforcement is particularly difficult. Finally, since value-added tax records are used in assessing income taxes, the understating of the volume of business due to value-added tax evasion also reduces the income tax assessment.

Estimates of the extent of income tax evasion are not very reliable. In 1979, however, a comparison of 1976 tax returns with national income data by the Ministry of Finance suggested that about 80 percent of wages and salary income was being reported, against only about 45 percent for other forms of income.

THE EXPENDITURE SYSTEM

Budget Procedures

The Italian budget is designed mainly as the basis for obtaining legal authorizations for spending. Substantive discussion of specific spending programs takes place mostly in connection with debate on individual expenditure laws. The current system does, however, provide the basis for a general review of the level of spending and revenue projected in the budget year and in the succeeding 3-5 year period. It also offers the opportunity to review and amend past expenditure programs, and presents a comparison of forecast budgets with economic policy goals.

Budgets must be submitted to Parliament by September 30 of the preceding year. Although the budget should be approved by Parliament by the end of December, this is frequently not done, so there is a procedure for provisional budget appropriations for up to four months of the new fiscal year, until the budget is finally passed. The budget law itself does not propose new expenditure or new taxation, which must be separately authorized by Parliament. The appropriations budget sets the limits at which the government may accept

---

*In 1980 the Ministry of Finance estimated that only 50 percent of the IVA due in 1977 was actually collected.

financial commitments based on existing expenditure laws and estimates the amount of revenue that can be raised under current tax
laws. In theory, all expenditure laws should fix exactly what sums
are to be spent, either in aggregate or yearly, and by what means
financing is to be provided. In practice, however, these laws are
frequently drawn up in nonspecific terms, leaving the fixing of annual
appropriations and funding to the subsequent annual budgets. Some
expenditure laws do provide for annual sums for multiyear expenditure, which have to be entered at the original nominal valuation in the
budget each year. Other compulsory multiyear expenditure allocations
are linked to movements in interest rates or the cost of living, or
other economic variables.

A significant part of each year's expenditures is previously
committed because of these multiyear expenditures, compulsory
expenditures, and other expenditure commitments such as continuing
transfers (as in the case of revenue sharing with the local governments).
For example, the 1980 appropriations budget showed that the increase
in multiyear expenditures accounted for 15 percent of the total increase
over 1979 and other compulsory expenditures for 103 percent.
(Changes in other expenditure items were actually negative.) On the
other hand, a 1978 law does provide a procedure for making some
adjustments in past expenditure commitments.

Appropriations on capital account that have not been spent are
automatically carried forward for up to five years, or indefinitely,
if the funds have actually been committed. Current account appropriations, if they have been actually committed, may also be carried
forward indefinitely. These accumulated but unspent appropriations,
residui passivi, are quite large, both in absolute amount and in relation to total budget expenditures. The residui attivi (assessed but
uncollected taxes and other revenues) have also been fairly large but
less so than the residui passivi. There is some evidence that both
residui are declining in importance, as a larger share of cash expenditure is made up of transfers, which can be made rather promptly,
and as current collections of taxes have been expanding. Table 4.2
shows the extent to which cash revenues and expenditures have been
the result of previous years' budgets.

It is commonly assumed that the existence of large residui
passivi must make the task of forecasting and controlling actual cash
expenditure rather difficult and the existence of large residui passivi
has been a constant source of debate. The relationship between annual
cash expenditure and residui, however, has historically been fairly
stable, particularly for current expenditure. More important than the
difficulty of forecasting such expenditures is the fact that long delays
in expending funds, especially on capital account, drastically limit

TABLE 4.2

Cash Expenditures and Revenues Arising from
Previous Years' Budgets, 1970-78
(percent of total)

	Revenues (Residui Attivi)			
	Direct Taxes	Indirect Taxes[a]	Total Revenue[b]	Expenditures (Residui Passivi)
1970	12.0	6.8	8.0	18.8
1971	12.3	4.3	10.1	18.5
1972	12.5	4.1	9.9	19.9
1973	12.7	3.0	8.2	21.5
1974	9.7	8.0	9.3	16.6
1975	5.9	3.2	5.8	17.7
1976	3.7	3.0	3.0	20.8
1977	2.5	1.9	3.5	17.1
1978	3.3	2.6	4.6	13.3

[a]Transaction taxes only (for example, IGE, IVA, registration, stamp, auto, TV).
[b]Including nontax revenues.
Note: The figures include a thirteenth month—the first month of the succeeding calendar year.
Source: Compiled by the author; data from Conto Riassuntivo del Tesoro, various issues.

the ability of the government to use expenditure policy as an effective tool of demand management and as a source of investment growth.

The Treasury finances its deficits mainly from the issue of currency, treasury bills, medium- and long-term bonds, drawings on postal savings, and borrowing from the central bank. Although legally the Treasury can borrow on current account from the Bank of Italy only up to 14 percent of the amount of government expenditure appropriations in the original budget estimates and subsequent amendments, it can obtain additional financing from the central bank through the bank's purchase of treasury and other government securities.

Budget Reform

By the mid-1970s concern about the growth of the public sector deficit and the desire to gain better control over expenditures pointed to the need to collect more comprehensive and consistent data about the expenditures of all components of the public sector and the need to project expenditure levels farther into the future. Traditionally the Italian budget process had been focused on the appropriations budget, rather than on actual cash receipts and expenditures. Some data on a cash basis had also been collected and published, but until early 1977 (under a 1976 law), cash budget forecasts were not regularly prepared and made public. Beginning in 1977, however, the Treasury was required to present to Parliament cash budget forecasts for the current budget year four times during the year (February, May, August, and November).

A further step forward was made in obtaining better data on the finances of the entire public sector and better control over its expenditures with passage of Law 468 of August 5, 1978. The main objectives of this budget reform law were to provide a clearer and more comprehensive picture of public expenditures and receipts, to set limits to the use of unspent appropriations (residui passivi) carried over from previous years, and to provide a tool for the government to alter expenditures under existing programs.

Starting with FY 1978 (calendar 1978) the annual central government's budget year was changed so as to begin on January 1 and terminate on December 31. Previously the fiscal year was the same as the calendar year, but the fiscal year was not officially closed until January 31 of the following year. This thirteenth, supplementary month allowed certain tidying up transactions to take place before the books closed—in particular, the collection and payment of taxes assessed for the fiscal year and the actual discharge of certain expenditure commitments for which the payment orders had been issued but not yet cashed by the end of December.*

---

*The basic published source of data on treasury cash operations, the Conto Riassuntivo del Tesoro, included a supplement to cover the thirteenth month before the 1978 reform. Data published by the Bank of Italy, however, showed the thirteenth-month operations, which actually occurred in the following year, as part of treasury operations in the second year. This resulted in some differences between the two presentations of cash data. There are also other Bank of Italy adjustments to the treasury data. Bank of Italy sources are cited in this book, unless otherwise indicated.

Starting with FY 1979 the government was required to submit not only appropriations budget figures when the budget was presented to Parliament, but also to prepare a cash budget on an experimental basis, for submission to Parliament by December 31, 1978. Beginning with FY 1980 annual budgets were drawn up and presented to Parliament, containing information on the residui, the appropriations (competenza) budget, and the cash (cassa) budget.

Multiyear Budgets

Another important innovation was introduced by Law 468 in the form of a requirement that (beginning with FY 1979) the government would have to prepare a multiyear appropriations budget covering a period of not less than three and not more than five years. (The first such budget covered the period 1979-81.) The multiyear budget, which must be updated annually on the occasion of the presentation of the annual budget for the following year, shows, separately, the trends of revenue and expenditures as estimated in accordance with prevailing legislation and a forecast of trends that would be consistent with the commitments and goals of national economic policy. It also indicates a limit on the recourse to financial markets for each of the years. The multiyear budget is only a planning device—it is not an authorization for collecting revenues nor for making expenditures. It is approved under the same law that provides for the approval of the annual budget.

Adjustment of Past Expenditure Commitments

Also created under Law 468 is a procedure to adjust revenues and expenditures in the budgets of the central government, the autonomous entities (which are included in the central government budget), and other public entities linked to central government finances. The ministers of treasury, budget, and finance are authorized to submit a "financial law" to the Parliament along with the budget, by which changes can be made in existing legislation relating to the budgets of these three parts of the public sector. This procedure makes it possible for the government to modify previous program commitments and is designed to make expenditure policy a more flexible tool of economic management. The financial law sets a maximum level of recourse to financial markets.

Changes in the Budget

The government must submit a bill to Parliament by the end of June each year, showing any proposed overall changes in original budget appropriations. Any other specific legislation that would cause an ad hoc change either in administrative or cash appropriations for a given fiscal year must be submitted to Parliament no later than October 31 of that year.

Standard Budget Accounting

Under Law 468 other parts of the public administration (such as local governments, hospitals, municipal enterprises, and ENEL) are required to conform their accounting systems to those adopted by the central government for the preparation of the annual appropriations and cash budgets, so as to permit a consolidation of all transactions pertaining to the entire public sector. These bodies are also required to provide the minister of treasury with figures on estimated revenues and expenditures for each year, to be included in the central government's multiyear budget.

EVOLUTION OF THE TREASURY CASH DEFICIT

Along with the growth of labor costs, the growth of the treasury cash deficit was the subject of much concern in the 1970s. Not only did the size of the deficit rise over time, but it was very high by international standards (see Table 4.3). Also, its financing was the principal source of rapid monetary expansion.

The exact size of the fiscal deficit varies, depending upon the breadth of coverage of the public sector employed. In 1978 the ratio of the various deficits to GDP under each of the main budget concepts was in the 11-13 percent range. For example the deficit of general government (the public administration, consisting of all levels of government, plus the social insurance institutes) amounted to 10.6 percent of GDP. The deficit of the public sector (which also includes the autonomous entities) amounted to 11.6 percent of GDP. The traditional measurement of the treasury cash deficit showed a deficit equal to 13.0 percent of GDP.

Italian fiscal deficits are high by international standards of the principal industrial countries. For example, in 1978 OECD statistics showed that the weighted average deficit of the public administration was 2.3 percent of GDP for the largest seven countries of the OECD, with the 10.6 percent deficit for Italy being far larger than that of the other countries: Japan 4.8 percent, the United Kingdom 3.9 percent, Canada 3.5 percent, Germany 2.7 percent, France 2.3 percent, and the United States 0.1 percent.[1]

Comparative EC statistics on 1978 revenues (including social insurance contributions) and expenditures of the public administration show that, on the expenditure side, Italy was more or less in line with its principal EC partners (about 47 percent of GDP), but that the

TABLE 4.3

Treasury Cash Deficits, 1970–78
(trillions of lire)

	Budget Deficit	Off-Budget Deficit				Total Deficit	Less Debt Consolidation	Net Deficit
		Minor Treasury Operations	Autonomous Entities	Postal Fund (local govern-ment, etc.)	Total			
1970	-2.4	0.3	-0.5	-0.6	-0.8	-3.2	—	-3.2
1971	-3.0	-0.5	-0.5	-0.7	-1.7	-4.7	0.3	-4.4
1972	-3.6	-0.8	-0.6	-0.8	-2.2	-5.8	0.2	-5.6
1973	-7.3	0.8	-0.3	-1.2	-0.7	-8.0	0.5	-7.5
1974	-5.2	-1.9	0.1	-1.9	-3.7	-8.9	0.3	-8.6
1975	-10.3	-4.1	-0.1	-2.0	-6.2	-16.5	2.4	-14.1
1976	-10.4	-1.7	-0.1	-2.5	-4.3	-14.7	0.4	-14.3
1977	-12.4	—	-0.4	-9.6	-10.0	-22.4	5.4	-17.0
1978	-33.4	3.3	—	-3.8	-0.5	-33.9	5.2	-28.7

Source: Compiled by the author from Bank of Italy annual reports.

ratio of Italian revenues to GDP was somewhat lower than the EC average (about 37 percent versus 43 percent. See Table 4.4.)

Italian source data on the treasury cash deficit (a different concept) reflects a considerably faster rate of growth of expenditures than of receipts (see Table 4.5). In the decade of the 1960s cash receipts (excluding social insurance contributions) averaged 17 percent of GDP and cash expenditures 18 percent. In the 1970s (1970-78) the corresponding average figures were 19 percent and 26 percent of GDP. As a consequence, the central government's cash deficit rose from an average of about 1 percent of GDP in the 1960s to almost 7 percent of GDP in the 1970s. Including off-budget deficit financing by the Treasury, the total treasury cash deficit grew from an average of 3 percent of GDP in the 1960s to 9 percent in the 1970s.

The growth of the central government's cash deficit did not have a corresponding effect on public consumption and public investment in the national income accounts, since these types of expenditures have declined as a share of total expenditures. In 1978 total purchases of goods and services amounted to only 4.2 percent of total cash budget expenditures, while direct investment was only 0.8 percent of the

TABLE 4.4

Ratios of EC Countries' Revenues
and Expenditures to GDP, 1978
(percent of GDP)

	Revenues	Expenditures	Deficit
Germany	44.0	46.8	-2.7
France	43.3	45.6	-2.3
United Kingdom	38.9	42.8	-3.9
Italy	36.8	47.4	-10.6
EC Average	42.8	46.8	-4.0

Note: Revenues and expenditures are those of public administration which includes social insurance contributions and benefits.

Source: Compiled by the author; data from European Community, Economia Europea No. 3 (July 1979).

TABLE 4.5

Treasury Receipts, Expenditures, and Deficit, 1960-78
(percent of GDP)

	Budget Receipts	Budget Expenditures	Budget Deficit	Total Treasury Deficit*
1970	16.9	20.8	3.9	5.1
1971	17.3	21.8	4.4	6.5
1972	16.3	21.1	4.8	7.5
1973	15.9	24.0	8.1	8.4
1974	16.6	21.3	4.7	7.8
1975	19.0	27.2	8.2	11.3
1976	20.4	27.1	6.6	9.1
1977	22.7	29.2	6.5	9.0
1978	24.4	39.6	15.1	13.0
Average, 1960-69	16.8	17.9	1.2	2.8
Average, 1970-78	18.8	25.8	6.9	8.6

*Includes net off-budget operations; excludes debt consolidation.
Source: Compiled by the author; calculated from data in Bank
of Italy annual reports and ISTAT, Conti Economici Nazionali 1960-
1978 (Nuova serie), Rome, 1979.

total. Within these two categories, purchases of goods and services
for the national defense accounted for 54 percent of such purchases.
General administration was second in importance (15 percent); public
safety was third (9 percent). Direct investment expenditures were
concentrated in the fields of industry (40 percent), transport and
communications (28 percent), and education (25 percent).

The direct effect of the rise in cash budget expenditures for
goods and services on aggregate demand was limited. There were,
however, large indirect effects of the growing deficit in the form of
transfer payments, both on current account and on capital account.
In addition to its indirect effects on growth and employment, the
deficit also had important consequences for monetary developments
(see Chapter 8).

In 1969 there was still some public saving available to finance public investment, in the form of a surplus on current transactions. In every year of the 1970s, however, the current account was in deficit, with the deficit in 1978 extremely large (even adjusting for the inclusion of some transfers included in the current account to finance debt consolidation).

CENTRAL GOVERNMENT DEFICIT

Receipts

During the 1970s (1970-78) the growth of central government cash revenue, despite some improvements due to the tax reform, did not keep pace with the rise in cash expenditures, with revenues rising on average per year by nearly 22 percent (see Table 4.6) and expenditures by 28 percent. In real terms total revenues rose on average by 7.4 percent per year and total expenditures by 12.4 percent.

In the post-tax-reform period 1974-78 direct taxes grew on average by 38 percent per year and indirect taxes by 22 percent. (Note that social insurance contributions are not included in tax receipts data contained in the central government's budget.) To a considerable extent the nominal growth merely reflected the rapid rate of inflation in that period. There was also, however, an increase in tax revenues in real terms. For the entire period (1970-78) real direct tax revenues increased on average by 12 percent per year, while indirect taxes rose much less—about 3 percent per year. In the period since the income tax reform (1974-78) real direct tax revenues grew on average by 18 percent per year, indirect tax revenues by 4 percent, and total tax revenue by more than 9 percent.

Some progress can be seen in the shifting of the tax burden from indirect to direct taxes (excluding social insurance contributions). Whereas in 1970 direct taxes accounted for only 27 percent of tax receipts, in 1978 the figure was 46 percent. There was also a tendency toward a relative increase in revenue from personal income taxes, compared to income taxes on businesses. For example, personal taxes accounted for 76 percent of the total in 1970, compared to 81 percent in 1978. This was the result of better collection of taxes on wages and salaries, of the progressivity of the personal income tax in a time of rapid inflation, and of the relatively poor profit performance of business. The decline in the ratio of tax revenue to total receipts (from 94 percent in 1970 to 86 percent in 1978) was largely due to the rise in transfer receipts, especially withdrawals from special treasury accounts for financing treasury transfer payments to the regions for consolidation of hospital debt and to the

TABLE 4.6

Growth of Cash Budget Receipts, 1970–78
(percent change)

	Direct Taxes		Indirect Taxes[a]		Total Receipts[b]	
	Nominal	Real[c]	Nominal	Real[c]	Nominal	Real[c]
1970	2.3	-4.2	14.7	7.4	12.0	4.9
1971	14.8	7.1	7.3	0.1	12.0	4.5
1972	20.0	12.9	—	-5.9	2.8	-3.3
1973	15.0	3.0	Reform 19.7	7.3	16.3	4.2
1974	Reform 42.9	20.6	23.1	3.9	29.2	9.0
1975	24.9	6.3	10.5	-6.0	28.9	9.7
1976	46.5	24.2	29.6	9.8	34.6	14.1
1977	36.2	14.6	27.2	7.0	34.8	13.4
1978	40.4	23.9	18.8	4.9	25.0	10.3
Average	27.0	12.0	16.8	3.2	21.7	7.4

[a] Does not include social insurance contributions.
[b] Including nontax receipts; excluding social insurance contributions.
[c] Deflated by GDP Deflator.

Source: Compiled by the author; elaboration of data in Bank of Italy annual reports.

TABLE 4.7

Average Tax Rates, 1970–78

	Direct Taxes[a]	Indirect Taxes[b]
1970	6.2	10.0
1971	6.5	9.8
1972	7.1	8.9
1973	6.8	Reform 8.7
1974	Reform 8.1	8.1
1975	9.1	8.2
1976	10.7	8.5
1977	11.9	9.0
1978	14.3	9.2

[a]Ratio of tax to net national income at factor cost (excluding employer's social insurance contributions).
[b]Ratio of tax to final domestic demand.
Source: Compiled by the author; calculations based on Bank of Italy and ISTAT data.

health insurance institutes for consolidation of the institutes' debts to the hospitals.

Tax revenue elasticity seems to have increased somewhat following the introduction of new indirect taxes in 1973 and the new direct taxes in 1974. In the period 1971-73 direct tax elasticity was about 1.4, while in the period 1974-78 it rose to 2.0. (This elasticity is measured as the change in direct tax revenue divided by the change in net domestic income at factor cost—excluding employer social insurance contributions.) For indirect taxes, the prereform figures for 1970-72 showed an elasticity of about 0.6 compared to 1.1 for the later period 1973-78. (Elasticity is measured by the change in indirect tax revenue divided by the change in final domestic demand.)

The pattern of average tax rates since the income tax reform of 1974 also shows a steady increase (see Table 4.7). In the period just prior to the reform (1970-73) the average direct tax rate was 6.6 percent (measured against net national income at factor cost, excluding employer social insurance contributions). In the period since the reform (1974-78) the average tax rate was about 10.8 percent and followed an upward trend. The apparent increase in tax elasticity and in the average tax, however, reflected in part the overlapping of the new system of nearly pay-as-you-go collections with continued collections of old taxes.

For indirect taxes the pattern is rather different. In the period 1969-72, prior to the reform in 1973, the average tax rate was 9.6 percent (measured against final domestic demand). Subsequently, the average rate dropped to 8.6 percent for the period 1973-78. The annual figures, however, show a general decline in the trend in] 969-74, which was arrested and reversed in the following period 1975-78. Since there were some indirect tax rate increases, particularly a package of increases in 1976-77, the rise in the average rate does not necessarily demonstrate improved tax collection capabilities.

Expenditures

A functional breakdown of central government budget expenditures shows that by 1978 social welfare expenditures and assistance to local governments had become the most important categories of on-budget expenditures (see Table 4.8). This contrasted rather sharply with the pattern for 1969, when educational expenditures and expenditures for economic assistance (such as capital transfers, endowment fund contributions, interest subsidies, and credits to other public bodies) were the two most important categories of expenditure.

In the period 1970-78 total cash budget expenditures rose on average by 28 percent per year, with current expenditures up 29 percent and capital expenditures up 27 percent (see Table 4.9). There was a very rapid rate of increase in current transfer payments (36 percent), particularly transfer payments to local governments (51 percent). In real terms, total cash expenditures grew at an average annual rate of 12 percent. Current expenditures grew by 13 percent, while capital expenditures grew by only 11 percent. Within current expenditures, real transfer payments rose by almost 20 percent per year.

Expenditures on compensation of personnel (salaries and pensions of government employees) grew at an average annual rate of 20 percent. Employment in the public administration grew fairly substantially, rising from 2.1 million in 1970 to 2.9 million in 1978. Salary rates, however, in the public administration (average annual increase of 10 percent in 1970-78) did not rise as fast as for workers in other major economic sectors. A very large part of wage and salary payments were to teachers (61 percent in 1978), police (12 percent), and military personnel (11 percent).

There was a dramatic increase in expenditures on interest payments on the public debt. While interest payments in 1970

TABLE 4.8

Functional Composition of Central Government
Cash Expenditures, 1969 and 1978
(percent of total)

	1969	1978
National defense	9.9	3.8
Public safety	4.6	2.2
Education/culture	18.7	11.0
Social welfare	14.6	21.4
Economic assistance	18.1	14.3
Assistance to local governments	4.8	19.4
Interest	2.8	7.7
Other	26.5	20.2
Total	100.0	100.0

Note: Data do not include thirteenth month.
Source: Compiled by the author; data from Ministry of Treasury, Conto Riassuntivo del Tesoro, December 31 Supplemento issues of 1969 and 1978.

represented only 5 percent of total central government expenditures,
by 1978 they represented 11 percent. Both the growing volume of
debt outstanding and generally high and rising interest rates in the
latter part of the decade accounted for the growing burden.

Despite the large increase in the share of total cash expenditures accounted for by interest payments, the trend toward a budget
consisting largely of transfer payments is clear. Thus, between
1969 and 1978 total transfers (both current and capital) rose from
42 percent of total cash expenditures to 56 percent of the total. All
of this shift was in current transfer payments.

The greatest increase in current transfer payments concerned
transfers to local governments. This included revenue sharing as
well as transfers to the regions for financing hospital benefits. Until
1974 hospitalization benefits had been financed partly by contributions
from the health insurance institutes and partly by borrowing from the
banks and by delays in paying suppliers. Because of the hospitals'
rising costs, by 1974 the health institutes had accumulated a large
debt to the hospitals. This debt was then taken over by the state and

has been gradually consolidated. In 1974 power over reimbursement to the hospitals for hospital benefits was transferred from the health institutes to the regions (effective January 1, 1975) and the National Hospital Fund was established. Until they were placed in liquidation in 1977 the health institutes turned over to the Treasury contributions

TABLE 4.9

Composition and Growth of Cash Budget Expenditures in the 1970s

	Share of Total		Average Annual Increase 1970-78	
	1969	1978	Nominal	Real
Current expenditures				
Personnel	31.5	18.2	19.8	—
Transfers, of which:	29.3	44.9	36.5	—
Autonomous entities	(2.7)	(2.4)	(28.2)	—
Local governments	(5.9)	(22.8)	(50.6)	—
Social insurance institutes	(8.1)	(11.7)	(46.1)	—
Interest	5.0	11.1	43.3	—
Purchases—goods/services	8.5	4.2	18.1	—
Other	5.3	4.1	35.3	—
Total current expenditures	79.6	82.5	28.6	12.8[a]
Capital expenditures				
Direct investment	2.3	0.8	13.7	—
Transfers	12.9	11.0	26.3	—
Credits and equity participation	5.2	5.7	42.1	—
Total capital expenditures	20.4	17.5	27.3	10.9[b]
Total expenditures	100.0	100.0	28.1	12.4[c]

[a] Deflated by public consumption deflator.
[b] Deflated by gross fixed investment deflator.
[c] Weighted by average shares of total over the period.
Source: Compiled by the author; calculated from Bank of Italy annual reports.

received to finance hospital benefits. Now health insurance contributions are paid directly to the Treasury, which then transfers funds to the regions for crediting to the regional accounts of the National Hospital Fund, which finances hospital benefits provided by the hospitals and clinics.

The rapid growth of public expenditures in the health field during the 1960s and 1970s reflected an increase in the number of people eligible for benefits, with the extension of health care to pensioners, self-employed workers, and retirees from government, and the introduction of social pensions (for those not otherwise covered). Also, the public health service structure was fragmented and inefficient, and cost-free medicines and loose control over eligibility encouraged demand for health services. In 1975, however, at least in quantitative terms, some aspects of Italy's health system exceeded the EC average: 10.6 beds per 1,000 inhabitants, compared to 7.8 beds, and almost two doctors per 1,000 inhabitants versus 1.6.[2]

Current budget transfers to social insurance institutes also rose substantially between 1969 and 1978—considerably more than did overall expenditures. In addition, there were large off-budget transfers from the Treasury to finance the residual deficits of the major pension fund (INPS).

The relatively small average annual increase in purchase of goods and services of 18 percent in 1970-78 shows the rather modest role that the growth of public consumption played as a direct influence on the growth of total demand.

In the capital account, direct investments grew quite moderately, at an average annual rate of 14 percent, while other capital transfers and credits and equity participations grew more rapidly. Direct investments constituted a very small proportion of total expenditures, falling from 2.3 percent of the total in 1969 to 0.8 percent in 1978. Other capital transfers and credits and equity participations were larger in absolute terms and accounted for about the same share of total expenditures in 1978 as in 1969. (This item includes some financing of deficits of the autonomous entities, especially the state railroads.)

Also included in the capital account are periodic endowment fund (that is, equity) contributions to the state holding companies and other public bodies. Amounts involved were fairly modest during the early 1970s, but grew later. For the entire nine-year period these contributions amounted to over 8.9 trillion lire, of which the largest shares went to IRI (31 percent), ENEL (20 percent), ENI (17 percent), and Mediocredito (10 percent). (Mediocredito is a medium-term industrial and export credit discount institute.) Late in the 1970s there was a perceptible increase in contributions to IRI to help in the financial restructuring of IRI companies, and to ENEL, which was faced with large capital investment requirements especially after the 1973–74 oil price increases.

OFF–BUDGET DEFICITS

During the 1970s (1970–78) the off-budget share of the Treasury's total cash deficit amounted to 25 percent of the total (including debt consolidation operations). These deficits consisted mainly of the financing by the Treasury of residual deficits of the principal pension fund (INPS), the autonomous entities (especially the state railroads, superhighways, and post and telecommunications), and the local governments (especially the municipalities). The deficits of these bodies, in turn, reflected the constant rise in Italian demand for social welfare benefits and public services, along with insufficient increases in social insurance contributions, an inadequate source of tax revenue (in the case of local governments), and insufficient increases in the public service rates charged by the autonomous entities.

Minor Treasury Operations

Minor treasury operations is an off-budget category that is highly complex. The most important components are interest payment transactions, financing of the social insurance deficits of INPS, and financing of the deficit of the postal and telecommunications system (see Table 4.10).

Statistically, one of the main items included in the total is interim payments by the Treasury to finance certain expenditures that were not previously recorded in the central government budget. Two major subcategories are the interest payments (or credits) on ordinary treasury bills that are in excess of (or less than) amounts originally budgeted, and net reimbursements with the postal savings system of amounts advanced by it to INPS to meet any shortfalls between insurance contributions and insurance benefits paid. Another main item in minor treasury operations concerns the management by the Treasury of certain accounts of various public entities such as the Cassa per il Mezzogiorno (Fund for the South), the autonomous entities (except for the post and telecommunications system), and the regions. (For discussion of financing of the post and telecommunications deficit, see the section below on the autonomous entities.)

Financing of social insurance deficits has become a matter of growing concern. The average annual amount of treasury financing of INPS deficits alone, in the six-year period 1969–74, was only 186 billion lire. In the succeeding four-year period (1975–78),

TABLE 4.10

Minor Treasury Operations, 1970-78
(billions of lire)

	Unappropriated Expenditures	INPS Financing	Postal System Financing	Other*	Total
1970	-108	-3	34	368	291
1971	17	76	-284	-316	-507
1972	-1	-871	-41	104	-809
1973	-311	153	-290	1,295	847
1974	-1,016	-585	-413	78	-1,936
1975	-1,175	-2,906	-387	365	-4,103
1976	-1,409	-3,181	-234	3,103	-1,721
1977	264	-2,255	-424	2,451	36
1978	652	-210	-617	3,531	3,356

*Including Cassa per il Mezzogiorno (Fund for the South) expenditures financed from foreign borrowing.

Note: The minor treasury operations consist mainly of interest payments.

Source: Compiled by the author; data from Bank of Italy annual reports.

however, such deficit financing averaged more than 2.1 trillion lire per year. There are a number of other social insurance institutes besides INPS, but INPS is the most important and the one with the largest deficit. It is responsible for the largest pension funds, the principal family allowance system, unemployment insurance, and wage supplement payments.

Data for the consolidated accounts of all the social insurance institutes shows that the total of social insurance contributions grew annually by 19 percent in the period 1971-78, while benefit payments grew by 20 percent. Since benefits already exceeded contributions in 1970, however, the absolute gap widened. In 1978 the shares of regular contributions received from employers, employees, and the government were, respectively, about 63 percent, 18 percent, and 19 percent. The Treasury was also responsible for covering residual deficits.

Of total benefits paid out by the social insurance institutes, pensions and income support (including relatively small unemployment insurance and wage supplement payments) were much the largest item, accounting for 83 percent of the total in 1978. The remaining benefit payments were for family allowances (6 percent) and health care (11 percent). These expenditures for health care do not, however, include direct transfers from the Treasury to the regions to finance hospitalization benfits under health system changes effective from 1975 onward. (Such transfer payments appear in treasury transfers to local governments, rather than in the accounts of the social insurance institutes. Consequently, the total cost of health benefits is understated in the consolidated accounts of the institutes.)

The table below shows the ratio of contributions to benefits of the social insurance institutes in the 1970-78 period; the figures include transfers by regions to the National Hospital Fund of funds received from the Treasury. The ratio generally declined in the latter part of the decade, dropping from 94 percent in 1970 to 75 percent in 1978.

Year	Ratio
1970	94.3
1971	89.9
1972	84.8
1973	87.7
1974	90.1
1975	78.3
1976	79.1
1977	79.4
1978	74.8

In addition to the social insurance institutes, there are a number of other public and private bodies that also provide social insurance benefits. In fact, in 1978 these bodies accounted for 34 percent of total social insurance benefits (reduced to 22 percent if hospitalization benefits provided by the regions are combined with benefits provided by the social insurance institutes). (See Table 4.11.) In addition to the regions, these organizations consist mainly of the autonomous entities and other public sector bodies that provide direct social insurance benefits, and other private and public bodies (especially with regard to severance pay). Total social insurance benefits from both the institutes and these other sources represented 19 percent of GDP in the period 1970-78 and 21 percent in 1978 alone. The annual

TABLE 4.11

Total Social Insurance Benefits by Category, 1970 and 1978
(billions of lire; percent of total)

	1970		1978	
	Amount	Percent	Amount	Percent
Pensions, income support*	5,314	50.4	29,718	64.0
Family assistance	1,058	10.0	2,261	4.9
Medical/hospital care	1,823	17.3	10,044	21.6
Severance pay	2,345	22.3	2,200	4.8
Other			2,195	4.7
Total	10,540	100.0	46,418	100.0

*Includes unemployment insurance and wage supplements for short-time work.

Note: Total benefits include benefits paid both by social insurance institutes and by other public and private bodies.

Source: Compiled by the author; calculated from Relazione Generale I (1974), p. 64; I (1978), p. 63, and other issues.

ratio of total insurance benefits to GDP for the 1970–78 period is shown below.

Year	Percent of GDP
1970	16.8
1971	18.0
1972	19.4
1973	18.9
1974	18.5
1975	20.3
1976	20.2
1977	19.7
1978	21.0

The rapid growth of pension benefits reflects in part the fact that in Italy the pension system (particularly disability pensions) has been used as a kind of parallel system for providing welfare and unemployment benefits. Of roughly 12.5 million pensioners in Italy in 1978, about 44 percent were recipients of disability pensions. Although average disability pensions are lower than average old-age pensions, disability pensions have been granted rather flexibly and are concentrated in the poorer areas of the country—suggesting the high incidence of socioeconomic beneficiaries. Also, about two million people are estimated to be receiving two pensions, costing about 10 percent of total pension expenditures.[3]

The pension system has had two important economic side effects: the indexation of pensions (see Chapter 3) overcompensates for inflation, contributing to the inflationary problem; and since pensions are still low in absolute terms, they tend to encourage pensioners to seek employment in the black labor market where they can continue to collect a pension while being (illegally) employed.

The relatively high portion of income received by the institutes from employer contributions compared to transfers from the government (apart from residual deficit financing) has led to periodic pressures for fiscalization of some of the heavy burden of social insurance contributions borne by employers. Pressure has centered on relief from health insurance contributions, in particular, on the grounds that health insurance is properly a community responsibility that should be borne by the state. In fact, there was a certain amount of fiscalization in the 1960s and 1970s, including rather sizable amounts in 1977 (653 billion lire) and in 1978 (almost 5.4 trillion lire).

Finally, one other item in minor treasury operations that bears mention is the management of public money, since these operations have sometimes been a source of net receipts to the Treasury. This is particularly true with regard to the regions, which relatively recently were assigned new spending authority but whose actual expenditures did not immediately catch up with the receipt of large transfer payments from the Treasury.

After three years of very large net outpayments in 1974-76, total minor treasury operations turned around in 1977 and 1978, with rather large net receipts for the Treasury in 1978. The main causes of the improvement were lower interest payments than those budgeted, much smaller off-budget financing of the INPS deficit, and large net receipts from the management of public accounts (especially of the regions).

Financing Autonomous Entities' Deficits

In addition to financing of the post and telecommunications deficit, which is recorded in minor treasury operations, the Treasury is also responsible for providing residual financing of deficits of the other autonomous entities through off-budget transactions. (Note that

TABLE 4.12

Cumulative Autonomous Entities' Deficits and Their Financing,
1970–78
(trillions of lire)

	Amount	Percent of Total
Receipts		
Sales of goods and services	19.1	56.3
Transfers from government*	12.9	38.1
Other	1.9	5.6
Total	33.9	100.0
Expenditures		
Personnel	20.6	46.6
Purchases of goods and services	9.4	21.3
Interest	2.9	6.5
Other	11.3	25.6
Total	44.2	100.0
Surplus/deficit		
By entity		
Post/telecommunications	-2.7	26.2
Railroads	-7.0	68.0
Highways	-1.0	9.7
Other	0.4	-3.9
Total	-10.3	100.0
By source of financing		
Off-budget treasury financing	2.4	23.3
Credit in budget	5.0	48.5
Other	2.9	28.2
Total	10.3	100.0

*Excluding deficit financing.

Source: Compiled by the author; data taken from Bank of Italy
annual reports and Relazione Generale (various issues).

the largest part of financing these deficits is anticipated in the budget itself, and recorded in the form of treasury advances to the autonomous entities shown in the capital account.) For the nine-year period 1970-78 the cumulative deficits of all the autonomous entities reached over 10 trillion lire (see Table 4.12). Budgeted transfers from the Treasury accounted for 38 percent of receipts, while income from the sale of their goods and services was 56 percent of the total. More than two-thirds of the deficits were due to operations of the state railroads. Over 70 percent of the cumulative deficits were financed by off-budget treasury financing or from credits in the budget itself.

Although there was considerable growth in the total deficits of the autonomous entities (mainly post and telecommunications and state railroads) at the beginning of the decade, the total deficit leveled out in the mid-1970s (1974 to 1977), before rising rather sharply in 1978 due to a doubling of the railroad deficit. Unlike the railroads and postal/telecommunications system, the state telephone company has not been a financial burden on the Treasury.

The rise in these deficits in the early part of the decade reflected reluctance to adjust public service rates in line with rising production costs. This was motivated by anti-inflation and income distribution aims. The energy crisis, however, and the growing problem of treasury deficits to some extent forced the approval of some increases in rates (see Chapter 6).

Financing Local Government Deficits

The Postal Savings Fund (managed by the Treasury) was the principal source of financing of residual deficits of the local governments in the 1970s. In the period 1970-78 total local government deficit financing by the Postal Savings Fund amounted to nearly 21.5 trillion lire, of which more than 9.3 trillion was in 1977 alone. The high level of financing in 1977 was partially due to transfers from the Postal Savings Fund to consolidate a large amount of debt previously accumulated with the commercial banks by the local authorities. Such off-budget financing declined significantly in 1978, as deficit financing was provided through regularly budgeted current transfers. On the other hand, 1978 data reflect large transfers to the regions for hospital assistance. In general, the heavy burden on the Treasury of local government financing arises from the elimination of most local taxing authority as a result of the tax reform, the growing need for urban services, and the inadequacy of control over local government expenditures.

Provisional budgets of the local authorities are subject to approval by the Ministry of the Interior before local governments can borrow from the Postal Savings Fund, but this did not prove to be an adequate control over local deficits. In the past, before approval was granted the local authorities borrowed short-term from the commercial banks and other financial institutions (at very high interest rates in the later years). Some authorities incurred such high interest rate obligations that repayments had to be rolled over with the banks for lack of funds. In 1976 a credit squeeze had a severe impact on local finances. In order to provide relief, a decree was issued in January 1977 to fund this short-term debt to the banks.* The funding took the form of the placement with the commercial banks of ten-year bonds bearing a 15 percent coupon. In 1977 the Postal Savings Fund provided over 4.3 trillion lire in such debt consolidation financing and in 1978 almost 2.3 trillion lire. As part of the refunding arrangements, however, from 1977 the local authorities were forbidden to engage in any more short-term borrowing from the banking system, except for temporary liquidity shortages. (They can borrow up to three months' revenue from the Treasury.) Although technically the local governments are responsible for interest and principal payments on the consolidated debt, to the extent that such payments increase future deficits these deficits will become eligible for financing from current treasury transfers.

Key developments in local government finance were the tax reform of 1973-74, the reforms of the hospital benefits system of 1974 and 1977, and some new limits placed on local finance in 1978. In the first case, the main effect was the virtual elimination of local taxing authority and the substitution of revenue sharing with the central government. In the second case, the main change was the transfer of responsibility for financing the cost of hospital benefits from the health insurance institutes to the regions. The third measures involved limits on hiring, on the rate of growth of some current expenditures, and on the size of urban transport deficits.

Under the tax reform, as a substitute for revenue formerly received from a variety of local taxes, local governments were assigned a fixed percentage increase in tax revenue off a base level of 1972-73. Initially the annual increase in such revenues was to be 7.5 percent or 10.0 percent, depending on the particular tax or level of local government. Subsequently, with inflation running at 15-20 percent, these shares were seen to be inadequate and the increase in revenue sharing had to be set each year (for example, 16 percent in 1979). Examples of increased control over local government spending

---

*Decree law No. 2 of January 17, 1977; converted into law 62 of March 17, 1977.

TABLE 4.13

Composition and Growth of Local Governments' Cash Budgets,
1970 and 1978

	Percent of Total		Average Annual Percent Change
	1970	1978	
Receipts			
Sales of goods and services	4.1	3.4	23.0*
Taxes	48.6	7.4	6.7
Transfers	32.1	62.0	40.5
Other	15.2	27.2	41.9
Total	100.0	100.0	31.0
Expenditures			
Purchases of goods and services	16.7	19.3	20.7
Personnel	32.6	30.8	18.2
Interest	11.6	6.6	19.0
Other	39.1	43.3	32.0
Total	100.0	100.0	26.1

*For 1971-78.
Note: Hospitals included from 1976 on.
Source: Compiled by the author; data from Bank of Italy annual
reports.

contained in November and December 1978 laws were a June 30, 1979
deadline for reorganization plans, a limit on new hiring, a limit of
11 percent on the growth of current expenditures in the 1979 budget,
and a 10 percent ceiling on the increase in urban transport deficits
and a requirement that any overrun of the deficit be covered by fare
increases.

Although the local authorities continue to generate a modest
amount of local tax revenue, current transfer payments, mainly from
the central government, constitute much the largest source of income
(Table 4.13). A relatively minor source of income is provided by
sales of goods and services by the municipal governments and other

municipal agencies. The ratio of income from such sales to total expenditures has declined somewhat, reflecting the rapid growth of expenditures and reluctance to raise the price of municipal services, particularly before 1975. Subsequently, the financial crisis of the mid-1970s forced some increases in urban public service rates.

On the expenditure side, a variety of transfer payments and capital expenditures grew quite rapidly in the 1970s, as did interest payments on local debt, although some relief from the previous steady rise was apparent in 1978 following the debt consolidation (at lower interest rates). Purchases of goods and services and personnel compensation grew relatively less rapidly.*

CONCLUSIONS

The Italian authorities sought to use tax and expenditure policies for countercyclical purposes during the 1970s (see Chapter 9), while recognizing the deficiencies in these tools. At the same time efforts were made to improve the long-term effectiveness of the tools themselves, through both tax and expenditure reforms.

It is still difficult to assess the degree of success of the 1971 and subsequent tax reform efforts. Both direct and indirect tax rates changed with some frequency, and the minimum income tax base was changed, as were deductions. Changes in the timing of tax payment requirements caused the overlapping of tax receipts from several years' income. Special one-time taxes were introduced and the transfer of most local taxing authority to the central government inflated its revenues. There is no doubt, however, that the extension of withholding at the source and the requirement for nearly current payment of taxes on income not subject to withholding have gone a long way to make the system more effective as a tool of economic management. Prompt collection of taxes became particularly critical during a period of high inflation, in order to protect the real value of revenues. There remain substantial pockets of income tax evasion, particularly

---

*Note that under the current system of financing hospital benefits, statistics on local government record the "grossing up" of both receipts and payments by the regional governments, since treasury transfers are recorded as receipts by the regions, but then are passed on as a transfer to the hospitals that provide services. There may be some timing differences in the receipts and payments of these transfers, however, so that in a given time period they need not wash out in terms of the effect on the regions' net budget surplus or deficit.

with regard to wages and salaries in the black labor sector, small-business and professional income, and the value-added tax on domestic sales. Also, use of the indirect tax tool is inhibited by the inclusion of most indirect taxes in the scala mobile basket.

The system of computerized tax rolls (anagrafe tributaria), which was to aid in tax collection by feeding into a computer financial and other information that could help the tax authorities to determine actual income, has been delayed for years. (Its full entry into operation is forecast for late 1981.) Nonetheless, it should eventually provide a useful tool for better tax collection. The recently greater use of selective audit techniques also holds some promise, as do cross-checks of personal income tax and value-added tax returns of small businesses. The value-added tax, too, is still inherently easier to collect than its predecessor and some efforts are being made to do so, such as requiring that a tax certificate document accompany goods in transit between production and distribution. Perhaps the most encouraging outcome of the tax reform effort was that tax evasion, no longer so easily available to the majority, is looked upon with much less acceptance than heretofore and political pressures for further reducing evasion are strong, especially on the part of the labor unions.

Italy's large budget deficits were more the result of a lower-than-average level of tax revenues compared to other EC countries, than to a higher rate of expenditures. If these very large deficits are to be reduced, it may be easier to concentrate on raising tax revenues than on improving expenditure control, although both are clearly necessary. In particular, the authorities should resist income tax indexing. One of the few forces operating in the Italian economy to control aggregate demand is fiscal drag. It permits real disposable income, despite its being protected by wage indexation, to be influenced by changes in economic conditions. This is not to say that occasional tax cuts to offset the effect of fiscal drag would be precluded. Increased awareness of the effect of progressive taxation on disposable income has already generated strong resistance to fiscal drag. But legislated tax cuts that can be designed to respond to particular economic conditions are a more discriminating tool than automatic adjustments. Until recent efforts at better control over expenditures can be seen to be effective, Italy cannot afford to give up a fiscal tool that works.

There is no reason, theoretically, why an efficient system of local government finance could not be based on adequate control over expenditures exercised locally, with financing provided by the central government. In practice, however, the disassociation of the taxing and the spending authority seems to have reduced fiscal discipline at the local level. Admittedly, the removal of most local taxing authority and the growing demand for public services in urban areas have presented very difficult problems for the local authorities. But the temptation to expand local expenditures and resist increases in local taxes and fees for services (such as urban transport fares) is hard to resist, when the resulting deficits could simply be presented to the central Treasury for financing.

To some extent the need to preserve some local responsibility for taxation has been recognized. Some taxes still are imposed at the local level, notably the tax on capital gains on real estate (INVIM). Proposals have occasionally been made for restoring additional authority to local governments and the authorized increase in existing local tax rates by up to 100 percent in 1978 and 1979 also reflected this concern. Indeed, the basic tax reform enabling law of 1971 called for new legislation to regulate tax revenues of provinces and municipalities. Although this has not been implemented, the original four-year deadline has been extended, so authority still exists to do so.

Force of necessity has, to some extent, overcome resistance to raising prices and public service fees charged by the autonomous entities and local governments for the services they provide. The authorities, however, have tried to achieve too many conflicting objectives through policies covering public service rates. These included sporadic attempts to limit the overall rate of inflation by holding down rates and the fixing of multiple rates for different categories of users for social reasons. It would be better not to burden public service rate policies with too many socioeconomic objectives. Also, sharp, ratchet-type rate increases are less desirable than an approach that continually keeps prices in rough synchronization with costs.

With the expanded cost of social insurance benefits, especially pensions and hospital care, a new look needs to be taken at the level of social insurance contributions and the relative burden borne by employers, employees, and the government. If the effect of raising benefits without raising employer and employee contributions is simply to increase inflation by monetary expansion to finance a larger budget deficit, then there may be little net gain in real income for the beneficiaries.

Italy still has a long way to go in making expenditure policy an efficient tool, either for overall demand management purposes or for accomplishing specific socioeconomic objectives through public expenditures. Until more adequate data are available on activities of non-central-government bodies, the authorities are acting in the dark in attempting to manipulate the economy with this tool of management. Even when the facts are known, there will remain a problem of exercising effective control over spending by such a large and diverse body of public agencies. Finally, there should be a reduction in the time it takes to actually spend funds, especially for investment purposes, if the public sector is to make a contribution to a revival of investment in general and social investment in particular.

A start has been made with the requirement for more uniform accounting of expenditures, the preparation of cash budgets, and the submission of multiyear appropriation budgets. The efforts of the central government to clean up the accumulated financial deficits of the local governments, health institutes, and hospitals have resulted in a recorded rise in treasury expenditures in the form of debt consolidation. The assumption of this burden is justified, provided new expenditure controls succeed in preventing the accumulation of such massive debts in the future.

Initially, the authorities have resorted to rather crude instruments for effecting better control over expenditures at the local level—for example, temporary freezes on hiring, prohibition of short-term borrowing, and quantitative limits on the growth of current expenditures. These measures may be necessary in order to have some immediate effect on spending. If adequately enforced, however, the budget reform of August 1978 would constitute a more lasting improvement, provided it succeeds in its aim of forcing both the central government and other parts of the enlarged public sector to plan ahead, reorganize, and regularly estimate the actual cash impact of their appropriation budgets. Even more important than such administrative reforms is the need for a broad-based political decision to exercise firmer control over expenditures in such politically sensitive areas as pensions, health insurance, and the cost of public services. The past record is not encouraging.

An examination of central government budget and off-budget cash operations by the Treasury reveals the growing extent to which the central government has become a mechanism for transferring resources to finance the local governments, the autonomous entities, and the social insurance institutes (see Figure 4.1). Furthermore, the transfers have been financed in large part through government borrowing and monetary expansion (see Chapter 8), rather than through taxation. This has had serious consequences for the growth of productive capacity and inflation. In 1978 the total of budget and net off-budget payments made to local governments, the autonomous entities, and social insurance institutes by the Treasury exceeeded 40 trillion lire (including debt consolidation), of which the local governments accounted for 47 percent, the autonomous entities 14 percent, and the social insurance institutes 39 percent (with transfers to the regions for hospital benefits shifted from local governments to the social insurance category) (see Table 4.14).

Very few of these expenditures by the Treasury were transfers on capital account for investment purposes. The bulk of them consisted of current transfers to finance municipal government services, health care, pensions, and railroad and postal services.

FIGURE 4.1

Transfers as Share of Treasury Expenditures, 1970–78 (percent of total)

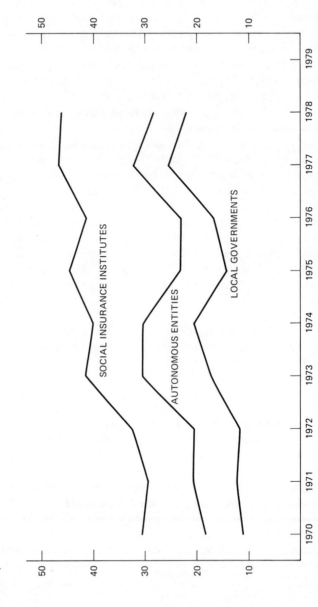

Note: Transfers are those to local government, autonomous entities, and social insurance institutes. Expenditures are cash budget and off-budget (net).

Source: Constructed by the author; data from Bank of Italy annual reports.

TABLE 4.14

Principal Components of Change in Treasury Cash Deficit, 1969-78
(trillions of lire; percent of change in total receipts or expenditures)

| | Amounts | | | Percent |
	1969	1978	Change	Change
Receipts[a]				
Direct taxes	2.6	21.2	18.6	41.9
Indirect taxes	6.4	24.9	18.5	41.7
Transfers[b]	0.2	5.0	4.8	10.9
Other	0.3	2.8	2.5	5.5
Total	9.5	53.9	44.4	100.0
Expenditures[a]				
Personnel	3.2	15.9	12.7	16.6
Transfers/credits to				
Local governments[c]	(1.2)	(19.3)	(18.1)	(23.6)
Autonomous entities	(0.7)	(5.6)	(4.9)	(6.4)
Social insurance institutes[c]	(0.7)	(15.7)	(15.0)	(19.6)
Subtotal	2.6	40.6	38.0	49.6
Interest (budgeted)	0.5	9.7	9.2	12.0
Purchases, goods/services	0.9	3.7	2.8	3.7
Other	4.0	17.9	13.9	18.1
Total	11.2	87.8	76.6	100.0
Deficit (including debt consolidation)	1.7	33.9	32.2	—

[a]Both current and capital transactions; expenditures include net off-budget expenditures.

[b]Mainly treasury drawings from special accounts for consolidation of debt of hospitals and health insurance institutes.

[c]Transfers to regions for hospital services are included with social insurance institutes figures.

Source: Compiled by the author; calculated from Bank of Italy annual reports and Relazione Generale data.

A comparison of the treasury cash budget deficit in the last year of the 1960s with that of 1978 shows the principal components of change between those two years. The growth of direct and indirect taxes was nearly the same in absolute amount, but there was a decided shift upward in the relative importance of direct taxes. The growth of expenditures (including both budget and net nonbudget spending) was far larger than that of receipts. Almost 50 percent of the expenditure increases were due to transfer payments to local governments, social insurance institutes, and autonomous agencies. One could say (arbitrarily) that 86 percent of the entire increase in treasury receipts was absorbed by these transfer payments. Italy needs to come to grips with the dramatic change in the Treasury's role in the economy as an intermediary for transfers of income.

The growth of the treasury cash deficit has had a number of serious economic consequences. First of all, there is a budget deficit on current account, as well as capital account. In other words, the budget no longer generates a source of public saving, but rather dissaving. At a time when the business sector, too, has difficulty saving because of pressure on profits from rising labor costs, a heavy burden is placed on the household sector to provide financing for productive investment. Disincentives to housing construction, a natural channel for household savings, have impeded that type of direct household investment. Inadequacies in Italy's capital market and poor business profit performance have limited the prospects of channeling household savings to business in the form of equity purchases, and the high leverage of Italian business makes debt financing a risky business. Even if the public sector were able to attract household savings designed to finance public investment, the history of difficulty in implementing public investment programs in the past is not encouraging.

The treasury deficit has to a large extent been financed through borrowing, including the creation of monetary base—partly from postal savings, but also from credit from the central bank. When faced with the need to limit domestic credit expansion in a highly inflationary environment, the monetary authorities have had to allow the Treasury to crowd out the private sector during periods of credit stringency. This effect on monetary developments could not fail to have an adverse effect on investment, employment, and inflation.

NOTES

1. OECD, Economic Outlook (Paris: July 1979), p. 41.
2. Bank of Italy, Annual Report (1977), pp. 214-15.
3. Sergio Gambale, "The Crisis in Public Finance in Italy," Banca Nazionale del Lavoro Quarterly Review No. 128 (March 1979): 73-90.

5

GROWTH, INCOME, AND EMPLOYMENT

Productivity gains independent of cyclical factors require
a high rate of capital accumulation which, however, is
not easy to reconcile with the maintenance of external
balance in view of the large import content of investment.
This, therefore, creates a viscious circle: the low productivity of the economy tightens the balance-of-payments
constraint and makes it necessary to restrict domestic
demand; this in turn slows down the rate of capital accumulation, thus preventing structural changes in industry,
the expansion of sectors able to increase output per employee and improvement of the trade balance.

Paolo Baffi
Governor, Bank of Italy
Annual Meeting, Rome, May 1977

INTRODUCTION

Real economic growth in Italy in the 1970s averaged only 3.1
percent.* Not only was this much lower than in the previous decade,
but growth also displayed a degree of volatility unknown in the earlier
period. The 1970s began with a period of relative stagnation following
the rapid growth of the late 1960s (Figure 5.1). While the business

---

*The following discussion of growth is based principally on
national income accounts prepared on a GDP basis using standard EC

FIGURE 5.1

Gross Domestic Product at Market Prices, 1970–79
(billions of 1970 lire seasonally adjusted at annual rates)

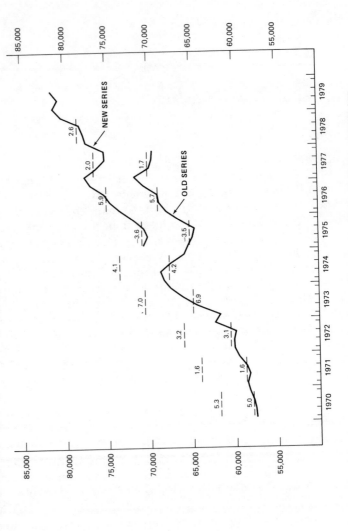

Source: Constructed by the author; data from Relazione Generale, and ISTAT.

cycle was probably peaking anyway, the real and psychological impact of the hot autumn of 1969 (see Chapter 2) certainly contributed importantly to a period of prolonged slow growth beginning in 1970 and continuing until late 1972. When recovery finally came it was very rapid, as Italy caught up with the generalized boom in the industrial world in 1972-73.

The shock of the 1973-74 oil price increases helped to drive Italy into sharp recession in 1974-75, with real output falling in the latter year by 3.6 percent. This was the first year of negative growth in the postwar period and the depth of Italy's decline in 1975 was the greatest among the seven largest OECD economies. Once again,

---

definitions. The series was originally introduced in 1974, but was also calculated in detail retroactively, beginning from 1970 and, for the principal components, going back to 1960. (No estimates were made for 1959, so annual changes for 1960 are not available.) Beginning with the 1978 national accounts, a revision of the GDP series was introduced. The main changes between the old (1974) and new (1978) series consist of the grossing up of certain items in the accounts to add some income and product that previously escaped statistical recording. The main gap was in the small-business sector especially involving noninstitutional labor (for example, black labor, second jobs, and foreigners working in Italy). On the sources side of GDP the major upward revisions in percentage terms were made in value added in the public administration and in industry (excluding construction). On the uses side of GDP, the greatest percentage changes were made in public consumption (including the transfer of some health expenditures from private to public consumption) and fixed investment. (In absolute amounts, the biggest revisions were made in value added in manufacturing and in private consumption.) On the income side of the accounts the major share of the revisions were in domestic wages and salaries (52 percent of the total) and in other factor income (44 percent). Despite the grossing up of some of the GDP components, annual percentage changes differ very little from the old series. Some ratios among the components do change, as a result of relative differences in the amount of adjustments made to the old data. For example, value added in agriculture has not been changed on the sources side, nor have exports of imports on the uses side of GDP. The new series is cited in the text and shown in the tables. In cases where new series data are not available (especially on the income side of the accounts) there is a specific notation that old series data have been used.

recovery was quite rapid in 1976. After the initial recovery from the oil crisis, however, Italy seemed to settle down onto a slower growth path than before the crisis. Although the balance-of-payments constraint on growth was considerably reduced, the underlying causes of many of Italy's problems had not been dealt with and future growth prospects remained hostage to inflation and balance-of-payments constraints.

In the employment field several developments stand out. Despite growth in real GDP of more than 31 percent between 1969 and 1978, employment grew by less than 5 percent. In absolute terms employment grew by only 950,000 jobs. The labor force, which had been declining quite steadily from 1960 to 1972, reversed itself, however, and began to grow after that date. The increasing participation of women was an important factor. Despite the sharp decline in real growth rates, the unemployment rate rose relatively little between the 1960s and 1970s (5.1 percent in 1960-69 versus 6.2 percent in 1970-78), and the rate did not change very much over the course of the business cycle. The composition of unemployment, however, changed dramatically, as the number of first-time job seekers grew from only 60 percent of the total at the end of the previous decade to 79 percent in 1979 (excluding marginal workers).

SOURCES OF GROWTH BY SECTOR

Shifts in the sources of growth of the Italian economy can be seen in the evolution of value added at market prices in real terms (1970 lire) among the primary,* secondary, and services sectors, including both services for sale and services not for sale—mainly the public administration. In the 1961-69 period the average annual percent change was 3.0 for the primary sector, 7.1 for the secondary sector, 6.3 for the tertiary sector, and 2.6 for services not for sale (the latter two figures based on the old GDP series). For 1970-78, corresponding percentages for the four sectors were 0.4, 3.1, 3.7, and 3.0, respectively. (The latter two figures include the percentage change for 1970 calculated on the basis of the old GDP series.) During the 1960s agriculture, and to a lesser extent services, had lost ground compared to industry. During the 1970s agriculture continued a rela-

---

*Agriculture is much the largest part of Italy's primary sector and "agriculture" is often used interchangeably with "primary sector" in this book.

tive decline, but at a slower pace, while the services sector became the most dynamic area of growth.

Primary Sector

Real growth in the primary sector during the 1970s (1970-78) was virtually nil. As can be seen in the table below, in four of the nine years there was negative growth. In fact, the record high level of value added in agriculture for any one quarter was reached in 1967 and not repeated in the 1970s (through 1978). Also, the absolute level of value added in the primary sector in 1978 was less than 2 percent higher than in 1967, 11 years earlier.

Year	Growth Rate
1970	-0.3
1971	0.5
1972	-7.4
1973	7.0
1974	1.9
1975	3.3
1976	-4.1
1977	-0.5
1978	3.5
Average	0.4

For the 1971-78 period marketable production of field crops grew on average by 1.3 percent per year (old GDP 1971-74). Production of tree crops (principally fruits, including citrus) grew very little, at 0.6 percent per year. The one relatively bright spot was livestock production where growing consumer demand reflecting the effects of a rising level of income provided an incentive to increased domestic production. Increased production averaged 3.2 percent per year—not dramatic growth, but better than elsewhere in this sector.

Criticism of neglect of the agricultural sector has been widespread, particularly in the wake of balance-of-payments problems in the mid-1970s, to which Italy's food deficit contributed. For example, Italy's food deficit was nearly four times higher in 1978 than in 1970, as seen below.

A very large part of the deficit was attributable to growing imports of livestock and meat, which rose from $0.8 billion in 1970 to $2.6 billion in 1978. After the initial jump in the food deficit to over $3 billion in 1973, however, the deficit remained in that range for five years, until a further sharp increase occurred in 1978. Although

Year	Food Deficit (billions of dollars)
1970	-1.2
1971	-1.5
1972	-2.1
1973	-3.4
1974	-3.3
1975	-3.2
1976	-3.2
1977	-3.5
1978	-4.4

the food deficit was still large, relative rates of growth of food exports and imports turned around in the latter part of the decade. Nonetheless, in the entire nine-year period the food deficit amounted to $26 billion, out of a total trade deficit of $33 billion. Of course, there is no reason to expect Italy to be self-sufficient in food, given its relatively sparse agricultural resources and its participation in the EC's Common Agricultural Policy (CAP). Still, long-term equilibrium in the foreign accounts requires that some attention be given to that aspect of developments in the agricultural sector.

An examination of relative prices (valued added deflator) and costs (unit labor costs) in the primary sector gives evidence of the profit squeeze in agriculture during the 1970s. While the value-added deflator rose on average by almost 14 percent, unit labor costs rose by nearly 19 percent per year. The general profit squeeze in the economy was particularly evident in agriculture, because although productivity grew more rapidly than in industry or services, this was insufficient to offset the even faster relative rise in nominal wages. The latter, in turn, was due partly to labor shortages in the north and center of Italy and partly to the effects of the wage indexation system under which the fixed lira value per point of wage adjustments results in higher percentage wage increases in low-pay sectors like agriculture than in higher-pay sectors.

Despite the profit squeeze, investment in the agricultural sector grew faster than in any of the other major economic sectors. In the period 1971-78 real growth of GFI in agriculture averaged 2.6 percent per year, and this sector's share of real GFI rose from 6.3 percent in 1970 to 8.0 percent in 1978. To some extent this reflected preference given to agriculture in the allocation of development credit. In fact, agriculture was the recipient of a growing share of medium and long-term credit granted by the special credit institutes, with the share of these credits going to agriculture rising from 3 percent in 1971 to 11 percent in 1978. (About 65 percent of these credits bear

subsidized interest rates.) The 11 percent share of credit going to
the agricultural sector in 1978 compared with agriculture's 8 percent
share of total gross fixed investment (current lire) that year.

Although Italian agriculture underwent great structural change
in the 1960s and 1970s, it remains backward compared to other developed countries. It is still characterized by a large number of small
production units. The average size of Italian farms was about 5 hec-
tares in 1978, and smaller in the south. Retail food outlets are numerous and small. The small size of producing and distributing operations
is typical of both the fresh food and the processed food branches of
the industry. There is considerable scope for cost reduction through
rationalizing the distribution system. Given its limited natural endow-
ments, Italy cannot expect to develop agriculture across the board,
but it does have some natural advantages of climate and location that
favor certain products, notably fruits and vegetables and their by-
products.[1]

On balance, the past record of very slow development in this
economic sector is discouraging. There are some signs of change,
however, in the increasing awareness of the need to assign a higher
priority to agriculture, the growth of livestock production, the reversal in the rates of growth of food exports and imports, and the
modest but steady increase in real investment even during a period
of low investment in the economy in general.

Secondary Sector

The main characteristics of the secondary sector during the
1970s were a deceleration in the overall rate of real growth, stagnation in the construction and public works component of the sector, and
increased volatility in industry.* On average, in the 1970-78 period,
industry grew at a rate of 4 percent and construction and public works
declined at a rate of 0.6 percent, for an overall growth rate of 3.1
percent. The table below shows the annual rates for the sector as a
whole.

---

*Unless otherwise specified, "industry" is often used inter-
changeably with "secondary sector" in this book, although the latter
also includes construction and public works.

Year	Percent
1970	6.2
1971	-0.2
1972	3.7
1973	9.1
1974	4.6
1975	-9.0
1976	10.0
1977	1.5
1978	2.0

Value added in construction and public works declined in real terms in four out of nine years, with only a modest growth (1 to 3 percent) during the remaining five years. The highest quarter of real output was the very first quarter of the decade. By 1978 the real level of value added in construction and public works was at virtually the same level as it had been a decade earlier in 1968.

The construction sector was troubled throughout the period by the low demand for investment in residential housing and by the slack demand for nonresidential construction, as management concentrated on investment in machinery and equipment, rather than new plant, in an attempt to offset the rising cost of labor and in the context of a generally high level of underutilized plant capacity. To some extent the poor performance of the housing construction sector may be exaggerated by the failure to record some residential construction built without regard to municipal codes (edilizia abusiva). This has occurred especially on the periphery of large cities, where housing shortages have been particularly acute. Also, some (legal) construction and home improvement work by homeowners escapes the statistics.

In reviewing changes in the Italian housing situation through 1977, Guido Dandri traced a sharp drop in the number of completed dwellings between the 1960s (1962-67) and the 1970s (1972-77), showing that a postwar peak of more than 450,000 dwellings was reached in 1964, which was never again achieved.[2] In fact, the average number of completions between the two periods fell from about 361,000 to only 198,000 units. Dandri roughly calculated that Italy needs about 300,000 new dwelling completions per year (more than double the number produced in 1977) in order for the existing state of housing adequacy not to be eroded.

A number of reasons have been cited for the decline in Italy's housing activity, including the adverse psychological effect of political developments from the formation of the first Center-Left government in 1963 onward; the 1963 extension of rent control to postwar housing and subsequent extensions of rent controls until the introduction of a complex fair-rent control law in 1978; declining profitability and rising uncertainty about future profitability; a rise in building costs faster than price rises for manufactured goods and a slow growth of productivity; the high nominal cost of money in some years, which made it impossible to cover mortgage payments out of rental income; a virtual paralysis of town planning; uncertainties about the effect of a 1971 housing reform that permitted municipal condemnation and purchase of private land and delays in obtaining building permits; and reduction in the backlog of demand for housing as a result of the 1960s housing boom.

A slowdown in the rate of growth and high degree of volatility in value added in industry (excluding construction) occurred in the 1970s. Growth fell from an annual average rate of 8 percent in the 1960s to 4 percent in the 1970s. Increased volatility can be seen in the sharp recovery (10 percent) of real output in 1973, following the 1971-72 period of stagnation, the 9 percent drop during the 1975 recession, and the even sharper recovery (up to 12 percent) in 1976.

Real value added in energy rose rather slowly compared to manufacturing. The poor rate of growth in energy production was concentrated in the period after the 1973-74 oil price hike. While value added had risen by more than 5 percent per year in the period 1971-73, there was very little growth thereafter (average 1.2 percent). Value added in real terms actually fell in 1974, 1975, and 1977, but this was offset by a strong recovery in 1976 following the 1975 recession and by a more normal growth of 5 percent in 1978.

Within the manufacturing sector (excluding energy) there were a few fairly bright spots: chemicals/pharmaceuticals, wood and wood products, metals and metallic minerals, and other manufactures. Growth in transport equipment was hurt by the adverse effect on demand for vehicles caused by the rise in the price of fuels. Chronically depressed textiles, clothing, and footwear continued to grow only slowly, as consumer demand for these products was not strong and foreign competition limited the growth of exports. The machinery and engineering industry suffered from slack demand for investment and nonmetallic minerals production suffered from stagnation in the construction industry.

The profit squeeze in the secondary sector was less severe than in agriculture, as measured by comparative price increases (value-added deflator) and unit labor costs. Average annual price increases were about 14 percent, while unit labor costs rose by more than 15 percent. Nonetheless, gross fixed investment in this sector fell on average in real terms by about 1.6 percent per year (1971-78).

Although more attention has been given to the development of large firms in Italy, especially in the public enterprise sector, Italian industry is still made up in large part of small firms. Usually this has been considered to be a disadvantage and symptomatic of the degree of underdevelopment of Italian industry. The existence of small, adaptable firms, however, may in fact be an advantage. For example, Manlio Germozzi of the Italian Confederation of Craft Industries has made a case for Italy's small craft industries' playing an important role in the modern economy.[3]

Contrary to what might have been expected, the number of firms in this industry has grown in recent years from 1.2 million units in 1968 to 1.4 million in 1976. Germozzi argues that the ability of the craft industry to grow during unfavorable cyclical conditions, the flexibility of response to change, and the employment opportunities for youth respond quite well to Italy's current growth and employment needs. While some branches of the craft industry have declined (clothing and textiles), others have grown (leather goods, construction, plastics). Also, the growth of the craft industry has been particularly strong in the highly industrialized north. This suggests that these small businesses have been able to prosper by subcontracting with larger firms and by producing goods and services that are not amenable to mass production.

Tertiary Sector

The real growth of value added in the tertiary sector, excluding services not for sale, was the fastest among the four sectors, including services not for sale. In the 1971-78 period, for commerce, lodging, and food services the average growth rate was 3.2 percent; for transport and communications, 4.2 percent; for banking and insurance, 4.9 percent; for rentals, 2.2 percent; and for others, 3.9 percent—an overall average rate of 3.5 percent. The annual rates for the sector are shown below.

Year	Percent
1971	3.5
1972	4.5
1973	5.5
1974	4.5
1975	—
1976	3.8
1977	3.2
1978	3.0

Although the rate of growth decelerated considerably from the average of 6.3 percent in the 1960s (1961-69—old series), falling to

3.7 percent in the 1970s (1970-78), the decline was less sharp than that in the primary and secondary sectors of the economy. Also, growth was much less subject to sharp cyclical swings than in industry, or to the irregularities of agricultural production due to weather.

The fastest rate of real growth in the services sector occurred in the banking/insurance industry, followed by transport and communications. The first area showed quite strong and steady growth, even in the 1975 recession. Growth in the transport/communications sector no doubt benefited from some shift from personal transport to public transport after the oil price increases of 1973-74. In contrast, commerce and public services (food and lodging), which had grown at a fairly good rate before the 1975 recession, still seem to be suffering some aftereffects of that trauma. In the other major sectors, rentals and miscellaneous services, growth was low for the former and moderately high for the latter. Growth in miscellaneous services, which includes a variety of nonessential services, had been quite rapid early in the decade, but seemed to suffer from increasing consumer uncertainties following the 1975 recession. On the other hand, some growth in this sector may be unrecorded because of the large number and small size of these service firms.

The profit squeeze in the service sector (excluding the public administration) was similar to that in industry, as prices (value-added deflator) rose at an annual average rate of 13 percent, compared to an increase of 15 percent for unit labor costs. Gross fixed investment in this sector (excluding the public administration) grew at a yearly real rate of 0.5 percent (1971-78), better than industry but worse than agriculture.

In a relatively less developed country such as Italy, where much attention has been devoted to industrialization, there has been a tendency to look upon the services sector as a stepchild in the development process—equating services with traditionally low-paying ancillary activities in the private sector and make-work jobs in the public sector. Except for tourism, relatively little public attention has been paid to development of the more modern types of private services typical of a postindustrial society. Given the fact that Italy's traditional industry must already compete with industrial products from developing countries with lower labor costs and the fact that there is an increasing pool of educated workers, employment and growth prospects in the services sector deserve more attention than they have received.

Services Not for Sale (Public Administration)

About 93 percent of real value added in the sector of services not for sale consists of services provided by the public administration.* The remainder consists of services provided by nonprofit organizations and domestic service. Real growth in this sector was modest but fairly constant in the 1970s (1971-78), as shown in the table below.

Year	Percent
1971	3.8
1972	3.8
1973	3.5
1974	3.3
1975	2.9
1976	3.3
1977	2.2
1978	1.7
Average	3.1

In the public administration alone the average real growth rate of value added was 3.2 percent, as employment in this sector grew by about 3 percent per year; in the other component of the sector, average growth barely exceeded 1 percent. For domestic service, however, the picture may not be complete, since some of such activity escapes the statistical record. Gross fixed investment in real terms in this sector declined on average by 1.9 percent during the 1970s (1971-78).

The temporary freeze on hiring by local governments imposed in 1977 and the 1978 budget reform were symptomatic of growing public demand for better control over the quantity and quality of output of the public administration, and increased determination by the authorities to gain that control. Given the past record, one should hesitate to suggest that this sector of the economy be stimulated to expand at a faster rate than in the past. Instead, priority attention should be given to greater efficiency through faster productivity growth.

---

*Because of the predominance of the public administration component of this economic sector, "public administration" is sometimes used interchangeably with "services not for sale" in this book.

INCOME AND ITS DISTRIBUTION

There were several developments in Italy's national income picture during the 1970s: rapid growth of nominal income, but a deceleration in the growth of real income; some increase in the share of total wage and salary income going to the primary sector and to the tertiary sector, while the share of industry remained quite constant and services not for sale (mainly the public administration) declined slightly; a closing of the per capita wage gaps among major sectors of the economy, with income in agriculture and in industry rising to meet the economywide average, and services income (including the public administration) falling relatively; a reversal in net factor income from abroad, from an addition to domestic income to a reduction; a shift in the distribution of national income toward wage and salary income, at the expense of other forms of factor income, especially profits, a slowdown in the rate of growth in gross disposable personal income and an increase in the propensity to save in the household sector; a serious worsening in the income and savings position of the business sector; and an enormous increase in dissaving in the public administration.

Net Domestic Wage and Salary Income at Factor Cost

Total net domestic income at factor cost (including social insurance contributions) rose rapidly in the period 1970-78. In 1961-69 wages and salaries had risen, on average, by 11.5 percent and other factor income by 9.5 percent, for an overall rate of 10.5 percent. For the 1970-78 period the average wage and salary increase was 18.9 percent and that of other factor income 12.9 percent for an overall rate of 16.5 percent. The annual rates are shown in the table below.

Year	Wages and Salaries	Other Factor Income
1970	16.9	6.1
1971	14.4	2.8
1972	11.6	10.1
1973	21.5	15.8
1974	24.5	17.4
1975	21.5	1.4
1976	22.1	27.4
1977	22.2	15.7
1978	15.4	19.5

Nominal wage and salary income rose more rapidly than did the combined total of other forms of factor income (profits, proprietorship income, interest, rent, royalties, and dividends). In the period 1973-77 alone, nominal wage and salary income rose each year by more than 21 percent. Although the recorded increase in 1978 was only 15 percent, the decline in the growth rate was in large part due to fiscalization by the Treasury of a part of social insurance costs normally borne by business. Without this special assistance, wages would again have risen by more than 20 percent. (See Chapter 3 for a discussion of the importance of social insurance contributions as a component of wage and salary income at factor cost.)

The growth of other types of factor income in nominal terms during the 1970s was generally lower and much more volatile. There was some relative improvement, however, beginning with the 1976 recovery, so that nonwage income in 1976-78 actually grew more rapidly on average (21 percent) than wages and salaries (20 percent). The strong effects on nonwage income of changes in the business cycle can be seen in the rise of only 1 percent in the 1975 recession versus a rise of 27 percent in the 1976 recovery.

By economic sector, in the period 1971-78 agriculture led the way in growth of wage and salary income at a rate of 21.9 percent. The tertiary sector was second (20.3 percent), with services not for sale (mainly the public administration) third (18.8 percent), and the secondary sector last (18.5 percent). Sectoral shares of the total wage bill did not change greatly in the 1970s, although there was a slight tendency for wages in the primary and tertiary sectors to grow in relative terms. On average for the period 1970-78 the four sectors accounted for the following shares of total wage and salary income: primary 4 percent, secondary 47 percent, tertiary 27 percent, and services not for sale (mainly the public administration) 22 percent.

Per capita (that is, per dependent worker) wage and salary income for the entire economy rose on average by 17.6 percent per year during the period 1970-78. Fastest growth was in the agricultural sector, which benefited from an average annual increase of 23.0 percent. This compared with 18.7 percent in industry and 15.7 percent in the services sector (including the public administration). This pattern of relative growth rates resulted in a reduction in per capita wage differentials among the various sectors. Agricultural workers, whose per capita income in 1970 had been only 40 percent of the average for the entire economy, by 1978 received 57 percent of the economywide average. In the industrial sector, there was also some relative increase, with per capita income in 1978 amounting to 102 percent of the average for the economy, compared to 97 percent in 1970. In the more highly paid services sector (including the public administration) the pattern was reversed. Whereas in 1970 salaries per worker amounted to 117 percent of the economywide average, by 1978 this had fallen to a ratio of only 105 percent.

Net Factor Income from Abroad

Duing the 1960s and early 1970s net factor income from abroad in Italy's national income accounts was positive. This was due to the rather substantial wage remittances from Italian workers employed outside Italy, which more than offset net outpayments of income on capital. While wage and salary income from abroad increased substantially in 1977 and 1978 after a period of stagnation, its growth did not keep pace with the rapid rise in Italian payments on foreign capital invested in Italy, in particular loan capital that had been borrowed to finance the large current account deficits of 1973-76. As a consequence, after experiencing a net inflow of factor income in 1970-73, the flow reversed and was negative in each of the succeeding five years.

On the labor income side, it seems rather unlikely that there will be substantial growth in the future, given the relatively improved prospects of employment in Italy compared to the 1960s and early 1970s and the less favorable climate for immigrant workers in neighboring European countries. On the other hand, such income in lira terms could be boosted by any future appreciation against the lira of the currencies of countries in which most Italian workers are located (for example, Germany and Switzerland). Such appreciation, however, would probably signal a weak Italian balance-of-payments position that would generate an offsetting outflow of factor income in the form of interest payments on foreign borrowing (or loss of interest earnings on official reserves). On the other hand, interest payments could decline in the early 1980s as a result of large debt repayments made in 1977-79. The size of these flows needs to be kept in perspective. In 1978 net foreign labor income and net income on capital were only 0.6 percent and 0.7 percent, respectively, of total net national income at factor cost.

Distribution of Net National Income at Factor Costs

The relatively faster growth of wage and salary income than of other forms of net national income at factor cost led to a substantial change in the distribution of net national income during the 1970s (Table 5.1). In 1970 wage and salary income (new GDP series) had accounted for 59 percent of total income; by 1978 the share had risen to 68 percent. While wages and salaries were becoming an increased

TABLE 5.1

Composition of Net National Income at Factor Cost, 1970–77 (percent of total, old GDP)

| | Wages/Salaries | Proprietorship | Other Factor Income | | Total |
			Net Interest/ Dividends	Retained Profits (before taxes)	
1970	60.3	28.7	8.5	2.5	39.7
1971	63.0	26.7	8.6	1.7	37.0
1972	63.1	26.1	8.8	2.0	36.9
1973	64.4	25.9	7.5	2.2	35.6
1974	66.2	21.8	10.9	1.1	33.8
1975	70.5	24.1	7.4	-2.0	29.5
1976	69.9	22.2	7.7	0.2	30.1
1977	71.6	22.0	8.3	-1.9	28.4
Average	66.1	24.7	8.5	0.7	33.9

Source: ISTAT, Bolletino (November 1978), p. 260.

TABLE 5.2

Wage/Salary Share of Factor Income, 1970-78
(percent of total; new GDP)

Year	Raw Data	Adjusted for Changes in Employment
1970	59.2	59.2
1971	61.7	60.9
1972	62.0	60.3
1973	63.2	60.9
1974	64.7	62.0
1975	68.9	65.8
1976	67.9	64.7
1977	69.1	65.7
1978	68.4	65.1

Source: Compiled by the author; elaboration of data from ISTAT, Conti Economici Nazionali 1960-1978 (Nuova serie), Rome, 1979.

share of the total, there was a corresponding drop in the share of both proprietorship income and corporate profits, while net interest income generally maintained its share (old GDP data).

To some extent the shift in income distribution was due to the shift in employment away from self-employment toward dependent labor. If the raw data are adjusted to take into account the effect of the shift in employment, the redistribution of income is somewhat less dramatic, but still perceptible (Table 5.2). There is some suggestion, however, in the period 1975-78 of a leveling off in the shift toward wages and salaries.

Growth of Factor Income in Real Terms

The sharp increase in wage and salary income in nominal terms masks a significant decline in the rate of growth of real wage and salary income. While net domestic wage and salary income in the 1960s in nominal terms had risen less (11 percent) than in the 1970s, when the increase was 19 percent, in real terms there was a substantial decline in the rate of growth between the two periods. When adjusted for inflation by the domestic private consumption deflator, the growth of real wages and salaries declined from 7.5 percent per year in the 1960s to 5.4 percent in the 1970s. For gross domestic nonwage factor income, the percentage change was +5.4 in 1961-69, and -0.6 in 1970-78. Furthermore, the relatively high figure for the 1970s is due to large increases in real income early in the decade— 11 percent in 1970 and 8 percent in 1971 and 1973. In fact, in the most recent five years of the period (1974-78) real wage and salary income rose on average by only 3 percent per year. The effect on consumer demand of the deceleration in the growth of real wage and salary income can be seen in the slowdown of growth of domestic private consumption in real terms. Whereas in the 1960s a 7 percent rate of growth in real wages and salaries was accompanied by a growth in real private domestic consumption of 6 percent, in the 1970s the comparable figures were 5 percent and 3 percent.

An examination of the effect of inflation on other forms of net factor income is also revealing in explaining investment behavior in the 1970s, since a large component of such income (especially profits and proprietorship income) constitutes an important internal source of financing of investment. The nominal growth of such nonwage income was insufficient to keep pace with inflation. In the 1960s net domestic nonwage income in nominal terms had grown on average by 10 percent. In the 1970s, nonwage income grew only moderately faster in money terms than in the previous decade (13 percent), while the price of investment goods (GFI deflator) rose much more rapidly (4 percent in the 1960s compared to 15 percent in the 1970s). The adverse effect on internal sources of investment financing, however, was alleviated to some extent by an average annual growth rate of depreciation allowances of 20 percent. (A 1975 tax reform permitted accelerated depreciation.) Nonetheless, even with the relatively faster growth of depreciation allowances, real gross domestic non-wage income fell on average during the 1970s. The effect of the general decline in real nonwage income can be seen in the weakness of gross fixed investment.

Gross Savings

The average propensity of the entire economy to save (gross national savings divided by gross disposable national income) declined somewhat in the 1970s relative to the 1960s and there was a dramatic shift in the sources of savings. (Gross disposable national income includes GNP, net current transfers from abroad, and net indirect taxes with the EC.)

TABLE 5.3

Gross National Savings, 1970–77
(percent of total, old GDP series)

Year	Business	Households/Nonprofit	Banks	Public Administration	Total	Savings Rate*
1970	16.4	74.8	4.2	4.6	100.0	24.1
1971	14.5	87.4	4.1	-6.0	100.0	22.6
1972	17.7	93.8	4.0	-15.5	100.0	21.8
1973	19.2	89.7	4.2	-13.1	100.0	22.3
1974	17.4	86.2	6.8	-10.4	100.0	22.0
1975	4.7	120.7	11.3	-36.7	100.0	20.1
1976	10.6	100.2	11.8	-22.6	100.0	22.2
1977	6.8	107.0	8.0	-21.8	100.0	22.7
1978	n.a.	n.a.	n.a.	n.a.	100.0	22.1

*New series.

Note: n.a. = not available.

Source: Compiled by the author; calculated from ISTAT, Annuario di Contabilità Nazionale (1977), pp. 48, 52, 56, 60; and Bolletino, November 1978, p. 259.

In the 1960s the overall propensity to save averaged 24.1 percent, falling to 22.2 percent in the 1970s (1970-78). A nadir was reached during the 1975 recession year at 20.1 percent. The relative importance (old GDP data) of the business sector declined as a source of gross savings, the household sector rose sharply, and the public administration generated negative gross savings in every year of the 1970s except 1970 (Table 5.3). The steady growth of negative savings in the public administration largely offset the growth of household savings and was a very important factor in explaining the decline in the savings rate of the total economy. At the same time, the shift in the sources of savings from the business to the household sector required that an efficient means be found for channeling personal savings back to the business sector to finance productive investment. Unfortunately, Italy's system of financial intermediation was another weak spot in the economy.

During the period of balance-of-payments weakness (1973-76) net foreign savings available to Italy made it possible to maintain a level of domestic investment greater than would otherwise have been possible.

Personal Income, Consumption and Savings (old GDP)

A review of developments in the national income accounts of the household sector in the 1970s (1970-77) is helpful in explaining the pattern of consumption and personal savings (Table 5.4). In Italy's national accounts the family or household sector includes on the income side the income from unincorporated business and on the expenditure side investment in unincorporated business and residential construction.

Wages and salaries and proprietorship income were by far the most important sources of gross personal income at factor cost, with net interest, rent, royalties, and dividends of relatively little importance. The annual rate of growth of wage and salary income exceeded that of proprietorship income, shifting the share of wages upward from about 59 percent of total gross personal income at factor cost in 1970 to 64 percent in 1977. Correspondingly, proprietorship income fell from 41 percent to 33 percent of the total. Although relatively small, interest income in the household sector rose in the latter part of the decade, reflecting the large payments made to households on the rising debt of the business and government sectors.

Current transfer receipts grew somewhat as a share of gross personal income, rising from 18 percent in 1970 to more than 21 percent in 1977. (Much the largest component of these transfers consists of social insurance benefits.) There was little change in the share of social insurance contributions of gross personal income. The other

TABLE 5.4

Disposable Personal Income and Consumption, 1970-77
(billions of lire, old GDP)

	Disposable Personal Income	Private (National) Consumption	Average Propensity to Consume
1970	46,512	36,696	78.9
1971	51,764	39,984	77.2
1972	57,244	44,061	77.0
1973	68,295	52,496	76.9
1974	82,835	65,275	78.8
1975	101,400	75,587	74.5
1976	121,859	92,003	75.5
1977	149,226	109,967	73.7

Source: Compiled by the author; data from ISTAT, Annuario
di Contabilità Nazionale (1974 and 1978).

major transfer payment, taxes on personal income and wealth, reflected some increase in the tax burden borne by the household sector.
The average tax rate (taxes divided by gross personal income) in
1970 was 4.5 percent; by 1977 it had risen to 6.5 percent. The net
result of transfers was a slower average annual rate of growth of
disposable personal income (18 percent) than of wage and salary
income alone (19 percent).

The relatively slower growth of disposable income than of
wages and salaries helps to explain the rate of growth of private
national consumption expenditures (17 percent in nominal terms),
which was lower than might have been expected, looking at wage and
salary increases alone. When deflated by the private consumption
deflator, gross disposable personal income rose by a rather modest
3.6 percent per year in 1971-77, compared with an average annual
increase in real national private consumption in that period of only
2.7 percent. The adverse psychological effect of deceleration in the
growth of real disposable personal income and the erosion of accumulated savings due to inflation no doubt contributed to a rise in the
average personal savings rate from 21 percent in 1970 to more than
26 percent in 1977. The annual rates, based on the old GDP series,
are shown below.

Year	Rate
1970	21.1
1971	22.8
1972	23.0
1973	23.1
1974	21.2
1975	25.5
1976	24.5
1977	26.3

This reflected an attempt by families to accumulate savings that, in real terms, would provide some protection against future uncertainties.

Business Income Savings and Investment (old GDP)

National income accounting data on corporate (or similarly organized) nonfinancial businesses in the 1970s (1970-77) show a pattern of moderate growth in nominal operating income; a sharp rise in the burden of interest payments; virtual stagnation in dividend contributions; a rise in the tax burden; considerable growth in the setting aside of reserves against future severance payments for workers; negative net corporate savings in every year of the 1970s; some shift in the sources of financing of investment away from internal funds toward borrowed funds; and an average annual decline in the real value of internally generated funds available for investments.

Gross operating income in the nonfinancial business sector rose on average by 16 percent in the period 1971-77, with year-to-year changes reflecting business cycle conditions. Interest payments grew sharply, particularly from 1974 onward, as the profit squeeze forced businesses to resort to fixed-interest external financing of investment. At the beginning of the decade interest payments absorbed a little over 28 percent of gross operating income. By 1977 they reduced such income by nearly 54 percent. Explaining the low level of equity investment in Italy and reflecting the poor record of profits, dividend disbursements by nonfinancial business were up only 47 percent between 1970 and 1977 in current lire, at a time when the cost of living had risen by 165 percent.

Corporate taxes during the first years of the decade (1970-74) were either stable or actually declining, relative to gross operating income. After the 1974 income tax reform, however, the average tax rose considerably, to more than 17 percent (1975-77), compared to an average rate of only 12 percent in the previous five years of the decade. The burden of allocations to reserves against future severance pay requirements also grew, from about 20 percent in 1970 to about 28 percent of gross disposable business income in 1977. While these reserves are retained by business and provide a source of (tax-free) cash flow and internal financing of investment, it was decided in 1977 to relieve business of part of this growth in these contingent liabilities by "unlinking" severance payments from the cost-of-living indexation mechanism. The recent growth of current payments of severance pay benefits has, in any case, reduced the importance of this source of business financing.

Net saving of the nonfinancial business sector was negative in every year of the 1970s. While net dissaving had been fairly modest in the early years (1970-73), averaging 610 billion lire per year, dissaving grew at an alarming rate in subsequent years, reaching nearly 9 trillion lire in 1977. The gross business savings record was less negative because of increasing depreciation allowances. Also, the poor savings picture was, to a modest extent, alleviated in the latter part of the period by an increase in government transfers to business: endowment fund contributions for public enterprise, fiscalization of some social insurance costs, and capital grants and interest subsidies, mainly for investments in the south.

The net effect of all these developments on the availability of internally generated investible funds was a very slow rate of growth even in nominal terms, averaging less than 11 percent per year in the period 1971-77 (Table 5.5). Since the gross fixed investment deflator in the meantime was rising by more than 16 percent per year, the real buying power of internal investment funds declined on average by about 5 percent per year. The consequences of such a pattern for real investment are obvious—slow growth of gross fixed investment and an increasing dependence on borrowed funds to finance even a low level of investment.

By the mid-1970s the weakness of the financial position of Italian business was already a matter of concern. A proposal was made in September 1976 by former Bank of Italy Governor Carli for converting fixed-interest debt to the banks into equity holdings.[4] After considerable public debate, the Industrial Restructuring and Reconversion Fund was created in August 1977 to provide financial assistance to manufacturing and mining industries in accordance with restructuring and reconversion plans approved by the Interministerial Committee for Coordination of Industrial Policy (CIPI). In addition, a December 1978 law authorized creation of consortia of commercial banks and special credit institutes, with prior approval of the Bank of Italy, to subscribe to shares and convertible bonds issued by industrial firms in connection with plans for reorganization of production and finances. Debt consolidation was also provided for under certain conditions.

TABLE 5.5

Investment Financing by Nonfinancial Corporations, 1970-77 (old GDP)

	Growth of Internal Investment Funds[a] (annual percent change)		Sources of Investment (percent of total)	
	Current Lire	Real Terms[b]	Internal Funds[a]	Borrowing
1970	n.a.[c]	n.a.[c]	42.2	57.8
1971	-13.8	-19.5	39.2	60.8
1972	26.5	20.0	43.6	56.4
1973	30.5	11.5	38.6	61.4
1974	10.3	-14.2	28.9	71.1
1975	9.7	-8.3	40.5	59.5
1976	2.1	-14.0	27.8	72.2
1977	9.2	-8.2	27.7	72.3
Average	10.6	-4.7	36.1	63.9

[a]Gross savings plus capital transfer receipts.
[b]Deflated by gross fixed investment deflator.
[c]Not available.
Source: Compiled by the author; calculated from ISTAT, Annuario di Contabilità Nazionale (1977); Bolletino (November 1978).

USES OF INCOME BY TYPE OF EXPENDITURE

The pattern of change in the components of national income described in the previous section accounts for the major variations in the types of GDP expenditures in the 1970s. The main expenditure developments are listed below:

A substantial slowdown in real growth of the economy, with investment stagnant, consumption exhibiting only slow growth and exports and imports both growing at a relatively fast pace, but export growth exceeding import growth,

A continued gradual shift in the composition of private consumption away from necessities and toward more discretionary purchases, but a slowdown in the rate of growth of total private consumption,

A rather steady moderate rate of growth of public consumption,

Almost no growth of real gross fixed investment, with investment in both residential and nonresidential construction particularly
weak,

Very modest growth of gross fixed investment in agriculture
and either stagnation or small negative growth in industry, services,
and the public administration,

Slightly slower growth of public investment than of private
investment,

Larger and more volatile inventory swings in the mid-1970s
than in earlier periods,

A rather remarkable adjustment in the net foreign balance in
real terms following the sharp worsening in Italy's terms of trade
and persistent current account deficits in 1973-76.

Composition of Demand

The composition of total demand for Italian goods and services
in real terms in the 1970s underwent some change, involving a slight
decline in private domestic consumption, stability in public consumption,
a significant decline in fixed investment, and steady growth of export
demand (Table 5.6). Private consumption fluctuated in the narrow
range of 53-55 percent of total demand and public consumption was
regularly 12-13 percent of the total. Gross fixed investment declined

TABLE 5.6

Composition of Total Demand, 1969 and 1978
(1970 lire)

	1969	1978
Private domestic consumption	54.0	52.8
Public consumption	12.7	12.6
Fixed investment	19.0	13.9
Inventories	0.6	0.5
Exports of goods and services	13.7	20.2
Total	100.0	100.0

Source: Compiled by the author; data from ISTAT,
Conti Economici Nazionali 1960-1978 (Nuova serie),
Rome, 1979.

TABLE 5.7

Average Annual Rates of Real Growth of GDP
Expenditures, 1960s and 1970s
(1970 lire)

	1961-69	1970-78
Private consumption	6.3	3.3
Public consumption	4.0	3.5
Gross fixed investment	5.5	0.1
Exports of goods and services	12.8	8.1
Imports of goods and services	11.0	6.2
GDP at market prices	5.8	3.1

Source: Compiled by the author; data from ISTAT,
Conti Economici Nazionali 1960-1978 (Nuova serie),
Rome, 1979.

from 19 percent in 1969 to less than 14 percent of the total in 1978.
In contrast, export demand for Italian goods and services rose from
14 percent of total demand in 1969 to about 20 percent in 1978.

The ratio of real exports to real GDP grew from 16 percent in
1969 to 24 percent in 1978, while the import ratio grew from 15 percent to about 19 percent. In current lire terms, the changes in the
exports/GDP ratio and imports/GDP ratio were more nearly alike,
the difference being accounted for by the worsened terms of trade
during the period.

Changes in inventories played a more important role in affecting
demand in the 1970s than had been the case earlier. During the 1960s
inventory demand, in the context of fairly steady real growth, tended
to be about 1 percent of domestic demand in real terms. With the
commodity price boom and the oil price rises of 1973-74, however,
and fairly rapid rates of real economic growth in 1973-74 and 1976,
inventory buildups were exceptionally large in those years, accounting
for 3.0, 3.0, and 2.5 percent, respectively, of domestic demand.
Conversely, there was a net liquidation of inventories in 1975, the
only year during the 1960s and 1970s when inventory change was
actually negative, both in real and in nominal terms.

An examination of the relative rates of growth in real GDP
expenditure components from 1970 through 1978 tells the story of

Italy's disappointing growth performance, particularly in the latter part of the decade (Table 5.7).

Private Consumption

In only two years of the 1970-78 period, 1970 and 1973, did real domestic private consumption exceed 3.5 percent growth per year. (Both years followed major wage contract increases.) This surprisingly slow rate of real growth reflects both a deceleration in the growth of real disposable personal income, as inflation picked up in the latter half of the 1970s, and a decline in the average propensity to consume. During the 1975 recession domestic private consumption actually declined in real terms, for the first time in two decades. Even in the recovery year 1976, when GDP rose by 5.9 percent, private consumption grew by only 3.5 percent. Indeed, in the three years following the recession, average real growth of private consumption was only 2.9 percent, suggesting that the impact of the recession and inflation on consumer behavior may have lowered the growth rate of private consumption more than a mere cyclical adjustment would suggest. Admittedly, the relatively low figure for 1977 (2.3 percent) reflected the impact of deliberate stabilization measures aimed at reducing inflation and strengthening the balance of payments. In 1979 there was a strong recovery, with growth in excess of 5 percent.

As one might expect, the composition of private consumption demand evolved over the decade away from concentration on purchases of necessities (food, clothing, shelter) and toward other forms of goods and services. In 1970 these three types of expenditure accounted for 54.4 percent of total consumption, with energy accounting for 3.4 percent and others for 42.2 percent. In 1978 food, clothing, and shelter comprised only 50.1 percent of the total, energy 3.8 percent, and others 46.1 percent. The annual growth rates for total real private consumption are shown below.

Year	Rate
1970	7.3
1971	2.9
1972	3.4
1973	5.8
1974	2.6
1975	-1.4
1976	3.5
1977	2.3
1978	2.9
Average	3.3

There were some other interesting shifts in consumption patterns. These included a slackening in the rate of growth of consumption of fuel and energy, from an average growth rate of 4.6 percent in the three years prior to the 1974 oil price increase to 3.9 percent in the succeeding five-year period (1974-78). The latter figure, however, reflects the effect of the 1975 recession, and consumption in subsequent years was rising rather rapidly. In 1978 alone, real energy consumption rose by 8.6 percent. The decline in the rate of growth of all other goods and services (including nonessentials) was rather striking: 5.8 percent versus 2.8 percent between the pre-oil-crisis and post-oil-crisis periods. In the latter category, where discretionary expenditures are substantial, growth of real consumption (1971-78) was relatively high in health (7.0 percent) and in recreation and education (4.1 percent) expenditures, compared to total private consumption growth during that eight-year period of 2.8 percent. Somewhat surprisingly, education/recreation expenditures rebounded from the 1975 recession, rising on average by 6.5 percent in the following three years.

The evolution of the structure of private consumption in Italy has been similar to that of other industrial countries. Overall growth of private consumption was typified by strong expansion in 1960-69, followed by relatively slower growth in the 1970s, in response to economic and sociological phenomena. In the earlier period the increase in discretionary income, consolidation of optimistic postwar expectations, and a shift in values toward a more consumer-oriented society contributed strongly to a pattern of consumption common to other developed countries. The more recent slowdown in growth requires some explanation. In part this may be due to approaching saturation of demand for some consumer products such as certain appliances and first-car purchases.

Gerardo Ragone, professor of economic sociology at the University of Naples, has suggested that in the period 1968-72 development of the youth culture in Italy, as elsewhere, profoundly changed the structure of Italian consumer demand and that the impact of the energy crisis beginning in 1973 added further to changes in consumption patterns.[5] The related growth of youth unemployment has also been an important factor.

Public Consumption

As discussed in Chapter 4, the large growth of public sector expenditures on current account did not generate a significant direct demand for government purchases of goods and services, but consisted mainly of a rise in transfer payments having an indirect effect on final demand. During the 1970s, except for 1971 and 1972 when public consumption grew by 5.8 percent and 5.3 percent, respectively, public consumption showed only a slow but steady rise, year in and year out. (The largest components of public consumption demand for goods and services, as measured by central government cash expenditure data, are for national defense, general administration, and public safety.)

Investment

The most troublesome aspect of developments in Italy's economic growth during the 1970s was the stagnation of real gross fixed investment. The ratio of GFI to GDP declined steadily from over 21 percent in 1970 to less than 17 percent in 1978, with an average for that period of 19 percent, compared to 22.2 percent for 1960-69. The annual ratios are shown below.

Year	Total	Machinery/Equipment
1970	21.4	8.2
1971	20.3	8.3
1972	19.9	8.1
1973	20.0	8.8
1974	19.9	9.0
1975	18.0	7.5
1976	17.4	7.7
1977	17.1	7.6
1978	16.6	7.3

The pattern was one of sharply reduced growth rates compared to the previous decade (1961-69) when average annual real growth of GFI was 5.5 percent (despite a significant drop in each of the two years 1964 and 1965). In comparison, average real growth in 1970-78 was 0.1 percent, as shown below. While there was a period of strong growth in 1973-74, this only made up for the failure of fixed investment to grow at all from late 1969 until late 1972. The decline in investment during the 1975 recession was nearly 13 percent. This was the sharpest drop in investment in the last two decades, although the trough was less prolonged than during the 1964-65 recession. Nonetheless, the recovery from the 1975 recession in 1976 was very modest, at 2.3 percent. In 1977 there was virtually no growth and in 1978 growth was again very slightly negative. In 1979 there was rather strong positive growth of GFI of more than 3 percent.

Year	Rate of Growth
1970	3.0
1971	-3.2
1972	0.9
1973	7.7
1974	3.3
1975	-12.7
1976	2.3
1977	0.0
1978	-0.4
Average	0.1

Much of the explanation for the poor growth of total fixed investment can be found in the rather steady decline in investment in construction, particularly residential construction, although nonresidential construction also did poorly (Table 5.8 and Figure 5.2). In fact, the highest quarterly level of real fixed investment in construction achieved in Italy during the past two decades took place in the first quarter of 1970. In 1978 the absolute level of investment in construction was lower than it had been a decade earlier in 1968. Total fixed investment in construction, which had grown in real terms by 5 percent in the 1960s (1961-69—old series), suffered an annual average decline during the 1970s (1971-78) of 1 percent. Similarly, residential construction fell on a yearly average by 2 percent and nonresidential construction declined by 1 percent.

Fixed investment in machinery and equipment (including transport equipment) in the period 1971-78 had a better growth record than did construction, growing on average by 1.6 percent (Figure 5.3). In fact, as a share of real GDP, machinery and equipment actually rose in the 1970s (1970-78) compared to the 1960s (old GDP) from an average of 7.6 percent to 8.1 percent. The average real growth rate for all of the 1970s was considerably boosted by the good rate of growth (15.5 percent) during the 1974 recovery from the previous period of stagnation. The drop in such investment during the 1975 recession, however, was particularly sharp (minus 19.1 percent). After recovery in the following year (8.4 percent) growth turned negative again in 1977 and 1978.

By EC standards capital accumulation in the form of machinery and equipment was low in Italy. The average ratio of such investment to GDP (real terms) in Italy in the period 1970-78 was 8.1. This compared with 8.9 in the United Kingdom, 9.0 in France, and 9.8 in Germany.

National income data (old GDP 1970-75; new GDP 1976-78) show that there was relatively little difference in the rate of growth of

TABLE 5.8

Growth of Real Gross Fixed Investment in the 1970s
(average rate, 1971-78; 1970 lire)

Category	Percent
Type of investment	
Construction	-1.4
Residential	-2.2
Nonresidential	-0.6
Machinery and equipment	1.4
Transport equipment	2.5
Overall average	-0.3*
Sector	
Primary	2.6
Secondary	-1.6
Tertiary	0.5
Services not for sale (including public administration)	-1.9
Overall average	-0.3*

*0.1 for 1970-78.
Source: Compiled by the author; calculated from ISTAT, Conti Economici Nazionali 1960-1978 (Nuova serie), Rome, 1979.

nominal fixed investment in the private as against the public sector (including both public enterprise and general government). During the period 1970-78, private investment in nominal terms grew at an annual average rate of 15.8 percent. This compared with growth rates of 16.0 percent for public enterprise and 13.4 percent for general government. Since private investment includes most investment in housing, however, the average growth rate for the private sector suffered from the stagnation in residential construction. In the industrial sector alone, average annual fixed investment grew by 19.0 percent in the private sector, but by only 14.2 percent for public enterprise. (Admittedly, the makeup of the two industrial sectors is not entirely comparable, since the public enterprise sector is dominated by large firms in heavy industry.) Growth of public enterprise invest-

FIGURE 5.2

Gross Fixed Investment (Construction), 1970–79
(billions of 1970 lire seasonally adjusted at annual rates)

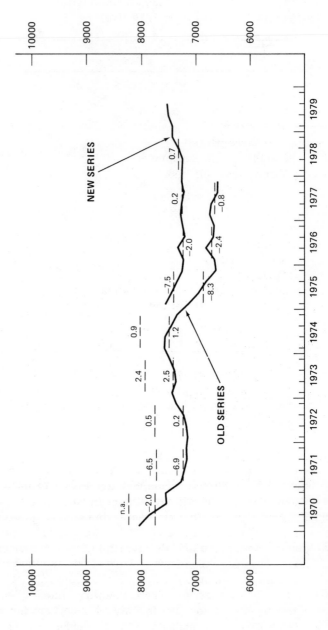

Note: n.a.—Not available.
Source: Constructed by the author; data from Relazione Generale and ISTAT.

FIGURE 5.3

Gross Fixed Investment (Machinery and Equipment), 1970–79
(billions of 1970 lire reasonally adjusted at annual rates)

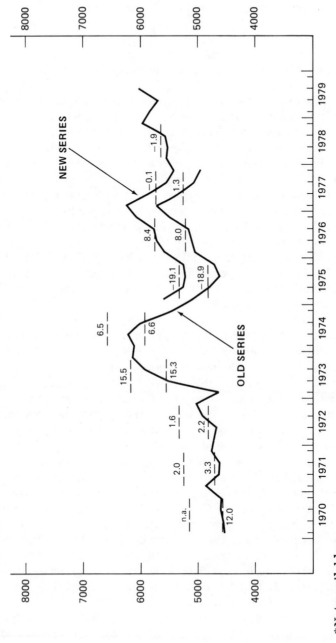

*Not available.

Source: Constructed by the author; data from Relazione Generale, and ISTAT.

ment in services was somewhat higher in this eight-year period, averaging 20.1 percent, than it was in private enterprise (16.8 percent). (The composition of service industries in these two sectors is quite different, and there is relatively little competition between them, except in the financial field.)

Investment by public enterprise in the industrial sector did seem to be somewhat more recession-proof than private enterprise in 1971-72 and in 1975. In the first period private enterprise (current lire) averaged 0.8 percent growth, while public investment averaged 13.2 percent. Similarly, in 1975 public investment rose by 16.7 percent compared to a decline of 0.6 percent for the private sector. One would expect investment by public enterprise to be less affected by cyclical fluctuations than private business, since much of its investment is in heavy industry requiring considerable lead time, or in the services sector (for example, transport and communications), which also requires long-term planning. Also, public enterprise has privileged access to financing through periodic equity contributions from government. A countercyclical pattern for public investment, however, was not apparent in the slow growth years 1977-78. This seemed to be due to a slowdown in social investment caused by a drying up of funds allocated in 1975-76 and by growing financial difficulties of the state holding companies.

There was a variety of reasons for the stagnation of real fixed investment in Italy in the 1970s. In the residential construction field, as discussed earlier, there were a number of regulatory and economic disincentives. In the nonresidential construction field, it probably could not be expected that new plant construction in the 1970s could continue at the same rate as in the 1960s, when Italy was still undergoing recovery from the war and building up its modern industrial structure for the first time. Without a doubt, the sharp increase in labor costs beginning at the end of the 1960s had an adverse impact on construction of new plant, both by immediately reducing profits available for investment and by causing management to shift investment toward labor-saving machinery instead of investing in new plant. The stagnation of fixed investment after the hot autumn of 1969 was prolonged. When recovery finally came in 1973 and 1974 much the largest increase in real investment was in the form of machinery and equipment, rather than in new plant. This was a pattern that was to persist throughout the rest of the decade, reflecting the continued sharp rise in unit labor costs and growing rigidities in the use of the labor force (see Chapter 3).

An annual business survey conducted by one of the large industrial special credit institutes, Mediobanca, provides some supplementary details on changes in the financial position of the Italian business sector. The survey covering 1968-78 included a group of

856 firms (188 public and 668 private) in industry, retail trade, food services, railroad and other transport, and some public services, representing about three-fourths of the corporations in these sectors. The following main developments stoood out: relatively low ratios of profits to sales and to equity capital; a cyclical pattern, but no clear trend in self-financing of investment; a rather steady increase in financial charges paid on borrowed capital; and a notable shift in the capital/liabilities structure of these firms away from equity capital toward short-term debt.[6]

In general, the weakening in the financial position of these firms was greater for public enterprise firms than for private firms. On the other hand, surveyed public enterprise did create relatively more new jobs and undertake relatively more new investment than private enterprise firms covered by the survey. For example, between 1969 and 1978 public enterprises accounted for only 36 percent of the total increase in gross sales, but hired 87 percent of new workers and made 56 percent of new investments. In turn, this active economic behavior resulted in public enterprises' earning only 24 percent of the gross profits of the 856 firms and accumulating 53 percent of the new debt outstanding.

The ratio of gross profits (operating profits plus amortization) to gross sales of the 856 firms averaged 3.3 percent in the first nine years of the decade (Table 5.9). Public firms had a lower profit ratio

TABLE 5.9

Gross Profits/Gross Sales Ratio (856 Firms) in the 1970s

Year	Public Firms	Private Firms	Total
1969	7.4	6.2	6.6
1975[a]	0.3	1.8	1.3
1976[b]	1.5	3.9	3.0
1978	1.2	3.3	2.5
1970-78 Average	2.8	3.7	3.3

[a]Recession
[b]Recovery
Source: Compiled by the author; calculated from Mediobanca, Dati Cumulativi di 856 Società Italiane (1968-78), Milan, 1979, pp. 34-37.

TABLE 5.10

Gross Return on Equity Capital (856 Firms) in the 1970s

	Public Firms	Private Firms	Total 856 Firms
1969	17.2	18.3	17.9
1978	4.8	18.6	12.4
1970–78 Average	8.9	17.3	13.5

Source: Compiled by the author; calculated from Mediobanca, Dati Cumulativi di 856 Società Italiane (1968-78), Milan, 1979, pp. 34-37.

than private firms. Even more striking was the sharp reversal in the relative profitability of public versus private firms between 1969 and 1978. Also, the effects on profitability of cyclical swings can be seen in the figures for one recession year (1975) and one year of economic recovery (1976).

A similar pattern of decline in profitability is seen in the ratio of gross return on equity capital (capital and reserves) (Table 5.10). Furthermore, the roughly equal rate of profitability of the public and private firms in 1969 was significantly changed, as profits of public firms fell sharply between 1969 and 1978 (and generally during the 1970s), while private firms generally maintained their rate of return.

There appeared to be no clear trend in the relative importance of self-financing as a source of total investment financing. The only sources of self-financing, however, were depreciation allowances and severance pay reserves, since net retained earnings were actually negative throughout the period. The business cycle showed up clearly in the figures on self-financing—for example, in the 1975 recession and 1976 recovery years (Table 5.11). (An annual survey by the Bank of Italy of a smaller group of firms shows a similar pattern of self-financing in these years.)

A rather steady rise in the burden of financial costs of borrowed capital was evident, particularly in the latter part of the decade, as the monetary authorities allowed nominal interest rates to rise as a tool for combating inflation and strengthening the balance of payments. The increase in the ratio of financial costs to gross sales of public enterprise was particularly large, rising from an average of 7.1 percent in 1970-73 to 9.1 percent in 1974-78. For private firms the percentages were 3.1 and 4.9 for the two periods, respectively, and for all of the 856 firms surveyed, 4.4 and 6.5 percent. A recent Confindustria study shows a rise in the weighted cost of borrowing of industrial firms from an average interest rate of 8.18 percent to 14.24 percent in these two time periods.[7]

The Mediobanca survey also shows some important shifts in the capital/liabilities structure of the 856 firms (Table 5.12). The two main changes between 1969 and 1978 were a drop in the percent of total capital and liabilities accounted for by equity capital and reserves from 20 percent to 14 percent and the rise in the importance of short-term debt from 26 percent of the total to 36 percent. The percent of depreciation and severance pay reserves, medium- and long-term debt, and other liabilities of the total changed relatively little over the period. As between public and private enterprise, the decline in the importance of equity capital was greater for the private firms (although still a higher proportion in absolute terms), while the growth of short-term debt was greater for the public firms.

While there is no doubt about the fact of stagnation in capital accumulation in the 1970s, it is hard to judge the extent to which low fixed investment will jeopardize future growth. Italy started out the 1970s with relatively new capital stock, as a result of investment in the 1950s and 1960s. A continued rapid growth of new plant construction was not needed, provided capital equipment was continuously

TABLE 5.11

Self-Financing Share of Investment Financing (856 Firms) in the 1970s

	Public Firms	Private Firms	Total 856 Firms
1975[a]	17.2	52.6	33.5
1976[b]	29.8	104.0	61.2
1970-78 Average	24.5	72.1	44.6

[a]Recession.
[b]Recovery.
Note: Self-financing includes retained earnings, depreciation allowances, and severance pay reserves.
Source: Compiled by the author; calculated from Mediobanca, Dati Cumulativi di 856 Società Italiane (1968-78), Milan, 1979, pp. 34-37.

TABLE 5.12

Structure of Business Liabilities and Capital (856 Firms),
1969 and 1978
(percent of total)

	1969	1978	Difference
Capital/reserves	19.9	13.8	-6.1
Public firms	17.4	13.0	-4.4
Private firms	21.8	14.6	-7.2
Depreciation allowance/			
severance pay reserves	31.0	28.2	-2.8
Public firms	26.7	24.9	-1.8
Private firms	34.2	31.4	-2.8
Medium- and long-			
term debt	19.9	20.3	0.4
Public firms	28.9	25.7	-3.2
Private firms	13.3	15.1	1.8
Short-term debt	26.2	36.0	9.8
Public firms	24.9	36.7	11.8
Private firms	27.0	35.3	8.3
Other	3.0	1.7	-1.3
Public firms	2.1	-0.3	-2.4
Private firms	3.7	3.6	-0.1
Total	100.0	100.0	—

Source: Compiled by the author; calculated from
Mediobanca, Data Cumulativi di 856 Società Italiane
(1968-78), Milan, 1979, pp. 34-37.

modernized. In fact, investment in machinery and equipment did
notably better in the 1970s than investment in new plant, and its
average share of GDP actually increased compared to the 1960s.
Stagnation in the early years of the decade, following the sharp rise
in labor costs, was probably offset by the strong recovery of investment in 1973-74. On the other hand, the subsequent period of further
stagnation in 1975-78 (including one recovery year, 1976) cannot help
but adversely affect Italy's growth potential and future competitive
position. Furthermore, the efficiency of the existing capital stock
due to the change in cost structures following the oil price increases
of 1973-74 has surely been reduced. In general, it appears that in

Italy's traditional industries capital equipment has been kept n
but capacity growth has been limited. The result has been the ε
ance of capacity bottlenecks when demand increases, and a failu.
shift the industrial structure toward newer growth industries.[8]

Foreign Sector

The effect on real economic growth of the net foreign balance
during the 1970s was relatively small in the early years of the decade.
With the need to adjust to the worsened terms of trade due to the increase in world commodity and oil prices, however, there was a significant shift in real resources from domestic uses to exports (see
also Chapter 7). On average, from 1961 to 1969 the annual increase
in domestic demand had been 5.6 percent, in foreign demand 12.8
percent, and in total demand 6.4 percent. For the 1970-78 period the
increases were 2.7 percent in domestic demand, 8.1 percent in foreign demand, and 3.6 percent in total demand. The annual figures
for this period are given in Table 5.13. Thus, a large surplus in the

TABLE 5.13

Importance of Foreign Demand, 1970-78
(percent annual change)

	Domestic Demand	Foreign Demand*	Difference
1970	6.8	6.0	-0.8
1971	0.9	7.2	6.3
1972	3.2	11.5	8.3
1973	8.2	3.8	-4.4
1974	2.8	9.9	7.1
1975	-6.1	3.7	9.8
1976	6.1	13.2	7.1
1977	0.6	6.7	6.1
1978	1.7	10.8	9.7
Average	2.7	8.1	5.5

*Exports of goods and services.
Source: Compiled by the author; ISTAT, Conti
Economici Nazionali 1960-1978 (Nuova serie), Rome,
1979.

foreign balance in real terms in the period 1975-78 was a significant positive factor in sustaining real growth. (This surplus was reduced during the 1979 recovery.)

The pattern of growth of exports and imports of goods and services (GDP concept), of course, reflected changes in the relative rates of growth in Italy and abroad and the relative price competitiveness of Italian exports. For example, Italian exports did not grow very fast in real terms in 1970 and 1973, when the attraction of strong demand at home reduced interest in exports and when capacity utilization in industry was relatively high. (Strike activity also played a part in 1973.) Conversely, in years of relatively slack domestic demand, such as 1971-72, 1975, and 1977-78, export growth helped to maintain total demand.

In the period 1970-73, which included two major rounds of industrial wage increases and little change in the lira exchange rate, Italy's competitive price position was no doubt hurt by the rapid rise in unit labor costs, and in 1974 Italy's relatively faster rate of inflation continued to hurt export prospects. Following exchange rate adjustments in 1973-74 and in 1975-76, however, exports began to grow rather well, despite the generally lackluster rate of growth in Italy's main markets in Europe in 1977-78. In those two years Italy recouped the market share it had had, and lost, earlier in the decade.

On the import side (imports of goods and services on GDP basis), slow growth reflected mainly the slow pace of economic activity in Italy. Import growth rather strongly reflected cyclical conditions,

Year	Percent of Growth
1970	15.9
1971	2.4
1972	11.4
1973	10.5
1974	2.2
1975	-9.6
1976	15.4
1977	-0.2
1978	8.1
Average	6.2

especially the effects of inventory speculation in 1972 and 1973. Conversely, during the 1975 recession liquidation of inventories contributed to a sharp fall of imports of goods and services in real terms. Following a long period of relative stagnation in real import levels from late 1975 until mid-1978, imports rose to very high levels in late 1978 and 1979.

EMPLOYMENT AND UNEMPLOYMENT

Population and the Labor Force

Italy's resident population grew at an average annual rate of 0.7 percent in the period 1970-78.* Whereas net migration had been steadily outward during the 1960s and in the first two years of the 1970s, by 1972 the direction of flow was reversed and there continued to be a net inward movement for the remainder of the decade. This source of net increase in the resident population helped to offset a decline in the number of net births during that period. The modest net inflow of migrants should continue for some time due to returning Italian pensioners.

The total labor force, which had been trending downward during the 1960s (average annual decline of 0.7 percent), generally continued to do so through 1972. The labor force touched bottom that year, however, and subsequently grew somewhat each year thereafter, averaging 1.2 percent for 1973-78 (Figure 5.4).

The turnaround in the labor force was in large part due to growth in its female component. In fact, between 1972 and 1978, the increase in the female labor force accounted for 81 percent of the total increase. This raised the proportion of women in the total labor force from 29 percent at the beginning of the decade to 32 percent in 1978.

The resumption of growth in the labor force was also accompanied by a reversal in the total participation rate (labor force divided by population) from a low point of 37.9 percent in 1972 to 38.9 percent in 1978 (Table 5.14). Italy's participation rate—low by industrial nations' standards—has mainly been due to low female workers participation and low participation in the higher age groups because of the exceptionally low legal retirement age (55 years for women and 60 years for men). The continued expansion of school attendance at higher levels also tended to reduce the participation rate. The reversal in the overall participation was due solely to a rise in the female

---

*All employment data cited in this section were taken from quarterly ISTAT labor surveys, unless otherwise noted. A new labor survey series began covering 1977 and subsequent years. ISTAT has reestimated data for earlier years and, unless otherwise specified, the statistics cited in this book are consistent with the new series. Note, however, that per capita (or per worker) income data shown earlier in this chapter are calculated from ISTAT employment data derived partly from the quarterly surveys, but also from other sources.

FIGURE 5.4

Labor Force and Employment, 1960–79
(millions of workers)

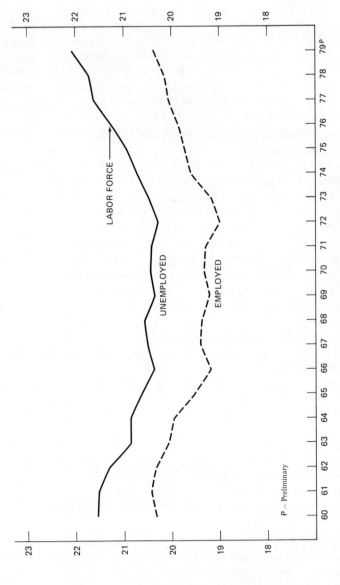

Source: Constructed by the author; data from ISTAT (New Labor Survey).

TABLE 5.14

Labor Participation Rate, 1970-78

	Men	Women	Total
1970	56.6	21.8	38.7
1971	56.0	21.7	38.4
1972	55.4	21.3	37.9
1973	54.9	21.8	38.0
1974	54.8	22.0	38.0
1975	54.6	22.4	38.1
1976	54.5	23.2	38.5
1977	54.1	24.4	38.9
1978	54.1	24.5	38.9

Source: Compiled by the author; data from ISTAT, "Note E Relazioni," No. 56 (1979).

participation rate. The higher overall rate should persist in the next few years, in view of the relatively large working-age group in Italy's population pyramid.

Employment

The pattern of average percent annual changes in employment, by economic sector, was quite different in the 1970s from that of the 1960s, as can be seen in the table below.

Sector	1960-69	1970-78
Agriculture	-5.3	-3.3
Industry	1.2	0.3
Services	1.1	2.5
Total	-0.6	0.5

The main factors behind the improved employment situation were a sharp decline in the average number of workers who had to be absorbed from the agricultural sector and a significant increase in the average number of new jobs created each year in the services sector. With the declining exodus from agriculture, demand for labor

TABLE 5.15

New Nonagricultural Jobs and Sources of Labor Supply,
1960s and 1970s
(thousands)

	1960–69 (10 years)	1960–69 (9 years)
New nonagricultural jobs		
Industry	793	189
Services	746	1,875
Total	1,539	2,064
Source of labor supply		
Exodus from agriculture	2,679	1,114
Decline in unemployment	370	-411
Change in labor force	-1,510	1,361
Total	1,539	2,064

Source: Compiled by the author; calculated from
ISTAT, "Note E Relazioni," No. 56 (1979).

for new jobs could begin to encroach on unemployment levels and
absorb some new entrants into the labor force. Whereas in the 1960s
nearly 270,000 workers per year left agriculture, during the 1970s
the exodus from that sector fell below 125,000 per year. In fact, for
the three years 1976-78 the average outflow of workers was only
61,000 per year.

In the meantime, there was a decline in the rate of new job
creation in industry, from an average of 79,000 new jobs created per
year in the 1960s to only 21,000 in the 1970s (Table 5.15). This decline in the rate of industrial job creation was due to stagnation in
the construction industry.

By far the largest number of new jobs created were in the services sector. In a period (1970-78) when 1.1 million jobs were being
lost in agriculture, the services sector was able to absorb 1.9 million
new workers, compared to only 0.2 million by industry. Indeed, the
growth of employment in the services sector was a very important
factor in reversing the pattern of change in total employment from an

average annual drop of 0.6 percent in the 1960s to an increase of 0.5 percent in the 1970s. Detailed data on composition of growth in the service sector are not available from ISTAT's labor surveys. Information obtained from other official sources, however—for example, the Ministry of Labor, social insurance entities, and state holding companies—show that in the period 1971-78 1.5 million jobs were created in the services sector (including services not for sale). Growth of employment in services not for sale (mainly the public administration) accounted for 48 percent of the total; commerce, lodging, and food services accounted for 19 percent; transportation and communications for 11 percent; credit and insurance for 7 percent; and all other services for 15 percent.

There was a continuing shift in the composition of the employed work force away from self-employment and toward dependent (wage and salary) work, although this pattern seemed to be slowing down in the latter part of the 1970s and there was actually an increase in the number of self-employed in 1974 and 1978 (Table 5.16). In 1960 the self-employed represented more than 42 percent of total employment. By the end of that decade the share had fallen to 34 percent. The decline continued generally throughout the 1970s, with the self-employed share of total employment falling to 29 percent in 1978. The largest part of this decline was, of course, in agriculture. Self-employed workers in agriculture had totaled 4.9 million in 1960,

TABLE 5.16

Changes in Employment, by Sector, 1970-78
(average percent annual change)

	Wage/Salary Workers	Self-employed	Total
Agriculture	-1.8	-4.1	-3.3
Industry	0.4	-0.6	0.3
Services	3.2	1.0	2.5
(public administration)[a]	(3.1)	(n.a.)[b]	(3.1)
Economy	1.4	-1.3	0.5

[a]1971-78
[b]Not applicable.
Source: Compiled by the author; calculated from ISTAT, "Note E Relazioni," No. 56 (1979).

2.9 million in 1969, and 2.0 million in 1978. While the self-employed in industry and services accounted for increasingly larger shares of the total, in absolute terms there was relatively little change in the number working in either sector between 1970 and 1978. In the construction sector, there was a tendency for the number of self-employed to rise, while the number of wage and salary workers in construction was generally falling. This suggests that negative growth in the construction sector was forcing workers to go out on their own to find employment.

Developments in the dependent labor force (wage and salary workers) showed some improvement in employment growth, with a 1.4 percent annual rate of increase in the 1970s compared to 1.1 percent in the 1960s. As with the self-employed, wage and salary workers in agriculture became a decreasing share of the total, falling from 10.6 percent in 1969 to 7.9 percent in 1978. The share of wage and salary employment in industry declined somewhat, from 49.6 percent in 1969 to 45.5 percent in 1978. Growth of employment in services (including the public administration) accounted for the remainder of the change, rising from 39.8 percent of the total in 1969 to 46.6 percent in 1978.

Short-time Work

The use of short-time work as a means of responding to a decline in demand was common in both the 1960s and 1970s. In Italian labor statistics short-time work was defined as a work week of less than 32 hours under the old labor survey and as less than 26 hours beginning with the 1977 survey. (The following data are based on the old survey through 1976 and the new survey thereafter.) The average number of short-time workers during the 1970s (1970-78) was 1.8 percent of total employment. Year-to-year variations reflected changes in the business cycle, with short-time work rising to a high of 2.3 percent of total employment in the 1975 recession year, but touching a low of 1.3 percent in 1970—that is, at the end of the late 1960s boom. Short-time workers were about equally divided between men and women during the period, with a slight tendency for the women's share to rise from about 51 percent in 1970 (old survey) to 54 percent in 1978 (new survey). Short-time work in the south, although higher than proportionate to the size of the southern labor force, did not show any perceptible change in its relative share over the 1970s, with its share averaging 40 percent of the total, compared to only a 31 percent share of the total labor force.

Unemployment

Considering the volatility of real growth, the rate of unemployment in Italy showed a considerable degree of stability and a rather low level during the 1970s, although there was some upward tendency in the trend. In 1960-69 the average annual rate had been 4.0 percent for men and 7.9 percent for women—5.1 percent overall. For 1970-78 the figures were 4.1 percent for men, 11.0 percent for women, and 6.2 percent overall. Annual unemployment rates for 1970-79 are shown below. In the 1960s unemployment rates had varied from 3.9

Year	Rate	Rate Excluding Marginal*
1970	5.4	3.6
1971	5.4	3.6
1972	6.4	4.2
1973	6.4	3.8
1974	5.4	3.4
1975	5.9	3.7
1976	6.7	4.1
1977	7.2	4.3
1978	7.2	4.7
1979	7.7	5.1

percent to 5.9 percent. In the 1970s the level was higher but the range was still narrow, from a low of 5.4 percent (1970, 1971, and 1974) to a high of 7.7 percent in 1979. The pattern of relative stability in the unemployment rate owed much to the increased job security the unions were able to obtain for their members during the 1970s and the fact

---

*An innovation in the labor survey introduced in 1977 was the inclusion of a new category of the marginally unemployed, which consists of those who, when first asked, state that they are not part of the professional work force (claiming to be housewives, students, pensioners, and so on), but when further queried, claim to be seeking work. The effect of the inclusion of this category of respondents among the unemployed in addition to the traditional counting of those previously employed and seeking reemployment, and new job seekers, is to boose the unemployment rate significantly—for example, the 1979 rate from 5.1 percent to 7.7 percent.

TABLE 5.17

Unemployment by Type
in 1959, 1969, 1979
(percent of total)

	1959	1969	1979
Previously employed	46.7	26.2	13.3
First job	30.1	39.6	51.0
Marginal workers[a]	23.2	34.2	35.7
Total	100.0	100.0	100.0

[a]Workers who initially claim not
to be part of the professional work force
(housewives, students, pensioners, and
the like) but then indicate that they are
seeking work.

Source: Compiled by the author;
data from ISTAT, "Note E Relazioni,"
No. 56 (1979).

that much of the impact of slack demand was absorbed through work
sharing, especially short-time work.

The extent of job security achieved by those already employed
is also clearly reflected in the declining proportion of the unemployed
(including marginal workers) who had previously held a job (Table
5.17). Whereas in 1969 26 percent of the unemployed were in this
category, in 1979 only 13 percent of the unemployed had been previously employed.

There was also a significant change in the relative rates of
unemployment among men and women (Figure 5.5). During the 1960s
total unemployment had averaged 5.1 percent; for the 1970s (1970–78)
it was 6.2 percent. Virtually all of the increase, however, was due
to a rise in the unemployment rate for women. In the first period the
spread between male and female unemployment rates had averaged
3.9 percentage points. In the second period it widened to 6.9 percentage points. To some extent this pattern is understandable, because
of growth in the female component of the labor force, involving the

FIGURE 5.5

Unemployment Rates, 1960–79
(percent of labor force)

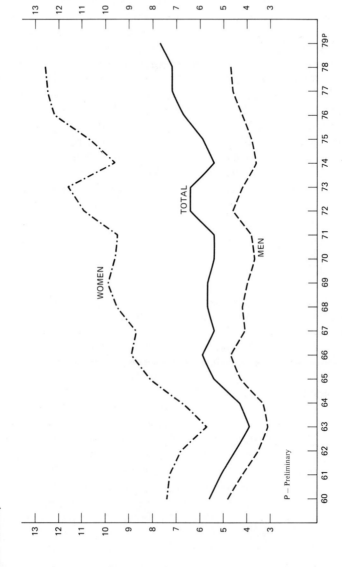

Source: Constructed by the author; data from ISTAT (New Labor Survey).

entry of relatively unskilled, first-time, women job seekers, and the addition of marginal women workers. Such workers would be more likely to be laid off or not to find new jobs during periods of economic slack than would experienced male employees. There was also an increase in the unemployment rate in the south, which was out of proportion to the very modest increase in the average unemployment rate for the whole economy. The figure for the south in 1978 was 10.0 percent, compared to 7.2 percent for the entire country.

The labor survey for 1978 shows that almost 76 percent of the 1.6 million unemployed were in the 14-29 age group. By educational level, 32 percent had no diploma or only an elementary school diploma, 35 percent had a junior high diploma, 29 percent a senior high diploma, and 4 percent a college degree. It is evident that, with the pattern of rising levels of formal education of the work force, more of the unemployed are apt to encounter thwarted ambitions, if the recent rate of real growth does not increase and rates of increases in unit labor costs do not moderate.

CONCLUSIONS

The chief characteristics of economic growth in Italy in the 1970s were increased volatility in growth rates and a generally lower rate of real growth than in the previous decade (in common with other industrial countries). Potential growth was adversely affected by a labor force that did not grow much during the decade and by a slowdown in the growth rate of productivity. There were some important changes, however, between the early 1970s and the late 1970s. The decline in the labor force that occurred in the 1960s continued into the early part of the next decade, but the labor force began to grow after 1972. In the earlier period withdrawals from the labor force were probably voluntary, or at least the necessary side effect of the migration out of agriculture and into industry and the movement from south to north. The later resumption of growth of the labor force was strongly influenced by the entry (and perhaps some reentry) of women into the labor force, as social customs changed, educational levels rose, and inflation created an incentive for women to work in order to help make ends meet.

The resumption in growth of the labor force and of employment, however, was accompanied by a slowdown in productivity per worker. Indeed, this factor may have been responsible for employers' taking on new workers, despite reluctance to accept what had become nearly a fixed cost. If productivity growth should settle down at the 1970s average of about 3 percent per year and the labor force continue to grow at about 1 percent per year, then real growth potential will be in the 3.5-4.0 percent per year range.

Among the sources of growth by economic sector during the 1970s, production in agriculture stagnated, although there was some growth in the livestock sector in response to changing consumption habits. The industrial sector was burdened by a declining construction industry, especially residential construction. In manufacturing (excluding construction) the picture was somewhat brighter, but the sector was troubled by sharp fluctuations in growth brought about by the shocks of the commodity boom and oil price hikes, and by the behavioral response of the public (retrenchment) and the policy response of the government (policy restraint) to those developments. The services sector continued its long-term growth trend, but was affected to some extent by the 1975 recession and may have been pushed to a somewhat slower growth path than previously. In the public administration there continued to be moderate but quite steady growth, as employment in the public sector grew fairly rapidly throughout the period.

The sharp rise in wage rates during the decade led to a substantial shift in the distribution of income in favor of wage and salary income versus nonwage income (especially profits). Apart from the immediate reduction in the ability of business to finance investment from retained earnings, the growing need to finance investment from borrowed funds weakened the capital structure of business and made firms more vulnerable to future economic shocks. To some extent the growth of depreciation allowances helped to offset increasingly negative net business savings, as did a growing level of capital transfers from government, but these offsets were insufficient to avoid the need for increased accumulation of debt, especially short-term debt, to finance investment. At the same time, the rise in disposable personal income of the household sector was less rapid than the rise in wage and salary income alone, since proprietorship income did not rise as fast and because net transfers (including taxes) became increasingly negative. The shock of recession and inflation evidently led households to save more, but this was insufficient to avoid a decline in the overall savings rate of the economy, in the face of low business savings and large negative savings by the public administration.

The components of aggregate demand expenditure changed relatively little during the period, apart from the continued expansion of the foreign sector, with export growth in real terms somewhat exceeding import growth. As between consumption and investment there was some shift in favor of consumption. This was more the result of a decline in real fixed investment, however, than of a rise in real consumption. Indeed, despite the rapid rise in nominal wage and salary income, private consumption did not grow very rapidly, as the household sector increased its average propensity to save. Also the deceleration in the rate of increase of real personal income and the erosion of accumulated personal savings due to inflation limited the growth of private consumption in real terms.

The most worrisome change in aggregate demand was the steady decline in the ratio of gross fixed investment to GDP, and virtually no growth in fixed investment during the 1970s. The persistent decline in demand for residential housing construction was particularly important, but there was also negative growth in the demand for nonresidential construction. While growth was positive for fixed investment in machinery and equipment, the growth rate was not high.

The major adverse factors that limited the growth of fixed investment were negative net saving in the nonfinancial business sector due to the profit squeeze, which was only partly offset by the growth of depreciation reserves and capital transfers from government; rather persistent excess capacity; periodically high nominal interest rates and restrictions on the availability of credit made necessary by the need to divert credit to finance the public sector deficit and the need to limit total credit expansion in order to resist inflation; a faster rate of price increase for investment goods than for consumption goods; inadequacies in the system for intermediating savings from the household sector to the business sector; and concern about the financial soundness of an Italian business sector that had become highly dependent on borrowed capital.

The net foreign balance became an important source of real demand after the oil crisis. Faced with a dramatic worsening in its terms of trade through OPEC monopoly pricing, Italy needed to effect an adjustment in its balance of payments in real terms. The combination of a sharp depreciation of the lira in late 1975 and early 1976, coupled with slow growth at home and somewhat faster growth abroad (including the OPEC countries), brought about a remarkable improvement in Italy's current account both in real and in nominal terms. The corresponding net export growth was a useful support for aggregate demand in the face of slow domestic demand. In fact, in general, export growth was a countercyclical factor during the 1970s.

Important structural changes occurred in Italy's labor force during the decade, notably including a rise in the women's share of the labor force; an increase in the participation rate from about 1973 onward; a reversal from generally negative growth of employment to some positive growth from 1973 onwards; a continued decline in self-employment but at a slower rate, associated with a slowing down in the exodus of labor from the agricultural sector; a concentration of new job creation in the services sector; and an apparent rise in structural unemployment, coupled with considerable resistance to cyclical unemployment due to the success of organized labor in obtaining a high degree of job security. The concentration of employment growth in the services sector (including government) may reflect simply the shift from industry to services that is going on in industrial economies. On the other hand, it may also reflect a retreat of some workers into marginal jobs due to an inadequate growth of new jobs in industry. The apparent rise in the unemployment trend reflects both the inability of the economy to generate a sufficient volume of new jobs and a mismatch between types of labor supply and demand. The virtual fixed-cost nature of employment (Chapter 3) has made business reluctant to increase overall employment levels. At the same time, the concentration of unemployment among women workers and first-time job seekers, especially youth, suggests that new entrants into the labor force may be seeking highly paid white-collar jobs (which they believe to be commensurate with higher educational levels) beyond the ability of the economy to provide them. By the late 1970s these shifts in labor-market conditions were beginning to have some effect on wage rate and employment prospects, despite evolution of a system designed to protect those already employed. The political parties, and union leaders themselves, could not ignore the growing political pressures being exerted by frustrated first-job seekers.

NOTES

1. See Lucio Sicca, "The Food Industry in Italy and its Growth Prospects," Banco di Roma, Review of the Economic Conditions in Italy Vol. XXXII No. 2-3 (March-May 1978): 121-36.

2. Guido Dandri, "The Evolution of the Italian Housing Situation from 1951 to 1978," Banco di Roma, Review of the Economic Conditions in Italy Vol. XXXII No. 2-3 (March-May 1978): 137-52.

3. Manlio Germozzi, "Craft Industry in the Italian Economy Today," Banco di Roma, Review of the Economic Conditions in Italy Vol. XXXII No. 4 (July 1978): 201-16.

4. See Mario Leccisotti, "Sul Problema del Risanamento delle imprese," Bancaria Vol. XXXIII No. 1 (January 1977): 28-33.

5. See Gerardo Ragone, "Sociological Aspects of the Evolution of Consumption in Italy," Banco di Roma, Review of the Economic Conditions in Italy Vol. XXXII No. 2-3 (March-May 1978): 105-19.

6. Mediobanca, Dati Cumulativi di 856 Società Italiane (1968-1978) (Milan: 1979).

7. Confindustria, Secondo Rapporto CSC sull' Industria Italiana (Rome: 1979), p. 24.

8. Angelo Girola, "Machine Tools: Advanced Technology for Italian Industry," Banco di Roma, Review of the Economic Conditions

<u>in Italy</u> Vol. XXXI No. 4-5 (July-September 1977): 221-39. Girola presents a fairly optimistic assessment of the status of Italy's capital equipment industry.

6

INFLATION

We realize today that the inflation of the last few years is
a different phenomenon from the violent explosions and
slow rises in prices that occurred in the past because of
its high rate, its persistence, its universality and the fact
that it is deeply rooted in expectations; we also realize
that it cannot be fully explained by a sudden, widespread
and persistent weakness on the part of central banks or by
the profligacy of governments and that it is perhaps related
to a more profound change in social relationships, through
which the mechanisms that determine prices—and hence
that universal price, the value of money—have themselves
been transformed.

Paolo Baffi
Governor, Bank of Italy
Annual Meeting, Rome, May 1979

INTRODUCTION

Inflation became the most serious and persistent constraint on
achieving an acceptable level of growth and job creation in Italy during
the 1970s. Faced with rapidly rising prices, the authorities were repeatedly forced to rein in the economy, especially through restrictive
monetary policies, leading to a pattern of "stop-go" growth. Despite
resort to such restrictive actions, after each burst of inflation the
underlying rate had ratcheted upward above the rate of the previous
cycle.

TABLE 6.1

Inflation Rates in Six Major Countries in the 1970s
(annual averages, consumer prices)

	1970-73	1974-78	1970-78
Italy	6.6	16.4	12.0
United Kingdom	8.0	16.2	12.6
France	6.3	10.7	8.7
Germany	5.3	4.8	5.0
Japan	7.4	11.5	9.7
United States	5.0	8.0	6.6

Source: Compiled by the author; data from IMF
International Financial Statistics (various issues).

While the problem of inflation was common to all the major
industrial countries in the 1970s, it was more severe in Italy than in
any other major country except, perhaps, the United Kingdom
(Table 6.1).

PRICE PERFORMANCE

Italy experienced both a steady rise in the underlying rate of
inflation (cost of living) and several sharp spurts of inflation during
the 1970s (Figure 6.1). In the early years (1970-72) the apparent
underlying rate of inflation fluctuated around 5-6 percent. In the following three years (1973-75), abstracting from the inflationary bulge
from the commodity and oil price rises, the underlying rate had moved
up to about the 10-11 percent range. In the last period (1976-78), excluding the large impact of the lira depreciation, the inflation rate
had risen to the 12-13 percent range. For the 1970-78 period, the
average yearly increase in the cost of living was 12.2 percent, compared to 3.7 percent in 1960-69.

In the first three years of the decade the rate of inflation was
relatively low by present standards, as can be seen in the table below.
(The inflationary impact of the 1969-70 wage settlements, however,
had already been felt in 1970, when the cost of living rose by 5.0 percent, compared to an average annual rate of only 2.0 percent in the
previous four years.) Slow growth, reflecting the adverse effects of

FIGURE 6.1

Cost of Living, 1970-79
(percent change from previous month)

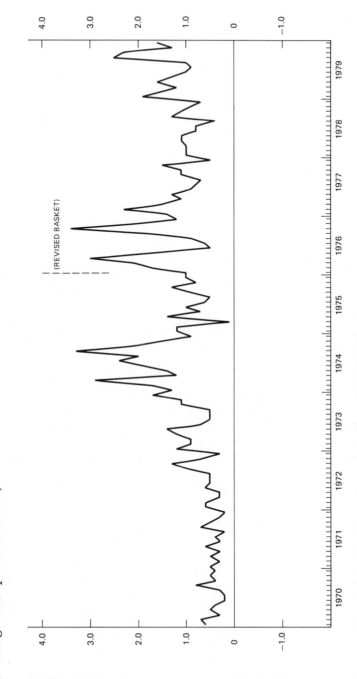

Source: Constructed by the author; data from ISTAT bulletins.

Year	Average Yearly Increase	December/December
1970	5.0	5.3
1971	5.0	4.7
1972	5.6	7.4
1973	10.4	12.3
1974	19.4	25.3
1975	17.2	11.1
1976	16.5	21.8
1977	18.1	14.9
1978	12.4	11.9

the hot autumn of 1969, helped to moderate demand pressures, the absence of major three-year wage contracts provided some respite, and the wage indexation system was less generous than it was later to become. In those first three years consumer prices rose, on average, by 5.1 percent, a somewhat higher rate than in the United States (4.5 percent) and Germany (4.7 percent), but lower than in France, Japan, and the United Kingdom. This relative price stability, however, ended in 1973. With heavy dependence on imported food, industrial raw materials, and energy, Italy suffered gravely from the rapid growth of commodity and crude oil prices in 1973-74. (In 1973 Italy imported about 18 percent of its food and was 79 percent dependent on imported oil for its energy.)

The deep recession of 1975 succeeded in slowing down the rate of inflation to about 11 percent (cost of living from December to December) compared to 25 percent in the previous year. Such a rate of inflation was still unacceptable, however, being more than double the level of inflation at the beginning of the decade and still generally higher than in other major industrial countries. With the resumption of growth in 1976 and the dramatic depreciation of the lira, the inflation rate again accelerated to 22 percent (December to December), nearly reaching the extremely high rates registered in the 1974 price boom.

A slowdown in growth in 1977-78, partly due to stabilization efforts by the authorities, helped to moderate price inflation once again. Even during this period of only 2-2.5 percent real growth, however, the rate of inflation persisted at about 1 percent per month. Given the fact that world commodity prices rose very little during this period, that the lira exchange rate was quite stable, that there were no major wage contract negotiations in industry, and that interest rates were declining, price rises of that magnitude in the context of slow economic growth were extremely disappointing. The resumption of faster economic growth late in 1978 and in 1979 both in Italy and abroad, a resurgence of commodity prices, further OPEC oil price increases, and a new series of three-year contracts in industry all led to a new round of price acceleration.

GDP Deflators

National income accounting deflators for the various components of Italian GDP show that most deflators rose in the range of 13-14 percent, on average, for the period 1970-78 (Tables 6.2 and 6.3). Price increases in this range occurred for GDP as a whole, in the primary and secondary sectors on the sources side of the accounts and for private and public consumption and exports on the expenditure side of the accounts. The main exceptions to price rises in this range were considerably higher rates of inflation for gross fixed investment (15 percent) and imports (16 percent).

Although there was considerable similarity in average rates of inflation in the different economic sectors over the nine-year period,

TABLE 6.2

GDP Deflators, by Sources of GDP, 1970-78
(percent annual change)

	Primary Sector	Secondary Sector	Tertiary Sector*	GDP
1970	3.2	8.9	6.2	6.8
1971	2.9	6.7	8.9	7.2
1972	10.1	4.8	7.4	6.3
1973	21.2	11.2	9.7	11.6
1974	13.9	21.6	16.5	18.5
1975	15.3	21.3	17.7	17.5
1976	21.3	16.8	16.6	18.0
1977	20.0	18.6	17.9	18.9
1978	13.4	12.8	13.7	13.3
Average	13.5	13.6	12.7	13.1

*Includes services not for sale.
Source: Compiled by the author; data from ISTAT, Conti Economici Nazionali 1960-1978 (Nuova serie), Rome, 1979.

TABLE 6.3

GDP Deflators, by Type of Expenditure, 1970–78
(percent annual change)

	Private Consumption	Public Consumption	Gross Fixed Investment	Exports of Goods and Services	Imports of Goods and Services
1970	5.0	6.3	11.0	6.2	3.5
1971	5.5	15.7	7.3	4.1	5.2
1972	6.4	8.0	5.4	2.3	3.7
1973	12.5	12.4	16.7	15.6	26.2
1974	20.8	16.8	28.5	36.6	57.2
1975	17.6	12.2	19.2	10.9	6.0
1976	18.1	17.0	19.0	20.5	24.0
1977	18.2	20.7	19.0	19.2	17.0
1978	12.7	18.2	11.3	7.2	4.5
Average	13.0	14.1	15.3	13.6	16.4

Source: Compiled by the author; data from ISTAT, Conti Economici Nazionali 1960–1978 (Nuova serie), Rome, 1979.

from year to year relative rates differed rather considerably. In the primary sector prices rose very rapidly in 1973, reflecting the world-wide food price boom, and relatively less rapidly in 1971 and 1974 when crops were fairly good. In the secondary sector price rises were relatively high in 1970 (reflecting the wage rate increases nego-tiated in 1969-70), in the economic recovery and oil price increase year of 1974, and in 1975 when the lira began to depreciate and unit labor costs in industry rose by more than 34 percent. In the tertiary sector price inflation was somewhat lower than in the other sectors, in part because the sector was less directly affected by the adverse impact of import prices during the price explosions of 1974 and 1976. Price rises for services not for sale (principally the public adminis-tration), however, rose faster than the economywide average.

On the expenditure side of the national accounts private con-sumption, because of its size, set the pattern for overall price move-ments. The deflator for public consumption was relatively low in 1975 and relatively high in 1971 and 1978. Real growth of public con-sumption in 1971 reflected a deliberate pump-priming expenditure policy and was the fastest in the decade. Furthermore, there were new wage contract rates introduced that year. Growth in 1978 was also relatively strong, being higher than in any of the preceding five years.

The deflator for gross fixed investment exceeded the overall GDP deflator significantly in 1970, 1973, and 1974. In the first year real demand was still relatively high from the previous cyclical peak and the immediate effects of the large wage increases in the engineer-ing sector from the 1969-70 wage settlement were felt. The latter two years were boom years for investment, making up for the stag-nation that occurred from early 1970 through the first quarter of 1973.

Export prices rose very rapidly in 1974, reflecting the impact of sharply increased costs of energy and raw materials. Italian ex-port price rises were relatively modest during the two years of slow-down in the growth of world trade in 1975 and 1978. Similarly, the import deflator grew rather slowly in 1975 and 1978, when commodity prices were falling or growing very little and price rises of manufac-tures were moderate due to recession or slow growth in most of the industrial countries.

Wholesale Prices

Italian wholesale prices, which are heavily influenced by changes in prices of imported materials, rose on average by 14 percent in the 1970-78 period (Table 6.4). Nonagricultural prices (including energy) rose more than did agricultural prices. Agricultural wholesale prices

TABLE 6.4

Wholesale Prices, 1970-78
(percent annual change)

	Agricultural Products	Nonagricultural Products	Total
1970	4.9	7.9	7.3
1971	2.2	3.6	3.4
1972	10.2	3.0	4.1
1973	27.2	15.2	17.0
1974	17.3	45.5	40.7
1975	10.8	8.2	8.6
1976	23.9	22.7	22.9
1977	17.7	16.4	16.6
1978	11.2	8.1	8.4
Average	13.9	14.5	14.3

Source: Compiled by the author; data from ISTAT bulletins (new series, net of value added tax from 1973 onward).

rose much faster than the average in 1973, exceeding 27 percent. Agricultural price movements were influenced by the EC's Common Agricultural Policy (CAP). In contrast to previous and subsequent periods, some EC agricultural prices were actually lower than world prices in 1973-74, which helped to shelter prices in EC countries from the world commodity boom. Gradual devaluation of the "green lira" between October 1973 and February 1974, however, and again in the first half of 1975, in line with earlier lira depreciation, concentrated some agricultural price rises in those time periods.* Nonagricultural wholesale prices (including energy) rose more rapidly than the overall index in 1974, the year of the largest OPEC oil price

---

*The "green lira" is an exchange note for the lira against foreign currencies which is used for EC agricultural pricing purposes. It is adjusted periodically to reflect changes in the actual market exchange rate for the lira.

increase. In that year nonagricultural wholesale prices increased by 45 percent, fuels and lubricants rose 137 percent, and the overall wholesale price index rose by 41 percent. Wholesale prices also rose very rapidly in 1976 and 1977, but at rather similar rates of increase for both agricultural and nonagricultural products, partly reflecting the across-the-board impact of lira depreciation on all imported goods. (There were green lira devaluations in the first half of 1976 which gave some boost to agricultural prices.) The economic slow-down of 1977-78 helped to keep wholesale price rises to only 8 percent on average for 1978. (Once again there were "green lira" devaluations in the first half of 1978.)

Cost of Living

On average the cost-of-living index rose somewhat less rapidly (12.2 percent) during the 1970s than either the GDP deflator (13.1 percent) or the wholesale price index (14.3 percent). The COL index consists of a weighted market basket of goods and services for a family of wage and salary workers. In addition, there is a consumer price index for the entire country. Movements of the two indexes are very similar. The latter index is used less commonly than the former as a yardstick of price inflation. The special scala mobile index used for wage indexation moved quite closely in line with both the COL and the consumer price index, except in 1974 when the OPEC oil price increase failed to be reflected in the scala mobile index because of the absence of gasoline in the scala mobile market basket. There was relatively little time lag between wholesale and retail price changes.

The pattern of COL price movements was one of relative stability in the first three years of the decade. This was followed by a moderate and rather generalized acceleration from mid-1972 through mid-1973, including a rise in prices late in 1972 in anticipation of the presumed inflationary effect from the introduction of the value-added tax on January 1, 1973. There was a sharp price acceleration from mid-1973 to late 1974, owing to large increases in the food and clothing and electric energy and fuel components of the index. These increases at the retail level reflected sharp world price increases for agricultural commodities, especially grains, fats and oils, and fibers in 1973 and crude oil in 1974. There was also some boost to prices from value-added tax increases on beef and luxury goods in 1974. The second round of sharp increases in the COL index occurred in 1976, a year of strong economic recovery following the 1975 recession, of sharp depreciation of the Italian lira, and of some indirect (including value-added) tax increases having a direct effect on retail prices. (The degree of acceleration in the cost of living in 1974 and

TABLE 6.5

Cost of Living, by Components, 1970-78
(percent annual change)

	Food	Clothing	Electricity/Fuel	Housing	Other
1970	4.5	7.5	6.5	5.5	5.2
1971	3.9	7.3	4.0	2.9	6.5
1972	6.1	6.1	-0.1	2.9	6.4
1973	11.8	12.0	0.9	5.7	9.7
1974	18.3	18.0	41.6	3.8	23.3
1975	18.4	15.3	5.1	13.0	18.2
1976	16.6	16.3	12.9	10.4	17.9
1977	17.6	23.4	29.5	5.8	18.2
1978	13.2	14.7	10.8	8.1	11.8
Average	12.3	13.4	12.4	6.5	13.0

Source: Compiled by the author; data from ISTAT bulletins.

1976 is more apparent in the December-to-December figures than in average changes for those two years; the December-to-December figures, respectively, were 25.3 percent and 21.8 percent, compared to average increases of 19.4 percent and 16.5 percent.) Slow growth in 1977 and 1978 brought some relief from inflation, with the average rise in 1978 having fallen to 12.4 percent and the rise over the course of the year (December-to-December) down to 11.9 percent.

Among the major components of the COL basket, average price increases in 1970-78 were highest for clothing, and in descending order of magnitude for miscellaneous goods and services, electricity and fuel, food, and housing (Table 6.5). Rent controls on some housing and reluctance to raise electric utility rates prior to the OPEC oil price increases helped to suppress price rises in those areas. The relatively sharp increase in clothing costs in 1977 apparently reflected the lagged effect of the sharp world price rises of cotton and wool in 1976. Electricity and fuel price changes were actually negative in 1972 and less than 1 percent in 1973 but took off later, as it became impossible to continue electric utility rates at pre-OPEC price increase levels. Food price rises, apart from changes in foreign and domestic supply conditions, were also influenced by very high unit labor cost increases in the agricultural sector.

Public Service Rates

Public service rate changes were important to both the rate of inflation and the size of deficits of various agencies in the public sector (see Chapter 4). In the four-year period 1970-73, efforts to repress inflation through relative stability in public service rates can be seen in the low average rates of increase for six of the seven types of rates (Table 6.6). In the following five years (1974-78), there is evidence that the authorities began to allow more rapid adjustments to cost increases. Despite this catch-up in rate movements, only two of the seven types of rates equaled or exceeded the rise in the overall consumer price index.

TABLE 6.6

Public Service Rates, 1970-78
(percent change)

	1970-73 (Annual average)	1974-78 (Annual average)	1970-78 (Cumulative)
Consumer price index	6.5	16.4	162.1
Autonomous entities' charges			
Railroad	0.6*	15.4	105.6
Telephone	20.0	8.3	178.4
Post/telecommunications	—	27.1	207.3
Local government charges			
Gas	2.8	12.5	88.9
Water	3.1	9.6	69.8
Urban transport	0.3*	19.4	138.9
ENEL (electricity)	-0.5	8.2	39.8

*1971-73.

Source: Compiled by the author; data from Bank of Italy annual reports (ISTAT consumer price data).

Although the unblocking of public service rates added somewhat to the recorded rate of inflation in the latter years of the decade, the need to reduce the continued burden on the Treasury of financing of deficits of local governments and autonomous entities that provide these services suggests that these rates cannot be allowed to get so far out of line with costs, even if a certain degree of subsidization may be considered socially and economically justified.

DEMAND-PULL FACTORS

While a sharp distinction between demand-pull and cost-push factors behind Italian inflation is rather arbitrary, it is useful to try to identify some discrete developments that contributed to inflationary pressures in particular periods and put pressure on the monetary authorities to provide accommodative monetary expansion. With two or perhaps three exceptional periods (including 1979), the pressure of excess demand on available capacity seems to have been a relatively unimportant cause of inflation during the 1970s. This conclusion is based on an examination of capacity utilization in the manufacturing sector, the amount of short-time work compensated by wage supplement payments, the number of total hours worked and the amount of overtime worked in large industry, fluctuations in inventories of finished goods in industry, the level of import demand, and changes in the money supply.

Bank of Italy calculations of capacity utilization in manufacturing for the period 1970-78 show that only in the first three quarters of 1970, the period from the third quarter of 1973 to the third quarter of 1974, and again in the fourth quarter of 1976 and the first quarter of 1977, did capacity utilization hover around the 95 percent level, suggesting the presence of generalized pressure on available capacity.* High capacity utilization in 1970 reflected the end of the late 1960s boom, but capacity utilization declined rather steadily until mid-1971. Both the 1973-74 and 1976-77 periods were at the peak of the recovery from stagnation in the early years of the decade and from the 1975 recession, respectively. By the end of 1978 and early 1979 capacity

---

*Bank of Italy data differ from a quarterly series contained in the business surveys of ISCO (the official National Institute for the Study of Economic Trends). The latter show lower absolute levels of capacity utilization—for example, about 78 percent in the 1973-74 period and 75 percent in the 1976-77 period, but the direction and magnitude of variations are similar.

utilization had risen fairly close to earlier peak levels, suggesting
that pressure on manufacturing capacity might again have been a
source of inflationary pressures in 1979. Apart from these relatively
brief periods, an overall insufficiency of manufacturing capacity does
not seem to have been an important factor behind price inflation.
There may have been exceptions at other times in certain sectors,
however, especially in the light of the low level of labor mobility in
Italy, which made it difficult to adjust to unexpected spurts in demand.
Also, it is still not clear to what extent the dramatic jumps in oil
prices have progressively made existing combinations of factors of
production no longer capable of producing at reasonably stable prices,
so that some capacity may have been made effectively obsolete.

Because of institutional limits on layoffs (Chapter 3), the typical
Italian response to cyclical variations in demand is reflected better
in data on short-time work than in unemployment figures.* Data on
the number of hours compensated for by wage supplement payments
to workers on short time, as shown in the table below, tend to confirm

Year	Short-Time Hours Compensated (millions)
1970	68
1971	200
1972	174
1973	127
1974	156
1975	345
1976	282
1977	250
1978	316

that the pressure of excess demand on productive capacity was probably a significant factor in the price rises of 1973-74, but this was
less clearly the case in the 1976 price explosion. Compensation for
short-time work in 1973 was lower than for any other year of the
period (except for 1970). In 1974 the next lowest number of short-
time hours compensated was recorded. Although the amount of compensated short-time work fell off in 1976 as the economy recovered,
the level was still well above that in all of the earlier years of the

----

*One would expect an inverse relationship between short-time
work and excess demand.

decade (except for 1975). This suggests that pressure on the available labor force, and hence on prices, was not a very important factor behind the sharp 1976 price increase, despite the relatively high rate of real growth that year. It should be recalled that this high growth rate followed negative growth in 1975 and to a large extent merely restored economic activity to a level reached before the recession. (To some extent the continuation of a relatively high level of short-time work in 1977 and 1978 may have been due to structural, rather than cyclical, phenomena.

Because of the declining trend during the 1970s in the number of hours worked (in accordance with union pressures to shorten the workweek and spread around available work), monthly hours worked in large industry and the amount of overtime employed were not very good measures of the relative pressure of overall demand on available capacity and, hence, on prices. The index of monthly hours worked by blue-collar workers in large industry (not available in 1970-71) shows a rather steady decline during 1972, a slight increase during 1973, a decline during 1974, stability at a low level in 1975, some recovery in 1976, a decline in 1977 and stability in 1978. This pattern generally followed the expected effects of the business cycle, but there was an absence of any dramatic increases or decreases in hours worked that would point to the presence (or absence) of strong demand pressures on prices. Similarly, contractual limits on the use of overtime limited the usefulness of this measure of the pressures of demand. For example, during the most recent period (1975-78), which included a sharp recession and rapid recovery, average overtime worked in large industry varied in the narrow range of 2.1 to 3.1 percent of monthly hours worked, except for the seasonally high month of August. In sum, data neither on total hours worked nor on overtime provide much evidence, pro or con, regarding excess demand as a cause of inflation.

Monthly ISCO business survey data on finished goods inventories lend support to the belief that excess demand was a significant factor behind price inflation in the period 1973-74, but probably not very important in the later price boom of 1976. In these monthly surveys businessmen are asked to characterize their inventories of finished goods as above normal, normal, below normal, or none. The balance between the percentage of replies indicating above normal against below normal (and none) gives a measure of opinions concerning the relative adequacy of finished-goods inventories. During a period of excess demand one would expect the majority of businessmen to indicate a below-normal level of finished goods on hand. In fact, this was true from the October 1972 survey through the August 1974 survey. The below-normal number of replies was particularly large from February 1973 through about May 1974. This period corresponded to the first (nonoil) phase of price acceleration in Italy during the 1973-74 price explosion. During the 1976 period of economic recovery and renewed price acceleration the business surveys again showed a sharp change in businessmen's evaluations of the adequacy of their inventories of finished goods compared to the preceding period. In absolute terms, however, businessmen seemed considerably more satisfied with the adequacy of the finished goods inventories than had been the case during the 1973-74 recovery. (To some extent the figures for 1976 may overstate the actual physical amount of such inventories compared to the earlier period, since it is generally believed that the high cost of carrying inventories during the 1975 recession led businessmen to improve management of their inventories and operate at a lower absolute level in the face of the same level of demand.) From late 1978 through mid-1979 the majority of businessmen were once again characterizing finished-goods inventories as significantly below normal, suggesting that a relative degree of demand pressure was again building up.

Some evidence of demand-pull inflationary forces can also be seen where excess domestic demand spills over into imports. There were three major periods during the 1970s when demand for imports of goods and services in real terms was particularly strong: late 1972 and early 1973, late 1975 and the last quarter of 1976, and late 1978 and early 1979. The sharp demand for imports in the third and fourth quarters of 1972 were more than usually anticipatory in nature. While real growth began to pick up around that time, there was little evidence that import demand at that early stage of recovery represented the spillover effects of excess demand. Rather, it was motivated by the buildup of inventories of raw materials as a hedge against further sharp world commodity price rises and in fear of lira exchange rate depreciation. By the second quarter of 1973 the sharp rise in real imports included fairly rapid increases in demand for both consumer goods and investment goods. Given the maturing of the recovery phase, this sharp growth may well have reflected some excess demand pressure. The strong recovery of import demand in late 1975 and early 1976 was not attributable to excess demand pressures but to initial restocking following the deep recession of 1975, when inventories had been sharply reduced. By late 1976, however, continued strong growth of demand for final consumer goods evidenced increasing demand pressures on capacity in the late phases of the 1975-76 recovery. Finally, the sharp rise in real import demand in the last two quarters of 1978 (and the continued high level in the first quarter of 1979) occurred too early in the recovery from slow growth in 1977-78 to give convincing evidence of demand-pull pressures, although it may have been a prelude to such pressures.

Rapid monetary expansion, closely linked with financing of a growing budget deficit, provides ammunition for those who attribute inflation in the 1970s to those causes. The evidence is mixed, however, with monetary expansion sometimes preceding and sometimes following episodes of price acceleration. The average rate of growth of the money supply (1970 through 1978) was 19.7 percent for M-1 (currency and coin and demand deposits with banks and the postal system) and 20.2 percent for M-3 (M-1 plus bank and postal savings deposits and ordinary treasury bills held by the public). The growth of the money supply was particularly rapid during four key phases of this period: during 1970, in the last half of 1973, in the last half of 1975 through the first quarter of 1976, and in the first quarter of 1978. For example, M-1 monetary expansion (measured by the seasonally adjusted increase at an annual rate for quarters ending in March, June, September, and December) reached rates of 26 percent and 27 percent in the March and December quarters of 1970, 31 percent in the quarter ending in June 1973, 31 percent in March 1976, and 28 percent in the March 1978 quarter.

The sharp rise in monetary expansion (M-1) in 1970 coincided with pressure to validate the sharp increase in wage costs following conclusion of the 1969-70 round of negotiations. The rate of monetary expansion, however, was not accompanied by an acceleration of price increases on the scale that occurred in later years. Possibly this was because the wage increase could still be absorbed by business by a cut in profit margins. Similarly, a close link between monetary expansion and inflation was absent in 1972. The ratcheting upward of inflation, which began in the last half of 1972, in fact followed a period of relatively slow monetary growth. In contrast, the acceleration of monetary growth in the last half of 1973 near the peak of the 1972-74 recovery period accommodated cost-push pressures from the 1973-74 world commodity price rises and the early 1973 wage rate increases under the three-year contract negotiations. The sharp deceleration in monetary growth during 1974, however, did not prevent a sharp rise in prices triggered by the OPEC oil price increase. The subsequent bulge in monetary growth in late 1975 and early 1976, designed to assist economic recovery from the 1975 recession, seems to have played a part in the 1975-76 lira depreciation and price explosion. Finally, the acceleration of money growth in early 1977 and in 1978 took place in a less buoyant growth setting than the earlier two periods of recovery, and in the absence of strong wage rate and nonoil commodity price pressures. In the absence of such cost-push factors, the reacceleration of inflation in early 1979 may have been partly attributable to excess monetary expansion.

COST-PUSH FACTORS

A number of strong cost-push factors contributed to Italian inflation during the 1970s. The strong increase in food and other raw material prices and the dramatic rise in the price of crude oil in 1973-74 were clearly cost-push phenomena of an exogenous sort. The acceleration of inflation in 1976, associated with the sharp depreciation of the lira exchange rate, also reflected to some extent the adverse effect on the lira of the sharp worsening in the terms of trade that had occurred in the earlier period. The constant erosion of the lira's value, however, due to persistently higher price and cost increases in Italy than in other major countries throughout earlier years of the decade, was another important cause.

The extent of cost-push pressures can be seen in data on the rise in unit labor costs, on changes in the price of materials, including imports—as a result of fluctuations in world prices and changes in the lira exchange rate—and on variations in the cost of money.

The rapid rise in unit labor costs in Italy, both in absolute terms and in comparison with other major industrial countries, was already discussed in Chapter 3. It will be recalled that for the period 1970-78 Italian data show that unit labor costs (per worker) for the entire economy rose on average by 14.6 percent per year. A comparison of relative increases in unit labor costs and corresponding prices (value-added deflators) in different sectors of the economy suggests that there was a declining opportunity for business to absorb labor cost increases by reducing profit margins. For the economy as a whole, unit labor costs rose more rapidly than prices in six out of nine years (1970-78), with costs rising on average by almost 2 percentage points per year more than prices. In the primary sector of the economy labor costs outpaced prices in eight out of nine years by an average of more than 5 percentage points per year. In industry labor costs rose faster than prices in six out of nine years, by 2 percentage points per year on average. In the services sector (including the public administration) labor costs and prices rose at about the same annual rate.

The rising cost of labor was, of course, not the sole source of cost-push pressures on prices. The price of raw materials and the cost of money also played a part. (A business survey of firms in industry and some services sectors showed that in the years 1974-78, as a percent of gross sales, labor costs were 22 percent, materials/ services costs 68 percent, financial costs 7 percent, and gross profits 3 percent.)[1] Raw materials costs, however, did not increase continuously at as high a rate as labor costs. Also the cost of money, although rising very rapidly, was a much smaller share of total business costs. Thus, cost-push pressures from the increase of labor costs were extremely important in affecting the rate of inflation.

Because of the openness of the Italian economy it was subject to substantial cost and price pressures from rising prices of imported goods and services, whether in the form of increasing prices of finished goods or, indirectly, through the rising costs of raw materials and intermediate goods used as inputs for Italian industry. In the period 1970-78 the ratio of imports to GDP in current lire averaged more than 21 percent, and following the oil price increases of 1973-74 the ratio rose to an average of about 24 percent in the next four years. Thus, changes in the price of imported goods and services had an important impact on domestic prices. (A Confindustria study in 1979 showed that on average, for six major industries, domestically produced materials accounted for 49 percent of gross sales, while imported materials accounted for 13 percent of sales. In other words, imported materials accounted for 21 percent of total materials.)[2] The impact of import prices on domestic inflation could take the form either of changes in world commodity price movements (typically denominated in dollars) or of changes in the lira exchange rate.

The inflationary push from increases in the price of imported goods and services was not a source of constant upward pressure on prices, as was the case with the wage/price spiral working through the scala mobile. Rather, it came in three bursts in 1973, 1974, and 1976. In those three years the deflator for imports of goods and services rose by 26, 57, and 24 percent, respectively. In other years, such as 1972, 1975, and 1978, the low rate of price increase for imported goods and services (4, 6, and 4 percent, respectively) actually helped to contain price inflation.

In 1973 and 1974 the main sources of the increases in import prices were rises in world prices of food, industrial raw materials, and energy, although lira depreciation also played a part. The Confindustria index of world commodity prices (dollar denominated and Italian trade-weighted) rose by 39 percent and 76 percent, respectively, in 1973 and 1974 (Table 6.7). (About 70-75 percent of Italian imports are food, raw materials, and intermediate goods.) In both years food price increases were large, at 55 percent and 42 percent, respectively. In 1973 the price of nonfood agricultural materials rose by 42 percent and in 1973 and 1974 minerals and metals rose by 56 percent and 45 percent, respectively. In 1973 the fuels price increase was 23 percent. In 1974 much the largest increase occurred for fuels (up 174 percent).

There was also a large depreciation of the lira late in 1973 and in mid-1974 which contributed to the rising costs of imports in those years (Table 6.8). Because the depreciation of the lira in 1973 took

TABLE 6.7

World Commodity Prices, 1970–78
(percent annual change)

| | Agricultural Products | | Minerals/ | | |
	Total	(Food)	Metals	Fuels	Total
1970	3.0	(5.4)	4.1	0.1	2.1
1971	1.0	(1.7)	−15.5	13.9	3.0
1972	17.6	(7.5)	2.1	8.0	11.6
1973	48.3	(55.0)	56.4	22.9	39.3
1974	18.5	(41.7)	45.0	174.0	76.0
1975	−2.7	(−7.8)	−27.0	2.8	−2.5
1976	15.4	(11.5)	37.6	6.9	12.5
1977	3.8	(7.6)	1.7	7.9	5.8
1978	5.8	(−0.2)	2.2	0.5	2.5
Aver-age	12.3	(13.6)	11.8	26.3	16.7

Source: Compiled by the author; data from Confindustria research office (dollar prices; Italian trade weights in 1977).

place at the end of the year, the recorded average change in the lira/dollar rate was almost nil between 1973 and 1972. Between the floating of currencies in February 1973 and February 1974, however, the lira/dollar rate dropped from its Smithsonian par value by 23 percent and the decline of the lira against the Bank of Italy's trade-weighted basket of currencies was 16 percent.

The increase in the lira cost of imported goods and services in 1976 was in large part due to the depreciation of the lira exchange rate. In that year the Confindustria world commodity index showed an increase of only 12 percent. In contrast, the lira exchange rate against the dollar declined by 27 percent and against the Bank of Italy basket of currencies by 11 percent. This sharp depreciation of the lira rate increased import prices, raised the cost of living index, caused automatic offsetting wage adjustments under the scala mobile system, and was clearly an important proximate cause of the acceleration of prices in 1976. (It should be noted, however, that there were also some significant nonautomatic increases in industrial wage rates in 1976, arising from the three-year round of wage negotiations of 1975–76.)

TABLE 6.8

Lira Exchange Rate Movements, 1970-78
(percent annual change)

	Lira per Dollar	Trade-weighted Lira
1970	—	n.a.
1971	1.4	n.a.
1972	5.7	n.a.
1973	0.1	-9.2
1974	-11.6	-7.6
1975	-0.4	-3.1
1976	-27.4	-10.8
1977	-6.1	-4.3
1978	3.8	-1.8

Note: n.a. = not available.
Source: Compiled by the author; calculated from
data in Bank of Italy bulletins.

The effect of increasing prices for raw materials and intermediate goods of both domestic and foreign origin can be seen in the sharp increases in wholesale prices in the three years 1973, 1974, and 1976. In those three years the index rose on average by 17 percent, 41 percent, and 23 percent. As in the case of prices of imported materials, however, the total index also displayed a degree of flexibility in the downward direction during periods of recession or of slow growth, as in 1975 (up 9 percent) and 1978 (up 8 percent).

In addition to examining the effect of rising costs of labor and raw materials on prices, it is also worthwhile to look at the effect of the rising cost of money on business costs. The annual Mediobanca business survey covering the period 1968-78 shows a faster rate of increase in financial costs for the nine-year period 1970-78 than in labor costs (average annual increases of 29 percent and 18 percent, respectively). During the same period the ratio of financial charges to gross sales increased from 4.1 percent in 1970 to a peak of 7.0 percent in 1977 (6.7 percent in 1978). Thus the higher nominal interest rate policy of the late 1970s contributed some modest upward cost pressures on prices. (This is not an argument for abandoning the use of interest rate policy as a tool of demand management, but does point

out the adverse feedback effect on costs of tight money in the context
of a highly leveraged business sector.)

PRICE AND RENT CONTROLS

In addition to general macroeconomic tools for influencing the
price level, Italy has exercised direct controls on rent and on the
prices of some goods and services. Rent controls had been in effect
from 1946 until a fair-rent law (equo canone) went into effect on
November 1, 1978. Under the old rent control law limits were placed
on rents stipulated under both pre-World War II and postwar housing,
with the limits periodically raised by law. The freeze did not apply to
luxury housing, which was periodically defined with reference to the
size of the taxable income of the tenant.

The 1978 fair-rent law created a system whereby rental
increases could be automatically adjusted in line with changes in the
cost of living. These adjustments, however, apply to a base rental
amount that varies according to a complex formula involving location,
condition of the building, age of the building, class of building (for
example, luxury), condition of the interior of the dwelling, and the
size (square footage). While agreement on application of the formula
to individual cases may be difficult, the law does provide for automatic adjustments without the need for new laws, once the classifi-
cation of the dwelling is established.

The possibility of fixing maximum prices for all goods and
services, including professional services by the Interministerial
Price Committee (CIP)is based on Law No. 347 of October 19, 1944.
That law states that the CIP may fix "prices of any merchandise, at
every level of exchange, including prices of imports and exports as
well as the prices of services including professional services." Since
the Constitution, however, establishes in Article 41 that "private economic enterprise is free," not all prices may be controlled simul-
taneously by CIP. The controls must be limited to those prices having
social utility or that concern "delicate aspects of economic life."
(Note that the establishment of the Common Agricultural Policy of the
EC effectively removed the Italian authorities' control over agricultural prices covered by the CAP.)

The 1944 price control law created both the central government's
CIP and Provincial Price Committees (CPP) designed to implement
a flexible system characterized by control over the maximum prices
of goods and services of preeminent importance to the national economy. Since 1968, in determining the economic sectors and the types
of goods and services over which it exercises control, the CIP must

abide by directives of the Interministerial Committee for Economic Planning (CIPE).

Organizationally, CIP is chaired by the president of the Council of Ministers (that is, the prime minister), or by a minister delegated by him. The committee is composed of ten ministers* and three experts, and is assisted by a consultative body, the Central Price Commission, which is divided into four subcommissions.† The provincial price organizations have a structure similar to that of the national organization.

Although the CIP was assigned broad powers for determining the prices of all goods and services, the list of goods and services that have been subject to control of one kind or another (that is, administered or placed under surveillance) has remained relatively stable. (There was an exception during a period of expanded control over prices between July 1973 and July 1974—see Chapter 12.) In large part, the prices fixed by CIP concern goods and services offered on a monopoly basis by autonomous state entities, by public enterprises, and by local governments. Some, however, are also sold by private business.‡

---

*Agriculture, Budget, Foreign Trade, Finance, Industry and Commerce, Public Works, Labor and Social Security, State Participations, Treasury, and Transport.

†The Central Price Commission is composed of representatives of the ministries represented on the CIP, the Foreign Trade Institute (ICE), ISTAT, and employers, workers, autonomous regions, and consumer associations. The four subcommissions are those for energy, for public services, for mining, chemical, and industrial products, and for food and agricultural products.

‡As of late 1979 the following items sold by public bodies were subject to price control (administered prices): urban and interurban telephone charges, radio and television subscription fees, railway fares and fees of the state railways, transport fees under concession arrangements, electricity rates, gas rates, water, general warehouse fees, elevator inspection fees, licenses for operation of sales stands in wholesale markets, fees for inserts in the legal announcement bulletin. For goods and services sold by private companies or individuals the list of administered prices includes solid fuels (coal and coke), petroleum derivatives, glass and cement, medicinal specialties, daily newspapers and newsprint, fertilizers, common soaps and household detergents, hotel rates, fees for olive crushing and wheat threshing and hulling of cereals, food products, edible olive oil and mixed seed oils, virgin olive cake, frozen beef, milk, salt, sugar,

Concerning procedures, there are no fixed rules as to the method by which CIP determines prices. In theory, prices must be fixed on the basis of cost, plus a fair margin of profit for producers and intermediaries. In practice, decisions are often made without a serious examination of those factors. In fact, CIP lacks important powers for investigating businesses in order to ascertain their costs. There is also a lack of personnel to carry out such investigations and methodically to supervise various sectors.

In addition to administered prices, some items are subject to a less formal type of price surveillance. Under authority assigned to CIP by the CIPE, the former is charged with monitoring the movement of these prices, through investigations and inspections. In 1977-79 there was a certain amount of liberalization of price controls by the transfer of some items from the administered price list to the under-surveillance price list.*

CONCLUSIONS

Italian inflation in the 1970s had a variety of causes, coming from both the demand-pull and the cost-push sides. Situations of general excess demand pushing against available capacity were quite rare, however. In contrast, cost-push factors were pervasive and continuous, coming both from domestic and from foreign economic developments.

Except for one or two rather brief periods toward the end of the recovery phases of business cycles (1973-74, 1976-77, and perhaps 1978-79) the pressure of excess demand on available capacity did not exert strong upward pressure on prices. Data on utilization of industrial capacity, variations in short-time work, fluctuations in finished

---

and insurance rates. In addition to these items, price control has not been delegated to the CIP for tobacco products and post and telegraph rates; these are controlled directly through ministerial decrees.

*As of late 1979 the following items were subject to price surveillance: aluminum, fungicides, over-the-counter drugs, schoolbooks, tin strips and rods, bread, dried pasta, milk and cheese products, "extra virgin" olive oil, cured meats and ham, fresh beef, pork, lamb, horsemeat, poultry and rabbits, frozen and canned foods, methane gas, gasoline, jet fuel, asphalt, lubricants, solvents, heavy fuel oil, home heating oil, some reinforced concrete, insulation, Thomas slag, and calcium cyanimide.

goods inventories, and the level of import demand tend to confirm this view. (Statistics on hours worked and on overtime did not give good evidence one way or the other, because of institutional limits on the length of the work week and restrictions on the use of overtime.)

The effective limits on the use of monetary policy dictated by the need to assure financing of a growing public sector deficit led to rapid rates of monetary expansion. An examination of relative rates of growth of the money supply and its timing suggests that rapid monetary growth in 1973, 1975-76, and 1978 played an independent role in facilitating the expansion of aggregate demand and placing upward pressure on prices during the two price explosions of 1974 and 1976 and may help to explain a reacceleration of prices in 1979. In contrast, rapid monetary growth in 1970 was not accompanied by dramatic price expansion and the relatively slow rates of growth in 1972 and 1974 did not prevent price acceleration in those years. Clearly, the very high rate of monetary expansion throughout nearly all of the 1970s (except briefly in 1975) greatly helped to accommodate other demand-pull and cost-push forces.

A constant cost-push factor was the rapid rise in unit labor costs, not due exclusively to automatic wage indexation adjustments, although these were critical in keeping the wage-price spiral going. The rise in world prices of imported food, industrial raw materials, and energy caused a dramatic exogenous impact on the Italian economy in 1973-74. This impact was perpetuated in time and multiplied in degree by the wage indexation system (see Chapter 3). The sharp depreciations of the lira in 1973-74 and in 1976 were due partly to the adverse effect on the balance of payments from the worsening of the terms of trade in 1973-74, but they also reflected the delayed effect of accumulated pressures on the exchange rate from generally faster unit labor cost increases in Italy than in other major industrial countries. Besides acting as a cost-push factor, the worsening in the terms of trade implied a reduction in real incomes, which consumers attempted to resist. Given the reduced supply of real goods and services available, real demand exercised stronger pressure on prices than before the worsening in the terms of trade. Finally, the rise in the cost of money, although more limited in its impact compared to the increase in labor, raw materials, and energy costs, also played a modest part in exerting upward cost pressures on prices.

The high rate of inflation in Italy in the 1970s had important effects on the distribution of income, the level and composition of growth and job creation, and the balance of payments.

Nearly all wage and salary workers and pensioners were progressively covered by the wage indexation system during the 1970s, and thus were automatically protected to some extent from inflation. The degree of protection, however, differed from worker to worker and indexation did not apply to other forms of income nor to financial or other assets. The extent to which different categories of wage and salary workers were protected from inflation varied considerably because new wage contracts often provided a fixed lira wage increase for all workers and because the unified lira value of each one point of scala mobile adjustments (after February 1977) was the same for all, without regard to level of income. As a consequence, blue-collar workers became better protected than white-collar workers, agricultural workers better than industrial workers, private sector workers better than workers in the public administration, and current income was better protected than accumulated financial savings.

The income of self-employed workers was not automatically protected against the effects of inflation. In fact, per capita proprietorship income rose (old GDP) series) less rapidly than did wage and salary income.

National income data (old GDP series) on income other than from personal services show rather modest amounts of interest income, rent and royalty income, and dividend income going to the household sector. In fact, net rental income was negative for the household sector throughout the 1971-77 period. Given the effects of rent control on at least part of rental housing, it seems likely that rental income was generally not very well protected from inflation, although some landlords may have escaped the controls, and potential or realized capital gains may have provided some compensation. The total of net interest income plus dividends, shown in GDP data, on average accounted for only 1.4 percent of gross personal income at factor cost. Net interest income rose quite substantially in absolute terms, however, with the rise in interest rates in the mid-1970s. The latter factor, plus the high rate of personal saving, increased the importance to investors of interest rates high enough to provide some positive return after inflation. In fact, interest rates paid to households were less negative in real terms late in the 1970s than earlier.

In a 1977 study of the real income from financial assets of Italian families in the period 1964-76, Giorgio Troi shows that in every year from 1969 onward interest earned in real terms was negative, with particularly large losses suffered in 1974 and 1976.[3] Although interest on short-term bank debt and medium- and long-term debt (mainly mortgage debt) paid by households was also negative in real terms from 1972 onward, the household sector still suffered large net losses because of its very large net financial asset position. According to Troi, cumulative losses in 1976 lira exceeded 54 trillion lira. While the study concentrated on the effect of inflation on current income from holdings of currency, financial deposits, and fixed-interest security holdings, Troi noted that there were also large capital losses during the period on bond portfolios of perhaps

2.6 trillion lire and on stock holdings of at least 10 trillion lire. It may be that other investments by Italian families, especially real estate, were more resistant to the ravages of inflation.

The effect of inflation on the net transfer portion of disposable income (old GDP data) reflects the fact that pension receipts are indexed. Conversely, the personal income tax is a progressive tax. In fact, in the period 1971-77 net transfers became increasingly negative for the household sector, as social insurance benefits and other current transfer receipts did not keep pace with the rise in social insurance contributions, income taxes, and other transfer payments.

When the household sector, as a creditor, lost from inflation, the corresponding debtors gained. Those debtors, however, were to a large extent public borrowers. To the extent that these borrowers provided subsidized public services and made transfer payments to lower income groups, there was some second-round compensation for some Italian savers. The business sector, which suffered a sharp drop in profits during the period, may also have received some compensation in the form of lower real interest payments on its debts. Weighted average interest rates paid by business in real terms were negative in six out of nine years in the period 1970-78. Still, business showed some natural reluctance to take advantage of these low real rates, because of fear that acceptance of a very high nominal rate over the long term was too risky, even in an environment of high inflationary expectations. The net effect of all this was that both Italian households and businesses were reluctant consumers and investors and real growth suffered.

The persistence of negative interest rates and of large losses on both current income and on financial assets of households is very troublesome in the context of an Italian economy that has become more and more dependent on the household sector for savings. One can wonder how long Italian families will continue to maintain such a high savings rate in the face of such losses and how a revival of productive investment can be achieved in such circumstances.

The balance of payments, too, felt the impact of inflation. While the depreciation of the lira in 1973-74 and 1975-76 was to some extent caused by the (exogenous) deterioration in Italy's terms of trade due to the commodity boom and the oil price increases, the steady erosion of the value of the lira from domestic inflationary factors also made a major contribution to the accumulated overvaluation of the lira which had to be corrected by these rather abrupt adjustments. While flexible exchange rates are supposed to provide a certain amount of leeway for rates to adjust to disparities in inflation rates, and have done so, it is clear that the openness of the Italian economy, coupled with a very effective wage indexation system, quickly tends to erode temporary competitive gains from such rate movements. Unless the basic causes of the inflation are dealt with, Italy can expect to continue to encounter periodic problems of growth and balance of payments.

Except for a relatively brief period in 1973-74 (Chapter 12), little attempt was made to employ comprehensive direct controls on prices. (The July 1973 action concerned mainly foodstuffs, prices of goods produced by large enterprises, and some rents.) Limited rent controls and administered prices, however, existed for a group of selected goods and services throughout the period. The 1973-74 experiment with comprehensive price controls and subsequent efforts at flexible price surveillance were not very effective. Indeed, the advent of OPEC monopoly oil pricing and the growing deficits of local governments and autonomous government agencies forced the authorities to raise the price of energy and other administered prices and public service rates and to accept a more flexible system for adjusting these prices to rising costs, in order to help conserve energy and reduce the burden on the Treasury.

While little can be done to avoid future inflationary impacts from abroad, domestic sources of inflation must be reduced and the mechanism that transmits and perpetuates inflation from both sources modified, if adequate rates of economic growth and job creation and balance-of-payments equilibrium are to be achieved in the future.

NOTES

1. Mediobanca, Dati Cumulativi di 856 Società Italiane (1968-78) (Milan: 1979).

2. Confindustria, Secondo Rapporto CSC sull' Industria Italiana Vol. 1 (1979), pp. 43-45.

3. Giorgio Troi, "Il rendimento del risparmio finanziario delle famiglie Italiane dal 1964 al 1976," Banca Nazionale del Lavoro, Moneta e Credito Vol XXX No. 118 (June 1977): 197-211.

7

THE BALANCE OF PAYMENTS

The oil crisis makes it necessary to adapt the structure
of our economy immediately to the changed terms of
trade between raw materials and manufactured goods.
First, two conditions must be fulfilled: the mobility of
the factors of production, so that they may be chan-
nelled towards the sectors more directly associated
with exports; and a rate of inflation no higher than that
existing in competitor countries. The hardening of
labour relations together with the uncontrolled growth
of money incomes have the opposite effect.

Guido Carli
Governor, Bank of Italy
Annual Meeting, Rome, May 1974

INTRODUCTION

For a country that was in chronic surplus in the 1960s, the
appearance of a balance-of-payments constraint in Italy in the 1970s
was a rude shock. Admittedly, there had been balance-of-payments
problems in 1963 and 1969, but these had been due principally to an
exceptional increase in capital outflows arising from confidence
problems in the political and economic fields. In fact, current account surpluses during the decade of the 1960s accumulated to a total
of nearly $12 billion—a very large amount for the size of Italy's
economy and second only to the United States among the OECD countries. Italy's large current surpluses, however, were to a considerable extent offset by persistent outflows of capital, which exceeded

$8 billion during the decade, and by generally negative errors and omissions, so that the cumulative overall surplus for the decade only slightly exceeded $2 billion.*

The 1960s' pattern of very large current account surpluses, largely offset by capital outflows, was sharply reversed in the 1970s. There were three distinct phases in Italy's balance-of-payments developments, shown in Table 7.1. The first period (1970-72) was essentially a continuation of the pattern that had prevailed during the 1960s. The second period (1973-76) encompassed the strongly adverse effects of the world commodity boom and oil price rises of 1973-74. The combined effect of these and other (economic recovery) factors forced Italy's trade, current account, and overall balances into massive deficit. In those four years the current account registered a deficit of $14 billion. Net capital inflows (of which 81 percent were compensatory borrowing) partially offset the current deficits, but the overall balance was still in cumulative deficit by $10 billion for the period. In 1974, alone, the current account deficit amounted to 4.7 percent of GDP.

There was a remarkable turnaround in Italy's balance of payments in 1977-78. Current account surpluses for the two-year period totaled nearly $9 billion; the capital account was in large surplus (despite repayments on old compensatory debt), and the overall balance reached a surplus in excess of $10 billion. (The current account continued in large surplus in 1979.)

----

*Balance-of-payments statistics in this book refer to the economic (that is, definitive) balance of payments, or to customs data in the case of some trade statistics. Although most original data are published in lire, they have generally been converted here into dollars. For the period 1960-71 the old par value of one dollar to 625 lire was used. For 1972-73 the Smithsonian central rate of one dollar to 581.5 lire was used, and for succeeding years the yearly average lire-per-dollar rate calculated by the Bank of Italy has been employed (1974, 650 lire; 1975, 653 lire; 1976, 832 lire; 1977, 882 lire; 1978, 849 lire). Two principal adjustments to published data have been made. The first consists of the transfer of hidden capital flight in some services accounts to the capital account for the years 1970-71, in order to be consistent with similar adjustments contained in published data for 1972-76. The second concerns the period 1960-76, where adjustments have been made to the net foreign position of the banks and to the overall surplus or deficit, to remove from the banks' foreign assets certain foreign exchange assets in the form of Italian export bills, which are really claims on residents. Published data from 1977 on already include this adjustment.

TABLE 7.1

Three Phases in Italy's Balance of Payments, 1970-78
(billions of dollars)

	Current Account	Capital Account	Compensatory Loans	Adjust- ments	Overall Surplus or Deficit
1970-72*	5.0	-4.3	(1.8)	-1.0	-0.2
1973-76*	-13.9	6.4	(4.9)	-2.5	-10.1
1977-78	8.8	1.5	(-1.5)	-0.1	10.2
Total	-0.1	3.6	(5.2)	-3.6	-0.1

*Current and capital accounts adjusted for hidden capital flight in services accounts.

Source: Compiled by the author; calculated from Bank of Italy annual reports.

In sum, the Italian balance of payments proved to be very resilient in the face of an enormous shock from the worsening in the terms of trade. Exports, aided by flexible exchange rates, did well and there was some progress in reducing dependence on imported oil. Export growth in real terms provided a useful underpinning during a time of weak domestic demand. The exchange rate depreciation also proved to be a boon to services income, particularly tourist receipts. When large deficits appeared, the authorities were at first able to attract capital inflows with considerable ease, but the massive Euromarket borrowing of 1973-74 put heavy strains on Italy's foreign creditworthiness and the authorities were then forced to resort to official borrowing and to a buildup of short-term bank debt. With a strengthened current account position in 1977-78 (and 1979), Italy restored its credit rating and established some margin of protection against future uncertainties.

TRADE, CURRENT ACCOUNT, CAPITAL ACCOUNT,
AND OVERALL BALANCES

Trade Account

Italy's trade account was typically in deficit during the 1970s. This did not necessarily create a problem, given the persistent surplus on services and private transfers. Only when the trade deficit got out of hand were there overall balance-of-payments financing problems. During the first three years of the 1970s the trade account was in approximate balance—a stronger showing than in the 1960s—but Italy was somewhat out of step with growth abroad and domestic demand was weak. When recovery from the post-1969 stagnation finally came, beginning around the third quarter of 1972, imports took off. This occurred at a time when inventories had been run down and when poor harvests and worldwide recovery were driving up world food and industrial raw material prices. In addition to the normal need to restock and the fear of further world price rises, there was growing unease about the stability of the lira exchange rate, which gave further cause for building up inventories of imported goods.

Beginning with the first quarter of 1973, Italy experienced eight successive quarters of large trade deficits (balance-of-payments basis) in the range of $0.8 to $2.5 billion per quarter, with a peak coming in the second quarter of 1974. By that time the effects of the quadrupling of crude oil prices by OPEC were also being felt. Negative real growth of GDP, however, which began in the third quarter of 1974 and continued for four more quarters (through the third quarter of 1975), brought some temporary relief. For a brief three quarters the trade deficit fell to modest levels. Then promptly with the recovery that began in the last quarter of 1975, imports rose again and the trade deficit was at least $0.5 billion per quarter for five of the six quarters from the fourth quarter of 1975 through the first quarter of 1977.

Imports were not the whole story. Exports, which rose at an average annual rate of 28 percent in 1973-74 (balance-of-payments basis in dollar terms), could not keep up with the growth of imports (45 percent) due to both volume and terms-of-trade factors. To some extent growth may have suffered from a decline in Italy's price competitiveness. Also, the attraction of rapid domestic growth and the approach to full industrial capacity utilization in the last half of 1973 and first half of 1974 no doubt acted to limit export growth.

With the improvement in Italy's competitive position from late 1975 and the relatively faster growth in many of Italy's export markets than at home, export growth accelerated while import growth was quite modest (average rise in dollar terms for the years 1975-78 of 17 percent and 9 percent, respectively). Both quantity and price factors were working to Italy's advantage during the two-year period 1977-78, as the quantity of exports rose on average by 9 percent, compared to import growth of only 4 percent in real terms. At the same time implicit dollar prices for exports were up on average by over 12 percent, against an average dollar import price rise of 9 percent.

Customs data (with imports on a c.i.f. basis) for the entire period 1970-78 show a cumulative Italian trade deficit of $33 billion. Much the largest deficit ($28 billion) was with the oil producers: Algeria, Indonesia, Iran, Iraq, Kuwait, Nigeria, Oman, Qatar, Saudi Arabia, United Arab Emirates, and Venezuela. Also there were deficits with Italy's EC partners ($7 billion), the United States ($3 billion), Canada and Japan ($3 billion), and other countries ($3 billion)—principally the developing countries, although there was a trade surplus with Europe of $4 billion. (Note that the inclusion of imports on a c.i.f. basis considerably adds to the size of the deficit.) By type of goods, the deficit was entirely in raw materials and intermediate goods ($103 billion)—attesting to the transformation nature of Italy's foreign trade. There were large surpluses in consumer goods ($46 billion) and investment goods ($24 billion). The deficit on food trade (including both final and intermediate goods and both fresh and processed food) and in energy products (coal, oil, and their products) more than accounted for the total trade deficit. Food, alone, showed a deficit of $26 billion and the energy balance a deficit of $56 billion. Furthermore, there was a tendency for both deficits to grow.

In each of the three periods of large trade deficits (1970, 1973-74, and 1976) the cyclical demand for imported raw materials and the crowding out of exports by the pressure of domestic demand were crucial factors. In 1974 the oil price increase was extremely important. The erosion of Italy's price competitiveness was also a significant factor in 1973-74 and perhaps in 1976, before the depreciations of late 1975 and early 1976 had made themselves felt. Italy's trade balance with its largest trade partner, Germany, was particularly volatile. In four years of the nine-year period (1970-78) Italy had trade surpluses (even with imports c.i.f.) ranging from $0.2 to $0.9 billion. There were even more frequent and larger deficits, however, ranging from $0.1 to $1.6 billion. The shift into large deficit with Germany in 1973 and 1974 was particularly troublesome, at a time when deficits with oil and other commodity exporters were hard to avoid.

Current Account

Changes in the current account balance generally followed those of the trade account (Table 7.2). The persistent surplus on services and private transfers, however, tended to reduce the deficit or contribute to the surplus on trade account. In the period 1970-72 the relatively strong trade account (balance-of-payments basis) was accompanied by substantial surpluses in services, following the pattern that had prevailed in the 1960s (Figure 7.1). During the balance-of-

TABLE 7.2

Current Account Balances, 1970-78
(billions of dollars)

	Trade	Services/Transfers	Current Account
1970	-0.4	1.5	1.1
1971	0.1	1.8	1.9
1972	-	2.0	2.0
1973	-3.9	1.4	-2.5
1974	-8.5	0.5	-8.0
1975	-1.2	0.6	-0.6
1976	-4.2	1.4	-2.8
1977	-0.1	2.6	2.5
1978	2.9	3.5	6.4

Source: Compiled by the author; data from Bank of Italy annual reports.

payments crises of 1973-76, however, the surplus in the services transfer account not only ceased to grow but even declined. In fact, there were 5 quarters out of 16 (not seasonally adjusted) when services and transfers were negative, adding to the deficit on trade account. In 1977-78 the improvement in the trade figures was accompanied by a sharp improvement in invisibles, with these items contributing to the growing account surplus. In fact, the current account surplus in 1978 amounted to 2.4 percent of GDP.

Capital Account

The capital account was in surplus in 17 out of 36 quarters during the period 1970-78 (not adjusted for hidden capital flight in 1970-71). The recorded figures, however, include net receipts (or repayments) from compensatory Euromarket loans of Italian borrowers at the request of the monetary authorities. These capital flows were not autonomous but were designed to help finance deficits in the current account and elsewhere in the capital account during times of weakness in the balance of payments. If these net capital flows are excluded, the capital account was in deficit in four out of nine years.

FIGURE 7.1

Balance of Payments, 1970–79
(millions of dollars, not seasonally adjusted)

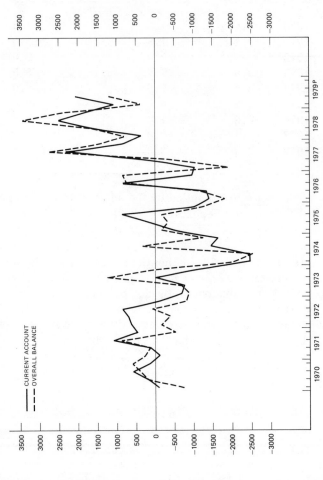

Note: Data for 1979 are preliminary.
Source: Constructed by the author; data from Bank of Italy annual reports and supplements to bulletins.

178

Overall Surplus/Deficit

The overall surplus or deficit measures the size of the balance-of-payments financing problem. It includes current account, capital account, and various adjustments (including errors and omissions), but excludes both official capital flows of the Bank of Italy and the Italian Exchange Office (Ufficio Italiano dei Cambi—UIC) and short-term foreign capital flows of the commercial banks. The overall surplus or deficit is thus calculated on a monetary-movements basis—that is, the sum of the change in the net foreign position of the official monetary authorities (the Bank of Italy and UIC), plus the net change in the foreign position of the commercial banks. The inclusion of the net foreign position of the commercial banks "below the line" as a financing item, rather than as an autonomous capital movement in the capital account makes sense in the Italian case, in that the monetary authorities have considerable authority (and use it) to influence the banks' foreign position both directly and indirectly.*

During the 1970s, however, there were large-scale borrowings and repayments of compensatory Euromarket term loans by various state-controlled special credit institutes and holding companies, at the behest of the central bank. Although these capital flows were recorded in the capital account of the balance of payments, they really constituted a form of indirect balance-of-payments financing. Thus adjustments should be made to the recorded surpluses or deficits, particularly in the deficit years 1973-76. In that period the financing problem that confronted the Italian monetary authorities (excluding the compensatory loans) was not a cumulative deficit of $10 billion, but one of $15 billion. Conversely, when the balance-of-payments situation improved in 1977-78, large repayments were made on the earlier compensatory loans. If a symmetrical adjustment were made for 1977-78 in the recorded cumulative surplus, then the "underlying" surplus was $12 billion, not $10 billion.

---

*In the text and tables of this book the overall surplus or deficit of the balance of payments is measured by these below-the-line movements and an adjustment is made to force equality with the above-the-line balance which is based on lire converted to dollars at current rates. Below-the-line monetary movements in dollars were obtained from the Bank of Italy.

EXPORTS

Export Performance

Italy's market share of the exports of all industrial countries (in dollar terms) averaged about 6.4 percent for the 1970s, as shown in the table below. (Industrial countries include the United States, Canada, Japan, Austria, Belgium, Denmark, France, Germany, Italy, Netherlands, Norway, Sweden, Switzerland, and the United Kingdom.) The pattern was one of a slight gain in market share in

Year	Percent
1970	6.3
1971	6.5
1972	6.7
1973	5.9
1974	6.0
1975	6.5
1976	6.2
1977	6.7
1978	6.9
Average	6.4

the early years of the decade (1970-72), a decline to a low point in 1973, and a general increase in market share to a high of 6.9 percent in 1978.

In that period Italian exports in dollar terms rose on average by 19.3 percent, compared with average export growth for the entire group of industrial countries of 18.7 percent. As already noted, the principal reasons for the loss of market share in 1973-74 (and briefly in 1976) were the pressure of domestic demand and the lagged effect of some loss of price competitiveness in those and earlier periods. Exports also suffered somewhat in 1973 and 1976 from strikes. The improvement in 1977-78 reflected improved price competitiveness. Also, the decline in labor mobility and the evolution of labor costs into virtually fixed costs during the decade put added pressure on business to sustain production at relatively high levels of capacity by pushing exports during periods of slack domestic demand, because a reduction in production levels did little to reduce variable costs. In addition, there may have been some incentive to shift resources from domestic sales to foreign sales, due to the relatively faster rise in Italian export prices than in wholesale prices, particularly after the lira depreciations that began in 1973-74.

TABLE 7.3

Growth of Exports, 1970–78
(customs data f.o.b.; percent annual change)

	Volume	Value (lira)	Value (dollar)	Price (lira)*
1970	7.1	12.6	12.6	5.2
1971	7.6	13.4	13.4	5.4
1972	12.7	15.9	24.6	2.8
1973	1.2	19.8	19.5	18.4
1974	7.7	52.6	36.8	41.7
1975	3.7	15.3	14.8	11.2
1976	11.7	36.3	7.0	22.0
1977	7.6	28.2	20.9	19.2
1978	10.8	18.8	23.4	7.2
Average	7.8	23.7	19.2	14.8

*Unit values.
Source: Compiled by the author; data from ISTAT bulletins.

Export growth in real terms was particularly strong in 1972, 1976, and 1978. The first two years were for the most part boom years in Italy's export markets. In 1978 Italian exports (and export profitability) were helped by the combined effect of a depreciation of the lira against the currencies of some of Italy's major trading partners and the appreciation of the lira against the dollar. Since a large part of Italy's (mainly primary/intermediate goods) imports are billed in dollars (45 percent in 1978), while a large part of its finished goods exports go to Western Europe, there was a significant gain in Italy's foreign exchange terms of trade.

A breakdown of the value, price, and quantity components of Italy's exports (customs basis) in the 1970s shows that, in lira terms, exports grew on average by almost 24 percent, owing to a growth in volume terms of 7.8 percent per year and of lira unit prices of 14.8 percent per year (Table 7.3). In this period, the growth in volume for investment goods exported averaged 7.5 percent per year, for intermediate goods 8.4 percent, and for consumer goods 7.2 percent. In terms of lira unit prices the average growth was 14.7 percent for investment goods, 15.9 percent for intermediate goods, and 14.0 percent for consumer goods. The value of exports in dollar terms, however, grew on average by only about 19 percent, showing the effect on data denominated in lire of the depreciation of the lira against the dollar. For the same reason, the average unit price of exports in dollars was less than 11 percent. Export values in lira terms were particularly inflated in 1974 and 1976 when the lira depreciated sharply against the dollar.

Although Italian export unit values in local currency rose more rapidly between 1970 and 1978 than in most other major industrial countries, from 1973 onward flexible exchange rates generally permitted Italy to retain or recover price competitiveness. After a worsening in its price competitiveness in 1974 and 1975 (despite considerable lira depreciation in 1973-74), Italy regained competitiveness with the large depreciation of 1976 and generally maintained it through the rest of the decade. The table below shows relative export unit values in manufacturing for Italy, compared to 13 other industrial countries, in dollar terms (1975 = 100).

Year	Relative Unit Value
1973	95.7
1974	96.4
1975	100.0
1976	92.9
1977	96.4
1978	91.2
1979 (2nd quarter)	91.9

Geographic Pattern of Exports

The pattern of Italy's exports by geographic area during the 1970s showed a predominance of trade with other European countries, which accounted for no less than 67 percent of Italy's exports in any year. The share was remarkably stable, although there was some slight tendency for a decline late in the period, as the growth of exports to the oil producers slightly impinged on the European share. Within Europe, trade with the EC accounted for no less than 45 percent of Italy's exports. The EC share did not fall, despite the rising share going to the oil producers, as export growth with the United Kingdom was particularly strong, following that country's joining the Common Market. (The U.K. share of Italy's exports rose from 3.6 percent of the total in 1970 to 6.1 percent in 1978.) Germany was Italy's most important market, accounting for 18 to 23 percent of

Italian exports. France was second with a remarkably steady 13 to 15 percent of the total.

Outside Europe, the major changes in Italy's direction of export trade were the sharp rise in the share of exports going to the oil-producing countries, the relative decline in importance of the U.S. market, the failure of exports to Canada and Japan to assume any significance, and the steady importance of the developing countries as a market for Italian products. The growing markets of the oil producers, which had absorbed only 4-6 percent of Italy's exports from 1970 through 1973, gradually accounted for an increased share, exceeding 12 percent in 1978. Within the oil-producer group the biggest gains were made in exports to Saudi Arabia and Iran. From exports of only $45 million and $103 million in 1973, respectively, the total rose to $1.24 billion and $905 million in 1978. In contrast, exports to the United States, which had accounted for 10 percent of the total in 1970, represented only 7 percent in 1978. Canada and Japan each represented only about 1 percent of Italy's export market throughout the entire period.

Exports by Type of Goods

On average during the period 1970-78 investment goods accounted for 21 percent of Italian exports, raw materials and intermediate goods (mostly the latter) for 43 percent, consumer goods for 35 percent, and unclassified exports for 1 percent. Over the period there was a decline in the share accounted for by investment goods, a rise for intermediate goods, and a decline for consumer goods. Most of the change took place rather abruptly in 1973 and 1974, due in part to the increases in world prices of energy products. Included in the intermediate goods category are exports of petroleum products, of which Italy is a fairly important exporter. Before the energy price rise, Italian exports amounted to $1.2 billion (1973). With the OPEC crude oil price increases of 1973-74, the price of petroleum products also rose abruptly, so that Italian refined exports reached $3.3 billion in 1978.

In the consumer goods area, motor vehicles were an important export and Italy had a surplus in consumer auto vehicles in every year of the period (1970-78), except 1978. Italy also had a very large surplus on a variety of other consumer goods which, after dropping in share of total exports with the rise in the price of intermediate goods exports in 1973-74, subsequently increased their share of the total. Included in this category are such important items as clothing, shoes, furniture, and appliances.

There was some decline in the share of investment goods exports, probably reflecting the generally weak demand for such goods in the period of slow recovery following the 1975 world recession. To some extent the relative decline in capital goods exports was compensated for by increased exports of replacement parts for such equipment.

IMPORTS AND ADJUSTMENT TO THE OIL DEFICIT

Import Performance

Imports of goods and services in the 1970s reflected changing rates of economic activity, including demand for imports to meet current production needs and for restocking or destocking, according to the phase of the business cycle. The effects of restocking can be seen in the recovery years of 1973, 1976, and late 1978. Conversely, import growth was low in periods of recession or slow growth, mainly in 1970, 1971, 1972, 1975, and 1977.

TABLE 7.4

Import Elasticity, 1960s and 1970s
(real terms)

	Δ Imports (Goods and Services) ÷ Δ GDP	Δ Imports (Merchandise) ÷ Δ GDP
1970	3.00	2.94
1971	1.50	0.25
1972	3.56	3.41
1973	1.50	1.60
1974	0.54	-1.34
1975	2.67	2.97
1976	2.61	2.59
1977	-0.10	-0.25
1978	3.12	2.92
Average 1970–78	2.04	1.68
Average 1961–69	1.62	1.57

Sources: Compiled by the author; calculated from ISTAT bulletins and Conti Economici Nazionali 1960-78 (Nuova serie), Rome, 1979.

TABLE 7.5

Growth of Imports, 1970-78
(percent annual change; customs data c.i.f.)

	Volume	Value (lira)	Value (dollar)	Price (lira)*
1970	15.6	20.0	20.0	3.8
1971	0.4	5.8	5.8	5.5
1972	10.9	13.8	22.3	2.6
1973	11.2	45.1	44.0	30.4
1974	-5.5	61.9	47.3	71.3
1975	-10.7	-5.7	-6.1	5.6
1976	15.6	45.8	14.4	26.2
1977	-0.3	15.5	9.0	15.8
1978	7.4	12.8	17.1	5.0
Average	5.0	23.9	19.3	18.5

*Unit values.
Source: Compiled by the author; data from ISTAT bulletins.

The income elasticity of imports of goods and services (GDP definition) showed a perceptible rise compared to the 1960s, but the elasticity of imports of merchandise alone (customs data) did not. Both concepts are measured as the ratio of the percentage change in the volume of imports to the percentage change in real GDP. The year-to-year variations are partially explained by relative price changes (Table 7.4).

The annual growth of imports of goods and services in real terms (GDP concept) averaged only 6 percent in 1970-78, down from an average growth rate of 11 percent in the 1960s, in line with slower economic growth rates in the 1970s. For merchandise imports alone (customs basis, c.i.f.) the volume increase averaged 5 percent, compared to 14 percent in the 1960s. In this period (1970s) the growth in volume for investment goods averaged 5.1 percent per year, for intermediate goods 4.4 percent, and for consumer goods 8 percent. In terms of lira unit prices, the average growth was 15.8 percent for investment goods, 20.0 percent for intermediate goods, and 14.5 percent for consumer goods. In fact, merchandise import volume fell in three of the nine years (1970-78), including a decline of nearly 11 percent in the 1975 recession year (Table 7.5). The index of the volume of merchandise imports, which averaged 124 in 1973 (1970 = 100), did not again exceed that level until five years later, when the average for 1978 was 129.

The index of unit values of imports (in lira terms) rose on average by more than 18 percent per year in 1970-78, compared to an average rise of less than 1 percent per year in the 1960s. In 1974 import prices rose by more than 71 percent. There were increases of 30 percent and 26 percent, respectively, in 1973 and 1976, years of generally strong world commodity price rises and, for Italy, currency depreciation. On the other hand, in years of slower growth, lower commodity price rises, and greater currency stability, import prices rose somewhat less rapidly than Italian wholesale prices.

Geographic Pattern of Imports

The pattern of imports by geographic area (customs basis, c.i.f.) was even more sharply affected by the oil price increases of 1973-74 than was the case with exports. In the early years of the decade the share of Italy's imports from Europe exceeded 60 percent and was tending to rise. By 1973 Europe accounted for 65 percent of Italy's total imports. After the oil price rises, the amount fell to only 56 percent in 1974, but in each succeeding year there was some restoration of the European share. Conversely, imports from the oil-producing countries, which had accounted for only 12 percent of Italian imports in 1973, rose to 23 percent in 1974, but trailed off in each succeeding year (through 1978). The share of Italy's imports from the United States also gradually declined over the period, from more than 10 percent in 1970 to less than 7 percent in 1978. Both Canada and Japan had only 1 to 1.5 percent of the market over the period, with little change apparent over time. The residual group of countries (mostly developing countries) accounted for a rather steady 12 percent of the market, on average.

Germany and France were much the most important trading partners for Italy in terms of imports. On average, Germany accounted for 19 percent of Italian imports. Before the growth of oil imports in 1974 Germany supplied about 20 percent of the total. Afterward, the share fell to about 17 percent and there was not much evidence of a recovery of market share. This was, no doubt, in large part due to the improved competitive position of Italy vis-à-vis Germany in line with the sharp depreciation of the lira against the mark. In contrast, Italian imports from France in succeeding years did recover from their 1974 low. For the entire period 1970-78, on average, imports from France accounted for 14 percent of the total.

As to the principal oil producers, Italian imports generally shifted away from heavy dependence on Saudi Arabia and Libya and toward somewhat greater dependence on Iraq, Kuwait, and Iran. In 1974 (the high point of market share for the oil producers) Saudi Arabia accounted for 7.4 percent of total imports, Libya 5.8 percent, Iraq 2.8 percent, and Iran 2.7 percent.

Imports by Type of Goods

By far the largest share of Italian imports consisted of primary materials and intermediate goods, which accounted, on average, for 72 percent of the total value of imports in 1970-78. The effect of price increases for oil and other primary materials in 1973-74 was a dramatic increase for this category of imports, from 67 percent to 78 percent of the total between those two years. Fuels alone (mainly oil) increased from 14 percent to 25 percent of total imports.

For the entire period investment goods accounted for 11 percent of total imports, consumer goods 16 percent, and unclassified imports less than 1 percent. Except for the sudden drop in the relative importance of investment goods between 1973 and 1974 due to the commodity and oil price increases, there was no clear pattern of increase or decrease in the share of investment goods of total imports. For consumer goods, the trend toward an increase in the share of the total, although interrupted in 1974, resumed subsequent to that period.

Dependency on Foreign Oil

The rise in the proportion of fuel imports to total imports in 1974 was the result of the sharp increase in the unit price of petroleum imports, upon which Italy is extremely dependent for its energy needs. In 1973 only 15 percent of Italy's total supply of primary sources of energy came from domestic production. Total energy imports provided 85 percent and oil imports alone accounted for 79 percent. Among types of energy, oil was much the most important, accounting for 74 percent of total uses of primary energy in 1973. By economic sector, domestic uses of final sources of energy were largest in industry (43 percent of the total), followed by agriculture/services/households (31 percent), transport (16 percent), and nonenergy (for example, petrochemical) uses (10 percent). Italy's electric energy production, too, depended heavily on oil-fired thermoelectric plants. Oil-fired plants had been steadily growing as a source of electric energy production in the postwar period. In 1960 only 7 percent of total electricity production was from oil-fired plants; by 1973 the figure was 62 percent.

TABLE 7.6

Crude Petroleum Imports, 1970-78

	Metric Tons (millions)	Volume Index	Unit Value Index (lire)	Dollar Value (billions)*
1970	113	100.0	100.0	1.8
1971	115	102.4	123.4	2.3
1972	120	106.4	120.0	2.5
1973	126	111.8	158.4	3.4
1974	117	104.4	536.6	9.7
1975	94	83.9	569.6	8.2
1976	101	89.4	757.6	9.1
1977	100	88.6	867.7	9.8
1978	108	95.8	851.7	10.8

*c.i.f.

Source: Compiled by the author; data from ISTAT bulletins.

After the 1973-74 oil price rises, Italy made some progress in reducing its dependence on imported oil. The volume of crude imports of 126 million metric tons reached in 1973 was the record high for the 1970s (1970-78) (Table 7.6). Even with a level of real GDP in 1978 that was 11 percent above that of 1973, crude imports were down 14 percent from the 1973 high.

The reduction in dependence on foreign oil, however, was due more to a shift in source of energy (toward natural gas) and to some reduction in oil imports for refining and reexport, than to energy conservation. In fact, the ratio of domestic uses of total primary energy to real domestic demand rose by 7 percentage points between 1973 and 1978. The ratio for oil, alone, was unchanged, but down from 1974-75. The annual ratios are shown below.

Year	Oil	Total Energy
1973	100.0	100.0
1974	105.1	105.2
1975	102.5	107.2
1976	101.1	106.9
1977	97.7	105.8
1978	100.3	107.2

Relatively little of the reduction in dependence on imported oil was due to an increase in domestic energy production. By 1978 domestic production accounted for only 15.6 percent of total primary energy sources, compared to 15.0 percent in 1973. Total imports still accounted for 84.4 percent of the total supply, against 85.0 percent in 1973. The main difference was that imported oil had dropped to 71.2 percent of total sources, compared to 78.6 percent in 1973, indicating that imports of other forms of energy (for example, natural gas) were making up the difference.

With regard to energy uses in these two years (1973 and 1978), exports accounted for 22.9 percent in 1973 and only 14.5 percent in 1978; the change in inventories was 1.2 percent in 1973, as against -1.5 percent in 1978; and domestic use in 1973 was 75.9 percent of the total, compared with 87.0 in 1978. In 1973 solid fuel accounted for 7.8 percent of total primary energy use, natural gas for 10.9 percent, oil for 73.5 percent, and hydro and nuclear for 7.8 percent. By 1978 the figures were solid fuel, 7.2 percent; natural gas, 15.5 percent; oil only 68.7 percent; and hydro and nuclear, 8.6 percent.

A shift in the pattern of use among economic sectors can also be seen in the decline in the share of final energy used in the industrial sector and in nonenergy uses (for example, feedstocks). In 1973 industry accounted for 42.7 percent of the total domestic use of final source of energy, transport for 16.4 percent, agriculture/services/households for 30.5 percent, and nonenergy for 10.4 percent. In 1978 the percentages were 38.9 for industry, 22.6 for transport, 32.2 for agriculture/services/households, and 6.3 for nonenergy. The use of oil to fuel electric energy plants also declined relatively after the peak reached in 1973, falling from 62 percent of total electricity production to 57 percent in 1978.

Adjustment to the Oil Deficit

In large part because of Italy's heavy dependence on imported oil the country experienced an unprecedented balance-of-payments crisis in the period 1974-76. (There had already been problems in 1973.) In 1977-78, however, the balance of payments greatly improved and the current account was in large surplus in 1978 (and in 1979). The importance of the balance-of-payments adjustment to the oil price rises of 1973-74 is worth special attention, particularly if the balance of payments is to be periodically subjected to such shocks by the OPEC cartel.

In 1973 the unit price of crude oil imports had already risen by 32 percent over the previous year, but in 1974 the increase was far greater, at 239 percent. In dollar terms the actual rise in the crude oil import bill between those two years was $6.3 billion, an increase from $3.4 billion to $9.7 billion. This increase represented 3.7 percent of Italy's entire GDP (dollar terms) in 1974.

Although there were other export and import price factors operating between 1973 and 1974, the oil import price increase was by far the most important cause of a decline in 1974 of 16 points in Italy's terms of trade (export unit value ÷ import unit value), following a decline of 9 points in 1973 due to both oil and other commodity price increases. The annual figures for 1970-78 are shown below. The

Year	Terms of Trade
1970	100.0
1971	99.9
1972	100.1
1973	90.9
1974	75.2
1975	79.2
1976	76.5
1977	78.8
1978	80.4
Average 1970-78	86.8
Average 1960-69	101.4

negative effect on Italy's balance of trade that year from the worsened terms of trade, alone, amounted to $9.6 billion (assuming no change in the volume of imports or exports in 1974).

While adjustment to the worsened balance of payments occurred over several years, with the improvement temporarily interrupted during the 1976 recovery, it is useful to compare the 1978 balance of payments, which was in large surplus, with the large deficit balance of 1974, in order to identify the areas of improvement between the two years (Table 7.7).

More than three-fourths of the turnaround of $14 billion in the current account occurred in the trade account, with the rest in services and transfers. Exports grew (in dollar terms on a balance-of-payments basis) by 84 percent, against an increase of only 36 percent for imports. About two-thirds of the improvement in the trade account was due to changes in the relative growth of export and import volumes. The volume of exports (customs basis) rose by 38 percent, against a 10 percent rise in imports (customs basis). The services account improved from a surplus of $0.5 billion in 1974 to one of $3.8 billion in 1978. All the improvement of $3.3 billion could be accounted for by the $3.3 billion

TABLE 7.7

Adjustment in Current Account Balance between 1974 and 1978
(billions of dollars)

Trade account				
Exports (f.o.b.) 25.3		Price factors	4.0	
Imports (f.o.b.) -13.9		Volume factors	7.4	
Balance	11.4	Balance*		11.4
Services	3.3	Services		3.3
Transfers	-0.3	Transfers		-0.3
Total current account	14.4	Total current account		14.4

*The volume factor is calculated by applying the percentage change in volume between the two years to the value of the initial year. The price factor is a residual, thus including the product of the change in quantity and the change in prices.

Source: Compiled by the author; calculations based on Bank of Italy and ISTAT data.

rise in the travel surplus, as changes in other service items cancelled each other out.

Looking at shifts in geographic trade patterns (customs basis) between the two years, it can be seen that the improvement in the trade balance of $10 billion (customs basis) was attributable to improved trade balances with Europe (52 percent of the total), the oil producers (40 percent), and the United States (10 percent). (Trade balances with other countries worsened.) Within Europe the sharp improvement in Italy's trade balance with Germany accounted for a full 25 percent of the entire improvement in Italy's trade balance. Stronger trade balances with France and the United Kingdom contributed an additional 21 percent of the total. (The trade balance worsened with Eastern Europe, Japan, and other countries—mostly developing countries—but only by modest amounts.) Among the oil producers, the largest improvements were with Saudi Arabia ($2 billion) and Libya ($1 billion). Trade deficits expanded with Iraq and Kuwait, but on a fairly small scale. The total improvement in dollar terms in Italy's trade balance with the oil producers was $4 billion, nearly all due to the growth of Italian exports to the oil producers (up by $5 billion) against very little import growth (up $1 billion).

Among different types of goods traded, by far the largest source of improvement in the trade balance came from an increase in Italy's traditional surplus on consumer goods. This accounted for 58 percent of the trade improvement, against 36 percent for investment goods, 5 percent for primary/intermediate goods, and 1 percent for unclassified goods. The improvement in the surplus on consumer goods trade amounted to $5.9 billion. All of the improvement was in the "other" category of miscellaneous consumer goods, while the balance on food and motor vehicles worsened. Within this "other" category, it appears that the main areas of gain were in such items as clothing ($0.9 billion), footwear ($1.4 billion), and furniture ($0.8 billion). The relatively small contribution made in the primary/intermediate goods group of merchandise obscured some rather large changes within the group. Thus, there was an improvement of $2.4 billion in the trade balance on industrial materials and an improvement of $1.2 billion for spare parts for investment equipment. The growth of the deficit on food and energy imports, however (in value terms but not in quantity terms), offset most of these gains.

There was a cost to domestic consumption or investment from the balance-of-payments adjustment in real terms between 1974 and 1978. For example, if the 3.56 trillion lire (1970 lire) improvement in the balance on goods and services (GDP concept) between 1974 and 1978 had been available for private consumption, the latter could have grown by an additional 8 percent above the 1974 base over the following four years. Alternatively, had such resources been allocated to fixed investment, there could have been a 24 percent increase above the 1974 base in those years.

SERVICES AND TRANSFER PAYMENTS

The net balance on services and transfer payments was in substantial surplus in every year of the 1960s and 1970s, ranging from a surplus of $0.5 billion in 1974 to one of $3.5 billion in 1978 (Table 7.2). (All the figures cited in this text include adjustments for hidden capital flight in some services and transfers. See the section on capital flight later in this chapter.) In 1978, service and transfer receipts represented 26 percent of all receipts on current account, against 74 percent for merchandise exports. Throughout the 1960s there had been a general upward trend in the surplus, but the pattern was much more erratic in the 1970s. After a drop in the surplus between 1969 and 1970, it grew in 1971 and 1972, only to drop back in 1973 and fall to a very low level by historic standards in 1974 and 1975. In 1976-78 the surplus rose exceptionally fast from $1.4 billion in 1976 to $3.5

TABLE 7.8

Cumulative Net Services and Transfer Accounts,
1970-78

Account	Billions of Dollars
Surplus items	
Travel*	21.3
Worker remittances*	6.8
Private transfers*	6.0
Subtotal	34.1
Deficit items	
Investment income	-5.6
Public transfers	-4.5
Transport/insurance	-4.4
Government services	-0.7
Other services	-3.6
Subtotal	-18.8
Net	15.3

*Adjusted for hidden capital flight.
Source: Compiled by the author; data from Bank
of Italy annual reports.

billion in 1978, contributing importantly to the strengthening of the
balance of payments.

The items in persistent surplus in the services/transfers
accounts during the 1970s were travel, worker remittances, and private transfers—especially emigrant remittances (Table 7.8). The persistent negative items were investment income, public transfers, the
transportation/insurance accounts, government services, and other
services. The latter category includes such items as banking commissions and trade expenditures, patents/royalties, insurance (other than
on foreign trade), film rights, border trade, and private technical
assistance.

The major changes in the services/transfers accounts during
the 1970s were an increase in the transport/insurance deficit due to a
substantial rise in the deficit on freight on merchandise trade; relative
stagnation in the travel surplus in 1970-74, followed by a dramatic
growth in 1977 and 1978; a sharp rise in the deficit on investment

income as Italy had to pay interest on a growing amount of foreign
debt in the mid-1970s to finance the oil (and other) deficits; slow growth
in receipts from worker remittances through most of the period until
1977-78, due to a reversal in the flow of Italian workers abroad and
to slow economic growth in the major European countries in which
they were employed; stagnation in net receipts from private transfer
payments (mainly emigrant remittances); and a temporary rise in the
mid-1970s in the deficit on other services, mainly due to the rise in
the cost of bank commissions on foreign loans and business expenditures.

Travel

    Net income from travel is by far the most important item in
Italy's services/transfers accounts and has been a constant surplus
component of the current account, as shown in the table below. There

Year	Travel Balance (billions of dollars)
1970	1.2
1971	1.3
1972	1.6
1973	1.7
1974	1.8
1975	2.3
1976	2.5
1977	3.9
1978	5.0
Total	21.3

was, however, a period of stagnation in the net surplus from the mid-
1960s until the early 1970s. The surplus, which had reached $1.1
billion as early as 1965, was only slightly higher ($1.3 billion) as late
as 1971. This was due both to a slump in receipts from foreign tourists and to sharp growth in foreign travel expenditures by Italy's increasingly well-off populace. In 1965 foreign travel expenditures by
Italian residents had accounted for about 0.5 percent of Italy's disposable personal income; by 1971 the figure had increased to about 0.85
percent. The reasons for stagnation of foreign travel expenditures in
Italy are unclear. Growth of income abroad was generally high and
Italy's relative price movements were not greatly out of line with those
abroad, although this may have begun to be a problem in the early
1970s. Perhaps the first postwar wave of U.S. tourism was exhausted

and the phenomenon of mass European tourism had not yet reached Italian shores.

The recovery of growth in the travel surplus late in the 1970s was clearly related to exchange rate movements that favored foreign tourist expenditures in Italy, and to a correspondingly sharp slowdown in the growth of Italian expenditures abroad. (Exchange restrictions on outward payments were a factor behind the slow growth of expenditures. See Chapter 11.) The average annual growth (in dollar terms) of travel receipts in the period 1972-1978 was 19 percent, compared to an increase of 10 percent in travel expenditures by Italians. Annual changes fluctuated strongly, influenced by exchange rate depreciations of the lira. In 1974 and again in 1976 travel receipts in dollar terms actually fell by 2 percent each, while Italian expenditures fell by 16 percent and 23 percent, respectively. In 1974 the drop was the result both of a decline in the number of tourist-days spent by foreigners in Italy and of a temporary adverse J-curve effect due to lira depreciation. With many foreign currencies buying more lire than before, foreign tourists were able to visit Italy and spend relatively less money (in dollar terms) than previously. For example, dollar expenditures per tourist-day rose by only 2 percent that year, compared to average annual increases of 11 percent in the previous four years. Similarly, the sharp rise in the cost of foreign travel helped to reduce the outward flow of expenditures by Italian residents. (The decline in travel receipts in 1974 may also have been related to the delayed effect of an outbreak of cholera in the Naples area in September 1973.) In 1976 the number of tourist-days rose by less than 2 percent and the J-curve effect contributed to an actual decline of 4 percent in dollar expenditures per tourist-day. The political uncertainties surrounding the 1976 parliamentary elections may also have hurt receipts in that year.

The strength of the travel account in 1975 was strongly influenced by the Holy Year, even though that was a year of world recession. The sharp rise in travel receipts in 1977 and 1978 was striking, with growth rates (dollar terms) of 49 percent and 32 percent, respectively. The increases were the result both of a substantial rise in the number of tourist-days spent in Italy and of a higher rate of expenditure per tourist-day. This was apparently due to reduced concern about political and economic instability, the favorable effect of large lira depreciation on travel to Italy by residents of such industrial countries as Germany, Switzerland, and Japan, and relatively more favorable price developments (deflated by exchange rate movements) in Italy than in some of Italy's competing countries in the tourist field.

While there was also a sharp percentage recovery in Italian travel expenditures in 1977 and 1978 (26 percent and 35 percent), the absolute level of foreign travel spending was remarkably low (only a little larger as a share of disposable personal income than in the mid-1960s). In fact, an earlier peak of $1.1 billion in Italian expenditure abroad reached in 1973 was not surpassed until 1978 ($1.2 billion).

The geographic pattern of travel receipts changed quite perceptibly during the 1970s. In 1969 the United States accounted for 20 percent of Italian travel receipts, the EC for 53 percent, other developed countries 15 percent, and developing countries (including Eastern Europe) 12 percent. In 1978 the pattern was United States 10 percent, EC 64 percent, other developed countries 18 percent, and developing countries 8 percent. The average annual growth of expenditures by Americans was only 9 percent during the period 1970-78, compared to 17 percent for total expenditures and 20 percent for the EC alone.

Whether or not the improvement in Italy's travel balance will endure will depend on a number of factors both in Italy and abroad: the rate of growth of national income abroad, especially in neighboring European countries; Italy's own inflation performance compared to that of its principal Mediterranean and West European rivals; the economic climate in Italy for the development, especially in the south, of new tourist facilities by small business; the expansion of infrastructure to support them; and changes in income growth and consumer preferences of Italian travelers.[1]

Worker Remittances

The second most important source of net foreign exchange income in the services/transfers accounts was worker remittances. These transactions provided the Italian balance of payments with net cumulative receipts of about $7 billion in 1970-78.

Worker remittances are a function of the number of Italian workers temporarily employed outside Italy, their length of stay abroad, the relative growth of income of host economies, and the exchange rate relationship between Italy and each of those countries. In practice, worker remittances are important mainly between Italy and other EC countries and Switzerland. The EC and Switzerland together typically accounted for about 70 percent of Italy's gross worker remittance receipts. During the 1970s improved economic conditions in Italy, slower growth in other parts of Europe, and the growing reluctance of some host countries to accept more foreign workers in their labor force tended to limit the growth of foreign exchange income from this source. Italy's membership in the EC protected Italian workers better than workers from non-EC areas. Also, having been longer in the business, Italian workers tended to be employed in relatively higher paying jobs than was the case with the more recently arrived workers from more distant places. For most of the period 1970-78 net income from worker remittances fluctuated in the range of $0.6 to $0.8 billion per year. Net receipts were relatively high in the good world growth year of 1973 and picked up noticeably in 1977 and 1978. The increase in 1977 may have been partly the result of delays in remitting earnings in 1976, a year of lira depreciation. Many workers abroad stood to gain by waiting for any additional appreciation of the currencies of the host country against the lira. Unlike tourist expenditures in Italy, there was no adverse initial J-curve effect on foreign currency earnings, since the Italians resident abroad directly earned and made remittances in these strong foreign currencies.

The geographic pattern of worker remittances was strongly centered on Germany and Switzerland, plus the remaining EC countries as a group, and the relative importance of different countries did not change notably between 1969 and 1978. The EC countries accounted for 50 percent of total gross earnings in 1969 and 53 percent in 1978. Germany provided 35 percent of the income in each of those two years. The second most important source of worker income was Switzerland, at 21 percent and 18 percent of the total in those two years. The United States, surprisingly, increased its share of the total from 7 percent to 9 percent between 1969 and 1978.

Private Transfers (Including Emigrant Remittances)

Some of the same factors affected emigrant remittance receipts as affected worker remittances, although the geographic pattern of transfers was rather different. One would expect that, with the end of net migration early in the decade, emigrant remittances would have been a relatively less dynamic source of foreign exchange, and this was the case. Gross receipts rose by only 117 percent between 1969 and 1978, versus 162 percent for worker remittances. The effect of the world recession on income available for remittances in 1974-75 can be seen in a dip in gross dollar receipts in those years. There was also a decline in 1976. In the latter year, some deliberate delays in repatriation of remittances in the hope of further lira depreciation may have played a part in the decline. This may also have been a factor in 1973 and 1974 during the earlier lira depreciation.

Italy gained relatively less in lira and dollar terms from the effect of exchange rate movements on the remittance of income earned abroad by Italian emigrants than on that earned by Italian workers. This was because emigrant earnings were less concentrated in the stronger currency countries of the EC and Switzerland. There was some relative increase in the share of those countries during the decade (from 37 percent of the total in 1969 to 46 percent in 1978, but this still fell short of the 70 percent share of total worker remittances that came from the EC and Switzerland in 1978.

In view of the trend of emigration patterns, it does not appear that substantial growth can be expected from remittance earnings in coming years.

Investment Income

The largest negative item in Italy's services/transfers accounts during the 1970s was the cumulative deficit on net investment income transactions of $5.6 billion (1970–78), shown in the table below. (The

Year	Investment Income (billions of dollars)
1972	-0.1
1973	-0.2
1974	-0.8
1975	-1.2
1976	-1.1
1977	-1.1
1978	-1.1
Total	-5.6

deficits in 1970 and 1971 were less than $100 million and have not been included here.) The balance in these accounts had not been, traditionally, very negative in the 1960s and the early 1970s. It was the dramatic worsening in Italy's net foreign financial position that came with the enormous balance of payments deficits of the mid-1970s that pushed the investment income item into large deficit. Substantial net deficits began in 1973, rose in 1974, and exceeded $1 billion in each of the next four years 1975–78—including 1978 when the rest of the balance of payments was strengthening.

On the receipts side, income came mainly from earnings on Italy's private foreign direct and portfolio investments abroad, earnings on commercial banks' foreign lending, and earnings on investment of official reserves (especially convertible currency holdings) by the monetary authorities. On the payment side, repatriation of income earned in Italy on foreign-owned investment, interest payments on foreign private and official compensatory loans to Italy, and interest on short-term borrowing by Italian banks were the principal items. The absolute level of receipts and payments fluctuated with the outstanding amounts of these various assets, and with relative interest rates and dividend yields in Italy and abroad.

There was a steady increase in receipts from 1970 to 1974. Although official reserves changed very little, Italy's commercial banks greatly expanded their Euromarket activities in 1970-73 and private Italian investment outflows were very large in the period 1969-73. Also, world interest-rate levels rose sharply in 1973-74, adding to the level of gross earnings on both private and official foreign assets.

With the advent of large balance-of-payments deficits in 1973-76, Euromarket borrowing initially protected the level of official reserves and the earnings on those reserves. Convertible currency reserves, however, dropped drastically in 1975 (and early 1976). In addition, the world recession of 1974-75 no doubt reduced earnings on Italy's investments abroad. With the strengthening of Italy's balance of payments in 1977 and 1978, convertible currency reserves rose to all-time highs (over $10 billion at the end of 1978, compared to $1 billion at the end of 1975). Also, rising world interest rates contributed to an increase in investment income receipts during these two years.

On the payment side, the rapid growth of compensatory foreign borrowing in the Euromarket and then loans through official channels, as well as the growth of the commercial banks' gross liabilities, greatly increased investment income payments, which peaked at $3.4 billion in 1974. The rise in payments reflected both the worsened net debtor position and higher Euromarket interest rates in 1973-74. Payments tended to decline after 1974, as did receipts, in line with lower world interest rates and a sharp reduction in both the commercial banks' assets and liabilities, which began in the last half of 1974. Also, the decline in payments may have reflected poor business conditions in Italy, which limited foreign earnings on investments there. Despite the repayment of a large amount of long-term foreign debt (especially official debt) in 1977 and 1978, a resumption of the rise in interest rates in those years once again boosted the absolute level of outpayments, in part due to the rising level of short-term net foreign liabilities of the commercial banks.

Whether the large net outflow of nearly $1 billion a year in the investment income account continues will depend on overall developments in Italy's current account, on world interest rate levels, and on the spread between the commercial banks' lending and borrowing rates. Also, the way in which the authorities manage the level and composition of Italy's foreign debt will influence the net investment income balance, because of the spread between interest rates on assets and on liabilities and the different interest rates applicable to different forms of debt.

Transport/Insurance

The negative transport/insurance balance was the third largest net drain on Italy's services/transfer accounts. This balance (including insurance on international trade only) was in persistent and growing deficit during the 1970s, although the growth of the deficit was not spectacular. The largest component was the deficit on merchandise freight. This net deficit increased, despite an equal rate of growth of receipts and payments from 1970 to 1978, because of the higher initial level of foreign payments on imports. Also, the growth of the deficit reflected growing merchandise imports, rather than rising freight rates. In fact, implicit freight rates tended to decline during the 1970s from an average of 7.9 percent in the first three years of the decade to only 5.4 percent in the last three years of the period (1976-78). Net receipts from ships' expenditures in foreign and Italian ports were another (smaller) negative item. In contrast, passenger traffic turned a surplus for Italy.

Government Services

Between 1970 and 1975 government services were a relatively unimportant item in the accounts, consisting of receipts from expenditures in Italy by foreign governments, international organizations, and the North Atlantic Treaty Organization (NATO) military forces. Net expenditures grew in the last three years of the period, however, to average $0.3 billion per year. This was due mainly to a variety of foreign expenditures by the Treasury for such purposes as salaries, building and training under government programs, and state pension payments.

Other Services

A catch-all category of other services was also in rather persistent deficit during the 1970s—$3.6 billion on a cumulative basis. There were deficits in every year of the period (1970-78) except 1976. The size of the deficit, however, declined from a peak in 1975 of $0.8 billion to only $0.3 billion in 1978.

The main causes of the fluctuations of the net balance were bank commissions and a group of miscellaneous services. With the large Euromarket term-loan borrowings of 1973 and 1974 and the growth of short-term borrowing by the commercial banks in 1976 and 1977, bank commission payments grew. Also, the increased effort to promote trade, especially with the oil producers, contributed to outpayments in that category. Net payments on patents and royalties were consistently negative, but with no very clear trend. Two other categories of other services were also regularly in deficit, but by very modest amounts: nontrade insurance and film rights. The residual category of other services was in both surplus and deficit at different times during the three-year period 1976-78, apparently due to border trade between Italy and Switzerland, which was affected by exchange rate movements.

Public Transfers

Net public transfer payments contributed a negative $4.5 billion to the services/transfers balance in the period 1970-78. Included in this item are reparation payments from World War II, various contributions by the government (mainly to international organizations), and private remittances. Much the largest item was contributions to international organizations. There was a particularly large negative balance for this item in 1978, which contributed one-third of the entire deficit for the nine-year period. This was due to complex financial transactions with the EC and mainly involved timing differences between receipts and payments (which reversed in 1979).

CAPITAL FLOWS

Pattern of Capital Flows

The principal features of Italian capital account developments during the 1970s were stagnation in the inflow of foreign investment in Italy, a sharp rise in foreign loans to Italy (especially compensatory loans from the Euromarket), a decline in Italian investment abroad, little change in Italian lending abroad, and sharp variations in net commercial credit flows.

The autonomous capital account in the 1970s (1970-78) experienced two distinct phases: deficits each year in the period 1970-73 and surpluses each year in 1974-78—when the effect of compensatory Euromarket loan transactions are removed from the capital accounts (Table 7.9).

Investment

Foreign investment in Italy in the 1970s averaged a little over $0.5 billion per year (including both direct and portfolio investment). There was surprisingly little fluctuation in the amount from year to year, except for net disinvestment in 1976, counterbalanced by a very large inflow in the following year. Direct investment inflows were by far the more important type of investment, as portfolio investment

TABLE 7.9

Capital Account, 1970-78
(billions of dollars)

	Recorded Balance	Less Euromarket Compensatory Loans	Autonomous Balance
1970	-0.6	1.5	-2.1
1971	-1.0	-0.2	-0.8
1972	-2.7	0.5	-3.2
1973	3.0	4.1	-1.1
1974	2.4	2.1	0.3
1975	-0.8	-1.0	0.2
1976	1.8	-0.3	2.1
1977	—	-0.6	0.6
1978	1.5	-0.9	2.4
Total	3.6	5.2	-1.6

Source: Compiled by the author; data from Bank of Italy annual reports and Bank of Italy Research Office.

flows were actually negative—to the extent of about $0.6 billion in the period 1970-78.

Cumulative foreign direct investment inflows amounted to $5.3 billion during the 1970s (1970-78). The largest beneficiary of this investment was the engineering sector with net inflows of $1.8 billion. The latter included a large Libyan investment in Fiat in 1977 of about $306 million and a mutual investment by Fiat and Iveco (a truck-producing company with German and other foreign participation) of about $420 million. Each of the remaining major economic sectors received net investment in the range of $0.3 to $0.5 billion—banking/insurance, retail trade, construction, food, oil and gas, and chemicals. At the end of 1978 foreign direct investment in Italy was valued at $7.9 billion—$1.5 billion from the United States, $2.5 billion from the EC, $3.2 billion from Switzerland/Liechtenstein/Luxembourg, and $0.7 billion from other countries. Of the total, $1.9 billion was invested in chemicals and energy, $2.7 billion in the engineering/metals/mining fields, $0.5 billion in the food industry, $0.4 billion in trade, $0.8 billion in the banking, insurance, and finance area, and $1.6 billion in other fields.

Data on foreign investment from Switzerland/Liechtenstein/Luxembourg may be misleading, since these countries, particularly the latter two, are often used as a pass-through for investment from other sources, including disguised Italian reinvestment in Italy after "laundering" abroad (for tax, exchange control, and other reasons).

The failure to grow of foreign investment in Italy is easily explainable: Italian economic growth and growth prospects worsened during the 1970s; profitability of Italian business declined (although it was generally higher for foreign companies than for domestic companies); local financing was as difficult (if not more so) for foreign-owned business to obtain as for Italian firms; tax collections tightened up as a result of various tax reform measures; labor conditions became more difficult than in most competing countries; and political, exchange rate, and exchange control uncertainties made long-term analysis of investment potential especially difficult.

Italian investment abroad amounted to a cumulative $3.6 billion in the period 1970-78. The pattern of direct investments was one of rather steady net outflows, with a peak in 1977 in connection with the mutual investments of Fiat and Iveco. Portfolio investments, however, sharply reversed from net investments abroad early in the decade (1970-73) to net disinvestment in the following five years (1974-78). Most of the earlier portfolio investment took the form of purchase of Eurobonds and foreign mutual fund shares. Cumulative direct investments resulted in a net outflow of $2.4 billion, while net portfolio investment (despite disinvestment late in the decade) amounted to $1.2 billion. Because of the turnaround in the portfolio investment account, the total amount of net investment outflows fell sharply during the 1970s.

The rather high rates of foreign investment by Italian residents in the early years can be attributed to a number of factors: slow growth in Italy during most of this period, making foreign investment relatively attractive; exchange rate stability, including exchange rate appreciation at the end of 1971 against the dollar and the currencies of much of the developing world in which the largest part of Italian direct investment is located; considerable freedom of capital movements with regard to direct investment; the need to establish some dependable sources of energy supply; attractive portfolio investment opportunities abroad during the 1972-73 boom; and presumably, good profitability in some less developed countries. Later in the decade some factors mitigating against investment abroad by Italians included the creation in January 1973 of a two-tier exchange market with a higher rate for capital movements (market reunified in March 1974); the imposition in July 1973 of a 50 percent non-interest-bearing deposit requirement on foreign investment outflows; the shortage of investment capital due to falling profits in Italy; and exchange rate uncertainty. Also, an exchange control amnesty law (Law 159 of April 1976) succeeded in attracting net disinvestments of Italian capital abroad of $601 million in 1976 and $61 million in 1977.

At the end of 1978 total Italian direct investments abroad amounted to $4.9 billion. The largest part of that investment (39 percent) was located in developing countries and smaller industrial countries, while 32 percent was in other EC countries, 9 percent in the United States, and 20 percent in Switzerland/Liechtenstein/Luxembourg. For the latter group of countries the figure includes both operating investments and investments in financial holding companies, which then reinvest the funds. The largest part of Italian direct investments abroad was in chemicals and energy (37 percent), with banking/financial holdings second (21 percent), engineering/metals/mining third (18 percent), and the remainder in food, retail trade, and other activities (24 percent).

Loans

There was an extraordinary growth of foreign medium- and long-term loan capital inflows to Italy (excluding trade credits) during the 1970s. The cumulative net amount exceeded $13 billion in the period 1970-78 (Table 7.10). Of that total, net compensatory borrowing in the Euromarket by state-related Italian borrowers accounted for over $5 billion. Net compensatory loan inflows occurred in 1970, 1972, 1973, and 1974, with net repayments made in each of the other years. Some special credit institutes (medium- and long-term investment banks) owned indirectly in various ways by the state, were the main organizations that borrowed in the Euromarket (especially IMI, Mediobanca, ICIPU, and CREDIOP). There was also one large loan by ENEL that was motivated, at least in part, by balance-of-payments considerations. Except for the ENEL loan, the loans were recorded in the balance of payments as private capital inflows, since they were not borrowings directly by the state, nor did they have formal state guarantees.

Before the explosion of Italy's balance-of-payments deficit in 1974, Italian institutions had already been active borrowers in the Euromarket on a large scale in 1970, 1972, and especially in 1973. These borrowings were principally motivated by the need for balance-of-payments financing and were made in large part at the behest of the Bank of Italy. After the difficult placement of some large bank consortia loans early in 1974, however, such large-scale borrowing virtually ceased until 1978. This was partly due to growing concern in the international banking community about the banks' exposure in Italy, but also reflected some reluctance on the part of the Italian monetary authorities to allow Italian borrowers to accept a widening

TABLE 7.10

Cumulative Net Foreign Lending to Italy, 1970-78
(billions of dollars)

Sector	Amount of Loans
Public borrowers (Cassa, ENEL, etc.)	$ 3.7
Banks/insurance/finance (including compensatory)	4.8
Communications	0.5
Construction	0.5
Metals	0.6
Engineering	0.6
Other (including EC loans)	2.7
Total	$13.4

Source: Compiled by the author; data from Bank of Italy annual reports.

in the premium over the London Eurodollar rate for fear of hurting Italy's already weakened credit rating. During the remaining years of Italy's 1973-76 balance-of-payments difficulties the authorities were forced to turn to foreign official lending sources and to short-term borrowing by Italian commercial banks.

In addition to the compensatory balance-of-payments loans, there was also a considerable growth during the decade in borrowing by other Italian bodies for other reasons. For example, the Cassa per il Mezzogiorno, which had long been a borrower abroad, continued to obtain loan capital for development of Italy's south, especially from the European Investment Bank (EIB) of the EC. ENEL borrowed to help finance investment in the electric energy sector, while IMI and CREDIOP borrowed to finance exports. In addition, there was a growing inflow of (nonmonetary support) "credits" from the EC. (This item includes various adjustments and imputations required to reconcile foreign exchange transactions data and economic balance-of-payments data.)

There was relatively little growth during the 1970s in the net outflow of Italian medium- and long-term loan capital, which averaged only $0.2 billion per year in the period 1970-78. In part this was the result of exchange controls. By far the largest share of these loans were to foreign banks and other financial institutions (including export credit), especially in developing countries.

Trade Credit

Net commercial credit fluctuated very considerably from year to year in response to changes in the rate of growth of exports and imports, relative interest rates in Italy and abroad and the availability of credit, exchange control measures, exchange rate considerations, political uncertainties, and export promotion efforts. The net balance on commercial credit flows (both short-term and long-term) varied from a net outflow of $1.7 billion in 1972 to a net inflow of $2.1 billion in 1976.

The relative rates of growth of exports and imports affected the net amount of commercial credit granted. In periods when exports were rising relatively fast, the corresponding export credit that accompanied such sales tended to increase (and similarly with imports). Thus, export growth would appear as an immediate improvement in the trade accounts, but this would be to some extent offset in the capital accounts by a corresponding outflow of export credit. Relative foreign and domestic interest costs of financing trade credit and the availability of credit also influenced commercial credit flows. In fact, interest rate policy in Italy was frequently motivated in part by balance-of-payments considerations, and manipulation of interest rate differentials between Italy and abroad was fairly effective in stimulating short-term capital flows in the desired direction.[2] (See the section on interest rates and capital flows later in this chapter, and Chapters 8 and 10.)

Terms of payment for merchandise trade were also affected by exchange rate expectations and by periodic variations in exchange control regulations over the extension and acceptance of trade credit (Chapter 11). Before the general floating of currencies in February 1973 the currency of payment used for Italy's exports and imports was not a question of great importance. After the experience of large rate movements in 1973-74 and 1975-76, however, Italian traders were more aware of the need to take this factor into consideration, and there is some evidence of shifts in the currency of billing in response to world exchange market conditions.[3]

Changes in political conditions in Italy also had some effect on trade credit through shifts in the timing of payment based on concern about economic policy shifts, as well as concern about exchange rate prospects. Attempts to preserve or build export markets were another factor affecting commercial credits, particularly at certain critical junctures during the 1970s, such as 1976, when foreign suppliers provided increased credit to Italian buyers at a time of Italian balance-of-payments difficulties in order to preserve their sales in the Italian market.

Conversely, Italian export promotion efforts, especially in the oil-producing countries and Eastern Europe, led to liberalization and expansion of the export credit guarantee program that encouraged an expansion of Italian export credits. In 1977, Law 227 simplified procedures, created a new coordinating agency, Sezione Speciale per l'Assicurazione del Credito all' Esportazione (SACE), and established a 5 trillion lire revolving authorization for annual credit guarantee ceilings. While annual export credit insurance had been extended in average amounts of $1.1 billion in the first five years of the decade, the annual average rose sharply after the reform to $3.4 billion per year in the succeeding four-year period. The largest portion of such guarantees was granted to cover credits for financing the export of Italian goods and services. Financial credits directly to foreign borrowers, however, were also an important component of the total, particularly in 1975-76, and guarantees of Italian construction projects abroad became important in the later years of the decade. The allocation of credit guarantees mainly favored the developing countries, which accounted for 65 percent of all guarantees issued during the decade (1970-1978); the socialist countries received 31 percent of the total, and developed countries 4 percent. At the end of 1978 total guarantees outstanding amounted to $14 billion, of which $9 billion were with the developing countries, $4 billion with the socialist countries, and $1 billion with developed countries.

The overall pattern of net commercial credit flows (including both short-term and long-term credit) was one of net outflows in the early years of the decade (1970-72), net inflows during the middle years when Italy was experiencing payments difficulties (1973, 1974, and 1976), and net outflows again when Italy's payments situation improved (1975 and 1977-78).

Medium- and long-term trade credit showed a net inflow in most years of the nine-year period, except for 1970, 1972, and 1978. This was due more to net repayments on Italian long-term credits than to any large increase in long-term credit extended by foreign suppliers to Italy, although there was some increase in the latter credits in 1975-76. With the strong improvement in the balance-of-payments situation in 1978 (and good export growth), there was a correspondingly large net outflow of Italian long-term trade credit to Italian customers abroad.

Net short-term credit flows fluctuated widely over time, as shown in the table below. As was to be expected, there were rather large net outflows of credit in the relatively good balance-of-payments years (1970-72, 1975, and 1977) and relative balance or net inflows during the weak balance-of-payments years (1973, 1974, and 1976). In 1978, however, the expected net outflow did not materialize, as inflows of short-term trade credit were quite large early in the year when Italian interest rates were rather high compared to foreign rates.

Year	Credit Flow (billions of dollars)
1970	-0.6
1971	-0.5
1972	-1.6
1973	-0.1
1974	0.4
1975	-0.6
1976	1.4
1977	-1.1
1978	—*
Total	-2.5

Capital Flight

The final component in Italy's capital accounts that deserves some attention is capital flight. While most countries do not attempt to quantify such capital outflows, the importance of the phenomenon in Italy requires that some consideration be given to the problem. The amounts of such illegal outflows reflect a variety of factors: political uncertainties, yield differentials on investments in Italy and abroad, the absence of a broad array of investment instruments in Italy, tax evasion, and currency speculation.

The techniques used in evading Italian exchange controls have varied over time and are a function of income, type of employment, and degree of financial sophistication (and honesty) of Italian residents, traders, and bankers. During the 1960s and into the early 1970s the favored way of exporting capital illegally was through the physical export of Italian banknotes, mainly across the border to Switzerland. The physical repatriation through the banking system of such banknote outflows provided the monetary authorities with a statistical measure of the volume of illicit capital outflows in this form.

At that time, Italian banknotes returned to Italy could legally be deposited to nonresident, convertible lira capital accounts. This "laundering" of Italian capital had two beneficial effects for its owners: it facilitated tax evasion on the original income and tax avoidance on the interest earnings on these "foreign" deposits; and it guaranteed the reexport of the capital in times of difficulties because of the convertibility feature of the accounts. Initially, in order to provide verification that the banknotes had really been returned from abroad, the authorities required in February 1970 that the returned notes be pre-

---

*Less than $100 million inflow.

sented to the Bank of Italy before being credited to accounts, rather than presented directly to the commercial banks for crediting. Subsequently, in June 1972, the authorities prohibited the deposit of repatriated banknotes to capital accounts, effectively putting an end to this channel of capital reinvestment, but not to the export of banknotes nor to capital flight, in general.

Following the June 1972 banknote measure, instead of repatriation of the banknotes through the banking system in the old way, banknotes were sold outside Italy at a discount to foreign tourists and to Italian emigrants and workers living abroad, particularly in Germany and Switzerland. The effect of these transactions was that lire were not purchased in Italy with foreign currency through the banking system, and therefore recorded tourist receipts and emigrant and worker remittances were understated in official balance-of-payments statistics. Another potential channel of capital flight consisted of underinvoicing exports and overinvoicing imports by Italian traders.

Because of the distortions in the balance-of-payments accounts during the period 1970-76 created by serious underrecording of tourist, worker remittance, and emigrant remittance receipts, the Bank ot Italy began to make explicit adjustments in the accounts in order to boost net receipts in the services/transfers accounts and to include a negative, hidden capital outflow in the capital account (shown under "other" Italian capital).*

Estimates of capital flight in the 1970s are necessarily very rough and must be used with caution. Repatriated banknotes in the early years and Bank of Italy calculations of hidden capital outflows in the mid-1970s suggest, however, that over the entire period capital flight amounted to about $8 billion.† The annual estimates are shown in the table below.

Although capital flight seemed to be greatly reduced after 1976 in response both to economic conditions and to exchange control regulations, it is too soon to conclude that the problem has been dealt with. Until the balance of payments again comes under pressure the system has not really been tested, and the volume of Italy's international

---

*These adjustments first appeared in the bank's annual report for 1973 and published data for 1972-76 include the adjustments. Calculations of hidden capital flight were also made for 1970 and 1971, but it is necessary to go back and adjust the published data for those years in order to have a comparable series. This has been done by the author.

†Capital flight is also suggested by the data on errors and omissions, which were nearly always negative during the 1970s.

FIGURE 7.2

Interest Rate Differentials and Capital Flows, 1970–79

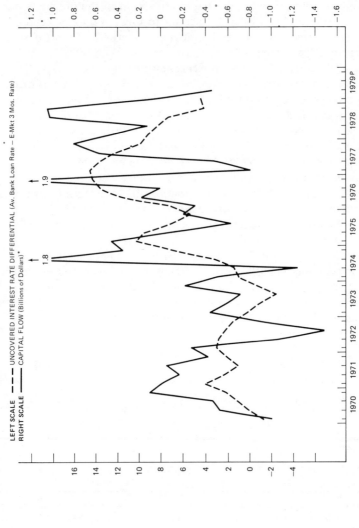

*Capital movements plus errors and omissions (excluding compensatory loans, short–term bank capital and official capital).

Note: Data for 1979 are preliminary.
Source: Constructed by the author.

Year	Capital Flight (billions of dollars)
1970	1.3
1971	1.2
1972	1.5
1973	1.1
1974	1.4
1975	0.8
1976	0.7
1977	—
1978	—
Total	8.0

transactions offers many opportunities for finding new channels for illegal capital exports. The main protection against a resurgence of capital flight is to prevent the emergence of the various incentives to capital flight that in the past have led to large capital outflows.

Interest Rates and Capital Flows

Because of the ability of the monetary authorities to exercise direct controls over short-term bank capital through manipulation of the net foreign position of the banks, Euromarket borrowing by state entities, and other capital outflows through exchange controls, it is difficult to assess the effect, in isolation, of interest rate policy on capital flows. Still, an examination of quarterly capital flows, which exclude bank capital and Euromarket compensatory loans, suggests that variations in interest rate differentials between Italy and abroad can have an important effect. This works mainly through trade-related credit (see the section on trade credit earlier in this chapter), and perhaps through unrecorded capital flows, showing up in errors and omissions. (For example, the existence of large Italian financial assets held abroad as a result of years of capital flight is believed to provide a source of foreign credit in times of domestic monetary restrictions.)

Figure 7.2 presents quarterly capital flows (excluding net bank capital and net Euromarket flows and including errors and omissions) plotted against interest-rate differentials between the average bank lending rate in Italy and the three-month Eurodollar rate in London (on an uncovered basis). The pattern shows a fair degree of correlation, although the effects of other factors, such as the prior import deposit in 1974 and the prior exchange deposit and export foreign financing requirements of 1976 (Chapter 11) also had an effect in stimulating capital inflows. (None of the large Euromarket borrowings by state entities in 1978 are considered to be compensatory, so they are included in the capital inflow.)

MANAGING SURPLUSES AND DEFICITS

The overall surplus or deficit in the balance of payments indicates the size of the financing problem that confronts the monetary authorities, which must be dealt with through variations in official assets or liabilities or by directly or indirectly effecting changes in the net foreign position of the commercial banks. The authorities may also directly affect the recorded surplus or deficit itself by use of compensatory loans recorded in the capital account. In fact, as discussed earlier, it is useful to calculate the overall balance net of such loans in order to determine the underlying surplus or deficit (Table 7.11).

The existence of overall recorded surpluses in 1970, 1971, 1977, and 1978 presented no serious financing problem. (There was actually an underlying deficit in 1970, which was offset by compensatory Euromarket borrowings.) Italian surpluses in the other three years were not so large as to create financing problems in the form of an undesirable buildup of reserves with inflationary domestic monetary effects. Even the large surpluses of 1977 and 1978 were tolerable in large part because of the need to accumulate foreign exchange for further repayment of accumulated foreign debt. In 1970 and 1971 the recorded surpluses were financed by an improvement in the net asset position of the monetary authorities, while the commercial banks' net foreign position did not change substantially. The relatively small deficit of 1972 was of acceptable size. The deficits in 1973–76, however, created serious problems.

In 1970, although there was a recorded surplus of $0.3 billion, the capital account included a net inflow from compensatory Euromarket loans of $1.5 billion—indicating that there was an underlying deficit on the order of $1.2 billion. A deficit of this size was troublesome, but the authorities had had some experience in the 1960s in dealing with a problem of this magnitude and Italy was creditworthy in the Euromarket. The combination of these compensatory borrowings and a reduction in the monetary authorities' net asset position was sufficient to deal with the problem. In 1971 the improvement in the current account moved Italy into overall surplus and the authorities were able to make net repayments on earlier compensatory loans. In 1972, although there was further improvement on current account, the capital account moved into large deficit, despite the resumption of some net compensatory borrowing. The overall recorded deficit reached

TABLE 7.11

Overall Balance-of-Payments Surplus or Deficit,
1970-78
(billions of dollars)

	Recorded Surplus or Deficit	Net of Compensatory Loans
1970	0.3	-1.2
1971	0.7	0.9
1972	-1.2	-1.7
1973	-0.5	-4.6
1974	-5.7	-7.8
1975	-2.1	-1.2
1976	-1.8	-1.4
1977	2.0	2.6
1978	8.2	9.1

Source: Compiled by the author; data from Bank
of Italy annual reports and Research Office.

$1.2 billion, or, adjusted for the compensatory borrowing, $1.7 billion. About two-thirds of the recorded deficit was financed by a worsening in the net reserve position of the monetary authorities, with the remainder covered by net short-term capital inflows through the commercial banks.

By 1973, when the world commodity boom and initial oil price increases occurred, Italy's balance-of-payments financing ability was already somewhat weakened by previous deficits, including fairly substantial Euromarket borrowing. The authorities were still able to draw on the Euromarket, however, through ENEL and the special credit institutes, in an unprecedented net amount of $4.1 billion (Table 7.12). This massive capital inflow allowed Italy to record an overall deficit of only $0.5 billion, although the underlying deficit was $4.6 billion. Furthermore, Italy's ability to draw further on Euromarket funds was seriously eroded. Most of the remaining small recorded deficit was financed by a decline in the official net asset position, while the commercial banks' foreign position was little changed. (There were also large short-term swap drawings from the Belgian and Danish central banks, which were converted in 1974 into short-term credit from the EC.)

In early 1974 Italian borrowers were still able to obtain some additional net Euromarket financing (over $2.0 billion for the year).

TABLE 7.12

Principal Sources of Balance-of-Payments Borrowing, 1973-76
(billions of dollars)

| | Official (Net) | | | Private (Net) | |
	EC[a]	IMF[b]	Bundes-bank	Euromarket Compensatory Loans	Short-Term Bank Credit
1973	—	—	—	4.1	0.1
1974	1.9	1.7		2.1	0.9
1975	—	1.2	-0.5	-1.0	-0.5
1976	0.5	—[c]	0.2	-0.3	2.7
Totals	2.4	2.9	1.7	4.9	3.2

[a]Medium-term credit and joint borrowing.
[b]Standbys and oil facility.
[c]Less than $100 million.
Source: Compiled by the author; data from Bank of Italy annual reports and Research Office.

That source of financing dried up, however, as foreign bankers became concerned about Italy's balance-of-payments position and prospects. Actually, standard measurements of a country's foreign debt repayment capacity, even then, did not show particularly high debt ratios; but the absolute amounts were large and the foreign banking community was surprised by the suddenness and size of foreign debt accumulation by a large industrial country that previously had not had much foreign debt. The effective closure of the Euromarket to Italian medium-term borrowing in early 1974 forced the authorities to seek alternative sources for financing subsequent deficits, including the remaining 1974 deficit of over $5.7 billion (after including the $2.0 billion in Euromarket borrowing early in the year). The major sources of foreign official credit drawn upon were an EC short-term credit later converted into a credit from the EC medium-term lending facility ($1.9 billion), a $1.2 billion IMF standby (drawings that year of $0.9 billion), an IMF oil facility credit of $1.7 billion (drawings of $0.8 billion), and a gold collateral loan of $2.0 billion by the German Bundesbank to the Bank of Italy. In addition, the authorities encouraged the commercial banks to increase their net short-term borrowing abroad, which rose by about $0.9 billion during 1974.

The recession of 1975 brought about a dramatic, if temporary, improvement in the current account, from a deficit of $8.0 billion in

1974 to a deficit of only $0.6 billion in 1975. This improvement helped
to reduce the overall deficit to only $2.1 billion. In fact, the financing
problem was less serious than this, since the recorded deficit included
the effect of the net repayment of nearly $1.0 billion on earlier Euro-
market credits—a deliberate effort on the part of the monetary authorities to restore Italy's international creditworthiness as soon as possible.
In 1975 the authorities drew the remaining amounts available under
the 1974 IMF standby and oil facility credit. They were able to repay
$0.5 billion to the Bundesbank and allow the commercial banks to
reduce their net foreign liabilities.

The economic recovery of 1976 once again led to an increase in
the current account deficit and to large exchange rate depreciation.
Although the current account was in deficit by $2.8 billion, the capital
account moved into large surplus ($1.8 billion), aided in large part by
net commercial credit inflows of $2.1 billion in response to policy
measures taken by the authorities, especially an increase in Italian
interest rates and a prior exchange deposit (aided by the desire of
foreign suppliers to retain their markets in Italy by providing additional trade credit). The size of the capital account surplus greatly
eased the financing problem, as the recorded deficit was only $1.8
billion. In fact, the underlying deficit (taking Euromarket compensatory loans into account) actually was smaller by the more than $0.3
billion in net repayment made on those loans, as the authorities continued efforts to restore Italy's foreign credit position. At the same
time, the authorities encouraged the commercial banks to increase
their short-term foreign borrowing. This was linked to a requirement
that Italian exporters who extended export credits of up to four months
would have to obtain financing in foreign currency from Italian banks
for 30 percent of the credit. As a consequence, the commercial banks
increased their net liabilities by $2.7 billion in 1976 and Italy's net
official reserve position actually improved by nearly $1 billion. Italy
continued to draw on foreign official sources of finance, including the
first tranche ($0.5 billion) of a $1.0 billion EC loan financed from an
EC joint borrowing in the Euromarket and an automatic drawing of
$0.2 billion from the Bundesbank under an option that permitted addi-
tional dollar drawings in line with any increase in the value of the
underlying gold collateral. The Italian government began negotiation
of a second IMF standby of 450 million special drawing rights (SDR)
in support of a strengthened stabilization program, but the agreement
was not completed until early in 1977.

The sharp improvement in Italy's current account in 1977 and
1978 dramatically changed Italy's overall balance-of-payments position.
The improvement in the current account was $5.3 billion in 1977 and
a further $3.9 billion in 1978. The capital account was virtually in
balance in 1977 and in surplus by $1.5 billion in 1978, despite net
repayments on earlier Euromarket compensatory loans of about $0.6
and $0.8 billion, respectively. In fact, the substantial surplus in the

capital account in 1978 was in large part due to Italy's renewed ability to draw on international capital markets in the ordinary way—that is, not through compensatory loans motivated by a critical need to finance a balance-of-payments deficit. Net loan receipts were particularly large for the Cassa per il Mezzogiorno, ENEL, IMI, and IRI. Official financing transactions in these two years were the reverse of the 1974-76 pattern, as repayments were made of $1.4 billion on EC medium-term credits, all of the IMF standby drawings (including a small initial drawing under the 1977 standby), about one-third of the IMF oil facility credit, and all of the outstanding $1.7 billion Bundesbank gold loan. (The second $0.5 billion tranche of the EC joint borrowing loan was drawn in 1977.) While both the current account and capital account positions were improving, the commercial banks continued to increase their net borrowing in 1977 by $4.0 billion, but made repayments of nearly $1.0 billion in 1978. In addition to large debt repayments, the 1977-78 surpluses permitted a massive buildup of official assets to unprecedented levels; convertible currency holdings reached $10.5 billion at the end of 1978.

CONCLUSIONS

The pattern of a strong Italian current-account position that had prevailed in the 1960s extended into the 1970s only through 1972. By 1973 the combined effects of very rapid growth of unit labor costs and exchange rate stability had eroded Italy's competitive position and there was already a serious balance-of-payments problem when the energy crisis struck. This required both a reduction in the oil deficit and in the earlier nonoil deficit (especially with Italy's EC partners).

Italy suffered a larger impact (for its economic size) than any other of the group of seven largest OECD countries, as a result of the 1973-74 oil price increases. Its adjustment between the years 1974 and 1978 was equally striking. The improvement was the result of slow domestic growth, exchange rate depreciation, and monetary and exchange control actions. There was a sharp decline in real growth in 1975 and slow growth in 1977-78, following the recovery of 1976 (Chapter 5). Italian interest rates were raised sharply in 1975 and again in 1976-77 (Chapter 8). The lira exchange rate depreciated significantly in 1973-74 and again in 1976, and exchange controls were reinforced (Chapter 11). The combination of slow import growth, improved price competitiveness, and capital inflows led to a remarkable turnaround in both the current account and the capital account. The growth of exports was in large part due to the ability of small and medium business to respond to new export opportunities (partly because they were able to avoid some of the costs and labor force rigidities faced by large business). The services accounts, especially travel, benefited greatly from exchange rate depreciation. The strengthening of the capital account was also helped by a high degree of world liquidity and an improvement in Italy's credit rating compared to some other debtor countries. There was, of course, a cost in real terms from the balance-of-payments adjustment, as real goods and services that might have been employed at home for increased consumption or investment had to be transferred to the oil producers.

By 1978-79 the large size of the current account surplus again raised the question of whether Italy, structurally, should be a net exporter of real resources and of financial capital, given its own level of development. (This was a theme that had also been heard regularly in the 1960s.) While the constant threat of new oil price increases mitigated against too rapid a reduction in the surplus, the existence of large current account surpluses, offset by capital outflow, was symptomatic of Italy's underlying inability to provide sufficient investment opportunities to employ domestic savings. The danger to future growth prospects of such a pattern of development is worrisome.

On the other hand, whether or not the strength of the current account will endure is open to question. To a considerable extent the 1977-79 improvement reflected a slow rate of real economic growth and of real imports, plus relatively moderate increases in import prices between 1974 and 1978. A return to a more acceptable growth path and the constant threat of oil price increases could jeopardize the current surplus. Also, a continuation of the rapid rise in unit labor costs and of enormous budget deficits could further accelerate price inflation. This would be incompatible with Italy's commitment to greater exchange rate stability in the European Monetary System (EMS), which will to some extent limit the use of exchange rates to offset rapid cost and price inflation. Prudent monetary policy can help to protect the balance of payments, but it cannot do the job alone.

NOTES

1. See Luigi Guantario, "Tourism in Italy: Its Situation, Problems and Prospects," Banco di Roma, Review of the Economic Conditions in Italy Vol. XXXII No. 1 (January 1978): 41-55.

2. See Enzo Rossi and Pietro Viola, "Leads and Lags della bilancia dei pagamenti dell' Italian negli ultimi anni e fattori che influiscono sul loro andamento," Bancaria Vol. XXXII No. 11 (November 1976): 1102-17. Rossi and Viola note that leads and lags in Italy respond promptly to interest rate differentials, especially through transactions by multinationals with access to many credit markets.

3. See Bank of Italy, Annual Report (Rome: 1978), p. 147.

8

FINANCIAL INSTITUTIONS AND MONETARY DEVELOPMENTS

The manoeuvering space allowed the Central Bank has shrunk and is still shrinking, as a result of the growing impact of decisions regarding the volume of government expenditure and its use, incentives to public and private sector investment and, above all, the definition of labour relations. . . . Should it become necessary to limit the overall volume of credit the reduction, owing to the rigidity of the public sector's demand, would mainly affect the directly productive sectors.

Guido Carli
Governor, Bank of Italy
Annual Meeting, Rome, May 1973

INTRODUCTION

The purpose of this chapter is to describe Italian financial institutions and their role in the economy and to outline the evolution of monetary developments during the 1970s. In Chapter 10 the use of monetary tools for specific countercyclical purposes will be examined.

The principal financial institutions in Italy are the Interministerial Credit Committee (Comitato Interministeriale per il Credito e il Risparmio—CICR), the Bank of Italy (Banca d'Italia) and the Italian Exchange Office (Ufficio Italiano dei Cambi—UIC), the commercial banks, the special credit institutes, and the securities markets.

Italy makes use of all the traditional monetary tools: bank reserve requirements, discounting by the central bank, and open-market operations. These instruments have been supplemented, however, by a variety of nontraditional monetary measures that are rarely used in such profusion in other industrial countries: control over the net foreign position of the banks, direct quantitative control over bank loans, bank portfolio investment requirements, and a number of exchange control measures that have monetary motivations and monetary effects.

The principal monetary target in the 1970s was control over the availability of credit, especially through control over the monetary base. Attention was also given, however, to interest rate policy, particularly with regard to its effect on the balance of payments. Subsidiary targets were sometimes set for total domestic credit expansion and credit to the Treasury by the central bank.

All of the principal measures of monetary growth—monetary base, total domestic credit, and money supply—grew at very high rates during the 1970s (1970-78). The monetary base grew at an average annual rate of 17.5 percent. The principal expansionary factor was the large and growing treasury cash deficit, which the monetary authorities felt it necessary to accommodate. Total domestic credit expansion grew on average by 18.4 percent per year. Of the total amount of such credit extended during the period the Treasury received 45 percent. The money supply as measured by M-1 grew at an average annual rate of 19.7 percent. The growth of the broadest concept of "money" (M-3) averaged 20.2 percent per year. In the period 1970-78, the three most important credit counterparts to the growth of M-3, on average, were credit to the Treasury (38 percent of the total increase in credit); short-term credit, especially bank credit to private business (22 percent); and long-term credit, especially lending the special credit institutes to industry and Postal Savings Fund lending to local governments (36 percent).

Interest rate policy was pursued more actively than in the 1960s in the face of balance-of-payments difficulties and the need to attract financial savings from the household sector to finance business and to provide a means of noninflationary financing of the growing treasury deficit. Real interest rates, however, were generally negative. The use of subsidized interest rates continued, mainly favoring small and medium industry, industry in the south, and agriculture; the cost of such subsidies grew rapidly.

FINANCIAL INSTITUTIONS

Official Monetary Institutions

The Interministerial Committee on Credit and Savings (hereafter called the Interministerial Credit Committee), a cabinet-level body chaired by the minister of the treasury, was created in 1947. Other members of the committee are the ministers of public works, agriculture, industry, foreign trade, budget, and state participations. The governor of the Bank of Italy also attends meetings of the committee. The committee has overall responsibility for establishing the basic guidelines of monetary, financial, and foreign exchange policy. It makes policy decisions in these fields, issues appropriate regulations, and provides implementing instructions to the Bank of Italy and other supervisory bodies.

Since 1926 Italy's central bank, the Bank of Italy, has carried out the usual responsibilities of a modern central bank. Although legally separate from the bank, since it was created in 1945, the Italian Exchange Office (UIC) has worked closely with the bank in exercising control over foreign exchange transactions and administering the country's official reserves. Specific responsibilities of the bank include lending to the Treasury in the form of overdrafts and through purchases of government securities, acting as depository for the required reserves of the commercial banks, supplying currency for the economy, supervising the financial soundness of the banking system, regulating new security issues, and exercising overall management of monetary policy under the guidance of the Interministerial Credit Committee. On the international side, the governor of the Bank of Italy is also president of the UIC and the two bodies share responsibilities for managing official foreign reserves, the Bank of Italy engaging in daily exchange market intervention and the Exchange Office managing reserve holdings and supervising exchange-control regulations.

Commercial Banks

The commercial banks are essentially short-term credit institutions dealing in loans and deposits of up to 18-months maturity. There are, however, some exceptions. The charters of public law banks, savings banks, and first-class pawn banks allow for medium- and long-term credit within certain limits. The ordinary credit banks and popular cooperative banks are allowed to invest up to 8 percent of their deposits in medium- and long-term loans (over 18-month to 60-month maturities). In addition, a few banks have special sections that are allowed to engage in medium- and long-term lending to particular economic sectors and some of the banks are stockholders in special credit institutes, which provides an indirect outlet for lending at longer term. (The common practice of rolling over short-term loans, in fact, also results in some short-term credit becoming virtually long-term.)

TABLE 8.1

Financial Structure of Commercial Banks, 1969 and 1978
(percent of total)

	End of 1969	End of 1978
Assets		
Bank reserves	11.8	11.7
Credit	68.3	65.8
Loans	(49.0)	(33.1)
Securities	(19.3)	(32.7)
Shareholdings	0.8	0.8
Interbank accounts	9.9	14.8
Foreign assets	9.2	6.9
Total	100.0	100.0
Liabilities/capital		
Deposits	71.1	71.3
Savings	(34.8)	(33.5)
Demand	(36.3)	(37.8)
Other clients' accounts	2.2	1.0
Interbank accounts	8.7	13.9
Foreign liabilities	9.3	9.1
Credit from central bank	5.8	0.9
Other liabilities (net)	0.7	0.9
Capital/reserves	2.2	2.9
Total	100.0	100.0

Source: Compiled by the author; calculated from
Bank of Italy annual reports and bulletins.

A comparison of the financial structure of the commercial banks
at the beginning of the decade and at the end of the period (Table 8.1)
shows a few important changes: a substantial decline in bank loans as
a share of total assets; a corresponding rise in portfolio investments;
a large increase in the importance of interbank accounts (both assets
and liabilities); and a decline in the relative weight of foreign assets.
    The commercial banks are organized in a variety of legal forms
and are generally grouped into the following categories: public law

banks, banks of national interest, ordinary credit banks, popular co-operative banks, savings and pawn banks, rural and artisan banks, and central institutes for the various categories of banks. Despite differences in origin, ownership, and lending patterns, monetary policy tools generally apply equally to all these commercial banks. (Before 1975 the savings banks were subject to different reserve requirements than the other banks, and the small pledge banks and rural and artisan banks are exempt from bank reserve requirements.)

Special Credit Institutes

The special credit institutes are medium- and long-term lending institutions. They are financed mainly from bond issues and, to a lesser extent, from savings deposits and savings certificates, deposits from the commercial banks, foreign borrowing, and other sources (Table 8.2). The institutes specialize in lending for industry (including small business), public works and public utilities, real estate (land and buildings), agriculture, and export credit. Some operate nationally, others only on a regional basis. Many of the institutes are owned either directly or indirectly by the government, but are particularly important sources of funding for private business. The institutes are also the source of most subsidized credit. (The commercial banks extend some subsidized credit to agriculture.) In 1970-78, 43 percent of new credit commitments by the institutes was in the form of credits with lower than market interest rates, especially benefiting small industry, industry in the south, and agriculture.

Securities Markets

Italy's securities market is rather large for the size of the economy, with net issue of stocks and bonds averaging 9.4 percent of GDP annually in the 1970s (1970-78). The market is heavily dominated by fixed-interest securities, especially those of the public sector and the special credit institutes. Financial intermediaries are more important than the public as holders of securities. For example, at the end of 1978 the commercial banks and the Bank of Italy were the largest holders of medium- and long-term securities (47 percent and 20 percent of the total), with individuals (19 percent); companies, other financial intermediaries, and nonresidents accounted for the remainder (Table 8.3). Stocks declined in relative importance in the 1970s, reflecting the poor profit and dividend record of Italian business. Shares are held mainly by companies and are typically unlisted. Bond issues have been relatively favored over stock issues by the tax system.

TABLE 8.2

Financial Structure of Special Credit Institutes,
1969 and 1978
(percent of total)

	End of 1969	End of 1978
Assets		
Loans	93.0	82.5
Domestic	(68.4)	(65.1)
For treasury account	(21.1)	(15.0)
Foreign	(3.5)	(2.4)
Other (securities, liquid assets, other)	7.0	17.5
Total	100.0	100.0
Liabilities		
Bonds	70.7	74.2
Deposits, savings certificates	6.7	7.7
Deposits of commercial banks	5.6	2.6
Public funds	5.3	3.8
Foreign currency loans	2.5	6.0
Other liabilities/capital	9.2	5.7
Total	100.0	100.0

Source: Compiled by the author; calculated from
Bank of Italy annual reports (appendixes).

Fixed-interest securities are subject to a definitive withholding tax of
zero to 20 percent (Chapter 4). Shares are subject to a 10 percent
withholding tax against total tax liabilities, although there were times
in the 1970s when an optional definitive withholding tax was on the
books. Shares were subject to double taxation (of corporate profits
and of shareholder dividends) until a tax reform of 1977 provided a
partial tax credit for stockholders.

Italy lacks a well-developed short-term money market, although
some efforts have been made to encourage such a market. Some reasons that a money market has not developed fully are the fact that
interest is paid on demand deposits; the resistance of the banks to

TABLE 8.3

Structure of Securities Markets, 1969 and 1978
(percent of totals; nominal values, excluding treasury bills)

	End of 1969	End of 1978
Type of security		
Bonds	71.8	85.4
Stocks	28.2	14.6
Issuers		
Bonds		
Public sector	26.8	45.3
Special credit institutes	29.4	31.7
Public/private enterprise	15.6	8.4
Stocks	28.2	14.6
Holders		
The public (individuals, companies)	58.8	29.4
Intermediaries	41.2	70.6
Bank of Italy	(7.0)	(19.9)
Commercial banks	(27.2)	(47.2)
Other	(7.0)	(3.5)

Source: Compiled by the author; calculated from Bank
of Italy annual reports.

creation of competing short-term instruments; the prevalence of over-draft lending by the banks, which leads to debt repayment rather than new investment in liquid assets when borrowers' liquidity increases; and for much of the 1970s, the lack of a treasury bill market open to the public that offered yields in line with short-term market conditions. The money market that does exist consists mainly of interbank deposits, secondary trading in treasury bills, and short-term operations in foreign markets (within the confines of prevailing exchange controls).

MONETARY TOOLS

Bank Reserve Requirements

Since January 1975 all commercial banks must hold minimum reserves against all deposits (both current accounts and savings deposits) of residents other than banks, including deposits of public bodies and the lira deposits of nonresidents. (Previously savings banks had requirements that differed from those of other banks.) Foreign currency deposits are not subject to reserve requirements. The martinal reserve ratio was initially set at 15 percent of the increase in deposits in the previous month, but was raised to 15.75 percent in February 1976. (In 1976 a one-time "extraordinary" reserve deposit was also assessed.) From January 1962 until January 1975 the maximum reserve ratio had been 22.5 percent and at least 10 percent of the difference between deposits and capital/reserves had to be in the form of cash deposits with the Bank of Italy. From September 1965 until January 1975, however, certain long-term fixed-interest securities were eligible as reserves against increases in time and savings deposits. The January 1975 reform required that all reserves be kept in the form of cash deposits with the Bank of Italy. Current interest paid on reserve deposits with the Bank of Italy is 5.5 percent, a rate that has remained unchanged since September 1970. Previous to that time (from June 1958) interest was paid at a rate of 3.75 percent.

Central Bank Discounting

Commercial banks do not have automatic access to central bank credit, but each individual bank is assigned a maximum discount ceiling. Criteria for setting individual ceilings include the size of the bank, its financial structure, its past use of central bank credit, and the comparative size of quotas of similar banks. Discounting may take the form of rediscounting of eligible paper, including agricultural warehousing and operating credits, or advances against collateral, either ordinary or with fixed-term maturities. Ordinary advances are by far the most important. Bank of Italy decisions on applications for credit depend on the effect of its lending on creation of monetary base, general bank liquidity conditions, and the particular liquidity position of the borrowing bank. Since 1969 penalties have been assessed against banks that make repeated use of fixed-term advances or whose borrowing under the ordinary discount facility exceeds a certain percent of required reserves. Changes in the discount rate were extremely infrequent in the 1960s, with only one change made in 1969. (From June 1958 to August 1969 the rate was 3.5 percent.) Beginning with the August 1969 increase in the rate to 4 percent, changes in the rate became much more frequent, with 18 changes in the basic rate in the period 1970-79. For a brief period in 1971-72 slightly lower rates (0.5 percentage points) were applied to advances than to discounts, while for some months in 1972-73 the rate for fixed-term advances was higher than the rates then applying to ordinary discounts and ordinary advances. The current (end-1979) discount rate is 15 percent, with penalty rates of 1, 2, and 3 percent assessed against banks that made use of fixed-term advances in the previous 150, 120, or 90 days, and 3 percent for banks whose discounts exceeded 5 percent of their required reserves at the middle of the previous calendar semester. (The special credit institutes, in principle, have no access to the discount window, but occasionally the Bank of Italy extends credit to relieve temporary liquidity pressures.)

Open-Market Operations

The Bank of Italy is limited by law to open-market operations in government or government-guaranteed securities. Until April 1969 operations could take place only in long-term securities, but subsequently operations in treasury bills were also permitted. (Through arbitrage, open-market intervention in government issues also affects the market for other bonds.) Open-market operations in long-term securities have generally been aimed at support of the government securities market in order to stabilize long-term interest rates so as to encourage investment and to provide an instrument of long-term savings for households with a minimum of price volatility. The need to let long-term interest rates respond to domestic inflation performance and to foreign interest rates, however, and the danger of losing control over the rate of expansion of the monetary base, have periodically overridden the general aim.

In the mid-1970s the monetary authorities sought to encourage the development of a more active short-term money market for treasury bills in order to influence the liquidity position of the banks, short-term interest rates, and household savings patterns. Beginning in September 1973 and in May 1974 the Treasury introduced the sale of 6-month and 3-month bills (rather than relying solely on 12-month issues). From January 1975 on, monthly auctions of these bills were the rule (with some exceptions). In March 1975 the Bank of Italy ceased to be a residual buyer of bills at a base price but competed with the commercial banks by bidding. Beginning in May 1975 the number of eligible bidders at the monthly auction was expanded to include the Exchange Office, social insurance institutes, special credit institutes, finance companies, and stockholders. (Individuals may buy bills through financial intermediaries.) From January 1977 the bank modified its secondary market operations in treasury bills by adopting more flexible criteria. Instead of determining the purchase price by applying a system of fixed margins to the tender prices recorded at the previous auction, intervention prices were adjusted more frequently in accordance with short-term monetary targets and market trends.

Control over Net Foreign Position of Banks

For Italy, use of control over the net foreign position of the commercial banks has become a traditional tool of economic policy management. Variations in the regulation of the banks' position have been rather frequent and have typically been dually motivated—by the desire to facilitate financing of balance-of-payments surpluses and deficits and the desire to influence domestic bank liquidity. In addition to direct controls over the banks' foreign position, the Bank of Italy has also used swaps (spot purchases of foreign exchange coupled with forward sales at a fixed rate) with the banks to create incentives for voluntary bank capital flows in one direction or another.

The present control encompasses the overall net position vis-à-vis nonresidents in foreign currencies and lire together. A balanced foreign currency position on a daily basis is required separately in U.S. dollars, EC currencies, and all other conto valutario currencies combined (the currencies of Austria, Canada, Japan, Portugal, Spain, Sweden, Switzerland, and Norway). Authorized banks (that is, those permitted to deal in foreign currencies) are not subject to any ceiling on their net foreign liability position, but are prohibited from maintaining a net foreign asset position. In addition, outstanding net forward transactions against lire are subject to a ceiling set individually for each bank.

Portfolio Investment Requirement

A bank portfolio investment requirement was introduced in June 1973 as a means of assuring a degree of stability in the demand for bonds at a time of rapid inflationary growth and of channeling the liquid financial savings of the household sector into medium- and long-term financing for businesses through the intermediation of the banks. The regulation specifies for six-month periods the percentage of the increase in bank deposits that must be invested by the banks in eligible bonds (calculated at nominal values), the floors or ceilings for particular types of bonds, and the minimum coupon rate of such bonds. The overall investment ratio has varied in the range 6.5 percent to 50 percent.* The minimum coupon rate has been set in the range of 7 percent to 10 percent. As an example, the requirement for the second half of 1979 was that the banks had to invest 6.5 percent of the increase in their deposits in real estate and agricultural improvement bonds that bore coupon rates of no less than 10 percent.

Direct Controls on Bank Loans

Direct quantitative controls over the expansion of domestic bank loans were introduced in July 1973 and remained in effect until March 1975. They were subsequently reintroduced in October 1976 and are still in effect. The joint aims of the regulation have been control over the overall rate of expansion of bank loans and the selective allocation of credit among the banks' borrowers. The regulations normally fix ceilings for a period of at least 12 months. As an example, the October 1979 regulation placed a ceiling of 16 percent growth in bank loans above a May 31, 1979 base for loans outstanding on May 31, 1980. The ceilings are usually set as a percentage growth over a base period, with separate ceilings established at intervals of every one to three months. The base amount has usually been the level of loans outstanding on a given date, but on one occasion was the average of bank loans over a previous six-month period. Rates of growth of bank loans (covering 12-month periods) have generally been in the range of 12-16 percent. At different times separate limits were set for loans to particular borrowers or for particular types of loans (for example, productive or financial loans or loans to the public administration), and various exemptions have been based on such factors as the size of the loan exposure with a particular borrower or the particular kinds of loans (such as electricity loans, foreign currency loans, loans to Friuli earthquake zone borrowers).

Prior Approval of Security Issues

Issues by public and private enterprise, local authorities, and public agencies require official permission of the Bank of Italy. Whenever any share issue or bond issue exceeds 500 million lire, approval

---

*For a period in 1973-74 the investment requirement was based on deposits outstanding as of a certain date; the investment ratio during the period varied in the range of 3 percent to 9 percent.

is required from the Interministerial Credit Committee. This control includes issues by the special credit institutes, which depend heavily on bond issues to finance their medium- and long-term lending. The regulation serves to control the level of lending activity of the institutes, which are not bound by bank reserve requirements, since they are not important collectors of deposits. The institutes must obtain the approval from the Interministerial Credit Committee, except for mortgage bonds available on tap—for example, savings certificates. Mortgage bond issues are limited by ceilings related to the size of the equity capital of the issuing institution, normally up to 30 times capital, but up to 50 times with Bank of Italy approval.

Deposit Measures

In May 1974 a prior import deposit was introduced to discourage imports and to absorb domestic liquidity. Importers were required to deposit in a non-interest-bearing account with the Bank of Italy for a period of 180 days the equivalent in lire of 50 percent of the value of their imports (c.i.f.) of certain products, chiefly consumer goods, in excess of one million lire (about 40 percent of total imports). In March 1975 the deposit requirement was entirely abolished.

In May 1976 a new deposit was introduced—a prior exchange deposit—again for both balance-of-payments and domestic liquidity absorption purposes. The requirement concerned virtually all purchases of foreign exchange (not just for imports of merchandise) in the amount of 50 percent of the value of the transaction. The deposits were made into a 90-day non-interest-bearing account with the Bank of Italy. In September 1976 the requirement was extended until April 1977, but at a declining rate: 45 percent from October 15, 1976, 40 percent from November 30, 1976, 25 percent from January 15, 1977, and 10 percent from February 28, 1977. The deposit was abolished on April 15, 1977.

Another deposit measure—a capital outflow deposit—also has had some derivative effect on domestic liquidity, although it was introduced mainly for the purpose of reducing capital outflows and strengthening the balance of payments. In July 1973 a 50 percent non-interest-bearing deposit requirement was introduced against outward transfers of Italian capital for direct investments, portfolio investments, financial loans, purchases of real estate, and personal capital movements. In addition, when foreign investments are transferred between residents against lire, the transfer is subject to the deposit requirement, regardless of the date when the investment was made. Reinvestment of funds in new issues or on the secondary market are exempt, if the original investment was made before July 27, 1973. The deposit is held with the banks that made the transfer and deposits are released only when and to the extent that disinvestment operations occur. Their release requires the prior approval of the Bank of Italy. Certain exemptions have been granted for bonds of EC institutions and, on an ad hoc basis, for some outward direct investments.

The Bank of Italy has also required borrowers to deposit the lira counterpart of the foreign currency proceeds of Euromarket loans with the bank in order to avoid the expansionary effect on domestic liquidity of compensatory foreign borrowing, mainly by the special credit institutes, at the behest of the Bank of Italy. In some cases where the borrowing was not made solely for balance-of-payments purposes, some drawdowns of the lira counterpart were allowed. Although some lira proceeds from such loans have been on deposit with the bank from 1969 on, the main period when freezing of lira counterpart occurred was in 1973-74 in connection with the massive resort to Euromarket borrowing during those years of balance-of-payments difficulties.

Foreign Financing of Italian Export Credit

Another mainly balance-of-payments-motivated measure with a fairly important effect on domestic bank liquidity was the introduction in May 1976 of a requirement that Italian exporters who extended export credit terms of up to 120 days obtain financing in foreign currency from Italian banks to the extent of 30 percent of the amount of credit granted. (This, in effect, permitted the repatriation of export proceeds of that amount in advance of the time when the foreign exchange income would otherwise have been received.) In September 1976 the foreign currency financing requirement was raised to 50 percent of the credit. In June 1977 the financing rate was reduced to 25 percent and in June 1978 the requirement was abolished altogether.

Approval of Foreign Lending and Borrowing

Generally, Italian exchange controls require approval by the Ministry of the Treasury or the Ministry of Foreign Trade of loans of any kind from nonresidents to residents and from residents to nonresidents, and the loans are subject to the rules governing the issue of domestic securities. (Approval for foreign bond issues in Italy is normally restricted to international institutions.) The extension and receipt of commercial credits are controlled. (See next section on control over export and import payment terms.) Loans and credits beyond a certain duration (generally 180-360 days) that are not connected with commercial transactions or with the performance of a service require the approval of the Ministry of Foreign Trade and are severely restricted.

Control of Import and Export Payment Terms

Italian exchange controls have long included regulation of the timing of import and export payments, aimed mainly at limiting the effects of leads and lags on the balance of payments, but the regulation also affects domestic credit conditions. The manipulation of payment terms was common practice in the 1970s, with measures to tighten payment terms by restricting advance import payments and delayed export receipts taken in 1970 and 1973 and measures to relax payment terms adopted in 1972, 1976, and 1978. ("Advance" means receipt in any month prior to the month of physical shipment of the goods; "delayed" means payment in any month after the month of physical arrival of the goods.) The degree of liberality of the regulations is measured by the length of the time period for advance payments and delayed receipts that can be automatically approved by the commercial banks under general authority granted by the exchange-control authorities. Automatic approval of advance import payments has been allowed for periods varying between 30 and 120 days and for delayed export receipts from 90 to 360 days (with 90 percent payment required in that time period and the remainder payable in all cases within 24 months). Currently the banks are allowed to authorize advance import payments of up to 120 days and delayed export receipts for up to 120 days. Payment terms that go beyond these limits require approval of the Exchange Office or of the Foreign Trade Ministry, depending on the time periods involved and whether or not the trading partner is in an OECD country.

MONETARY TARGETS

From the mid-1960s control over changes in the monetary base became the principal monetary target in Italy. The original selection of this target was based on some evidence that the link between changes in the monetary base and final economic policy objectives was more stable than for some measure of bank reserves alone. Also, the relative underdevelopment of the money market in Italy and the desire to keep long-term rates low to encourage investment limited the ability and desire of the Bank of Italy to aim at control over interest rates as a principal monetary objective. Faced with difficult and complex economic and financial problems in the mid-1970s, the authorities were forced to expand the number of intermediate monetary targets and to adopt a variety of nontraditional monetary policy instruments in order to achieve final economic policy aims. Control over the monetary base, however, continued to be the principal intermediate monetary objective. Relatively little attention was given to control over the money supply.[1]

Selection of the monetary base as a target reflected the key role that control of the monetary base of the banks could play in regulating bank credit and hence, total domestic credit expansion. In fact, from 1974 onward, the authorities also experimented with setting specific monetary targets (ceilings) on total domestic credit expansion (Chapter 10).[2] This concept included bank credit (bank loans and portfolio investments), plus special credit institute loans, and bond issues. In addition, the authorities also sought to influence the composition of total credit on a sectoral basis.

Attempts to control the monetary base and the credit multiplier in order to influence bank credit expansion included changes in reserve requirements and manipulation of short-term interest rates (such as the treasury bill rate) and of long-term bond rates. In addition, there were periodic measures to affect monetary base on a one-time basis— for example, prior deposits. Use of direct controls in the form of the portfolio investment requirement and ceilings on bank loans were designed mainly to influence the composition of bank credit, rather than its volume. When ceilings on bank loans were in effect, however, the banks typically were near their limits. This indicated that the ceilings had an important rationing effect and also an effect on the growth of the demand deposit component of money supply.

Open-market operations and manipulation of the spreads among different short-term and long-term interest rates were also aimed at affecting the composition of credit. Thus, by the late 1970s, through variations in reserve requirements, bank loan ceilings, portfolio investment requirements, treasury bill rates, and the net foreign position of the banks, the monetary authorities had a variety of tools for affecting changes in all the principal forms of commercial bank credit.

In the market for longer-term credit, manipulation of interest rates, directly or through open-market operations, and the prior approval requirement for bond issues were designed to affect the supply of credit from the special credit institutes and the bond market.

The latest version of the monetary and financial sector of the econometric model of the Italian economy describes the evolution of monetary policies in the latter part of the 1970s.[3] Notwithstanding the many innovations in monetary policy, some aspects of the basic approach to monetary policy remained valid over the years: attention to the relationship between the monetary base and bank credit; recognition of the importance of the structure of time lags within which the process of multiplication of the monetary base occurs; and assignment of importance both to total bank credit expansion and (to a lesser extent) to its allocation.

The somewhat curious coexistence of measures aimed at influencing changes in the monetary base, at the same time that direct monetary controls were being used, was specifically commented on in the revised model. The conclusion was that the employment of numerous policy instruments did not constitute simply a different way of obtaining a single credit result, but actually helped to achieve an array of financial results that a single instrument by itself (that is, use of the traditional monetary tools) would not be able to achieve. It was recognized, however, that such a system has heavy costs. The disadvantages of continued use of direct controls were also expressed by the governor of the Bank of Italy at the annual meeting of the bank in 1977. He was concerned that the controls would reduce the efficiency of financial intermediaries in allocating resources because of the abrupt changes of course created by new regulations; would result in a forced redistribution of incomes due to shifts in the level and structure of interest rates; would provide reverse subsidized credit to the Treasury; if kept in place too long, would lead to fear that their elimination would amount to a leap into the unknown; would encourage the state to bring pressure to bear on the banks to invest in its securities, rather than making an effort to generate public savings; and would transfer additional credit risk to the banks because, in the context of unstable financial markets, households place more of their savings in liquid bank deposits.

MONETARY DEVELOPMENTS

Despite the resort to a wide array of both traditional and nontraditional monetary measures, average annual growth rates of all major monetary aggregates were very high in the 1970s: monetary base up 17 percent, total domestic credit up 18 percent, and money supply up 20 percent (Table 8.4).

Monetary Base

The monetary base is defined as the liquid claims on the rest of the world, the government, and the Bank of Italy by the Italian private sector, both banks and nonbanks. It includes currency and coin; demand deposits with the Treasury, Postal Savings Fund, and Bank of Italy; postal savings; treasury bills (only those held by the banks at times when bills were eligible to meet bank reserve requirements);

TABLE 8.4

Relative Growth of Monetary and Other Financial
Aggregates, 1970-78
(average annual percent increase)

Financial Aggregate	Percent
Monetary base	17.5
Total domestic credit	18.4
Bank lending	
Bank loans	17.8
Portfolio investments	26.1
Special credit institute loans	15.5
Net security issues	37.2
Money supply	
M-1	19.7
M-3	20.2

Source: Compiled by the author; calculated from
Bank of Italy annual reports and bulletins.

the banks' unutilized rediscount quotas; some required financing of
agriculture warehousing bills; and convertible currency not tied up as
a result of existing regulations concerning the net foreign position of
the banks.*

The sources of monetary base creation are broken down into

---

*The inclusion of postal savings held by the public on the "uses"
side of the accounts and as an item in the treasury accounts on the
"sources" side reflects the fact that treasury borrowing from postal
deposits (which are held with the Postal Savings Fund, a separate department of the Treasury) is one common way of financing the treasury
deficit. If the public were to shift its savings out of postal deposits,
this would create a demand for alternative financing for the Treasury,
especially from the central bank. Thus, inclusion of postal deposits
in monetary base facilitates analysis of the role of treasury financing
as a source of monetary base creation. Nonetheless, official statistical data sometimes show monetary base figures both including and
excluding postal deposits.

four parts: the foreign sector, the Treasury, central bank credit, and "other." The foreign sector's effect on monetary base is the result of changes in Italy's balance-of-payments position, including changes in the net foreign position of the commercial banks. The Treasury's effect on monetary base depends upon the extent to which the Treasury's cash deficit is financed through borrowing from postal savings, treasury bill issues to the commercial banks (only through 1975 while treasury bills were still usable as part of required reserves), the issuance of treasury coinage, variations in small demand deposits held with the Treasury by the public and the banks, and borrowing from the Bank of Italy/Exchange Office through the purchase of treasury bonds, treasury bills, open-account loans, or other means. Central bank creation of monetary base comes about as a result of Bank of Italy lending to the banks through various forms of discounts and advances, and briefly in 1975-76, Exchange Office refinancing of exports. The "Other" sector of the monetary base accounts includes special accounts to record the effects of monetary policy measures designed to reabsorb monetary base creation (for example, prior import deposits, prior exchange deposits, and deposits of the frozen counterpart of foreign compensatory borrowing) and some miscellaneous items involving nongovernment securities, deposits of the special credit institutes, and some other accounts of the Bank of Italy and Exchange Office. Although the distinction is to some extent arbitrary, for analytical purposes the sources of creation of monetary base are sometimes broken down between autonomous factors that affect changes in the monetary base of the commercial banks and policy intervention factors. (See Chapter 10 for an analysis of monetary base developments employing this distinction.)

Monetary base targets are published at least annually, with revisions of the target and of other financial flows updated every month or two. An annual target is published in the Ministry of Budget's program and forecast report submitted to Parliament at the end of September and a revised target is often published in the annual report of the Bank of Italy at the end of May or otherwise made public through speeches or parliamentary testimony. The lack of emphasis on targets for periods of less than 12 months is justified by the rather long time lags between changes in the monetary base and changes in bank credit—on the order of six quarters. The target is based on an estimation of the demand for credit, related to GDP forecasts in real and nominal terms, including the investment component. The amount of expansion of the monetary base required to meet bank credit demand is estimated and the level of bond issues to be authorized is determined. Subsequently, if the GDP forecast does not appear to be reaching the desired outcome, the authorities must decide what revision in the monetary base target is required or what change in the level of

TABLE 8.5

Growth of Monetary Base, 1970-78
(percent)

	Total	Excluding Postal Deposits and Adjusted*
1970	11.1	12.3
1971	17.3	14.3
1972	15.8	12.9
1973	19.3	18.4
1974	13.1	15.4
1975	19.4	21.0
1976	17.4	12.9
1977	19.2	18.6
1978	24.6	23.1
Average	17.5	16.5

*Corrected for changes in bank reserve requirements.

Note: 1960-69 average annual growth was 9.4 percent.

Source: Compiled by the author; data from Bank of Italy annual reports and bulletins.

long-term interest rates is needed to pull real demand back to the desired path.

The growth of the monetary base in the 1970s (1970-78) averaged 17.5 percent per year, compared to 9.4 percent in the 1960s (Table 8.5). There were particularly rapid rates of growth in 1973, 1975, and 1978. In 1973 the main cause was a sharp increase in the size of the treasury deficit and the fact that 91 percent of the financing of the deficit was through creation of monetary base. (In a year of economic recovery it was difficult for the Treasury to place its longer-term issues with the banks and the public.) The rapid increase in 1975 reflected a 73 percent rise in the treasury deficit, nearly half of which was financed by creation of monetary base. The less contractionary impact of the foreign sector was also a factor, as the balance of payments temporarily improved during that recession year. In addition, the release of prior import deposits accumulated in the previous year increased the monetary base. In 1978 there was a combination of very large financing of a much larger treasury cash deficit and a significantly expansionary foreign sector, as the balance of payments was in surplus on both current and capital account.

Based on Bank of Italy adjustments* to exclude the effect of changes in bank reserve requirements (and excluding changes in postal savings), the rate of monetary base increase in the period 1970-78 was 16.5 percent versus 17.5 percent for the unadjusted figures.[4]

By far the most important source of monetary base creation in the 1970s (1970-78) was the treasury cash deficit, which accounted for more than 94 percent of the cumulative total (Table 8.6). The foreign sector, as a result of a strong balance-of-payments position late in the period, contributed 13 percent of the total monetary base creation, credit to the banks from the central bank resulted in net extinction of monetary base by about 1 percent, and other (mainly monetary base absorption measures) led to a further destruction of monetary base by more than 6 percent. This pattern in the sources of monetary base creation was in rather sharp contrast to that of the 1960s, when the Treasury was a much less important source of monetary base creation and central bank credit to the banks much more important.

Although the major problem in managing changes in the monetary base concerned cyclical and trend growth, the monetary authorities also had to contend with some seasonality in the accounts. For example, the relative strength of the current account of the balance of payments in the third quarter of the year, due mainly to tourist receipts, created a foreseeable source of monetary base creation from the foreign sector. There was also a certain amount of seasonality in monetary base creation from the treasury cash deficit in the last quarter of the year, as expenditures accelerated at the end of the fiscal (and calendar) year. Central bank lending to the banks, too, showed a certain degree of predictability in the second quarter of the year, and

---

*The adjustment to the monetary base is designed to correct the statistical series for variations in the reserve coefficient due either to changes in the legal reserve ratio or to the voluntary behavior of the banks. The adjustment is necessary in order to be able to calculate intertemporal comparisons of the credit multiplier so as to evaluate monetary policy and especially bank behavior, and in order to be able to analyze the effects on the process of credit multiplication of changes in the "effective" reserve coefficient (that is, including changes in the banks' voluntary behavior).

TABLE 8.6

Sources of Cumulative Creation of Monetary Base, 1960s and 1970s

| | 1960-69 | | 1970-78 | |
	Trillions of Lire	Percent	Trillions of Lire	Percent
Foreign sector	1.1	10.8	7.5	13.3
Treasury deficit	6.8	65.8	53.3	94.4
Central bank credit	2.8	27.3	-0.5	-0.9
Other	-0.4	-3.9	-3.8	-6.7
Total	10.3	100.0	56.5	100.0

Source: Compiled by the author; data from Bank of Italy annual reports.

especially in the fourth, when end-of-year withdrawals for the holidays led the banks to resort to central bank credit, and in both quarters when the banks needed temporary liquidity, partly to offset the effects of tax payments by their clients.

Foreign Sector

For a four-year period in the middle of the decade Italy's balance of-payments deficits made a contribution to limiting the rate of expansion of monetary base. In 1973-76 the deficit on current account was a significant contractionary factor—in 1974 alone, over 5.8 trillion lire. Capital movements, however (including short-term commercial bank flows) also played a part in affecting the creation of monetary base. In 1972 and 1975 capital outflows contributed to a net extinction of monetary base through the foreign accounts. Capital inflows partially offset the contractionary effect of the current deficit in 1973 and 1974, completely offset the contractionary influence of the current account deficit in 1976, and added to the expansionary effect of current account surpluses in 1977 and 1978. (See Chapter 7 for a discussion of balance-of-payments developments during this period.)

Treasury

In only three of the 36 quarters in the period 1970-78 did the Treasury fail to create monetary base from financing its cash deficit.

(The constant growth of the treasury deficit is discussed at length in Chapter 4.) In fact, the most important problem in managing the monetary base during the entire period was the constant pressure on the Bank of Italy to provide financing of the deficit in the least inflationary way possible. The annual percentages of the total deficit financed by the creation of monetary base are shown in the table below. Financing

Year	Percent
1970	92
1971	55
1972	73
1973	91
1974	86
1975	47
1976	80
1977	-4
1978	29

the treasury deficit without creation of monetary base was, of course, easier during periods of relatively slack credit demand. At such times the commercial banks were able to invest surplus funds in treasury issues (and were interested in doing so), including some medium- and long-term issues, and the public found it attractive to invest some of its liquid savings in these instruments. This situation prevailed during the 1975 recession and again during the slow growth that took place in most of 1977-78. In contrast, during the economic recovery periods of 1972-74 and 1976 the Treasury was forced to resort more extensively to the creation of monetary base, mainly credit from the central bank.

The three quarters when treasury financing operations actually resulted in some destruction of monetary base were the second quarter of 1977 and the second and third quarters of 1978. This development reflected the success of the Bank of Italy in finding financing for the Treasury through large sales of treasury bills to the banks and the public (in the second quarter of 1977 and second quarter of 1978), and through large sales of medium- and long-term treasury bonds (in the second and third quarters of 1978). The success in placing new treasury issues with the public resulted in an actual extinction of monetary base by the Treasury's operations for 1977 as a whole (the only year of the 1960s and 1970s when this occurred). Despite a continued high level of sales of these issues to the public in 1978, however, the massive increase in the Treasury's cash deficit that year led to the second highest creation of monetary base by the Treasury in Italy's history. More than three-quarters of the monetary base increase occurred in the last quarter of 1978 when the treasury deficit grew very sharply and unexpectedly.

Central Bank Credit

Central bank credit to the commercial banks was not a very important factor behind the growth of monetary base over the entire period. In fact, cumulative credit in the nine years (1970-78) was negative by about 500 billion lire. Thus, the Bank of Italy's task with the banks was mainly to provide some credit in the short term to meet immediate liquidity needs, since ample liquidity was being provided them mainly through the treasury deficit.

Other Sources

Until 1972 the other sources of monetary base creation were of little importance. In fact, the important components of this account are really not so much sources of creation of monetary base as reabsorption of monetary base through policy interventions, followed by some re-creation of monetary base when deposits originally made to absorb monetary base are released. The main items in the account are prior import and prior exchange deposits and the frozen counterpart of compensatory borrowing abroad (see Chapter 10).

Uses of Monetary Base

The uses of monetary base by the public consist of changes in the holdings of currency and coin, postal savings, and small accounts with the Bank of Italy and the Treasury. Fluctuations in the public's monetary base are predictably seasonal, with increases typical in the second and fourth quarter, in connection with preparation for the summer and Christmas holidays. Variations in the currency and coin component are dependent on transactions demand for this part of the money supply, and demand for postal savings varies with the financial savings rate and the relative attractiveness of competing savings instruments. During the 1970s (1970-78) currency and coin typically represented about 6.5 percent of the annual increase in total financial savings of households, while postal savings represented about 8.5 percent. Although the proportion of postal savings declined somewhat, the decline was small. Also, the new competition for household financial savings in the form of treasury bills does not seem to have affected postal savings as much as investments in other fixed-interest securities. In any case, fluctuations in the monetary base holdings of the public tend to be fairly predictable, leaving fluctuations in the total monetary base to be reflected more strongly in the monetary base of the commercial banks.

The impact on bank credit of changes in the banks' monetary base (total reserves) depends on the level of bank liquidity (and net free reserve), relative interest rates on bank loans and on securities, and the prevailing array of monetary regulations. Bank of Italy data show adjusted bank credit multipliers in the range of 4 to 6 for the years 1970-78, as shown in the table below. The multiplier is calculated as bank credit (bank loans and portfolio investments) divided by bank reserves (that is, the banks' monetary base, including both required reserves and bank liquidity), and is adjusted for changes in bank reserve requirements.

Year	Multiplier
1970	4.8
1971	4.4
1972	4.7
1973	5.2
1974	5.5
1975	5.6
1976	5.7
1977	5.8
1978	5.7

At the beginning of the decade the banks had rather large net borrowed reserves (bank liquidity less debt to the central bank), reflecting the effects of strong credit demand during the earlier business cycle recovery phase that extended into 1970. In the subsequent two years, until the latter part of 1972, the banks accumulated net free reserves in the face of relative stagnation in economic growth and in credit demand. With the beginning of recovery late in 1972 net bank reserves turned negative and remained negative (except briefly in the third quarter of 1973) until the last quarter of 1976—that is, not only through the recovery phases of 1972-74 and 1975-76 but also in the 1974-75 recession year, although net borrowed reserves were significantly reduced during the latter period. The banks again had net free reserves in the latter half of 1977 and in 1978 (except for small net borrowed reserves in the third quarter of 1978). The sudden and massive increase in the Treasury's creation of monetary base at the end of 1978 boosted the banks' net free reserves in the last quarter of 1978 to unprecedented heights, but reserves turned negative through the first three quarters of 1979.

Total Domestic Credit

Total domestic credit (TDC) expansion grew at an average annual rate of 18.4 percent during the 1970s (1970-78). This concept includes

credit to the Treasury and credit to the rest of the economy from the
banks, the special credit institutes, and bond issues (by local governments, state holding companies, and private companies). It is used
principally to measure the competing demand for credit from the
government and the business sector. Credit to the business sector
grew particularly rapidly in 1973 and 1975-76. Rapid growth in credit
to the Treasury occurred in 1975 and 1978. (See Chapter 10 regarding
performance against TDC targets.) On a cumulative basis for the entire nine-year period credit to the Treasury accounted for 45 percent
of the total, with its annual rate varying in a range from 34 percent
in 1973 (a year of economic recovery and strong credit demand from
the business sector) to 58 percent in 1978 (a year of unprecedented
growth in the treasury deficit). At the end of 1978 outstanding credit
to the Treasury represented 41 percent of all domestic credit outstanding. To some extent, however, the "crowding out" effect of
treasury demands on credit was offset by rising government transfers
to the business sector, especially in the latter part of the decade.

Bank Loans and Investments

Italian banks increased their loans on average by 18 percent
per year and their portfolio investments by 26 percent per year in
1970-78 (Table 8.7). The relative rates of growth of the two types of
credit reflect a number of economic and regulatory factors, including
the demand for credit for working capital in relation to the prevailing
level of business activity, the relative attractiveness of interest rates
on bank loans versus securities, the existence (or not) of quantitative
credit controls on bank loans, the demand for long-term funds for
investment, and the existing regulation (if any) on the banks' portfolio
investments. The slower rate of growth of loans compared to portfolio
investments was also partly due to the consolidation of hospital and
local government debts to the commercial banks by the Treasury in
particularly large amounts in 1975, 1977, and 1978. In addition,
from January 1977 onward, the local governments were forbidden to
borrow from the commercial banks, which resulted in large net repayments on earlier loans in 1977 and 1978.

The commercial banks are restricted mainly to short-term
lending, which accounted, on average, for 81 percent of all bank loans
in the 1970s. The 19 percent of medium- and long-term loans were
those permitted under various exceptions to the general rule (discussed earlier). The vast majority (94 percent) of all bank loans were
denominated in lire. There were occasions, however, when foreign
currency loans were very important (54 percent of the total rise in
bank loans in 1977). Most lending was to domestic business, particularly private industry. At the end of 1978, 87 percent of all loans
were to domestic business, 68 percent of such business loans were

TABLE 8.7

Relative Growth of Bank Loans and Bank Portfolio
Investments, 1970-78
(percent)

	Bank Loans*	Portfolio Investments
1970	20.5	6.6
1971	15.5	28.3
1972	19.0	25.7
1973	21.7	35.0
1974	21.3	22.6
1975	16.7	26.3
1976	23.6	12.1
1977	11.1	50.6
1978	10.8	27.4
Average	17.8	26.1

*Based on Credit Risk Center data and not adjusted
for hospital and local government debt consolidation.
Source: Compiled by the author; data from Bank of
Italy bulletins.

to industry, and 83 percent of the loans were to private business.
Average annual rates of growth of bank loans were greater for domestic business (18.5 percent) than for the public administration (11.1
percent), and greater for public enterprise (19.5 percent) than for
private enterprise (18.1 percent). Within the public administration,
the average annual growth rate was 8.4 percent for loans to local
governments and 31.2 percent for loans to social insurance institutes.
Loans to households and nonprofit organizations grew at an annual
rate of 19.1 percent, loans to credit institutes at 27.6 percent, and
loans to nonresident business at 29.3 percent. The overall rate was
17.8 percent. The quarterly pattern of bank lending in the period
1970-78 mirrors business demand for operating capital during different phases of the business cycle. As would be expected, bank loans
grew rapidly in the 1972-74 recovery and the 1975-76 recovery.

The average annual rate of growth of lending to the public administration was very high (23 percent) in the period 1970-76. The

accumulation of debt in the case of local governments, hospitals, and health insurance institutes, however, eventually forced the Treasury to engage in large-scale debt consolidation and to limit further accumulation of bank debt in the case of local governments and hospitals. In fact, bank loans to the public administration declined by 27 percent and 30 percent in 1977 and 1978, respectively. Bank lending to households and nonprofit organizations grew at a somewhat higher than average rate, but was not very large in absolute terms. Lending to households consisted mainly of mortgage credit and to some extent discounting of consumer credit for large-ticket consumer durables, but the development of consumer credit in Italy has been slow.

Shifts in the portfolio holdings of the commercial banks in the 1970s consisted mainly of a sharp increase in holdings of treasury bills, a large decline in bonds of the state holding companies, and a fairly large increase in securities issued by the special credit institutes (Table 8.8). These changes reflected the growth of the treasury deficit and efforts to obtain financing of the deficit in ways that minimized the creation of monetary base. Changes in the composition of portfolio investments also depended on whether or not particular securities were eligible for inclusion in bank reserve requirements (before the 1975 reform) or eligible for inclusion in the banks' portfolio investment requirements (from 1973 on). The more favorable tax treatment of public debt issues (and to a lesser extent of special credit institute bonds), compared to that of business enterprise, was also a factor in portfolio investment choices. Finally, within these policy constraints, relative interest rates, credit risks, and sectoral demand affected the banks' portfolio investment decisions.

On average the banks increased their portfolio investments by 26 percent per year in 1970-78. Higher than average purchases were made in the case of treasury bills, bonds of the special credit institutes in the industrial field, and medium- and long-term government bonds. The smallest increase among the major categories of portfolio investments occurred in the case of bonds of the state holding companies (ENEL, IRI, ENI, and EFIM). Given the growing financial difficulties of public enterprise, this was not surprising.

Special Credit Institutes Lending

The special credit institutes operate in the medium- and long-term credit field, financed mainly by their own bond issues. Credit from the institutes is the chief source of external long-term business financing, so there is a close link between this financial variable and real investment. To some extent, however, the link is attenuated by the fact that the commercial banks also extend some long-term credit—for example, for housing—and that the institutes extend credit for some purposes not linked to investment, such as export credit and

TABLE 8.8

Commercial Banks' Portfolio of Fixed-Interest Securities in the 1970s
(percent of total)

| | Outstanding | | Average Annual Percent Change* |
	End-1969	End-1978	
Treasury bills	18.2	26.0	37.4
Government bonds	28.7	26.9	26.8
Special credit institute bonds	34.2	38.1	28.0
Industrial	(19.9)	(24.9)	(30.4)
Other	(14.3)	(13.2)	(25.0)
State holding company bonds	16.3	7.5	15.3
Other	2.6	1.5	21.7
Total	100.0	100.0	26.1

*1970-78.
Source: Compiled by the author; data from Bank of Italy bulletins.

agricultural operating credit. Also, loan procedures of the institutes require that disbursement of credit be made only after the investment being financed has been carried out. In the interim, short-term pre-financing by the commercial banks is common. The time lag between investment completion and disbursement extends up to nearly eight quarters, but is concentrated in the second to fifth quarters. Consequently, correlations between the institutes' credit operations and investment must be made with these time lags in mind. (There are published data on loan commitments by the institutes that provide a better measure of current policy regarding the relative "ease" of long-term credit.)

The rate of increase in lending (disbursements) by the institutes averaged almost 16 percent per year in 1970-78, as shown in the table below, but was less than the 18 percent growth of lending by the commercial banks. This reflected the relative stagnation of investment demand (Chapter 5). The overall rate of growth of lending to the domestic business sector was 16.3 percent; to the foreign sector (export credit), 13.1 percent; and to the Treasury for public works, 13.2 percent. The relatively high average growth rate for loans to

Year	Percent
1970	13.8
1971	20.8
1972	18.1
1973	27.1
1974	10.2
1975	19.1
1976	9.7
1977	10.2
1978	10.1

industry (17.1 percent) was a function of sporadically strong credit demand for long-term investment (for example, 1973). Although the rate of increase in direct loans for public works rose significantly (24.7 percent), this was offset by a slow growth of loans on treasury account for public works (13.2 percent), as the Treasury shifted toward financing public works of the central government, the state railways and state highways, by its own bond issues rather than through CREDIOP (Consorizo di Credito per le Opere Pubbliche). The slow growth of real estate credit (14 percent) was due to persistent stagnation in residential construction. The relatively low average rate of growth of credit to agriculture (12.3 percent) masked a significant increase in the later years of the decade. For example, in the period 1975-78 credit to agriculture increased at an annual average rate of 19 percent.

Data on new loan commitments for the period 1970-78 confirm the increased attention to agriculture. Whereas in the early years of the decade, 1970-75, commitments to agriculture represented only 8.5 percent of the total, in the last three years (1976-78) the share going to agriculture averaged 12.1 percent of the total. The relative growth of loan commitments to agriculture was at the expense of the housing sector, as the shares of industry (that is, industry and export credit) and services changed very little between the two periods.

New loan commitments broken down between loans with interest rate subsidies and those at market rates show some shift away from subsidization. for the entire nine-year period subsidized loans represented 43.4 percent of the total. This figure, however, is inflated by the high proportion of subsidized credits approved in 1970 and 1971 (75 percent and 65 percent, respectively). Excluding those two years, the average share of the total represented by subsidized credits is reduced to 36 percent. The largest beneficiaries of subsidized credit were industry and agriculture, with subsidies to housing and services relatively less important. In the period for which data are available (1973-78) 63.1 percent of subsidized loan commitments were in favor of industry (including export credits) and 20.4 percent for agriculture. Subsidized loans for housing and services were 7 percent and 9.5 percent, respectively. There was some shift in favor of agriculture and housing at the expense of industry in the latter part of the period.

Security Issues

Major developments in Italy's medium- and long-term securities markets (excluding treasury bills) during the 1970s were a continued deline in the relative importance of shares versus bonds; a large increase in the relative importance of bond issues by the public sector compared to share and bond issues by business enterprise; and a dramatic shift in the relative importance of security holdings by the public compared to holdings by financial intermediaries (see Table 8.3).

The decline in the importance of shares is not surprising in the light of the general weakness in business profits over the period. This also helps to account for the decline in total security holdings of the public since the public is more apt to hold equities than are financial institutions. The average yield on stocks in 1978 was 4.91 percent—a record high for the 1970s, when yields ranged from a minimum (annual average) of 2.50 percent in 1973 to the 1978 maximum. In comparison, the average yield on government issues in 1978 was 11.18 percent and on other bonds 13.51 percent.

The growth of bond issues by the public sector mirrors the rise in budget deficits and the consolidation by the Treasury of the debts of local governments, health institutes, and hospitals (Chapter 4). There was very little change during the period in the relative importance of bond issues by the special credit institutes as a whole, nor between those of the industry/public works institutes and the real estate/agricultural institutes. The relative decline in bond issues by business enterprise involved mainly state holding companies (other than ENEL) and private companies, although issues by private firms were never of much importance. (Private bond issues represented less than 1 percent of total security issues outstanding at the end of 1978.) Within the group of public enterprises with bond issues outstanding (ENEL, ENI, IRI, EFIM, and IRI/Autostrada), ENEL issues predominate, accounting for two-thirds of all the bond issues outstanding of this group at the end of 1978.

The shift toward more government bond issues brought with it a shift toward greater importance for financial intermediaries in the securities market, as the Bank of Italy was frequently forced to provide financing for the Treasury through purchase of treasury securities. Also, the commercial banks fell heir to treasury securities issued to consolidate bank loans to local governments and health institutes. (In addition to increased holdings of these long-term government securities, the banks acquired large amounts of treasury bills as a result of the growth of open-market operations in the bills.) Manipulation of the banks' portfolio investment requirement also contributed to the growth of bond holdings by financial intermediaries. The principal beneficiaries of the portfolio investment requirement were bonds issued by the special credit institutes to finance agriculture, industry, and housing credit.

Although individuals more than doubled their holdings of securities between the end of 1969 and the end of 1978, their share of total securities outstanding sharply declined. Nonresidents' holdings of Italian securities rose slightly in absolute terms from 2.1 trillion lire at the end of 1969 ($3.3 billion) to 3.6 trillion lire at the end of 1978 ($4.3 billion), but their share of total issues outstanding fell from 5.9 percent to 2.3 percent. Securities holdings by companies, too, declined as a share of the total from 13 percent to 8 percent, reflecting mainly the declining importance of stock issues held in intracompany and intercompany accounts.

During the 1970s (1970-78) almost half (45 percent) of net annual medium- and long-term security issues were treasury or treasury account issues (excluding treasury bills), and almost half (44 percent)

TABLE 8.9

Net Security Issues, 1970-78
(average percent of total)

By Type of Security:	100.0
Bonds	84.8
Stocks	15.2
By Issuer:	100.0
Public Sector:	48.2
Treasury/Treasury Account*	45.0
Other	3.2
Special Credit Institutes:	43.9
Industry/Public Works	30.3
Real Estate/Agriculture	13.6
Business Enterprise:	7.9
ENEL	7.7
Private	-0.5
Other	0.7

*Excludes Treasury bills.
Source: Compiled by the author; data from Bank of Italy annual reports.

TABLE 8.10

Purchasers of Stocks and Bonds, 1970-78
(average percent of total nominal value)

	Stocks	Bonds*
The public		
Individuals	19.5	12.4
Companies	62.0	0.1
Nonresidents	14.8	0.1
Subtotal	96.3	12.6
Financial intermediaries		
Bank of Italy	0.5	27.6
Commercial banks	0.4	57.9
Other	2.8	1.9
Subtotal	3.7	87.4
Total	100.0	100.0

*Excludes treasury bills.
Source: Compiled by the author; data from Bank of
Italy annual reports.

were issues of the special credit institutes (Table 8.9). Of the remainder, ENEL issues were by far the most important item.

The basic pattern of security purchases in the period consisted
of: purchases of stock by companies and to a lesser extent individuals,
and commercial bank and central bank purchases of bonds (Table 8.10).
Companies purchased more than 60 percent of all stock issues, compared to 20 percent for individuals. Commercial banks purchased
nearly 60 percent of all bond issues, compared to less than 30 percent
for the Bank of Italy and about 12 percent for individuals.

Growth in the purchase of bonds by the Bank of Italy was attributable mainly to purchase of treasury bonds. The commercial banks'
purchases were concentrated in bonds of the special credit institutes,
involuntary acquisition of consolidated local government debt issued
by the Treasury's Postal Savings Fund, and voluntary purchases of
new (in 1977) variable-interest, two-year treasury certificates.

The poor performance of Italy's stock market can be seen in the change in the market value of outstanding shares. At the end of 1969 the market value was actually higher than at the end of 1978 (20.0 trillion lire versus 18.9 trillion lire). Also, the relative underdevelopment of the market can be seen in the extent to which it was dominated by unlisted securities. Whereas during the previous decade (1961-69) listed shares were, on average, 47 percent of total shares outstanding (based on average market values), the average for the 1970s (1970-78) was only 32 percent. The ratio of listed securities to the total declined without interruption from 1970 to 1977, but recovered somewhat in 1978 as a result of large listed share issues by public enterprises (especially IRI subsidiaries). Since there was little public interest in these securities, they were placed mainly with parent companies. (In Italy public enterprise is not necessarily entirely owned by the government; shares of some public enterprises are listed and traded on the stock exchange.)

Similarly, data on gross issues of listed and unlisted shares show that, on average, listed shares accounted for only 20 percent of gross new issues, compared to 80 percent for unlisted shares. Two-thirds of gross issues were sold by private enterprise, against one-third by public enterprise. The growth of share issues by public enterprise in the latter part of the decade to some extent explains the growth of unlisted shares, since share issues by public enterprise are less likely to be listed than are those of private companies. (1978 was exceptional.) For outstanding stocks (average market value), listed shares comprised 32.2 percent of the total and unlisted shares 67.8 percent. Individuals held 25.5 percent of the total, companies 49.4 percent, nonresidents 19.7 percent, the banking system 3.1 percent, and other intermediaries 2.3 percent.

Sectoral Financial Operations

The chief characteristics of external financing of industry in the 1970s were heavy dependence on bank lending (mainly short-term operating credit) and on loans from the special credit institutes for long-term investments (Table 8.11). Bond issues were relatively unimportant because of the "crowding out" effect of public sector issues, tax discrimination in favor of government issues, and the effects of the portfolio investment requirements levied on the banks. Share issues were more important, involving mainly intracompany or intercompany financial operations, although individual purchases were considerable. Capital endowment fund contributions from the Treasury to the state holding companies were of significance for the public enterprise sector, particularly in 1976-78. Other (minor) sources of financing consisted of foreign borrowing and receipts of indemnity payments

TABLE 8.11

External Sources of Financing of Industry, 1970–78
(average percent of total)

	Public Enterprise	Private Enterprise	Total
Bank loans	31.1	58.6	48.3
Special credit institute loans	19.5	23.4	22.3
Bond issues	14.3	0.1	5.5
Stock issues	11.9	15.7	14.5
Capital endowment contributions	17.9	—	6.0
Other	5.3	2.2	3.4
Total	100.0	100.0	100.0

Note: For 1970–72, percentages were calculated for the manufacturing sector only.
Source: Compiled by the author; data from Bank of Italy annual
reports.

from the government for former electricity company holdings, which
had been nationalized in 1962.

In the late 1970s the shift in the relative dependence of public
enterprise away from financing from the special credit institutes and
toward capital endowment contributions from the Treasury was a
reflection of the greater weakening of the financial position of public
enterprise than of private companies (Chapter 5). This made it necessary for the government to come to the rescue with larger injections
of new equity capital. The major change in the sources of industrial
financing for private enterprise took the form of a decline in the relative importance of stock issues, with the difference made up mainly
by greater resort to bank loans.

In the housing sector, nearly two-thirds of total financing came
from internal (mainly household) savings, with the special credit institutes in the real estate field providing the second most important
source of financing (Table 8.12). There was considerable stability in
the relative importance of internal savings, while public funding grew
in importance in the later years, in contrast with a slight decline in
the relative importance of mortgage credit from the special credit
institutes.

TABLE 8.12

Sources of Financing for Housing, 1972-78

Source	Average Percent of Total
Internal savings	64.1
Public funds	5.3
Bank loans	12.8
Special credit institute loans	16.3
Bond issues	1.4
Insurance companies	0.1
Total	100.0

Source: Compiled by the author; data from Bank of Italy annual reports.

Data for 1970-78 on the annual allocation of household financial savings among different savings instruments confirms the growing importance of financial intermediaries. Thus, direct credit to the business and government sectors of the economy by the household sector, in the form of purchases of stocks and bonds issued by business and the purchase of treasury bills or accumulation of postal deposits, were relatively unimportant, accounting for only 1, 8, 3, and 9 percent, respectively, of the growth of total household financial savings (Table 8.13). The remainder of household financial savings (excluding currency and coin) required the intermediation of financial institutions, most notably the commercial banks. In fact, nearly 60 percent of the average annual increase in household financial savings took the form of increased bank deposits—demonstrating a strong preference for liquidity. The public's demand for liquid bank deposits reflects the fact that interest rates on these deposits vary to accommodate changes in households' financial asset portfolios, so that there is little need for households to seek out higher returns on other forms of financial assets or to shift into real estate investment. Also, the asset choice of households is to some extent limited by government actions—such as the adverse effect on real estate investment of earlier rent controls and the 1978 fair-rent law—and foreign exchange controls on foreign investments. Finally, rapid inflation has reduced the willingness of households to invest in long-term financial assets.

Over the course of the nine-year period there was considerable
stability in the allocations of new financial savings to currency and
coin, postal deposits, miscellaneous deposits and certificates, stock
purchases, and insurance reserves. In contrast, investments in
foreign financial assets, which had averaged 10 percent of new savings
in the first three years of the decade, virtually disappeared in subsequent years. Investments in fixed interest securities (excluding treasury bills) varied quite widely, growing rather rapidly in years of slow
economic activity (1971, 1972, and 1975) and by very little (or there
was actual disinvestment) in years of faster growth (for example,
1970, 1974, and 1976). In the latter years, families preferred to
build up liquid assets in the form of bank deposits to finance rising
consumption and rising prices. Household investments in treasury
bills was a relatively late-arriving phenomenon, being of importance
mainly in the three years 1976-78. In the first two of these years the
growth of investment in treasury bills was, in part, at the expense of
other fixed-interest security purchases. However, in 1978 the combined total of these two forms of savings set a record.

TABLE 8.13

Allocation of Household Financial Savings,
1970-78
(average annual increase)

Form of Savings	Percent
Currency/coin	6.6
Bank deposits	58.7
Postal deposits	8.6
Treasury bills	3.0
Other deposits/certificates*	2.7
Bonds	8.0
Stocks	1.4
Insurance reserves	6.7
Foreign assets	4.3
Total	100.0

*Includes treasury bills through 1972.
Source: Compiled by the author; data
from Bank of Italy annual reports.

TABLE 8.14

Money Supply and Income Velocity of Money, 1970-78

	Money Supply (percent annual change)		Income Velocity (nominal GDP ÷ money supply)	
Year	M-1	M-3	M-1	M-3
1970	27.2	13.6	2.02	1.20
1971	18.8	17.1	1.85	1.11
1972	17.5	18.3	1.73	1.03
1973	24.1	23.2	1.67	1.00
1974	10.4	15.5	1.86	1.07
1975	12.2	23.5	1.88	0.98
1976	19.7	22.8	1.96	1.00
1977	21.6	23.8	1.95	0.98
1978	26.1	24.0	1.80	0.92
Average	19.7	20.2	1.86	1.03

Sources: Compiled by the author; calculated from Bank of Italy bulletins (data adjusted for revision in net foreign position of commercial banks) and ISTAT, Conti Economic Nazionali 1960-78 (Nuova serie), Rome, 1979.

Money Supply

The money supply in the hands of the public as measured by M-1 rose on average by 19.7 percent, and as measured by M-3 at 20.2 percent per year over the nine-year period 1970-78 (Table 8.14). M-1 consists of currency and coin, bank current deposits in lire and foreign exchange, deposits with the Bank of Italy, current account postal deposits, and deposits with the Treasury. M-3 consists of M-1 plus bank savings deposits, postal certificates, and treasury bills. (M-2 is the same as M-3, less treasury bills.)

Annual rates of growth were high throughout the period for both M-1 and M-3. M-1, however, because it measures the more liquid forms of monetary assets, reflected cyclical changes in the transactions demand for money more than did M-3—for example, in 1973, 1975, and 1976 (Figure 8.1).

The income velocity of money as measured by M-1 declined in the 1970s compared to the 1960s. (Or, conversely, the demand for

FIGURE 8.1

Changes in Money Supply (M-1), 1970-79
(percent change over end of previous quarter, seasonally adjusted)

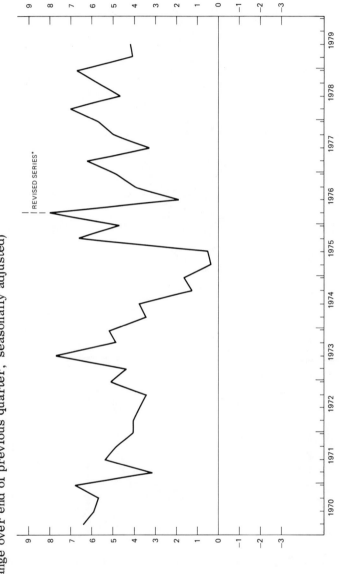

*Minor revision due to change in recording of net foreign position of banks.
<u>Source:</u> Constructed by the author; data from Bank of Italy Research Office.

FIGURE 8.2

Changes in Money Supply (M-3), 1970-79
(percent change over end of previous quarter, seasonally adjusted)

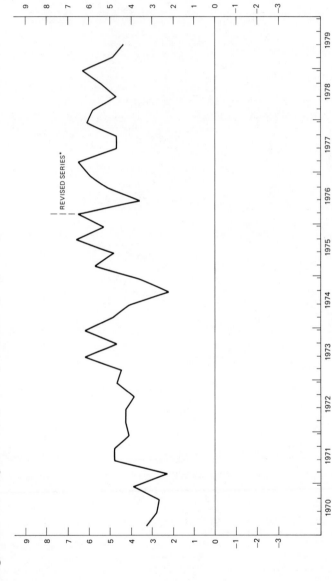

*Minor revision due to change in recording of net foreign position of banks.
Source: Constructed by the author; data from Bank of Italy Research Office.

256

money tended to rise.) M-1 velocity, which had averaged 2.72 in the 1960s fell to an average of 1.86 in the 1970s. There was some indication, however, that the ratio was stabilizing during the 1970s. There was a somewhat similar decline in the income velocity of money as measured by M-3 between the 1960s and the 1970s (1.36 versus 1.03). Except for a temporary increase in 1974, this measure of velocity tended to decline generally throughout the 1970s. At the beginning of the decade (1970) M-3 velocity stood at 1.20; in 1978 it had fallen to 0.92.

To some extent the downward trend in velocity was interrupted in years of fast economic growth, when households increased the turnover of their liquid assets. This is discernible in the figures for 1974 and 1976. Although it is not yet clear whether the long-term declining trend in velocity has begun to level out, there is some indication that this is so. In the past, declining velocity meant that a relatively fast rate of growth of the money supply resulted in a less than proportionate increase in prices. This provided some offset to rapid monetary growth.

The declining trend in velocity (or the rising demand for money) is a peculiar phenomenon in Italy.[5] Not only is the demand for money generally higher than in other major countries but the trend is also unusual. The fact that demand deposits bear interest has sometimes been cited as an explanation for high money demand, but payment of interest has been common for many years. Perhaps the chief explanatory factors are the shift in the distribution of income toward wages and salaries in the household sector, a rising personal savings rate, the strong liquidity preference of households, the rise in nominal interest rates paid on bank deposits between 1973 and 1978, and a relative lack of choice of investment instruments. A redistribution of income in favor of wages over profits is likely to result in the need for financial intermediation in an inflationary environment in which the household sector has a high liquidity preference. In fact, during the 1970s liquid deposits as a share of household financial savings tended to become more important and less liquid assets less so (for example, stocks, insurance reserves, and foreign assets). This was a natural reaction of considerable instability in the securities and foreign exchange markets. Finally, investors' choice was limited by exchange controls on investments abroad, the lack of a developed mutual-fund industry, and the undeveloped market for listed shares. From 1977 onward treasury bills (included in M-3 but not M-1), and variable-interest treasury certificates did increase the choice for savers.

Rates of growth of two measures of money (M-1 and (M-3) generally followed the same pattern over the 1970s, with some differences in timing and with changes in M-1 somewhat more volatile than M-3 (Figures 8.1 and 8.2). (Rates of growth are measured here as the change in three-month periods ending in March, June, September, and

December over the preceding three-month period, seasonally adjusted.)
There was a general acceleration in money growth (M-1 and M-3) from
late 1972 to late 1973—that is, in the period at the beginning of the economic recovery from the previous two years of stagnation. In the case
of M-1, monetary growth declined sharply during the later phase of
the cycle to a trough during the 1975 recession. The deceleration in
the rate of monetary expansion was less striking and less prolonged
in the case of M-3, which generally grew at a declining rate beginning
only in the fourth quarter of 1973 and extending to the third quarter of
1974. The discrepancy between rates of growth suggests that continued
growth of nominal income of the household sector was being allocated
to savings deposits rather than demand deposits, with the reduced need
for money for transactions purposes during the 1974-75 recession.

There was a renewal of monetary expansion in the early phase
of the second recovery period through early 1976, followed by a brief
period of deceleration in the middle of 1976. In 1977 and 1978 monetary
expansion under both measurements rose to, and stabilized at about
the level of, previous peak rates (roughly 5.5 percent per quarter). In
fact the long-term trend of money growth, especially for M-3, seemed
to stabilize at about 5.5 percent per quarter for the six-year period
1973-78. Only during the 1974-75 recession was there a serious interruption (Figure 8.2). The persistence of such a high rate of growth of
money supply in 1977-78, two years of relatively low real growth and
relatively moderate cost-push pressures, appeared to be a significant
factor behind the continued high rate of inflation in that period.

The financing counterpart to monetary creation has been discussed
earlier in connection with the expansion of various forms of credit from
the banks, special credit institutes, and security markets. During the
period 1970-78, about 87 percent of the increase in total financial
assets held by the public took the form of monetary assets included
under the broadest definition (M-3), while 13 percent of the average
annual increase was invested in other forms of financial assets (other
deposits and certificates, bonds, shares, foreign assets). Sixty-nine
percent of the counterpart in financing provided to borrowers consisted
of lending to domestic business (and households) and 38 percent in
lending to the Treasury, while other forms of credit declined. Financing
of the economy (business and households) was concentrated in short-
term operating credit by the commercial banks, medium-term loans
by the special credit institutes, and medium- and long-term bond issues
subscribed to by the banking system.

Interest Rates

Interest rate movements in the 1970s were a function of demand
for credit from business for operating capital and investment, and from

the Treasury for financing the cash deficit; the domestic supply of
credit available (under prevailing monetary regulations) from the
banks, the special credit institutes, the securities markets, and the
household sector; interest rate movements and liquidity conditions in
foreign credit markets; regulation of interest rates by the monetary
authorities and the bank cartel; subsidization of some interest rates;
and expectations concerning the "inflation premium" needed to provide
some real return on capital.

The relatively stable interest rates of the 1960s made possible
by such monetary practices as the frequent pegging of long-term bond
rates, the sale of treasury bills "on tap," and the more stable economic environment in terms of growth and inflation could not continue
in the 1970s. The growing links of Italian financial markets with international markets also made it more difficult to insulate the economy
from changes in monetary conditions abroad. On the other hand, the
Italian monetary authorities were able to take advantage of large international financial markets as a vehicle for exercising control over
domestic liquidity and the balance-of-payments position, notably
through control over the payment terms for trade credit and the banks'
net foreign position, and through compensatory Euromarket borrowing
(Chapters 7 and 11).

The most important interest rates for business borrowers were
the bank lending rate on short-term credit, interest rates charged by
the special credit institutes on medium- and long-term borrowing,
and to a lesser extent, long-term yields on bond issues (especially
for public enterprise, which had more ready access to the bond market
than did private enterprise because of preferential tax treatment available until the end of 1975). The principal interest rates on sources of
funds for the lending institutions were the rates paid on ordinary bank
deposits and the rates paid on bond issues by the special credit institutes. Also important was the short-term rate paid on interbank deposits, which was the most accurate (and volatile) measure of day-to-
day money market conditions. (The treasury bill rate became important
late in the decade.) Finally, short-term Euromarket interest rates
had an important effect on trade credit and on short-term bank capital
flows (within the limits allowed by exchange control regulations). In
some periods Euromarket rates on term loans were significant. For
households and the Treasury, postal savings rates and state bond
issue rates were important.

Some interest rates were set administratively. Both the prime
bank lending rate and maximum bank deposit rates were usually set
by the bank cartel (either formally or informally), while there were
periodic variations in the subsidized interest rate granted by the
special credit institutes and the interest rate paid on postal savings
in line with a "reference rate." Beginning in 1977 the reference rate,

on the basis of which subsidized lending rates are determined under the law, was automatically set every two months on the basis of the cost of borrowing.

Although the bank cartel (headed by the larger banks under the aegis of the Italian Banking Association) attempted to set a minimum prime rate for bank loans and a range of maximum bank deposit rates (depending on the size and maturity of the deposit), competitive conditions often led to divergencies from the recommended rates. Also, there were frequent occasions when strong pressure was exerted on the banks by the public and the Bank of Italy and Treasury to modify cartel rates.

Interest rate movements also reflected the strength of domestic credit demand and the status of the balance of payments. There were some periods when high interest rates generally suited both domestic growth and balance-of-payments considerations, as in the high growth, high inflation, and large balance-of-payments deficit years 1973, 1974, and 1976. Similarly, relatively lower interest rates in 1977 and 1978 were appropriate to periods of slow growth and strong balance of payments, although the still high rate of inflation and the existence of accumulated foreign debt were limiting factors. Something of a dilemma occurred in the early years of the decade 1970-72 and in the recession year 1975, since there were grounds for keeping interest rates low to escape from a long period of stagnation in the first case, and from the deep recession of 1975 in the second. In the first three years of the decade the balance of payments on current account was quite strong, but there was a persistent problem of capital flight that inhibited a move to lower rates. In 1975, although the balance of payments improved sharply with the recession, there was still a deficit on current account and in the overall balance and there were expectations that any recovery would re-create balance-of-payments problems (as it did).

Interest rate movements reflected the combined effects of demand for credit and monetary policy measures aimed at controlling its supply (Chapter 10). The pattern of interest rate movements during the 1970-78 period can be broken down into six periods: a general decline in rates from mid-1970 to mid-1973 during a period of economic stagnation and monetary ease; an extremely sharp rise in rates from about mid-1973 to the end of 1974, during a period of fairly rapid real growth an extremely rapid rise in inflation triggered by commodity and oil price increases, an enormous balance-of-payments deficit, and tighter monetary policy; a sharp drop in rates from late 1974 (or early 1975) until late 1975 as Italy experienced negative real growth and a deceleration of inflation; another sharp rise in rates from late 1975 to about mid-1977 in connection with recovery from the recession, a continued balance-of-payments deficit, a renewed increase in inflation following the sharp depreciation of the lira, and resort to a number of restrictive monetary measures; a significant downturn in rates from mid-1977 to late 1978 coincident with slow real growth, lower rates of inflation, and a much strengthened balance of payments; and a new upturn in rates from about the third quarter of 1978 through 1979, as real economic activity picked up again, world and domestic prices began to rise more rapidly, and the monetary authorities adopted a more restrictive policy stance.

During most of the nine-year period short-term interest rates exceeded long-term rates and average real interest rates paid by business were negative. Only in 1970 and for three quarters (from the last quarter of 1972 through the second quarter of 1973) did long-term rates (private bond yields) exceed short-term rates (average bank lending rate). Despite the unprecedented rise in nominal interest rates (peak average bank lending rate of 19.32 percent for the second quarter of 1977), real rates were generally negative. For example, deflating the weighted average annual interest rate paid by business (Confindustria calculation) by the deflator for value added in industry, only in 1971-72 and in 1978 were the interest rates paid by business positive (Table 8.15). In 1974 and 1975, during the height of inflation, real rates averaged a negative 9 and 8 percent, respectively.

The commercial banks' lending rates reflected the cost of various types of deposit liabilities: domestic deposits (which were bid for competitively despite cartel "maximums"), interbank rates, and foreign rates (Eurodollar short-term rates in London). Bank lending rates moved parallel with interbank borrowing rates, which tended to respond very promptly to changes in credit conditions. Lending rates also reflected changes in Eurodollar rates quite closely (but with a slight lag) from the beginning of 1970 to about the end of 1975. Subsequently Italian bank lending rates and Eurodollar rate movements diverged sharply. Exchange rate movements and public expectations explained much of this discrepancy, as Italian monetary authorities pushed up interest rates to protect the balance-of-payments position, lenders demanded a higher "inflation premium," and Italian rates had to be kept high to offset the forward discount of the lira. With the dramatic improvement in Italy's balance of payments in 1977 and 1978 and some improvement in the inflationary situation, it was possible for Italian rates to come down from their previous high levels, despite the concurrent rise in short-term Eurodollar rates. By 1979 Italian and Eurodollar rates were again moving in the same general direction.

Long-term interest rates charged on special credit institute loans (both subsidized and ordinary) mainly reflected the cost of bond issues by the institutes. Prior approval of new bond issues and the fixing of minimum coupon rates on securities eligible for meeting the commercial banks' portfolio investment requirements were tools used to influence the cost of money to the special credit institutes. Long-term rates on loans by the institutes also generally followed the direction of movement of short-term commercial bank lending rates, but were insulated from the extreme rise in short-term rates in 1974, 1976, and 1979. Nonetheless, long-term rate movements were still quite sharp by previous Italian standards; for example, the average nonsubsidized rate for loans by the industrial special credit institutes rose from 8.71 percent in 1973 to 12.00 percent in 1974 (Table 8.15). These long-term rates also followed short-term rates upward during the 1976 rise in rates, averaging 15.70 percent for that year.

Since the special credit institutes depend principally on obtaining funds from bond issues in the market, they could not expect to be completely protected from the impact of short-term rate increases, even though the portfolio investment requirement levied on the commercial banks helped to limit that impact. Even the subsidized rates charged by the special credit institutes underwent some change, with the average subsidized rate rising each year from 1972 through 1977, but falling back in 1978. Nonetheless, the rise in subsidized rates did not keep up with the rise in market rates and the degree of subsidy "spread" rose in each year from 1974 through 1978. The cost of

TABLE 8.15

Real Interest Rate Paid by Business, 1970-78
(percent)

	Weighted Average Interest Rate Paid by Business	Rate of Inflation (Deflator for Value Added in Industry)	Real Interest Rate
1970	8.77	8.93	-0.16
1971	8.53	6.70	1.83
1972	7.61	4.78	2.83
1973	7.81	11.18	-3.37
1974	12.33	21.64	-9.31
1975	13.01	21.30	-8.29
1976	15.16	16.79	-1.63
1977	16.45	18.63	-2.18
1978	14.62	12.79	1.83

Source: Compiled by the author; weighted average rate data from Confindustria, Secondo Rapporto CSC sull' Industria Italiana Vol. I (Rome: 1979): 22.

TABLE 8.16

Interest Rates Charged on Industrial Loans
by Special Credit Institutes, 1970–78

Year	Ordinary Rate	Subsidized Rate	Spread
1970	9.78	4.68	5.10
1971	9.78	4.61	5.17
1972	8.98	4.56	4.42
1973	8.71	4.60	4.11
1974	12.00	5.29	6.71
1975	12.00	6.48	5.52
1976	14.45	6.58	7.87
1977	15.70	7.83	7.87
1978	15.45	7.23	8.22

Source: Compiled by the author, data from Confindustria, Secondo Rapporto CSC sull' Industria Italiana Vol. I (Rome: 1979): 22.

interest rate subsidies rose accordingly, both on credits to industry (28 percent annual average increase) and for all sectors (also 28 percent), with the absolute cost rising from 311 billion lire ($0.5 billion) in 1970 to 1.8 trillion lire ($2.1 billion) in 1978.

CONCLUSIONS

During the 1970s Italy's financial institutions themselves did not change greatly, although the pattern of financial flows among them did. To a considerable extent the redirection of financial flows was a response to the imposition of nontraditional monetary tools employed in an effort to exert better control over the rapid expansion of monetary aggregates. (See Chapter 10 for a discussion of the use of monetary policy for countercyclical purposes.)

The principal Italian financial institutions in the 1970s comprised a system of commercial banks specializing in short-term lending, especially to the private business sector. Many of them had access to nationwide or regional systems of branches and were active in international markets. Medium- and long-term lending were the preserve of the special credit institutes, which lent mainly to private and public enterprise. In a period of slow growth of long-term investment these institutions grew somewhat less rapidly than did the commercial banks. The Italian securities market was a large and rapidly growing one, strongly dominated by fixed-interest securities issued by public bodies and by the special credit institutes as borrowers, and by the commercial banks and the central bank as lenders.

There were few encouraging signs of structural change in Italian financial institutions. The rapid growth of the commercial banks was in part a reflection of the financial weakness of business, which was heavily dependent on external sources of finance, particularly short-term credit. The increasing concentration of savings in a household sector, which insisted upon a high degree of liquidity in its financial savings, imposed a growing burden of intermediation on the banking system. The special credit institutes continued to play a useful intermediating role in supplying long-term credit for business investment, including the extension of subsidized credit to some favored sectors. The cost of interest rate subsidies, however, grew considerably with the sharp increase in nominal interest rates. The securities market became more and more dominated by bonds rather than stocks, by the public sector rather than business enterprise (either private or public), and by dependence on the banking system rather than on the public to purchase its issues. Foreigners retreated from the market. The stock market suffered from low current yields and capital losses. A growing share of new issues were for intracompany and intercompany accounts and the great majority of new share issues were unlisted, in a market where the number of listed shares was already very small. Alternative financial institutions such as mutual funds were slow to develop in this environment.

The monetary authorities made some effort to improve the quality of the traditional monetary tools available for monetary management. The system of reserve requirements was revised in early 1975 to make changes in reserve ratios simpler and more readily usable. Subsequently this tool was, in fact, used only occasionally. After practically no use of variations in the discount rate in the 1960s, the central bank changed the rate rather often in the 1970s. Efforts to expand the use of open-market operations centered on adoption of a system of auctioning of treasury bills, with different maturities open for sale to an expanded group of purchasers, including the public. This was coupled with a more active central bank role in the secondary market both for treasury bills and for longer-term government issues. Use of regulations to control the net foreign position of the banks, already in the 1960s considered a traditional monetary tool for Italy, continued to be a means of affecting domestic liquidity, but was used mainly for dealing with balance-of-payments financing problems, particularly after Italy had virtually exhausted its credit in the Euro-bond market in 1974.

Faced with serious inflation and balance-of-payments problems, the authorities adopted a number of nontraditional measures to deal with immediate problems. Thus, in an effort to gain better control over bank credit expansion, quantitative controls over the growth of bank loans were introduced; a portfolio investment requirement was imposed on the commercial banks to help deal with the problem of intermediating household savings; and a variety of exchange controls were employed. The latter included prior import deposits, prior exchange deposits, obligatory foreign financing of Italian export credits, manipulation of the terms of payment for imports and exports, imposition of a non-interest-bearing deposit for most outward capital flows and the freezing of the lira counterpart of compensatory borrowing in the Euromarkets. The need to resort to an increasing array of direct controls, however, was viewed by the monetary authorities as a very mixed blessing, reducing the efficiency of financial institutions.

The authorities continued to give priority attention to control over the monetary base, but additional targets were set for total domestic credit expansion, bank loan growth, and credit from the central bank to the Treasury (see Chapter 10). More attention was paid to interest rates. Interest rate stability, which had been an important goal in the 1960s to encourage investment, became impossible to achieve in the context of rapid inflation, periodic balance-of-payments difficulties, and the need to provide savers with some incentive to save in such an unstable environment. Notwithstanding the innovative use of such a variety of monetary tools, the expansion of the money aggregates (monetary base, total domestic credit, bank credit, and money supply) was extremely large.

By far the most important source of monetary base creation was the growing treasury cash deficit. This constant source of expansion was periodically supplemented, or partly offset, by balance-of-payments developments, with the foreign sector providing some contractionary impulse in the mid-1970s and some expansionary stimulus later in the decade. Central bank credit to the banks was minimal, other than to meet short-term liquidity needs. The relative importance of bank loans declined in comparison with the banks' portfolio investments. Bank loans to business grew faster than loans to the public sector, but this partly reflected a prohibition on local governments' borrowing from commercial banks after they had fallen deeply in debt to the banks. The growth of long-term credit to business by the special credit institutes was relatively low because of the stagnation in real investment. Securities markets were inundated by treasury securities issued to finance the budget deficit. The rapid expansion of the banks' monetary base led to high rates of increase in bank lending and in the money supply, which was only partly offset by a decline in the income velocity of money.

Interest rates were allowed to rise sharply in the face of rising rates of inflation and in an effort to protect the official reserve position. Real rates were still generally negative, however, except early in the decade and in 1978. Unfortunately, the business sector did not respond to this incentive because of other impediments to investment.

NOTES

1. See Giacomo Vaciago, "Monetary Policy in Italy: The Limited Role of Monetarism," Banca Nazionale del Lavoro Quarterly Review No. 123 (December 1977): 333-48.

2. See Warren D. McClam, "Targets and Techniques of Monetary Policy in Western Europe," Banca Nazionale del Lavoro Quarterly Review No. 124 (March 1978): 3-27; see also English language abridged version of the Bank of Italy's annual report for the year 1978, Rome, 1979, pp. 158-59.

3. Bank of Italy, "Modello Econometrico dell' Economia Italiana," II Edizione M2 BI, Settore Monetario e Finanziario (Rome: 1979).

4. Bank of Italy, Bollettino, "La base monetaria aggiustata" (April-September 1978): 243-61.

5. See OECD, Demand for Money in Major OECD Countries, Economic Outlook Occasional Studies (Paris: OECD, 1979).

II
THE USE OF
ECONOMIC POLICIES

9

FISCAL POLICY

If, in conditions of full or near full employment, people
demand more services from the Government, the regional
and local authorities and the autonomous Government
agencies while refusing to bear the cost by paying higher
taxes, then they are asking the economy to provide more
resources than it can offer. The shortfall in resources is
met from abroad, by importing more goods and services
than are exported. This behavior can be likened to that of
a country which, instead of taxing its own citizens, thinks
it can tax the citizens of neighboring countries.

Guido Carli
Governor, Bank of Italy
Annual Meeting, Rome, May 1974

INTRODUCTION

In the fiscal field the task of the Italian authorities in the 1970s
was twofold: reform of the tax and expenditure system so as to make
fiscal policy an effective macroeconomic policy tool (see Chapter 4),
and use of fiscal policy as a countercyclical device, which will be discussed later. In the long run, the more important task was fiscal reform. The tax and expenditure system at the beginning of the decade
was such as to make the exercise of fiscal policy management highly
ineffective. The tax system was too complex, depended too much on
indirect taxes, was subject to widespread evasion, and was collected
(if at all) with such delays as to make the timing of the effect of tax
measures unpredictable and sometimes perverse. The expenditure of

269

central government appropriations, too, was subject to long delays, particularly with regard to spending on capital account. This made use of the public expenditure tool unpredictable and sometimes poorly timed to deal with current economic problems.

Nonetheless, the Italian authorities made use of both their taxing and spending authority during the 1970s in efforts to influence real and financial variables, while recognizing the continued inadequacy of these tools. Approval of tax and expenditure packages followed the stages of the business cycle. For example, there were major expenditure packages in 1971, 1975, and 1978 (years of stagnation or recession) and major tax packages in 1974 and 1976 (years of strong growth). At the same time, however, there was a continuing need for higher taxes or a slower growth of expenditures, if the long-term upward trend in the treasury deficit was to be arrested.

USE OF TAX POLICY

While tax measures were aimed in large part at affecting total demand, there were often subsidiary objectives, typically involving attempts to shift the composition of demand (for example, from consumption toward investment) or to provide selective tax relief for particular groups such as low income taxpayers and sometimes business. Thus, to help low income groups, there were increases in the tax-free allowance in 1970, 1974, and again during the 1975 recession year. Similarly, a special tax deduction for low income taxpayers was created as part of the 1976 tax-increase package and a further special deduction was allowed in 1978, a year of slow growth but high inflation. There were business tax incentives included in the period before the introduction of the value-added tax at the beginning of 1973, in the 1975 minireform (in the form of revaluation of assets, incentives to mergers, and improved deductions for interest costs to business), and again in 1977 with a partial elimination of double taxation of dividends by the introduction of a tax credit and by making the local income tax and real estate capital gains taxes eligible as deductions against the corporate tax.

There was little use of across-the-board tax cuts as a means of stimulating demand, although at the end of 1975 there was an important upward shift in personal income tax brackets to offset the effects of fiscal drag. There were no generalized personal income tax rate increases, but a surtax on high incomes was a part of the 1974 tax package. Also, the corporate tax rate was raised from 25 percent to 35 percent in 1974. Flat-rate withholding taxes on interest and on dividends were increased on several occasions, with the former of particular importance because of the Italian savers' preference for fixed-interest assets. Thus, the dividend withholding flat tax was increased from 30 percent to 50 percent in 1976 and the withholding tax on postal and bank deposits was progressively raised from 15 percent to 16 percent in 1976, 18 percent in 1977, and 20 percent in 1978. The increase in the dividend tax was mainly a political maneuver, but the interest tax measure had perceptible revenue consequences. (In 1978 the latter tax generated the second largest source of income tax revenue, after the personal income tax.) One of the advantages of the tax has been that while appearing to be a politically popular tax on unearned income, in fact it affects a large enough number of middle and low income earners to generate significant amounts of revenue and can be used to affect real personal income.

The combination of fiscal drag, some higher tax rates, and improved tax collection methods led to a shift in the relative burden of direct and indirect taxes toward the former. Whereas in 1969 direct taxes represented only 29 percent of total central government tax revenue, in 1978 they accounted for 46 percent of the total. (Figures exclude payroll taxes.)

Because automatic growth of revenues from income taxes could be counted on, due to fiscal drag and new collection procedures, most tax rate changes concerned indirect taxes and public service rates. In part, this was because of the desire to discourage energy consumption by raising manufacturing and the IVA taxes on gasoline (which also had the advantage of not being included in the scala mobile basket). Also, the reduced resistance to increases in public service rates meant that it was possible to change these rates more frequently than before. Although public service charges are generally included in the scala mobile basket, on one occasion it was possible through some manipulation of the type of charge included in the basket to prevent full pass-through of rate increases. This was done in 1977 in the case of newspapers, urban transport fares, and electric rates.

There were also a number of increases in the IVA, with the luxury rate rising from 18 to 30 percent in 1974 and then to 35 percent in 1977. The standard rate was also increased from 12 to 14 percent in 1977. At various times the stamp, registration, consumption, and concessions taxes were raised and both the 1974 and 1976 tax packages included special one-time taxes on motor vehicles.

It is difficult to separate out the revenue effects of the tax reform (particularly the improvement in collection procedures) from the effects of specific tax measures taken for current demand management purposes. The one across-the-board tax relief measure, which had some countercyclical motivation (the end-1975 shift in tax brackets to reduce fiscal drag), may have contributed somewhat to inflation in 1976, since by the time the cut took place, the economic recovery had already begun. Still, tax revenues generally followed the desired pattern associated with changes in cyclical conditions, particularly in the case of indirect taxes. Thus the growth of total tax revenues was especially fast in the main years of recovery and of significant tax increase measures (1974 and 1976) at 29 percent and 36 percent, respectively, and relatively low in the periods of stagnation or recession (1971-72, 1975, and 1977-78). (See Chapter 4 for a discussion of tax elasticities and the growth of revenue in real terms.)

USE OF EXPENDITURE POLICY

On the expenditure side, there were major reflation packages in 1971, 1975, and 1978, whose chief beneficiaries were small business, exports, housing, agriculture, and southern development. In addition, there were periodic measures to fiscalize part of the social insurance costs normally borne by business through their assumption by the Treasury. Fiscalization measures were taken in 1971, 1972, 1977, 1978, and 1979.

The variety of expenditure measures taken had different effects on actual government spending levels. For example, there were a number of measures involving direct budget appropriations and expenditures for such purposes as: interest rate subsidies on loans, capital grants, endowment fund contributions to Mediocredito, ENEL, and the state holding companies, and appropriations to establish loan funds for housing and other purposes. There were some measures that set limits on the level of guarantees that could be extended (for export credits, in particular) and other measures that authorized the Treasury or other public bodies to borrow in the capital market. In many cases multiyear programs were involved. Thus the impact on final demand of these measures is hard to trace and could vary widely. Interest rate subsidies concerned actual budget expenditures, but they depended upon the granting of credit. Endowment fund contributions also involved direct budget expenditures, but their initial impact was simply to improve the financial position of the recipient, which later would use the funds either to relend, repay debt, or make direct investments. The appropriation of loan funds, too, depended upon the subsequent processing of loan applications, and spending might occur considerably later. Changes in guarantee ceilings did not involve any government spending at all, except in rare cases of default on loans covered. Appropriations for capital grants (for example, for southern development) had an effect on final demand only after approval and disbursement for specific investment projects.

The direct effects of expenditure measures in stimulating the economy through public consumption and public investment were fairly limited, since the growth of public spending was so heavily concentrated on transfer payments. In 1969 treasury cash expenditures for purchases of goods and services amounted to 8.5 percent of total budget expenditures, and direct investments to 2.4 percent. By 1978 the corresponding figures were 4.2 percent and 0.8 percent. The counterpart to the relative decline in the direct impact of treasury expenditures on final demand was the rapid growth of transfer payments, which increased from 42.1 percent of total budget expenditures in 1969 to 55.8 percent in 1978. This does not mean that increases in treasury expenditures did not impact on final demand, but that demand was affected indirectly, and less predictably than if direct expenditures for final goods and services had been involved.

Neither cash budget data nor national income data give much evidence that current expenditure operations played an important countercyclical role. On the one hand, budget data show a rapid rate of growth in purchases of goods and services in the strong growth years of 1970 and 1974 and a very slow rate of growth in the recession year 1975. On the other hand, growth was fairly rapid in 1977-78, which was consistent with demand management objectives, and not rapid in 1976 when stimulus was not needed. In short, the record was mixed. National income data also show a somewhat mixed picture.

TABLE 9.1

Relative Rates of Growth of Public and Private
Consumption, 1970-78
(percent)

	Private Consumption*	Public Consumption*
1970	12.7	9.8
1971	8.6	22.3
1972	10.0	13.8
1973	18.9	14.8
1974	24.1	20.4
1975	16.0	15.9
1976	22.2	20.1
1977	20.9	23.4
1978	16.0	22.3

*Current lire.
Source: Compiled by the author; data from ISTAT,
Conti Economici Nazionali 1960-78 (Nuova serie), Rome,
1979.

TABLE 9.2

Relative Rates of Growth of Public and Private Fixed Investment, 1970-78
(percent)

| | Private Investment* | Public Investment* | | |
		Overall	General Government	Public Enterprise
1970	11.3	25.2	21.2	27.0
1971	-2.7	17.4	2.8	23.6
1972	4.3	9.1	-3.5	13.6
1973	34.0	10.3	14.2	9.0
1974	39.2	18.8	17.9	19.0
1975	-0.6	16.7	21.3	15.1
1976	21.9	21.5	24.7	20.0
1977	21.0	14.3	9.6	16.7
1978	13.6	4.1	12.8	—

*Current lire.
Note: Old GDP series 1970-75; new series 1976-78.
Source: Compiled by the author; data from Bank of Italy annual reports.

During the stagnation of 1971-72 public consumption did rise more rapidly than private consumption (averaging 18 percent versus 9 percent). (See Table 9.1.) Again in 1977-78 the growth of public consumption outpaced private consumption (average growth of 23 percent versus 18 percent). But in the critical recession year 1975 the reverse was true, as public consumption grew at the same rate as private consumption (16 percent).

The record of countercyclical behavior is also mixed with regard to public fixed investment, which was supportive of total demand during the 1971-72 period of slow growth and in the 1975 recession (old GDP data), but failed to play that role in 1977-78 (new GDP data). (See Table 9.2.) Thus public investment (including investment both by general government and by the public enterprises) averaged 13 percent in 1971-72, compared to less than 1 percent for private investment. Similarly, in 1975 public investment rose by 17 percent versus a decline of about 1 percent for private investment. In 1977-78, the pattern was reversed, with public investment growing by an average of only

9 percent versus 17 percent for private fixed investment. As between public investment by government and by public enterprise, only the public enterprises provided a countercyclical stimulus in 1971-72, while both types of investment helped to support demand in 1975 and both generally failed to do so in 1977-78. In fact, there was no growth, even in nominal terms, in fixed investment by public enterprise in 1978. This weakness of investment by public enterprises reflected their increasing financial difficulties growing out of earlier efforts to sustain investment growth (see Chapter 5).

The effects of the fiscalization of part of social insurance costs borne by business as a result of measures taken in 1971, 1972, 1977, and 1978 can be seen in the figures for increases in total dependent labor costs in those years and in 1973. In the absence of such measures labor costs would have risen by 1 percent more in each of the years 1971, 1973, and 1977. In 1972 the corresponding reduction in labor costs was 1.5 percent and in 1978 the relief provided amounted to a very substantial 5 percent. Use of this technique is one of the more effective ways for public expenditure to have a prompt economic effect, since it provides a partial offset to the too rapid rise in labor costs. This adds to the already large treasury deficit, however, and is a second-best solution to moderating the rises in labor costs themselves.

The effects of expansionary measures that did not impact directly on aggregate demand in the 1970s are more difficult to trace. To a large extent stimulus efforts took the form of loans and interest rate subsidies on loans. In the case of housing, it appears that the stimulus measures of 1971 and 1975 did have some marginal impact on housing investment, with a lag. New loan commitments by the special credit institutes rose substantially in 1971 (up 14 percent). By 1973 and 1974 housing investment turned up moderately, growing by 3.2 percent and 2.7 percent in real terms, after little or no negative growth in the prior two years. A sharp increase in special credit institute commitments in 1973 (up 64 percent) and in expenditure of public funds (up 25 percent) apparently also contributed to the rise in housing investment in 1973-74. Since these were already years of economic recovery, however, the timing of the impact of the earlier measures was not optimal from the cyclical point of view. Although there was a similar sharp increase in housing loan commitments and in the expenditure of public funds in 1975, real investment in housing in that year and in the succeeding two years was either negative or minimal. In any case, the relatively modest impact of housing measures adopted by the government is due to the fact that the principal source of housing finance is household savings. Housing loans on average accounted for only 29 percent of total housing finance in 1972-78 and direct expenditure of public funds for only 5 percent of the total.

In the case of agriculture, the 1971 and 1975 stimulus measures seemed to have a more perceptible effect. Total loan disbursements to agriculture rose by 90 percent in 1971 and by 140 percent in 1975. New commitments also rose substantially in those years, and increased credit availability contributed to the good rate of growth of real investment in agriculture in 1971-72 (average 4.2 percent) and in 1975-76 (average 6.2 percent). Also, the timing of the countercyclical impact was generally better than in the case of housing, which was subject to longer delays.

The sharp increase in the export credit guarantee ceiling in 1975 (from 1.4 trillion lire to 2.5 trillion lire) resulted in a very sharp rise in guarantees actually extended that year. Although the new guarantee level declined somewhat in each of the succeeding three years, the absolute level remained well above that of the early years of the decade. The increase in guarantees may have played a modest part in the good performance of exports in 1975 (despite the fall in world demand) and in the succeeding years. There were too many other factors, however, especially lira depreciation and changes in relative rates of growth in Italy and abroad, to attribute too much importance to this factor. The increased guarantee ceilings may have had some special importance in the expansion of Italian exports to nontraditional markets, such as Eastern Europe and the Middle East.

In addition to the various expenditure packages so far discussed, the government took steps aimed at income maintenance. In fact, during the period 1970-78, 25 percent of all current transfers from the central government were to the social insurance institutes. The table below shows the annual percentage change in such transfers. In

Year	Percent Annual Change
1970	109.3
1971	-12.2
1972	-13.9
1973	99.5
1974	-20.8
1975	75.5
1976	-31.7
1977	90.8
1978	118.1

part, the level of transfers varied automatically in line with prevailing cyclical conditions, but it also reflected legislated changes in social insurance benefits, changes in the current financial position of the insurance institutes, and (in 1976-78) transfers for consolidation of debt of the health institutes.

The sharp increase in transfers to the social insurance institutes in 1970 was the result of the major reform of the pension system in 1969. The rise in 1973 reflected a large increase in minimum pensions introduced late in 1972. The rise in 1975 reflected both the effect of the recession and of legislated increases in family allowances, short-time work supplements, and pensions. In 1977 and 1978 consolidation of health insurance debt contributed to the rise, and in 1978 the extension of the linkage of pensions to industrial wage rate increases and a large rise in the minimum pension also played a part. To the extent that the rise in transfers to the institutes in 1973 resulted in any increase in final demand that year, it was ill timed from the countercyclical point of view. A less serious criticism can be made with regard to the sharp increase in 1970. Although that was still a year of strong growth on a year-to-year basis, the stagnation of 1971-72 had already begun.

The effect on income maintenance can be seen more clearly in data on the composition of changes in disposable personal income during the 1970s. (For 1970-77 social insurance benefits constituted from 17 to 20 percent of gross personal income.) In the periods of slow growth, 1971-72, and especially in the 1975 recession year, the rate of increase in social insurance benefits did have the expected countercyclical effects; that is, in those three years such transfer receipts grew faster than did wages and salaries and helped to sustain gross personal income (see Table 9.3). Conversely, in the recovery year of 1974 the opposite was true. For 1976 and 1977 the figures do not show the expected countercyclical pattern. Social benefits grew faster than wages in the 1976 recovery year, when such income support was not particularly needed. (This adverse cyclical effect was at least partly accidental, reflecting a more generous method of calculating pensions, that had been approved in the 1969 reform law but did not go into effect until 1976.) In 1977, when growth slowed down, social insurance benefits did not rise faster than wages. (It seems likely that, with the pension reform of 1978, social insurance benefits in 1978 did help to sustain personal income. For example, fiscal data show an increase in total social insurance payments of about 24 percent, compared to about 18 percent in 1977.)

In addition to income support for the general populace, periodic wage contracts with employees in the public sector also were a source of income support to the economy, but were tied to the accident of contract termination dates rather than to prevailing cyclical conditions. (The wage bill in the public administration is about 20 percent of the total.) New contracts were negotiated with civil servants in late 1970, 1973, 1976, and 1979. Although salary increases in the public administration generally did not keep pace with blue-collar wages nor with white-collar wages in other sectors, there were substantial increases due to these contracts recorded in 1971 (9 percent), 1973 (21 percent), and 1976 (16 percent). The timing of large increases in 1973 and 1976 was not appropriate in cyclical terms. The relatively low rates of wage rate increases in the 1970s, however, did have some restraining effect on the growth of the total wage bill. (The low rate of increase was partially due to less frequent scala mobile adjustments in this sector than elsewhere.)

Under the 1974 and 1977 IMF standby agreements and commitments made under EC loans, Italy accepted ceilings on financing of the treasury cash deficit and on the deficit of the enlarged public sector (see Table 9.4). Italy stayed within the ceilings on the treasury deficit for 1974, 1976, and 1978, but considerably exceeded the 1977 ceiling. It also failed to meet the ceiling on the enlarged public sector deficit in both 1977 and 1978. Failure to meet the 1977 deficit ceilings was caused by shortfalls in receipts due to slow growth, changes in taxation of joint income tax returns required by a Constitutional Court decision, decreased yields from abolished taxes, and other factors. In 1978 the larger than targeted deficits reflected such factors as

TABLE 9.3

Relative Rates of Increase in Wages and Social Insurance Benefits of Households, 1970–77
(percent)

	Wage/Salary Income	Social Insurance Transfer Receipts
1970	16.9	n.a.*
1971	14.5	18.5
1972	11.2	14.4
1973	21.4	19.1
1974	24.5	17.5
1975	21.3	35.9
1976	22.0	23.9
1977	22.0	18.4

*Not available.

Note: Old GDP series; 1978 not available.

Sources: Compiled by the author; data from ISTAT, Annuario di Contabilità Nazionale (1977), pp. 47, 51, 55, 59; Bolletino (November 1978), pp. 255–58.

TABLE 9.4

Performance against EC/IMF Fiscal Ceilings, 1974-78
(trillions of lire)

	Financing of Treasury Cash Deficit		Enlarged Public Sector Deficit	
	Ceiling	Actual*	Ceiling	Actual*
1974 (IMF)	9.2	8.6	n.a.	n.a.
1976 (EC)	13.8	13.2	n.a.	n.a.
1977 (IMF)	13.1	16.2	16.5	21.6
1978 (EC)	28.0	27.4	31.5	33.3

*Rounded to nearest 100 billion lire.
Note: n.a.—not applicable.
Sources: Compiled by the author; data from Bank of Italy annual reports and IMF.

continued fiscalization of employer health insurance contributions, IVA tax concessions for industrial reconversion, the effect of inflation on government wages and pensions, the rise in interest payments, transfers to the social insurance institutes, and endowment fund contributions to IRI and ENI.

CONCLUSIONS

The use of fiscal policy for countercyclical purposes was probably more effective on the tax side than for expenditures, although efforts in both areas relieved at least some of the burden placed on monetary policy. Except perhaps for the end-1975 measure to reduce the effects of fiscal drag, tax policy measures were correctly attuned to the requirements of countercyclical policy. They had the advantage over expenditure policy of being more immediate in their impact and were, in general, appropriately addressed to shifting demand from consumption toward investment. The increases in the corporate tax rate and in the flat withholding tax on dividends, however, were not consistent with the need for encouraging investment, and periodic measures to raise revenues clearly fell far short of meeting the rapid long-term trend of growth of expenditures and of keeping the treasury deficit under control.

Occasional measures to stimulate demand through expenditure packages had relatively little direct effect on aggregate demand because of the small size of public consumption and direct government investment. Public investment, however (including that by public enterprise), did help to sustain investment demand to some extent. Stimulus measures not directly impacting on final demand (for example, loan programs) probably helped agriculture and exports to a modest extent. Income support measures, including the automatic stabilizers, were also appropriately countercyclical in most cases. Set against these positive results was the unacceptable long-term trend of growth of public expenditures, which contributed to excessively expansionary fiscal and monetary developments (see Chapters 4 and 8).

10

MONETARY POLICY

There is, to my mind, something profoundly unsatisfying
in having to direct central bank action in such a way as to
. . . constrain the volume of credit potentially expressed
by the flow of monetary base because it is not possible to
regulate the flow [and] in having to channel the flow of
credit because, in the absence of adequate budget and incomes policies, the free decisions of market operators
are distorted by inflationary or exchange rate expectations.

Paolo Baffi
Governor, Bank of Italy
Annual Meeting, Rome, May 1976

INTRODUCTION

The burden of countercyclical economic policy management fell
heavily on monetary policy in the 1970s. The chief aims of monetary
policy were to control the global expansion of domestic liquidity, influence the cost of credit, allocate credit among different sectors,
and manage the flow of international capital both for balance-of-payments and for domestic liquidity purposes. The principal problem
encountered was the constant creation of liquidity on a large scale
through financing of a growing treasury cash deficit (see Chapter 4).
This made it difficult to control the overall expansion of domestic
liquidity and avoid the crowding out of credit needed for private productive investment. The tools used to accomplish monetary aims
were numerous and complex, involving traditional monetary instru-

ments, direct monetary controls, and exchange controls having both a balance-of-payments and a domestic monetary effect.

Monetary policy shifted during the 1970s, with about five years of relatively expansionary measures (1971, 1972, 1975, 1977, and 1978) and about four years of mainly contractionary measures (1970, 1973, 1974, and 1976). Results of attempting to use monetary policy to influence real growth, inflation, and the balance of payments were mixed.

CONTROL OVER MONETARY BASE

The first aim of monetary policy was control over the growth of the monetary base, particularly the monetary base of the banks. For analytical purposes the Bank of Italy sometimes attempts to distinguish between autonomous sources of creation of the banks' monetary base and policy intervention sources. While the distinction is somewhat arbitrary, the approach does help to isolate particular sources of monetary base creation that are not readily subject to control by the monetary authorities (autonomous factors) and to separate out the effects of different policy intervention tools that can be used to add to or offset monetary base created in the autonomous sectors.

In every year of the 1970s the autonomous factors that create monetary base generated more than enough liquidity, and policy intervention had to move in the direction of reabsorption of excess liquidity. The range of annual increases in the monetary base of the banks was 14-29 percent (Table 10.1 and Figure 10.1). There were rather high rates of expansion in 1971, 1977, and 1978, low rates in the three years 1972-74, and intermediate rates in 1970, 1975, and 1976. Behind these rates of growth were a variety of autonomous factors and a plethora of monetary policy measures aimed at affecting the growth of the banks' monetary base. Despite resort to a wide variety of tools, the monetary authorities were unable to prevent a rather high rate of expansion of the banks' monetary base throughout the decade.

The autonomous foreign sector was a major source of absorption of monetary base in 1972-76 and a significant source of expansion in 1977-78 (see Chapter 7). For the entire period, however, it had a neutral effect on the growth of the banks' monetary base.

The treasury cash deficit grew rather continuously, except for a brief decline in 1976. The rates of increase were especially large in 1971, 1975 (partly due to the cyclical effect of the recession), 1977, and 1978 (see Chapter 4). The net effect of the various autonomous factors on the monetary base of the banks, in the absence of counter-action by the monetary authorities, would have been monetary base

TABLE 10.1

Autonomous and Policy Factors Affecting Monetary Base
of Banks, 1970-78
(trillions of lire)

	Autonomous Factors[a]	Policy Factors[b]	Net Change	Percent Change in Banks' Monetary Base
1970	1.9	-0.7	1.2	20.0
1971	4.7	-3.2	1.5	21.8
1972	3.7	-2.5	1.2	13.9
1973	3.4	-1.6	1.8	18.2
1974	3.3	-1.2	2.1	17.9
1975	13.2	-10.5	2.7	20.3
1976	12.0	-8.7	3.3	20.2
1977	22.9	-18.3	4.6	23.5
1978	38.2	-31.2	7.0	28.7
Totals	103.3	-77.9	25.4	Average 20.5

[a]Includes foreign sector (other than net foreign position of banks
and compensatory loans), treasury cash deficit (net of treasury currency issues), and change in deposits of special credit institutes.

[b]Includes changes in net foreign position of banks, net compensatory Euromarket borrowing, financing of treasury deficit with postal
deposits and nonmonetary base sources, central bank credit to banks,
and other factors (principally changes in prior deposits and in frozen
counterpart of Euromarket loans).

Source: Compiled by the author; calculated from Bank of Italy
annual reports.

growth in the range of 28 percent to 157 percent per year in the 1970s,
or an average annual growth rate of more than 72 percent (Table 10.2).

Among the policy measures that influenced the banks' monetary
base, manipulation of the net foreign position of the banks (through
exchange controls) was not particularly important in the early years
of the decade, 1970-73 (Table 10.3). Subsequently, balance-of-payments
considerations often overrode domestic monetary considerations. Measures to affect the banks' foreign position were to a limited extent used

FIGURE 10.1

Percentage Change in Banks' Monetary Base, 1970–79
(over end of same quarter of previous year)

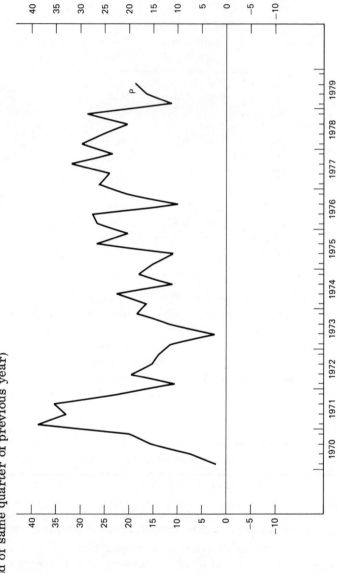

Note: P indicates preliminary.
Source: Constructed by the author; data from Bank of Italy bulletins.

TABLE 10.2

Autonomous Factors Affecting Monetary Base of Banks, 1970–78 (trillions of lire)

	Foreign Sector	Treasury Cash Deficit	Other [a]	Total Autonomous	Effect on Monetary Base of Banks [b] (percent change)
1970	-0.8	3.2	-0.5	1.9	33.0
1971	0.6	4.8	-0.7	4.7	66.6
1972	-1.1	5.8	-1.0	3.7	42.8
1973	-2.8	8.0	-1.8	3.4	34.9
1974	-5.0	9.0	-0.7	3.3	28.3
1975	-0.9	16.5	-2.4	13.2	97.8
1976	-1.2	14.6	-1.4	12.0	73.2
1977	2.3	22.4	-1.8	22.9	116.8
1978	7.7	33.9	-3.4	38.2	157.4
Totals	-1.2	118.2	-13.7	103.3	Average 72.3

[a]Includes part of treasury deficit that is financed by currency issue and changes in deposits of special credit institutes.

[b]Percent growth of monetary base of banks if no countervailing policy action were taken.

Source: Compiled by the author; calculated from Bank of Italy annual reports.

TABLE 10.3

Policy Factors Affecting Monetary Base of Banks, 1970-78
(trillions of lire)

	Net Foreign Position of Banks	Compensatory Loans	Postal Savings	Non-Monetary- Base Finance of Treasury	Central Bank Credit to Banks	Prior Deposits	Frozen Counterpart	Other	Total
1970	0.1	0.9	0.2	-0.3	-1.3	0.0	-0.2	-0.1	-0.7
1971	—*	-0.1	-1.1	-2.2	0.1	0.0	0.1	0.0	-3.2
1972	0.3	0.3	-1.4	-1.6	0.9	0.0	-0.7	-0.3	-2.5
1973	0.1	2.6	-1.8	-0.7	0.3	0.0	-2.2	0.1	-1.6
1974	0.6	1.3	-0.8	-1.3	1.4	-1.2	-1.1	-0.1	-1.2
1975	-0.2	-0.6	-2.3	-8.7	-0.4	1.2	0.6	-0.1	-10.5
1976	2.6	-0.3	-2.6	-2.9	-1.5	-3.5	-0.6	0.1	-8.7
1977	3.5	-0.5	-3.1	-23.2	0.2	3.5	0.6	0.7	-18.3
1978	-1.2	-0.7	-4.4	-24.0	-0.2	0.0	0.8	-1.5	-31.2
Totals	5.8	2.9	-17.3	-64.9	-0.5	0.0	-2.7	-1.2	-77.9

*Less than 100 million lire.
Source: Compiled by the author; calculated from Bank of Italy annual reports.

to bolster official reserves in 1972 and 1974 and, conversely, the banks were instructed to reduce their net foreign indebtedness when the balance of payments improved temporarily in 1975. The capital inflow of 1972 was in keeping with domestic reflationary policies, but the inflow in 1974 contributed an undesirable addition to domestic liquidity. (In fact, the authorities eventually placed a ceiling on the increase in net foreign liabilities in July of that year.) In 1976 and 1977 there were very large increases in these short-term capital inflows (reflecting the re-imposition of direct controls on lira bank loans late in 1976). In 1976 this was necessary for balance-of-payments reasons, even though it added to the problem of domestic liquidity. In 1977 the inflows continued and, while a case can be made on balance-of-payments grounds for a further strengthening in Italy's foreign reserve position, it seems questionable that this source of liquidity creation should have been allowed to expand on the scale it did. In 1978, a perceptible reduction of these debts conformed both to the much improved balance-of-payments situation and to the need for some offsets to the very rapid rate of creation of monetary base from the treasury deficit. (The decline also reflected some liberalization of direct controls on bank loans in lire.)

A similar combination of balance-of-payments and domestic liquidity considerations motivated the resort to Euromarket compensatory loans, especially in 1973-74, and the contemporaneous sterilization of much of the lira counterpart of those loans. The need for the foreign exchange income was obvious and the inadvisability of feeding domestic liquidity during this period of relatively strong growth was equally evident. The subsequent repayments on these loans and release of the counterpart in 1975-78 were sufficiently modest and spread out over time so as not to create liquidity problems.

The inclusion as a policy intervention item of drawings on postal savings to finance part of the treasury deficit reflects the option available to the Treasury to make use of this relatively noninflationary source of deficit financing and even to influence the growth of postal savings to some extent by changing the interest rates paid on such savings. There was a steady increase in this source of treasury financing, except for a drop in 1974. A substantial increase in interest rates in October 1974 and again in July 1976 contributed to the resumption of growth.

By far the most important means of avoiding monetary base creation, especially in the latter part of the decade, consisted of financing part of the treasury deficit through the sale of long-term and short-term securities to the banks and the public. This was easier in times of ample liquidity and slow growth. Thus, sales of treasury bonds were most important in 1971-72, 1975, and especially 1977-78. Sales of treasury bills became very important in 1975 and 1977-78.

The Bank of Italy had already run into trouble in the late 1960s in trying to peg bond prices, and the problem of reconciling stability in bond prices and interest rates with the need to control monetary base and to use the interest rate policy tool arose repeatedly during the decade. In the primary market, the Bank of Italy was a residual buyer of government bonds, thus providing direct deficit financing, but in the secondary market its operations were aimed at control of liquidity and interest rates. At the beginning of 1970 the bank had completely stopped intervention in the bond market, except in nine-year treasury bonds, but it later resumed intervention. Once again in 1973, the governor of the bank complained that bond price support had made it impossible to carry out an adequate long-term interest rate policy. In fact, the introduction of a portfolio investment requirement, which will be discussed later in this chapter, was an alternative means of trying to stabilize the bond market. In early 1974, with the sharp rise in inflation and in interest rates at home and abroad, the authorities had to reduce intervention to allow interest rates to rise. Support of the bond market was again temporarily abandoned in June. In early 1975 the bank was once more intervening to curb short-term fluctuations in rates and to help insulate investors from possible capital depreciation, but by late 1975 and early 1976 the goal had changed again, as the bank became a net seller of bonds. No longer was the main concern the avoidance of capital losses for investors, but the need to permit long-term rates to move upward sufficiently to provide a current yield incentive to savers. By 1977 the bank was primarily interested in restoring a positive yield curve, following a period of very high interest rates in 1976, by helping short-term rates to decline at a faster rate than long-term rates.

Open-market operations in short-term treasury securities were not very important before 1976 because of the relative lack of development of the market. By 1977-79, however, the expansion of the banks' holdings of treasury bills was such as to permit the authorities to use open-market operations as the main means of controlling the banks' monetary base. Given the existence, however, of the bank portfolio investment requirement for long-term bonds and direct credit controls over bank loans, the banks' purchases of BOTs (treasury bills) tended to be a residual.

The usual pattern of open-market operations consisted of net official purchases of bills at the monthly auctions, with the bills then sold off through secondary market operations. Thus, in 10 of 11 quarters (fourth quarter of 1976 to second quarter of 1979) there were net primary market purchases, but in every quarter there were net secondary market sales. In 7 of 11 quarters there were net sales overall, exerting a contractionary force on the banks' monetary base. The contractionary effect was particularly large in 1977, when the Bank of Italy effected net sales of bills of more than 10 trillion lire. (In 1978 net sales were less than 4 trillion lire.)

The growth of the treasury bill market was a mixed blessing. On one hand, it enlarged the sector of the securities market that was subject to wide fluctuations in interest rates and it permitted both banks and nonbanks to accumulate reserves of secondary liquidity that were virtually risk-free, paid market rates, and could be easily converted into monetary base. On the other hand, the authorities' open-market interventions became more effective when carried out in an increasingly efficient market. In addition, the possibility of carrying out open-market operations in both short-term and long-term securities made it possible, to some extent, to isolate long-term notes from changes in short-term notes by use of a market-related instrument, rather than by administrative controls.

Central bank credit to the banks was rarely an important source of increase in the monetary base of the banks. Lending was generally for seasonal or other short-term liquidity purposes. There were perceptible increases in the banks' monetary base from central bank credit in 1972 and 1974. In the first case, most of the credit was extended in the last quarter, when the economic recovery was already under way. A large part of this credit was seasonal, however, and was repaid in the succeeding quarter. The growth of central bank credit in 1974, too, was concentrated in the fourth quarter, when the recession of 1974-75 had just begun. There had also been a considerable extension of such credit, however, in the second quarter as well, when the need for an additional source of liquidity was less clear.

Imposition of a prior import deposit in 1974 and a prior exchange deposit in 1976 were emergency measures taken at a time when use of the traditional monetary tools was clearly failing to have as large and immediate an effect on inflation, the exchange rate, and the balance of payments as was deemed necessary. In the case of the 1974 measure, the initial motivation was twofold—to slow down imports and to absorb monetary base. Shortly after it was introduced, however, primary emphasis was given to its domestic monetary effects. The major monetary impact of the measure occurred in the second and third quarters of 1974 (see Figure 10.2). By the third quarter, the 1974-75 recession was already under way, but the impact of the prior deposit seems to have been too late and too small to be credited with much importance as a cause of the slowdown. The risk of adopting such a measure was that the deposits would eventually have to be released at a time when the injection of additional liquidity might be unwelcome. Fortunately, such an increase in liquidity during the 1975 recession year proved to be fairly tolerable.

In the case of the prior exchange deposit imposed in May 1976, the size of the net monetary impact was far larger in the year it was

FIGURE 10.2

"Other" Creation of Monetary Base, 1970–79
(change from previous quarter in billions of lire, not seasonally adjusted)

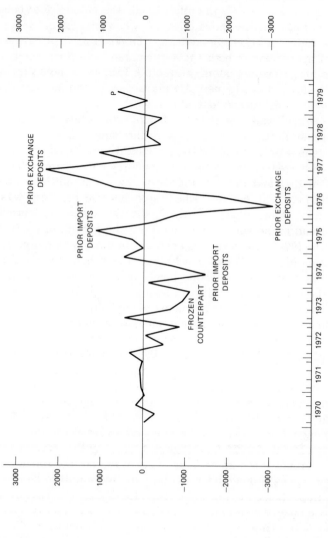

Note: P indicates preliminary.
Source: Constructed by the author; data from Bank of Italy bulletins.

introduced than for the earlier prior deposit measure (3.5 trillion lire versus 1.2 trillion lire). The deposit had a rather sharp, if temporary, effect on the growth of the banks' monetary base, but rapid growth resumed and real economic activity continued to grow for another three quarters. Also, the release of the accumulated deposits in 1977 was less well timed than the earlier deposit. While economic growth was still modest and monetary policy generally expansionary, the release of the deposits added liquidity beyond what was required.

Occasional action was taken to reabsorb bank liquidity through changes in the reserve requirement. In January 1975 a major reform of the system was introduced, but this was aimed principally at simplifying the system by eliminating the use of securities as eligible reserves and requiring that all reserves be held in the form of cash with the central bank. This did facilitate an increase in the reserve ratio in February 1976 from 15 percent to 15.75 percent. Also in February and September special reserve deposit requirements of 0.5 percent and 0.5 percent were assessed against deposits outstanding at the end of December 1975 and June 1976, respectively. The amount of bank liquidity that was sterilized by these two measures was fairly substantial, at about 750 billion lire and 500 billion lire, respectively.

DIRECT CONTROLS ON BANK LOANS AND INVESTMENTS

In 1973 the monetary authorities concluded that indirect control over bank credit through controlling the monetary base of the banks was insufficient. In order to exert a more immediate effect on bank credit, they introduced direct quantitative limits on bank loans.* The July 1973 measure imposed a 12 percent limit on the growth of bank loans between the end of March that year and the end of March 1974. The limits applied mainly to loans to customers who had outstanding

---

*The Bank of Italy's econometric model assumes a time lag of six quarters between changes in the banks' monetary base and changes in bank credit, with the maximum effect felt in the third and fourth quarters. [Bank of Italy, Modello Econometrico dell'Economia Italiana: Settore Monetario e Finanziario (Rome: 1979), p. 71.] The increased proportion, however, of bank credit, now represented by short-term treasury bill holdings, has probably reduced the lag. This may also be true as a result of the imposition of direct controls requiring close monitoring of credit maturities, but the relatively short time period when these conditions have prevailed make econometric testing difficult.

loans of 500 million lire or more. Direct ceilings on bank loans were continued for a second year, with a maximum increase of 15 percent between March 1974 and March 1975. The controls were allowed to lapse during the recession of 1975, but with the sharp acceleration of inflation in 1976 direct controls were reimposed in October 1976 and they remain in effect. Since October 1976 new ceilings have been set periodically, calling for rather steady but modest annual growth rates of 15-16 percent. Major exemptions are permitted for foreign currency loans and loans to customers whose outstanding loans are below a certain size (100 million lire through July 1980). The exception for foreign currency loans was particularly important in 1977 when more than half of the rise in bank loans took that form. (The growth of these loans was also related to a requirement introduced in 1976 that Italian exporters finance part of their export credit abroad—see Chapter 11.) During most of the period since their introduction the ceilings appear to have exercised some restraint on the volume of bank loans. Only in mid-1978 did loans subject to the ceiling fall as low as 95 percent of the limit, and on a few occasions they exceeded the limit.

The use of a bank portfolio investment requirement beginning in June 1973 was closely related to bank reserve requirement arrangements and also to direct credit controls. The portfolio investment requirement had originally been introduced as a modest means of channeling a larger share of financial savings into productive investment and of protecting the long-term bond market from the effects of a restrictive credit policy. At that time it was also possible to use certain eligible securities to meet bank reserve requirements, so the new portfolio requirement was mainly a supplement to the reserve requirement. With the reform of the reserve requirement system in January 1975, however, all reserves had to be held in the form of cash. Consequently, the portfolio investment requirement was expanded so as to permit the authorities to continue to influence the amount and composition of the banks' securities portfolios on a substantial scale. With the January 1975 reform of reserve requirements, the percentage of deposit increases to be invested in eligible securities was substantially raised—to 40 percent of the increase between December 1974 and May 1975 for the first half of 1975. Another innovation was the fixing of a minimum coupon interest rate for eligible securities as a means of influencing medium- and long-term interest rates. Subsequent changes in the regulation reflected the desired mix of bank loans and portfolio investments, with the portfolio requirement being relaxed in times of credit ease and vice versa. In the midst of a recession, in July 1975 the ratio was reduced to 30 percent. During the 1976 recovery (in June) it was raised to 42 percent. During the slow growth period of 1977-78 there were further relaxations. In January 1977 the ratio was reduced to 30 percent and in September 1978 to 6.5 percent.

FIGURE 10.3

Relative Growth of Bank Loans and Portfolio Investments, 1970–79
(percent change from same quarter of previous year)

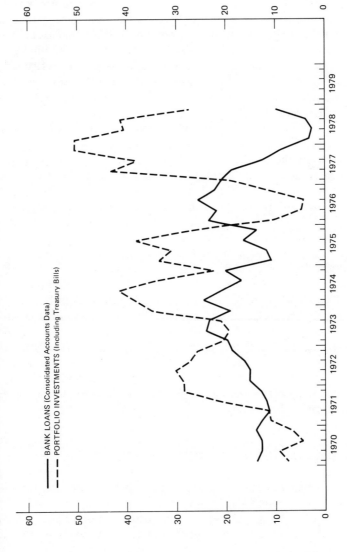

BANK LOANS (Consolidated Accounts Data)
PORTFOLIO INVESTMENTS (Including Treasury Bills)

Source: Constructed by the author; data from Bank of Italy bulletins.

Throughout the period several types of securities were always excluded from eligibility for meeting the investment requirement: shares, ordinary treasury bills, and municipal bonds. At various times most state bonds and those of autonomous entities, special credit institutes, and public and private enterprises were eligible. The major shifts in relative investment priorities consisted of the inclusion of agricultural bonds (1973) and mortgage bonds (1975) and the deletion of state bonds (1975). These changes reflected some new attention being given to development of the agricultural sector, continued stagnation in the housing sector, and a decision to remove state bond issues from the list (such bonds already benefiting from tax exemption). Also, it was hoped that the removal of this guaranteed means for placing state issues would exert some pressure to reduce the treasury deficit.

The use of the two direct controls over bank loans and portfolio investments was aimed mainly at credit allocation, rather than control over the total amount of bank credit. By manipulating the two requirements and varying the eligibility of various types of bonds, the authorities could both change the mix of (short-term) bank loans and (long-term) portfolio investments and channel long-term credit into different economic sectors (see Chapter 8).

Figure 10.3 shows the relative rates of growth of bank loans and investments in the 1970s, revealing the combined effects of cyclical conditions and changes in regulations. For bank loans, there can be seen high rates of expansion during the economic recovery periods (1972, 1974, and 1975-76), and a deceleration of loan expansion due to imposition of ceilings in 1973 and their reimposition in 1976. Rates of growth of portfolio investments tended to move in the opposite direction, as the banks invested excess liquidity in securities during periods of slow business-loan demand (1971-72, 1974-75, and 1977-78). Some shift to portfolio investments due to the imposition of ceilings on bank loans can be seen in 1973 and 1976 and the attraction of high-yield, risk-free, liquid treasury bills shows up in 1977-78.

TOTAL DOMESTIC CREDIT TARGETS

Italy agreed to ceilings on total domestic credit expansion (see Chapter 8) under IMF standby agreements of 1974 and 1977 and EC loans of 1974 and 1976 (which call for economic policy commitments as long as the loans are outstanding). This venture into monetary targeting was not a success. In only one out of seven instances did Italy comply with the ceilings (Table 10.4). Although the ceiling for the 1974-75 standby year was respected, credit expansion considerably overshot the mark in 1976, 1977, and 1978. In 1976 the rapid

TABLE 10.4

Performance against EC/IMF Ceilings
on Domestic Credit, 1974-78
(trillions of lire)

| | Total Domestic Credit Expansion[a] | |
	Ceiling[b]	Actual
1974-75 (IMF)[c]	21.8	21.5
1976 (EC)	29.5	33.3
1977 (EC)	30.6	35.8
1978 (EC)	46.0	49.0

[a]Rounded to nearest 100 billion lire.
[b]Ceilings were also set for April 1975/March 1976,
April 1977/March 1978, and a preliminary ceiling for
CY 1977, which are not shown here. (All those ceilings
were exceeded.)
[c]Period of 4/1/74-3/31/75.
Source: Compiled by the author; data from Bank of
Italy annual reports and IMF.

credit expansion reflected mainly the much faster than anticipated
recovery from the 1975 recession. In 1977 the sharp rise in financing
of the treasury cash deficit in the last quarter caused a break in the
domestic credit ceiling. In 1978 there was also an excess of credit to
the public sector, but mainly to bodies not included in the treasury
cash deficit definition (see Chapters 4 and 9).

MONEY SUPPLY

An examination of the behavior of growth in the money supply
(M-1 measured by change from quarter to quarter, seasonally adjusted)
around the turning points in real economic activity (GDP in 1970 lire)
shows the following pattern. First, there was a steady deceleration of
money growth from the fourth quarter of 1971 until the third quarter
of 1972. This was a period of slow growth, with the beginning of the
recovery in real economic activity and the turnaround in the rate of
money growth both occurring in the fourth quarter of 1972. This does
not suggest that monetary expansion was an important stimulus to

recovery. Second, during the subsequent recovery (in 1973-74) money growth initially accelerated, but there was a sharp deceleration in the rate of increase that began four quarters ahead of the downturn in real activity; that is, there was a drop in the rate of monetary expansion from a peak of about 31 percent in the second quarter of 1973 to a trough of less than 2 percent in the first quarter of 1975. A decline of this magnitude certainly had a restraining effect on growth. Third, the next turning point, in 1975, showed a reversal in the rate of growth of the money supply and of real activity coinciding in the third quarter of 1975. This suggests that monetary ease did not lead to economic recovery. Fourth, for the subsequent downturn, although there was a sharp temporary deceleration in money growth in the second quarter of 1976, money growth then accelerated again until the second quarter of 1977, coincident with the beginning of the downturn in the real economy. This does not give evidence that tight money contributed to the economic slowdown. The month-to-month pattern does, however, show a somewhat earlier downturn in money expansion, which may have had some restrictive effect on the real economy. Fifth, the resumption of a faster rate of money growth from the third quarter of 1977 through 1978 (except for the second quarter of 1978) preceded the recovery that began in the first quarter of 1978 and may have contributed to that recovery.

In sum, evidence of a prompt impact from changes in money growth on real activity was mixed. Slow money growth seems to have helped to decelerate real growth in 1973-74 and perhaps in 1976, while faster growth did not seem a very important source of recovery in 1972 and 1975, but may have played a role in 1978.

INTEREST RATES

While concentrating their efforts on controlling the volume of the various monetary aggregates during the 1970s, the Italian authorities also followed a rather active interest rate policy through the use of a variety of tools (see Chapter 8).* These included changes in the

---

*In the Bank of Italy's econometric model the principal channels through which monetary aggregates affect real aggregates are the cost and availability of long-term credit (especially from the special credit institutes) and the cost of short-term bank credit and the level of business liquidity. Thus, control over both short-term and long-term interest rates is considered to be an important intermediate economic goal.

rate for central bank discounts and advances and in penalty rates; open-market operations in treasury bills and long-term bonds by the Bank of Italy; use of moral suasion with the banks to adjust the prime rate and bank deposit rates; setting of a minimum coupon rate for securities eligible for the portfolio investment requirement; and modification of subsidized interest rates on medium- and long-term credit.

The discount rate became a frequently used tool of monetary policy, signaling changes in the authorities' monetary stance. (Actual use of the discount facility was modest.) While the discount rate (for example, the rate on ordinary advances) had been changed only once in the entire decade of the 1960s, it was changed 18 times in the 1970s, including four changes in 1976 alone. Variations in the discount rate sometimes led and sometimes lagged market rates (Figure 10.4). In early 1970 a rise in the discount rate preceded increases in the banks' lending rates and in longer-term rates. With the slowdown in growth in the rest of the period 1970-72, however, market rates tended to decline first, followed by catch-up reductions in the discount rate. During the period of greatest financial difficulty, 1973-76, the discount rate was used quite actively to attempt to lead market rates. Thus, in the third quarter of 1973 a sharp jump in the rate from 3.5 percent to 6.5 percent in September helped to trigger a sharp rise in market rates. For example, the average bank lending rate rose from 8.57 percent in the third quarter of 1973 to a peak of 17.9 percent in the first quarter of 1975. (In the meantime, there had been a further rise in the discount rate in March 1974 to 9 percent.) By that time, however, bank lending rates needed no upward push from the authorities, in the context of very rapid inflation in 1974 and a good rate of real growth during most of that year. In fact, the authorities lost no time in relaxing interest rate policy, with cuts in the discount rate of 1 percentage point each in December 1974 and May and September 1975. For a time the discount rate fell well below its normal relationship to bank lending rates, but bank lending rates dropped sharply to close the gap, reaching a low point of 12.25 percent in the last quarter of 1975.

Economic recovery and severe balance-of-payments difficulties led to discount rate increases in February 1976, first from 6 percent to 7 percent, and then to 8 percent. In the following month there was an unprecedented rise of 4 percentage points in the rate, to 12 percent. In October, faced with heavy pressure on the lira in the exchange market, the rate was again increased, to 15 percent—a record high for Italy. The banks' average lending rate also rose quickly between the first and second quarters from 12.81 percent to 17.63 percent. Although money market rates (the interbank rate) began to fall back from the peak and continued to decline through 1978, the bank lending rate lagged somewhat, continuing to rise to a peak of 19.71 percent in the

FIGURE 10.4

Discount Rate and Interest Rates on Business' Borrowing, 1970–79

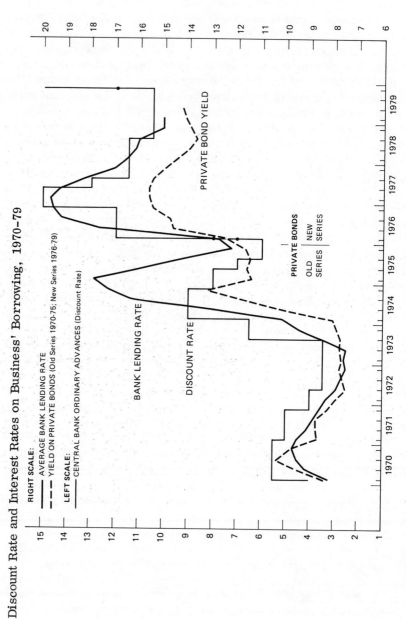

Source: Constructed by the author; data from Bank of Italy bulletins.

298

first quarter of 1977. By the second quarter, however, bank lending rates were also coming down, reflecting the reduction in real economic activity that began in the second quarter of 1977. The monetary authorities once again led market rates downward, with a cut in the discount rate in June 1977 by 2 percentage points to 13 percent and a second cut in the rate in August by 1.5 percentage points, to 11.5 percent. The pattern of declining interest rates in Italy generally continued through 1978, although there was some leveling out and even some increase in the latter part of that year. The decline was ratified by another discount rate cut of 1 percentage point in September 1978, to 10.5 percent. The resurgence of inflation late in 1979 triggered sharp increases in the discount rate, which again reached 15 percent at the end of the year.

Because of the underdevelopment of the treasury bill market, open-market operations in short-term government issues were not very important in the early years of the decade. The principal money market rate was the interbank rate. This rate responded rather quickly to changed monetary conditions, including discount rate changes. Like the bank lending rate, it considerably exceeded the usual relationship with the discount rate in 1974-75, but otherwise followed the discount rate. With expansion of open-market operations in treasury bills in 1977-79, the authorities had a more direct means of influencing short-term rates. The bill rate and interbank rates tended to track closely together, since bills and interbank deposits were competing vehicles for investment of liquid bank funds.

Although the authorities periodically sought to assure some stability in the bond market through open-market operations and manipulation of the portfolio investment requirement, they could not avoid allowing prevailing cyclical conditions to have an effort on long-term rates. Both the special credit institutes' long-term (nonsubsidized) lending rates and yields on private bonds followed the same general pattern as short-term bank lending rates during the 1973-74 period of monetary restrictions and again in the 1976-77 period of monetary restraint. "Operation twist" efforts to allow short-term rates to rise more than long-term rates can be seen, however, in the increased spread between the average bank lending rate and private bond yields, which reached peaks of 6.45 percentage points in the first quarter of 1975 and 4.48 percentage points in the third quarter of 1976. Nonetheless, medium- and long-term rates (at least in nominal terms) were very high by historic standards, especially in the later period.

The authorities and the public occasionally exercised some pressure on the banks to bring about desired changes in both lending rates and bank deposit rates set by the banking cartel. For example, in September 1975 the Bank of Italy asked the banks to reduce their lending rates by 2 percentage points, and in 1977 it urged further reduction.

In fact, the prime lending rate responded quite promptly to changing credit conditions, while deposit rates were rather "sticky." The prime rate moved with even greater frequency than the discount rate, but did not follow the rather precipitous decline in the latter during the 1974-75 recession. In retrospect, monetary and balance-of-payments developments might have been less troublesome in late 1975 and early 1976 had the somewhat higher interest rate level favored by the cartel been followed. On the other hand, there is room for criticism of the low rate policy for bank deposit rates favored by the banks. During the period 1970-74 the maximum suggested rates paid on savings accounts of 20 million lire or more (maturities of up to 18 months) never exceeded 6 percent and were as low as 4.5 percent through February 1975, compared to an average bank lending rate of 17.9 percent in the first quarter of that year. (The failure of the banks to raise suggested deposit rates earlier meant that cartel ceilings were not, in fact, respected.) Cartel deposit rates rose much more nearly in line with actual rates paid, beginning in March 1975, when the maximum suggested rate for savings deposits was raised from 4.5 percent to 12 percent. There were subsequent reductions in the suggested rates in May, June, and October 1975 and then increases again in March and April 1976, along with the general rise in interest rates during the financial crisis of that year. At the end of 1979 the maximum suggested rate payable on savings deposits stood at 10.25 percent.

The reluctant adoption in March 1975 of deposit rates that followed more closely the trend of market rates reflected a growing awareness on the part of the banks that the public was beginning to take an interest in competing forms of financial investments that offered higher returns and considerable liquidity—that is, treasury bills. The narrowing of the spread between bank borrowing and lending rates was a positive development. It meant that higher deposit rates would provide some incentive for personal savings. It also meant that in the future the narrower spread might force the banks to be more selective in their credit policy, improving the prospect of eventual relaxation of direct credit controls.

A fairly modest additional interest rate policy tool exercised in the latter part of the 1970s was the setting of a minimum coupon interest rate for securities eligible for purchase by the banks to meet their portfolio investment requirement. Introduced in January 1975, the minimum rate was at first set in the range of 7-8 percent. The rate was unified at 8 percent in December 1975, raised to 9 percent in June 1976, and to 10 percent in January 1977. That rate was still in effect at the end of 1979. (The rate took on less importance, however,

with the sharp reduction in the portfolio investment requ
was introduced in September 1978.)

Even subsidized interest rates on loans by the speci
institutes did not escape the general rise in interest rates
part of the decade. These subsidized rates (for example, in
credit) varied in the approximate range of 4.5 percent to 5 p
from the beginning of the decade through the third quarter of
After that, there was a modest rise in the rates through 1975.
was a period when short-term bank lending rates were actually falling.
The subsidized rates, however, were still very low in absolute terms
and the growing cost to the Treasury and to Mediocredito of financing
the subsidies led to a gradual increase in the rates, without regard
to the cyclical movement of rates. After a temporary dip in subsidized
rates in the first quarter of 1976 the rates resumed climbing through
the third quarter of 1977, a period of general increases in other interest rates as well. In May 1976 there had been approved an enabling
law for reforming the system of subsidized credit. In February 1977,
implementing the reform, it was decided that subsidized interest
rates of the special credit institutes should thenceforth be fixed every
two months and automatically linked to the cost of raising funds for
the institutes. This had the advantage of relating subsidized rates to
changes in market conditions, so that lending would not be interrupted
because lending notes became unremunerative.

CONCLUSIONS

In the 1970s the Italian monetary authorities faced the difficult
task of having to drive the economy with the accelerator in the permanent "down" position because of the continuing generation of monetary
base on a large scale by treasury deficits (see Chapter 4). Ironically,
the weakening in the balance of payments in the period 1972-76 brought
with it some useful monetary offset to the expansionary pressure of
the treasury deficit, but the balance-of-payments deficit itself posed
other grave problems. Conversely, when the balance of payments improved in 1977-78 it began to contribute a new source of monetary base
creation. Against these two major sources of autonomous monetary
base creation the authorities used a variety of policy measures to
avoid the creation of excessive monetary base for the banks or to reabsorb monetary base. While changes in the business cycle allowed
for some relative tightening or relaxing of monetary restraint from
time to time, in every year of the decade policy measures had to be
negative; that is, the brake always had to be applied to a greater or
lesser extent.

Periodic resort to tight credit generally had the desired effect of slowing down economic activity, but relaxation of credit restraints did not always succeed in stimulating recovery. The effectiveness of restrictive monetary policy during the periods of monetary restraint was heightened by the progressive weakening of the financial structure of business, especially public enterprise, which had become highly dependent on borrowed capital. Similarly, the constant pressure on profits from rising unit labor costs offset some of the improvement in business liquidity that would normally be expected during the early part of recovery stages of the business cycle and the profit squeeze also strengthens the effectiveness of credit control.

The central bank made a serious effort to depend principally on market-oriented monetary tools, aimed at maneuvering the monetary base of the banks as its principal monetary target. As early as 1973, however, this was determined to be an insufficient technique for dealing with emergency problems, and the authorities embarked upon a period of rather comprehensive direct controls over bank loans and portfolio investments. This was done with some reluctance, as shown by the temporary abandonment of controls on bank loans in 1975. When the balance of payments improved and the economy slowed down in 1977-78, the authorities again partially dismantled some of the earlier sets of controls, especially the portfolio investment requirement.

Except for the overly relaxed monetary policy adopted to boost Italy out of the 1974-75 recession, which contributed to the lira crisis of 1975-76, the authorities probably did as good a job of dealing with the symptoms of Italy's economic problems as could be expected. Measures used to control the monetary aggregates were innovative and fairly effective, although occasionally their timing went slightly awry. The more active use of interest rate policy was a useful complement to traditional efforts to exert control over credit availability. Even the most sophisticated and timely actions to absorb liquidity creation, however, were no substitute for cutting off excess liquidity at the source. To do that the treasury deficit had to be reduced, if not in absolute terms, at least relatively. This was not within the power of the central bank.

11

EXCHANGE CONTROLS AND
EXCHANGE RATE POLICY

The recent experience in a number of countries, and more
specifically in Italy, leads us to conclude that the important
role assigned to exchange rate flexibility in the present
international context should not be allowed to have the perverse effect of fixing in the price system short-run fluctuations caused by speculative and seasonal factors. . . . In
some countries the high degree of wage indexation is
another factor which, by interaction with the inventory
cycles and destabilizing capital movements, limits the
effectiveness of an approach to the problem of external
adjustment that relies largely on exchange rate changes.

Paolo Baffi
Governor, Bank of Italy
Annual Meeting, Rome, May 1977

INTRODUCTION

For a country faced with an immediate balance-of-payments
problem there are three main options that can be exercised until such
time as the nation can effect internal adjustments: finance the deficit,
impose (or strengthen) exchange controls, and let the exchange rate
move. In the Italian case, history suggests that the first two are typically the favored choices. This is because Italy has had considerable
success in turning around a balance-of-payments deficit, given time
and tight monetary policies, which seems to justify temporary financing
of deficits. Also, long experience with exchange controls, which are
not politically unpopular and which can be fairly effective because the

lira is not internationally important, make resort to this technique
appealing. Finally, Italian authorities have traditionally been skeptical
of the ability of exchange rate movements to turn around the trade account because of presumed low elasticities and because of the fear of
inflationary feedback from a depreciating currency.

Italy's exchange control system is highly complex, despite considerable de facto freedom, especially for current payments. The
basic exchange control law grants a monopoly over foreign exchange
transactions to the state, which may then delegate authority to engage
in foreign exchange operations. The maximum regulatory authority is
the Exchange Control Directorate of the Ministry of Foreign Trade.
The next level is the Italian Exchange Office and the final (most liberal)
level is the system of banks authorized to deal in foreign exchange.
Most current account transactions (goods and services) are liberalized,
with some exceptions for imports—mainly from the socialist countries
and Japan. Most capital movements are subject to some form of control, although inward capital flows and direct investments, in general,
are treated more liberally than other forms of capital movements. [1]

Italy's exchange control system reflects both long-term views
about the liberalization of international capital movements and short-
term considerations related to prevailing balance-of-payments and
monetary conditions in Italy. Italian dedication to freedom for current
account transactions has been fairly constant, although a certain degree of trade protectionism exists. Officials have been particularly
aware of the importance of freedom for international travel transactions
because of the importance of tourism to Italy's balance of payments
and because of the penchant of some countries (including Italy itself)
to impose controls on travel, even though travel is protected by international commitments in the IMF and OECD. There is no questioning
of the desirability of freedom for capital movements as a means of
encouraging the efficient allocation of resources across international
boundaries, particularly for direct investment. There is still a feeling,
however, that Italy is a poor country with scarce capital resources
(witness the underdeveloped south), which cannot permit an unrestricted
approach to capital movements. Italian experience with chronic problems of capital flight in times of political, social, and economic crisis
strengthens this view, and has led to frequent manipulation of capital
controls. Although controls are not completely effective, their com-
prehensiveness and the fact that the lira is not widely used in international finance make resort to controls attractive. Also, exchange
controls are politically more acceptable than some alternative restrictive measures would be.

The preference of the Italian authorities for exchange rate stability is one of long standing. After the initial readjustment of the lira
rate following World War II the lira par value was never changed until

the general Smithsonian realignment of December 1971. Even during the days of IMF par values (with 0.75 percent margins) the Bank of Italy regularly intervened to limit movements within this already narrow band. There persisted a belief that, for Italy, exchange rate movements would not help much to adjust the trade account. This was because the import price elasticity was low, due to Italy's dependence on imported food, energy, and industrial raw materials. Also, it was believed that foreign demand for Italy's exports was not very price-elastic. Since the lira had never experienced any substantial rate movement, it was hard to prove or deny this thesis before the general floating of currencies in February 1973. Once rate movements on a significant scale were permitted, Italy was immediately struck by large lira depreciations in 1973-74 and then again in 1975-76, which were accompanied by very rapid price inflation. This experience generated great concern about the existence of a vicious circle of lira depreciation and domestic inflation and further sensitized Italian officials to the inflationary risks of lira depreciation. As soon as possible after the 1976 balance-of-payments crisis, the authorities again sought to restore rate stability through regular intervention in the market. The need for exchange rate adjustments to offset disparities in relative price movements was not denied, but this was not a favored tool of adjustment.

EXCHANGE CONTROLS AND EXCHANGE RATE POLICY

Exchange control measures used during the 1970s were complex and frequent. Most measures concerned capital movements, although variations in the travel allowance and the prior import deposit of 1974 and the prior exchange deposit of 1976 all affected current transactions. Even a summary listing of the measures used to affect capital flows is a long one:

Prior licensing.
Fifty percent deposit for capital outflows.
Control over payment terms on trade credit.
Control over the net foreign position of commercial banks.
Requirement that mutual funds selling in Italy invest 50 percent of
    proceeds in Italian securities.
Limitations on the import and export of bank notes.
Emergency limits on inflows and prohibition of paying interest on
    foreign deposits.
Time restrictions on the right to hold foreign currency in residents'
    accounts.

Required foreign financing of advance import payments and of export
credit.
Amnesty on illegally exported capital and criminal penalties for vio-
lation of controls.
A foreign exchange tax.

In addition to exchange controls, a variety of methods for influencing exchange rate movements were tried in the 1970s. Market intervention by the Bank of Italy in the spot market was a day-to-day occur-
rence. In principle the bank very rarely intervened in the forward
market, but normally left forward rates to be determined by market
forces.* Intervention margins varied from 0.75 percent under the IMF
par value regime, to 2.25 percent under the EC "snake"† in which
Italy participated in 1972-73, to no margins during the float from 1973
to early 1979, and to 6 percent margins (against EC currencies) under
the European Monetary System (EMS) introduced in March 1979. The
dollar was the principal currency used for intervention, except for
considerable use of EC currencies for snake operations and the
(planned) greater use of EC currencies under the EMS.

On three occasions the exchange market was closed: in August
1971 immediately following the first dollar devaluation, in June 1972
in connection with the departure of the pound sterling from the EC
snake, and in January 1976 during the lira exchange crisis. Actually,
closure of the market meant that official quotations and Bank of Italy
intervention were suspended, but trading continued among the banks
and their clients.

There was one discrete adjustment in the exchange rate at the
time of the Smithsonian realignment, with a revaluation against the
U.S. dollar, the French franc, the U.K. pound, and (de facto) against
the Swiss franc, and devaluations against gold, the German mark,
and the Japanese yen. Italy experimented with a dual exchange rate
system in 1973-74 with a managed float of the ordinary rate and a
freely floating rate for financial transactions. During that period the
financial rate was always quoted at a discount, sometimes a fairly
large one. The market was reunified in 1974, however, and a single

---

*As of December 31, 1978, authorized banks were allowed to
engage in forward transactions up to 360 days in major convertible
currencies when dealing with other banks, or up to 180 days when dealing with nonbanks. Outstanding net forward transactions against lire,
however, were subject to a ceiling set individually for each bank.

†An arrangement limiting the fluctuation of EC currencies within
the margins.

managed float continued until the system was modified by Italian participation in the EMS in 1979.

USE OF EXCHANGE CONTROLS

The pattern of varying periods of restrictions and relaxations of exchange controls fits calendar years rather well. This is partially due to the fact that seasonal factors in the balance of payments tend toward a weak lira at the beginning and end of the year. This, added to any cyclical or structural weakness of the lira, has tended to trigger exchange crises at the turn of the year. The years of restrictive exchange controls (and weakness in the lira rate) were: 1969-70, 1972, 1973, 1974, and 1976. A generally more liberal policy prevailed in 1971, 1975, 1977, 1978, and 1979. (See Chapter 7 for a discussion of balance-of-payments developments during the 1970s.)

Italy started the decade with a balance-of-payments problem related to the disturbances of the hot autumn of 1969. Although the current account was in surplus in both 1969 and 1970 there were large capital account deficits and the overall balance was in deficit in both years (netting out compensatory Euromarket borrowings in 1970). A number of restrictive measures were taken. In 1969 the banks were required to eliminate their net foreign asset position and in 1970 they were allowed to move into a net foreign liability position (related to the amount of their export credit financing). Prior authorization was required for purchase of foreign mutual funds in 1969. In the same year Italian bank notes in denominations of more than 10,000 lire, repatriated from abroad, could no longer be credited to capital accounts, and in 1970 the bank notes had to be transmitted directly to the Bank of Italy for control purposes, rather than to commercial banks. Payment terms on trade credit were tightened in 1970. Reflecting the effects of these measures, there was a short-term inflow of bank capital of $0.7 billion in 1969 and approximate balance in 1970. Repatriated bank notes (a measure of capital flight) fell from $2.3 billion in 1969 to $1.3 billion in 1970. (See Chapter 7 for discussion of capital flight techniques.) Outward portfolio investment, however, continued high and net commercial credit was also a large negative item in the capital accounts.

In 1971 the balance of payments was in surplus on current account and overall. This permitted a slight relaxation of credit terms for exports from Italy and in December, just before the Smithsonian realignment, emergency measures were taken to prevent speculative capital inflows in anticipation of revaluation of the lira against the dollar and some other currencies.

In June 1972, despite a large current account surplus, the lira came under pressure, following the floating of the pound sterling. The exchange market was briefly closed and Italy was allowed to intervene in dollars rather than in EC currencies as a means of helping keep the lira inside the EC snake. Repatriated bank notes could no longer be credited to capital accounts and the banks were allowed to have a net foreign debit (but not a net asset) position. For the year there was a net inflow of bank capital of $0.4 billion. Repatriated bank notes still amounted to nearly $1 billion, but this measure of capital flight disappeared from the recorded data as illegal exports of capital had to be diverted to new channels.

The then unprecedented deficit of 1973 (current account deficit of $2.5 billion and overall deficit of $4.6 billion, adjusted for Euromarket compensatory borrowing) triggered three waves of exchange control measures. In January payment terms on advance import payments and delayed export receipts were tightened, the holding period permitted for residents to keep foreign currency on deposit in capital accounts was reduced, and a dual exchange market system was created. In February the travel allowance was reduced, the ordinary lira floated, and the holding period for foreign currency was further reduced. In July prior approval of import payments in advance of contract terms was moved to the more restrictive level of the Foreign Trade Ministry, a 50 percent non-interest-bearing deposit was imposed on most capital outflows, the banks were required to maintain a balanced position on a daily basis in specific foreign currencies, and foreign financing was required for advance import payments. Balance-of-payments data for 1973 showed a small surplus on trade credits (after a very large deficit in 1972), and advance import payments declined slightly as a share of all payments. Travel expenditures grew very rapidly, however, (27 percent), and the outflow of Italian loan and investment capital rose slightly compared to 1972. (Note, however, that the effects of these measures, especially those not taken until July, were to a considerable extent not apparent in annual statistics until the following year.)

The continued balance-of-payments problems of 1974 elicited still further restrictive exchange control measures. There was a tightening of rules for the import and export of bank notes, and the travel allowance was made available on a per-year rather than per-trip basis. A 50 percent prior import deposit was imposed in May and a limit placed on the net foreign liabilities of the banks to avoid too big a buildup of debt and to reinforce restrictive domestic monetary policy. The dual exchange market was abolished in March because it had not proved to be effective and had been supplanted by other measures, especially the 50 percent deposit on capital outflows. Reflecting the effects of the travel measure, travel payments by Italians fell by

16 percent in 1974 (taking into account the hidden capital flight adjustment). Following introduction of the prior import deposit, the volume of merchandise imports (seasonally adjusted) fell in June and July, rose in August, and then fell in each of the succeeding six months. Foreign financing of Italian imports increased as foreign exporters sought to protect their Italian markets. (Net trade credit turned strongly positive in 1974 to the extent of $0.6 billion.) The decline in imports, however, following imposition of the prior import deposit, seems to have reflected the slowdown of economic activity in Italy rather than being the effect of the deposit itself. Despite the limit on increases in the net foreign liabilities of the banks, there was a net capital inflow from that source in 1974 of $0.9 billion, which took place before the measure was introduced.

In 1975 the temporary improvement of the balance of payments that accompanied the 1975 recession allowed some relaxation of earlier measures: the prior import deposit was abolished in March; the requirement for foreign financing of advance import deposits was abolished in May; and the ceiling on net foreign debt of the banks was removed in June. Despite these liberalization measures, and reflecting the economic recession, imports fell in volume and value and the banks repaid about $0.5 billion in foreign debts.

The exchange crisis of end-1975 and early 1976 once again led to a new battery of restrictive measures. At first, in January, there had been a relaxation of payment terms on trade credit (which was later correctly criticized for its bad timing). Within less than three weeks, however, the authorities—having virtually exhausted convertible currency reserves through heavy exchange market intervention— were forced on January 21 to withdraw from (close) the exchange market. (The market reopened on March 1.) In succeeding months a series of restrictive measures were taken. In February the composition of financial instruments that travelers could take out of the country was restricted; the holding period for deposits in residents' foreign currency accounts was reduced; and special emigrant savings accounts in foreign currency were created to attract an inflow of emigrant remittances. In March foreign financing was required for advance import payments, a new amnesty law was approved for those who had illegally exported capital, and new penalties (including criminal sanctions) were imposed for exchange control violations. In April a prohibition on the export or import of lira bank notes in denominations greater than 10,000 lire was imposed. In May a new 50 percent, non-interest-bearing, prior exchange deposit was assessed against nearly all purchases of foreign exchange, including both current account and capital account transactions (if not already covered by the earlier 50 percent deposit on capital outflows), and foreign financing was required of 30 percent of export credits with maturities of up to

120 days. In October a 10 percent foreign exchange tax was assessed on purchases of foreign exchange (later in the month reduced to 7 percent after having been temporarily lifted at the end of the initial two-week period), and the amount of foreign financing of export credits was raised to 50 percent. By September it was possible to announce the time schedule for phase-out of the prior exchange deposit, and in December the phase-out plan for the foreign exchange tax.

The exchange control measures of 1976 were the most drastic of all those taken in the postwar period, in keeping with the seriousness of the 1976 exchange crisis. Although the amount of the overall balance-of-payments deficit in the three quarters at the height of the crisis (the fourth quarter of 1975 through the second quarter of 1976) did not equal that in the two months at the peak of the earlier crisis in 1974 (first two quarters), the ability of the authorities to resist further lira depreciation had been considerably weakened in the intervening period by the accumulation of additional foreign private and official debt. The Bank of Italy's convertible currency reserves again were low ($2.3 billion at the end of September 1975), and by the end of January 1976 had fallen to only $1.0 billion.

The impact of the exchange control measures can be seen in some of the statistics for 1976. Travel payments by Italians fell by 23 percent (dollar terms). Worker and emigrant remittances rose in lira terms, but not in dollar terms. In the following year, however, there were increases in dollar terms of 53 percent each in these receipts, probably reflecting some deliberate delays in remittances for exchange rate speculation reasons. The share of advance import payments of total payments and of delayed export receipts of total receipts both fell (contributing to a relative improvement in leads and lags). The amnesty law eventually resulted in repatriation of a little over $600 million in 1976 and $60 million in 1977. The prior exchange deposit coincided with a considerable drop in imports of goods and services in real terms (GDP concept, seasonally adjusted) in the second quarter and in the succeeding quarter, although there was some recovery in the final quarter of 1976. For the three quarters after the prior exchange deposit measure was introduced, however, imports of goods and services generally leveled off, despite the continued growth of real economic activity. This contrasted with the earlier import deposit in 1974, when the downward turning point of the business cycle occurred at the same time as the import measure and reinforced it.

The imposition of the 10 percent exchange tax in October coincided with a pickup in imports of goods and services in volume and value terms in the fourth quarter, partly a reaction to the initial negative effect of the earlier measures. Also, the lira had begun to decline somewhat after an initial period of recovery (May-August). The tax, in effect, constituted an asymmetrical devaluation of the lira (on the import but not on the export side). It had the advantage that it could be reversed by the authorities, if further rate depreciation was later deemed unnecessary. Any need at all for the tax can be questioned—at least in retrospect—and particularly the extension of the tax beyond the initial two-week period. Although the trade account remained in deficit in the third and fourth quarters, the current account was in surplus in the third quarter and the capital account and overall balance in surplus in both quarters. Furthermore, during the initial two-week period of the tax, the amount of exchange market intervention required to calm speculative fears had progressively declined.

The effect of the foreign financing requirement of export credits was a very large inflow of short-term bank capital borrowed by the Italian banks in Euromarkets for relending to Italian exporters. In 1976, the net foreign debt of the banks grew by $2.7 billion. This source of foreign financing was the single most important support for the official reserve position that year. Also, the measure tended to create a new, permanent source of financing for Italian exporters.

The recovery of the balance of payments from the latter half of 1976 through 1978 allowed a substantial dismantling of the exchange controls introduced in 1976. In February 1977 the foreign exchange tax was completely abolished. In April the prior exchange deposit came to an end. In October the travel allowance was increased and regulations on the export of Italian bank notes were relaxed. Travel payments rose that year by 26 percent in dollar terms, but receipts were rising by 49 percent and the overall balance of payments could accommodate the increase. Imports of goods and services in real terms fell imperceptibly, along with slow growth. In 1978 there were further liberalization measures: the 50 percent deposit for capital outflows was somewhat relaxed; the foreign financing of export credits was abolished in June; the composition of the travel allowance was liberalized; payment terms for advance imports were made easier; and the holding period for residents' foreign currency accounts was slightly lengthened. Most important, at least symbolically, was the decision by the government in December for Italy to participate in the new European Monetary System. Travel payments again rose rapidly (35 percent), but so did receipts (32 percent). The inflow of short-term bank capital for the year as a whole was even greater than in the previous year, at $4.0 billion. This was, again, the single most important support for official reserves. By then, however, reserves were also much strengthened by the very large current account surpluses of 1977 and especially 1978.

TABLE 11.1

Lira Exchange Rate Movements, by Currency, 1973–78
(percent change in lire per foreign currency unit)

	Dollar	German Mark	French Franc	Swiss Franc	British Pound	Japanese Yen	Trade-Weighted
Prefloat changes							
Smithsonian (12/71)[a]	7.0	-5.7	6.9	1.5	6.9	-8.8	—
General float (2/73)[b]	0.1	-2.2	-2.1	-6.9	8.7	-4.8	—
Postfloat changes[c]							
1973	-0.3	-19.1	-13.2	-13.2	-3.2	-9.1	-9.2
1974	-11.6	-14.6	-3.1	-18.6	-6.5	-3.2	-7.6
1975	-0.4	-5.4	-12.4	-15.3	4.8	1.3	-3.1
1976	-27.4	-24.6	-14.3	-31.8	-3.4	-27.7	-10.8
1977	-6.1	-14.9	-3.2	-10.5	-2.9	-17.5	-4.3
1978	3.8	-11.2	-4.9	-29.4	-5.7	-23.3	-1.8
Cumulative[d]	-44.9	-142.8	-68.0	-207.7	-20.8	-117.2	-44.2

[a]Change from previous IMF par value to Smithsonian central rate (market rates for Swiss franc).

[b]Change between Smithsonian rate and rate at beginning of general float.

[c]Calculated on basis of change in yearly averages (except for 1973, when calculated on basis of change between yearly average and rate at beginning of float in February).

[d]Calculated on basis of change between general float (2/14/73) and average rates for December 1978.

Source: Compiled by the author; calculated from Bank of Italy, Bollettino No. 1–2 (1979): 242–43.

USE OF EXCHANGE RATE POLICY
(THE VICIOUS CIRCLE)

In retrospect it is surprising to note that the lira was revalued against several currencies at the December 1971 Smithsonian realignment (Table 11.1), but the image of the lira as a weak currency had not yet developed. Despite the recorded balance-of-payments deficit of 1969 and the underlying deficit of 1970, the surplus of 1971 and the long period of large current account surpluses and extreme rate stability in the 1960s caused the lira to be viewed as a fairly strong currency. The relative strength of the lira, however, was short-lived. Between the Smithsonian realignment and the general float that began in February 1973 the lira had already depreciated against the German mark (2 percent), the French franc (2 percent), the Swiss franc (8 percent), and the Japanese yen (5 percent). Only against the dollar (virtually no change) and sterling (up 9 percent) did the lira hold its own. *

With the beginning of generalized floating, the lira immediately dropped substantially (Figure 11.1). It declined especially against EC currencies after the lira's dropping out of the snake, and to a lesser extent, against the dollar. This occurred roughly in the period February to July 1973. For the month of July the trade-weighted value of the lira (Bank of Italy index) had declined by nearly 14 percent from the base point on February 14, 1973. † Between February and July (monthly averages) the lira had fallen by less than 1 percent against the dollar alone. This first phase of depreciation of the lira tended to lag balance-of-payments developments. The overall balance of payments had already been in deficit in the last quarter of 1972 and in the first quarter of 1973. Resistance to rate movement had been traditional and Italy was still in a position to finance a considerable deficit from reserves and foreign borrowing.

The introduction of the dual exchange market in January 1973 represented an attempt on the part of the authorities to insulate current

---

*Lira exchange rates are traditionally quoted in lire per foreign currency unit. This technique has been used here. Strictly speaking, references to a decline in the lira rate really refer to a rise in the rate for the foreign currency and the percentage changes are not identical.

†IMF data concerning movements in Italy's effective exchange rate show a greater degree of depreciation than the Bank of Italy trade-weighted index. The IMF index is based on changes in the lira rate against 20 other currencies, weighted by trade flows and taking into account price elasticities and feedback effects on domestic costs and prices.

FIGURE 11.1

Changes in Lira Exchange Rate, 1970–79
(percent change from previous month)

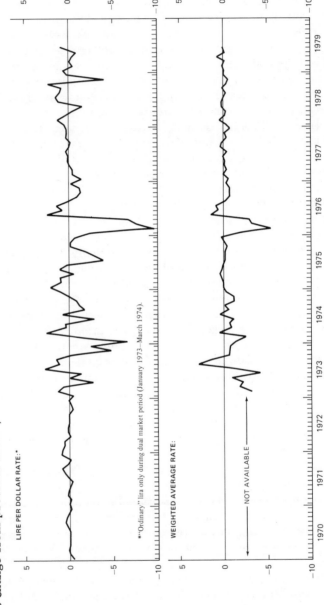

Note: "Ordinary" lira only during dual market period (January 1973–March 1974).

Source: Constructed by the author; data from Bank of Italy bulletins.

314

account transactions from exchange rate instability generated by volatile capital flows. The capital account had been in persistent deficit
in 1972, with quarterly deficits in the range of $0.4 to $1.1 billion
each, or $2.7 billion for the year. It was hoped that the dual market
system would provide a market-oriented means of rationing demand
for foreign exchange for financial transactions through a floating rate
for such transactions, but in the following month Italy was also forced
to let the ordinary lira float. This to some extent undercut the raison
d'être of the dual market system. The float of the ordinary lira was
a managed float, however, while the financial lira floated freely.
(During the existence of the dual market the average monthly spread
between the ordinary rate and the financial rate for the dollar ranged
between 0.8 percent in April 1973 and 7.5 percent in March 1974.)
At the same time, the authorities did not depend upon the financial
lira rate movement alone to accommodate demand for foreign exchange;
they continued to apply traditional exchange controls. This, too, tended
to reduce the importance of the financial market. Finally, it proved
difficult in practice to separate completely the financial and current
account transactions. The authorities were under constant pressure
to make exceptions for certain types of transactions by providing them
access to the (less depreciated) ordinary lira exchange market rate.

It is difficult to assess what impact the dual market really had.
Recorded data on capital flows show surpluses for three of the four
quarters after its introduction, but this was the period of maximum
Euromarket compensatory borrowing and there was, in fact, an underlying deficit in the capital account. It seems more likely that the cost
of the 50 percent deposit requirement on most capital outflows that
was introduced in July 1973, coupled with some rise in interest rates
in the latter half of 1973, were more important disincentives to capital
exports.

A second and more serious round of rate depreciation resumed
in late 1973 and carried forward into 1974 (covering the period October
1973 through February 1974). Although the overall balance of payments
showed a surplus in the third and fourth quarters of 1973, this was
due entirely to capital account surpluses, in large part generated by
well-publicized Euromarket borrowings by various public entities.
As the full impact of the oil crisis hit, the current account went into
deficits of $2.5 billion in both the first and second quarters of 1974
and the overall balance also into unprecedented deficits. The lira rate
clearly could not withstand such pressures, despite the massive borrowing in the Euromarket. Furthermore, the $1.2 billion borrowed
by Mediobanca in February 1974 proved to be the last such loan for a
long time, as the market received still another Italian borrower with
some reluctance. The lira depreciated quite sharply both against the
dollar and against currencies in general. The drop in the dollar rate

between October 1973 and February 1974 was nearly 16 percent and
the trade-weighted lira dropped by more than 5 percent. The lira continued to be generally weak during the rest of 1974 and the depreciation
against the dollar and against the basket of currencies for 1974 (year-
over-year) was about 12 percent and 8 percent, respectively.

In 1975 the lira on a weighted-average basis changed relatively
little (down 3 percent), as the balance of payments improved temporarily during the recession. There was considerable movement, however, against the dollar: appreciation in the first half of the year and
then depreciation in the latter half. The result for the year as a whole
was almost no change in average yearly rates.

The resumption of very large quarterly current account and
overall deficits exceeding $1 billion each in the last quarter of 1975
and the first two quarters of 1976 led to prompt and sharp depreciation
of the lira both against the dollar and against the basket of currencies.
After a futile attempt to defend the rate late in 1975 and in the early
days of 1976, official convertible reserves were nearly exhausted,
prospects of further large foreign borrowing were poor, and there
was no alternative to letting the lira fall. The lira decline against the
dollar was 29 percent between December 1975 and April 1976, and
14 percent against the basket of currencies. With the series of restrictive measures introduced in 1976 and the improvement of the
balance of payments in the third quarter (partly for seasonal reasons)
the lira recovered somewhat in May–July from the April lows, after
which it again gradually lost some ground both against the dollar and
against the basket at the end of 1976 and early 1977. (At its most depreciated point in the first week of November 1976, the rate was 947
lire per dollar, including the effect of the 7 percent exchange tax and
the 50 percent prior exchange deposit.) For 1976 as a whole the drop
of the lira against the dollar was 27 percent and against the basket of
currencies 11 percent.

With the strengthening of the balance of payments in 1977 and
1978 there was relatively little movement in the trade-weighted lira
(down 4 percent and 2 percent, respectively). There was a perceptible
decline against the dollar in 1977, however (6 percent on average), and
a rise in 1978 (4 percent). In 1978 the combination of a rise in the lira
against the dollar and a fall against EC currencies helped the balance
of payments by minimizing the increase in imports costs (because a
large portion are dollar-invoiced), while improving Italy's competitive
position in its principal EC export markets.

The first major decline of the lira (in 1973-74) was generally
accepted by the Italian authorities as an inevitable result of the energy
crisis and of accumulated increases of Italian costs and prices in excess of those of other countries. The even sharper depreciation of the
lira in early 1976, in contrast, raised serious concern about whether

the rate movement had overshot the mark and whether such depreciations would constitute an additional source of inflationary pressure
through the workings of a vicious circle. The vicious-circle argument
suggested that floating rates permitted overshooting to occur—especially when due to speculative attacks—that the rate did not always
recover from its excessive depreciation, that once the price effect
of the initial movement had been built into domestic prices it would
not be reversed, and that (especially in a highly wage-indexed economy)
the initial price movement fed back through wage rate adjustments
and tended to perpetuate the inflationary impact.[2]

One need not believe that the existence of a vicious circle is a
generalized problem in a flexible rate system; but given the openness
of the Italian economy to shocks from abroad (including further oil
price hikes), the extent and efficiency of wage indexation, the record
of frequent speculative attacks on the lira, the poor record on inflation
and expectations of more of the same, it is easy to understand Italian
concern about this danger. The case has not been made, however, that
better control over monetary expansion and over the economy in general would not have prevented much of the depreciation of 1976. Also,
there was some correction to apparent "overshooting" of the rate after
the initial depreciation, especially taking into account the effective
rate due to the exchange tax and the prior exchange deposit. Finally,
the question of the extent to which rate movement can help to adjust
the trade account is not yet settled. After the 1976 depreciation there
was slower import growth and, particularly, faster export growth (of
both goods and services). In any case, if Italian inflation rates persist
in exceeding those abroad, in the long run there will be no alternative
to allowing some rate movement to compensate.

CONCLUSIONS

The use of exchange controls in Italy is so common and widely
accepted that it would be unrealistic to expect any significant abandonment of the basic system, particularly control over capital movements.
The use of such controls, however, simply results in suppressing
problems that eventually must be dealt with. In particular, the chronic
problem of capital flight will not be resolved until better opportunities
for investment of domestic savings have been created. As long as the
problems faced in the 1970s persist, exchange controls will continue
to be used. In such circumstances they can make a modest contribution
to economic policy management. Fortunately, there is not a great deal
of enthusiasm for controls on the part of Italian monetary authorities,
particularly the draconian ones employed in 1974 and 1976.

Traditional resistance to using the exchange rate as a balance-of-payments adjustment device because of fear of the effects of depreciation on domestic inflation has some justification, but persistently higher inflation in Italy than in other industrial countries will leave no choice but to permit exchange rate depreciation. Furthermore, the favorable response of exports and services (especially tourism) in 1977-79 to earlier rate depreciation is encouraging. This suggests that Italian doubts about the utility of flexible rates in bringing about balance-of-payments adjustment may have been exaggerated.

NOTES

1. International Monetary Fund, Exchange Arrangements and Exchange Restrictions (Washington, D.C.: IMF, 1979).
2. Giannandrea Falchi and Maoro Michelangeli, "IMF Surveillance of Exchange Rates and Problems of the Vicious Circle," internal document, Bank of Italy Research Office, April 1977; Morris Goldstein, "Downward Price Inflexibility, Ratchet Effects, and the Inflationary Impact of Import Price Changes: Some Empirical Evidence," IMF Staff Papers (November 1977), pp. 569-612.

12

WAGE, PRICE, AND
EMPLOYMENT POLICIES

If we are convinced that an increase in employment in a
sound monetary environment can be achieved only if conditions are created in which the use of resources is
profitable and the expected rate of return stable, a policy
regarding the cost and mobility of labour linked to precise
objectives for investment and employment must be formu-
lated through negotiation of a social contract.

Paolo Baffi
Governor, Bank of Italy
Annual Meeting, Rome, May 1978

INTRODUCTION

One can question whether the Italian government had any coherent
wage, price, or employment policy during much of the 1970s. Certainly, the specific policies adopted and the actual economic behavior
of labor, management, and government could not (and did not) lead to
the desired pattern of steady economic growth, reasonable price stability, rising employment, and balance-of-payments equilibrium (see
Chapters 5-7).

A principal cause of the labor discontent that led to the hot
autumn of 1969 had been a feeling within the labor movement that workers had not received their fair share of the pie from the growth of the
economy in the 1960s, and that social welfare had been neglected.
Labor aspired to the same level of compensation being paid in other
EC countries and social benefits on an EC scale.

319

In the early years of the decade business did not strongly resist wage demands in the hope of assuring labor peace and with the intent of passing added costs on in the form of price increases. At first Italian exports were sufficiently competitive internationally so that intolerable balance-of-payments problems were avoided. The agreement of management to reform of the scala mobile indexation system in 1975 was motivated by the wish to avoid constant wage negotiations. Yet it is remarkable that this critical reform was agreed to by Confindustria and the three labor confederations with practically no participation by government. In fact, the agreement was later endorsed by government and applied in other sectors of the economy as well. Considering the economic impact the reform had on the ability of government to manage the economy, a more active role in reform of the system was certainly called for.

The government did not pursue an active incomes policy, especially in the early years of the decade. When it was drawn into wage negotiations, it was always under strong political pressure to come down on the side of the unions. Frequent appeals by the central bank stressed the need to tie wage increases to productivity growth in order to remain competitive internationally, but governments found it difficult to resist pressures for wage and social benefit increases and a series of such benefits were readily adopted.

All parties gave lip service to the objective of increased employment. In the face of rapidly rising unit labor costs, however, businesses increasingly directed investment toward labor-saving machinery and equipment, with adverse consequences for employment growth. When employment did not grow very much, or actually fell (as in 1971-72), there were some escape valves that relieved the pressure. First of all, there was the possibility of emigrating to another European country to find work. Second, the slow growth of employment partially reflected the more or less voluntary decline in the labor force due to the exodus from agriculture. Finally, the growing success of the unions in obtaining job security and income support through social reforms kept those already employed reasonably content. As time passed, however, the demand for labor in neighboring EC countries declined, Italian workers were less willing to go abroad to seek employment, and the labor force began to grow, particularly as women and youth moved into the labor market. More and more the unemployed consisted of the young, the better educated, and discontented, first-time job seekers.

Except for a fairly small number of administered prices and a brief experiment with more comprehensive price controls in 1973-74, the government did not depend heavily on direct price controls to restrain inflation. In the early years of the decade political resistance, and even deliberate government action, held public service rates and administered prices at levels unjustified by rising costs, but this led to large and growing deficits in parts of the public sector, particularly the railroads, ENEL, and the local governments.

By 1973 excessive cost and price rises had already contributed to a serious balance-of-payments problem. To this were added the sharp increases in oil and commodity prices in 1973-74. A period of deep recession (1975) and continuous balance-of-payments problems (1973-76) followed. By late 1976 the situation had reached such a state that there was a general recognition that the old pattern could no longer be allowed to continue and some corrective measures were taken, including some efforts to deal with the rise in unit labor costs; but with some improvement in economic conditions in 1977-79, pressures to deal with basic problems subsided.

WAGE AND EMPLOYMENT MEASURES

From the beginning of the decade until late 1976, virtually all the measures taken in the wage and employment area consisted of adding new wage and social benefits for labor. Even before the hot autumn of 1969 (that is, in February of that year) there had been a major pension reform that introduced a more generous formula for calculating pensions, tied them to changes in the cost of living, created a social pension for those workers not otherwise qualifying for a pension, established a minimum pension level, and made other changes in the system. In March of that year a decision was made to eliminate regional wage differences gradually (to be completed in July 1972). In the hot autumn of the year, wage negotiations began which culminated in generous wage settlements.

In May 1970 the new Workers' Statute recognized the right to form unions, to assemble in plants, to check off union dues, to prevent unjust dismissals, and to enjoy other work benefits. In December the government negotiated a contract with its own employees which, although less generous than in other sectors, resulted in contractual wage rates rising by more than 9 percent between 1970 and 1971.

In 1971 a pace-setting Fiat contract provided for union participation in establishing work conditions concerning piecework, wage grading, the work environment, and organization of assembly-line work. In 1972 national contracts also dealt with these work-rule issues and regional wage rate differentials ended on schedule (in accordance with the 1969 agreement). Unemployment benefits were improved in industries experiencing restructuring and were extended to agricultural workers.

In 1973 the government negotiated a very generous contract with government employees, which raised contractual wage rates by more than 21 percent that year. Pensions were raised by 30 percent, effective at the beginning of the following year, and family allowances and unemployment benefits were increased. A 1974 Fiat agreement with the union contained a commitment not to discharge any employees in 1975 and to consult the union before reducing hours worked. Although the agreement was peculiar to Fiat, it was symptomatic of the extent to which job security had been achieved, even in a year of deep recession.

January 1975 was the occasion for a revision of the scale mobile wage indexation system that provided for gradual unification of the absolute amount of each point of wage adjustment for all economic sectors at the highest (industrial) level. (There were still some exceptions in the financial sector at higher levels.) The 1975 recession also led to some other benefits for labor. Supplementary wage payments for short-time work were expanded to permit payment for longer periods of time and to provide compensation equal to 80 percent of the normal wage instead of the 66 percent previously paid. Minimum pensions were linked to industrial wage rate changes, as well as to the cost of living, with the aim of assuring some rise in pension income in real terms.

At the beginning of 1976 a more generous method of calculating pensions went into effect, as had been provided by the 1969 reform law. Also early in the year, in the face of financial problems in some industries partly related to the recession, funds were provided to GEPI (a state industrial management and holding company responsible for assisting firms in trouble) in order to provide wage guarantees for up to six months equal to 80 percent of the worker's normal wage. By the fall of the year, however, the accumulation of new balance-of-payments problems and accelerated inflation showed that some action had to be taken on labor costs. The government had been negotiating a new standby arrangement with the IMF for some time without being able to conclude an agreement, and other sources of foreign credit had dried up in the absence of a program agreeable to the fund.

The government asked the three union confederations and Confindustria to develop some measures that would help to contain the rise in unit labor costs, and acted to limit the growth of public sector deficits by approving a large package of direct and indirect tax rises and public service rate increases.

For the first time in the 1970s, union leaders found themselves in the position of being asked to concede some economic benefit, instead of making demands for new benefits. The seriousness of Italy's problems was undeniable and union leaders showed some disposition to make sacrifices. A serious effort was made by the government to obtain agreement to a significant modification in the scale mobile system, which was widely acknowledged to be a key factor behind the continued growth of inflation. Proposals were made to exclude the

effect of rising import costs from the basket in order to avoid the perpetuating of cost-price pressures coming from abroad. Suggestions
were made to exclude indirect tax increases when calculating wage
adjustments. This reflected the government's recognition that the use
of indirect tax policy to restrict the growth of consumption was being
thwarted by wage adjustments that offset the price increases caused
by indirect tax rises. It was also proposed that the frequency of adjustments be reduced from quarterly to semiannually, or that one or more
quarterly adjustments simply be omitted, in order to interrupt the
wage-price spiral.

Agreement was nearly reached on reducing the frequency of
adjustments to a semiannual basis. Last-minute opposition by the
Socialist-led UIL, however, caused the other union leaders to retreat.
Also, a February 1977 decree concerning fiscalization of health insurance costs contained provisions that would have excluded increases
in indirect taxes from scala mobile adjustments and would have introduced tax penalties against firms that agreed to supplementary wage
benefits at the plant level, but these two parts of the decree were not
ratified by Parliament.

In the end, the only concessions to limit the rise in labor costs
that could be agreed to in late 1976 and early 1977 were very modest.
They consisted essentially of wage restraint at plant-level bargaining;
some modest agreements on overtime, work shifts, and internal labor
mobility; unlinking of severance pay from cost-of-living adjustments;
some minor changes in the type of prices included in the scala mobile
market basket with regard to newspapers, urban transport fares, and
electric rates (resulting in one-time prevention of about a 1.5 point
increase in the scala mobile index); the elimination of anomalies in
the form of higher than standard scala mobile adjustments (over
2,389 lire per point) in a few (mainly financial) sectors; a forced loan
to the Treasury through the payment of scala mobile adjustments in
the period September 30, 1976 through April 30, 1978 in the form of
treasury bonds for workers having an annual income in excess of
8 million lire, and payment of half of the adjustments in that form to
workers with income in excess of 6 million lire but less than 8 million
lire; and the abolition of seven holidays. (While these negotiations were
going on, the government also began negotiation of a new labor contract
with government employees that contributed to rises in contractual
wage rates of more than 16 percent both in 1976 and in 1977.)

The various minor modifications in the scala mobile permitted
the government to include a commitment in the April 1977 IMF standby
to a ceiling of 26 points (18.2 percent rise) in wage adjustments between January 1977 and April 1978. (Italy eventually met the target
with 2 points to spare—that is, a rise of 16.8 percent.)

In June 1977, as a partial quid pro quo with the unions, the government passed a law aimed at gradually reducing youth unemployment by creating 600,000 new jobs for young workers in the public and private sectors. (This remained a goal in subsequent economic plans, but performance fell well short of the objective. Between 1977 and 1978 employed youth, 14-29 years old, fell by 45,000.)

The urgency that had characterized the tripartite negotiations of late 1976 and early 1977 receded as the balance-of-payments constraint and pressures from foreign lenders became less important factors. Still, the earlier attitude of union leadership that the economy could somehow adjust to labor demands, made without regard to productivity growth, changed perceptibly and there was greater recognition of the limits to new wage demands, if the employment situation were to improve. In early 1978 the three confederations endorsed wage restraint and supported greater labor mobility in return for promised policies to stimulate investment and new jobs. In December 1978 a limit was placed on the adjustment of higher than minimum pensions arising from the link with industrial wages. A new round of major contracts was negotiated, beginning in late 1978 and finally concluding in mid-1979. The results of the contracts were relatively modest, estimated at about 10 percent (in addition to scala mobile adjustments) extended fairly evenly over a three-year period.

PRICE MEASURES

Generalized attempts during the 1970s to limit price increases by direct measures were sporadic and not very successful. Rent controls were regularly extended throughout the period until July 1978 when a fair-rent law (equo canone) was finally passed. The earlier controls did not apply to luxury housing and were, to some extent, evaded. Although the immediate reaction to the fair-rent statute was unfavorable, the law does provide a system for automatic annual adjustments in rents based on a complex formula, once the initial base is determined.

With the acceleration of price inflation that began after the hot autumn of 1969, the government made occasional efforts to restrain general price rises in an administrative way. Late in 1971 the provincial prefects were urged to use the power provided in 1944 and 1947 laws to fix the local price of some basic necessities. In late 1972 in the province of Rome the government experimented with limiting the increase in some food prices to the prices charged at food stands run by the provincial agency responsible for providing a source of popularly priced foods. This effort was abandoned in favor of stronger appeals for self-restraint. Late that year a release of butter from EC stockpiles was used as an anti-inflation device (as has also been done with frozen beef and powdered milk). With the imposition of the new value-added tax on January 1, 1973, the rates applicable to some foods, textiles, and building costs were introduced at reduced levels to limit the price impact. (These items had formerly been exempt from the old sales tax.)

The only major effort at comprehensive price controls was a one-year experiment begun in July 1973. The approach began with a temporary freeze and then evolved into a system of prior approval. The freeze was initially for about 90 days (but briefly extended) and measures concerned a group of 21 food and other necessities, plus products produced by large firms (those that had had a turnover of at least 5 billion lire in the first half of 1973). Price lists were posted and consumers were encouraged to report violations, which they did for a time, but eventually this approach failed. The price control authorities initially resisted approval of price rises but were soon forced to concede increases in the face of rapid rises in costs. The major oil price increases of 1973 and 1974 and the depreciation of the lira put strong pressures on the price control system. After a brief period of relative price stability (cost-of-living increases of 0.5 percent per month in July–September), the monthly inflation rate exceeded 1 percent in each of the succeeding months of 1973 and did not fall below 1 percent per month again until December 1974. By June 1974 the price control program was abandoned, although the prices of some products continued to be administered and others became subject to surveillance.

While trying to resist general price increases, from about 1974 onward the authorities were also confronted with the problem of permitting administered prices and public service rates to ise in a politically and economically acceptable way. The energy price explosion and the growing problem of public sector deficits by the mid-1970s succeeded in overcoming much political opposition to price and public service rate increases. In fact, the package of such measures approved in late 1976 raised little political opposition.

There were gasoline price rises twice in 1973, twice in 1974, once in 1975, three times in 1976, once in 1977, and once in 1979. Electric rates rose in 1974, 1975, 1976, and 1978; railroad fares were raised in 1975, 1976, 1977, 1978, and twice in 1979; and there were a number of increases in city gas, postal, and telephone rates. In the case of city gas and petroleum products, semiautomatic systems for triggering price modifications based on calculations of the effect of the changes in different cost variables were adopted in 1977 to mitigate the political problem of having to make repeated ad hoc adjustments. Also, laws concerning local government finance for 1978 and 1979 required that any larger than forecast deficit of urban transport companies would have to be covered by fare increases. In 1978, after long debate, the government began requiring token payments for medicines received under health insurance programs, and over-the-counter drugs and even pasta were removed from the list of administered prices.

CONCLUSIONS

The relative hands-off attitude of government to labor negotiation during much of the 1970s was politically understandable, but increasingly risky from the economic point of view. Eventually the government was forced to intervene to adopt some sort of incomes policy. When it did so, economic circumstances were so grave that there was at least some recognition on the part of labor leaders that a change in priorities was required.

It is hard to believe that wage-price pressures can be sufficiently controlled without a significant modification of the scala mobile.[1] Despite the nearly complete protection of wages from cost-of-living increases as a result of the 1975 reform, labor negotiations have been conducted as if this were not the case, with the result that wages have tended to be doubly protected, both by the scale mobile and by negotiated increases. The unions are correct in saying that wage adjustments only follow previous price rises, but the system has become such an efficient means of perpetuating inflationary pressures from whatever source that it is in need of change. Various techniques could be used, but politically and economically, one of the better ways would be the one that nearly succeeded in 1976—a reduction in the frequency of adjustments.* This would be in line with practices in other countries, would reduce the effective coverage of the system, and would restore the role of union leadership in negotiating wage rate changes (instead of nearly all the change being automatic). Negotiated wage adjustments would at least offer some opportunity for shaping wage gains to current economic realities.

In addition, the use of indirect taxation should be freed, at least to some extent, from the scala mobile, either by removing tax changes from computation of adjustments or otherwise limiting the inflationary

---

*Bank of Italy estimates show that quarterly adjustments, as opposed to annual adjustments, cause the price index to rise by at least one-third more over a two-year period as the result of any autonomous inflationary push. (Bank of Italy, Report for the Year 1977 [abridged English version] [Rome: 1978]: 146.)

feedback effect. Greater freedom to use indirect taxes is particularly necessary, because of the usefulness of such taxes in affecting the composition of demand.

Italy now has a system of social benefits that can compare with that in other major industrial countries. It is already having difficulty financing these benefits. Unless the central government is able to reduce its own deficit sufficiently to permit it to continue subsidizing these benefits without resort to massive monetary creation, then the real value of those benefits will be eroded by inflation. Also, unless a closer and more visible link is maintained between rising benefits and the level of contributions, there may well be continued financing problems.

A shift in emphasis from wage increases toward employment growth has generally been accepted in Italy, at least in principle. Italian workers, especially in the industrial sector, have achieved rough equality of pay with their EC colleagues, even though average productivity still falls short of that in other EC countries. Indeed, the generous wage gains made in the past now threaten to impede employment growth for those young people who have benefited from educational reforms earlier supported by the labor movement.

The increased priority given to new job creation makes sense, and specific microeconomic efforts to deal with the problem are worth trying.[2] The results of the youth employment program of 1977, however, have been disappointing. In the long run there is no substitute for providing better incentives for business investment across the board if enough jobs are to be created. Fiscalization of employer social insurance costs, which has an immediate effect on costs, can play a part. It can be justified as a proper responsibility of government (provided the budget situation improves enough to accommodate any additional financial burden). Tax incentives may help, but wage restraint is still the key.

There is not much positive that can be said about past efforts to control prices with direct controls. Public service rates must move in general accord with cost increases. A case can be made for some subsidy element in certain cases, but not to the extent that the monetary financing of the resulting deficits feeds inflation throughout the entire economy.

A more active incomes/employment policy must be supported by complementary monetary and, especially, fiscal policies. Unless those policies can be made more effective, the economic and political environment will not be right for asking sacrifices from workers in the form of wage restraint. The labor movement will be looking particularly at a reduction in the budget deficit as an indication of a reduction of waste in government, and will be pressing for an increase in job-creating public investments.

NOTES

1. See Franco Modigliani and Tomaso Padoa-Schioppa, "The Management of an Open Economy with '100% Plus' Wage Indexation," Princeton University, Essays in International Finance No. 130, (Princeton, N.J.: 1978).

2. See Ettore Massacesi and Maria Finzi, "The Labour Market in Italy," Banco di Roma, Review of the Economic Conditions in Italy Vol. XXXI No. 3 (May 1977): 117-36.

13

OUTLOOK

In addition to the immediate goals, the objective of the
stabilization programme was to launch a policy which
would again give the economy scope for faster growth,
which had been impeded by the worsening of the terms
of trade as a result of the oil crisis. . . . We have not
succeeded, nor are we anywhere near to succeeding, in
shifting domestic demand from consumption to investment; this is the necessary condition for setting in
motion the virtuous circle which will increase productivity, produce a lasting improvement in foreign trade
and allow a larger and steadier expansion of domestic
demand.

Paolo Baffi
Governor, Bank of Italy
Annual Meeting, Rome, May 1978

The Italian economy ended the decade on a positive note in 1979.
Growth was considerably faster than the average for the decade, in
excess of 5 percent. Employment grew by over 1 percent. The balance
of payments was in very large surplus on current account (over $5
billion) and in the overall balance (over $2 billion). The main sour
notes were a reacceleration of inflation (cost of living) to nearly a
16 percent rate, compared to 12 percent in 1978, and another rise in
the unemployment rate (to 7.7 percent versus 7.2 percent in 1978).
The economic recovery brought with it a fairly rapid rise in productivity (about 4 percent) and a slight moderation in the rise in unit labor
costs (about 13 percent). The treasury cash deficit was virtually

unchanged compared to the previous year and there was a modest deceleration in the growth of the money aggregates, with the monetary base up about 19 percent (compared to 25 percent in 1978) and the money supply (M-3) up about 23 percent (compared to 24 percent). Although 1979 was a relatively good year, there was little to suggest that any basic problems had been resolved. Efforts in 1978-79 (the Pandolfi Plan) to follow up the stabilization measures of 1976-77 by moderating the rise in real wages and shifting public expenditures toward investment were thwarted by the fall of governments and the need for early parliamentary elections. Also, the relatively good economic environment reduced the urgency for strong corrective action.

Over the medium term, Italy is likely to continue to experience faster growth of unit labor costs than other major industrial countries. To avoid such an outcome would require a greater moderation in wage rate increases, both from contractual and from automatic adjustments, than seems likely. There has been some moderation in the growth of contractual rates, but any significant modification of the scala mobile will still be tenaciously resisted. In addition, there does not appear to be much prospect of limiting the further growth of employer social insurance contributions. Unless existing labor rigidities are relaxed, productivity growth will continue to suffer. Union leaders have shown some recognition of this fact, but hard-won gains in working conditions are not likely to be given up. On the other hand, the growing political pressures from unemployed youth may exert some restraint on labor costs. If these problems are not addressed directly, then growth of the black labor market will be the only way in which business can survive.

The treasury deficit is still not under control, despite tax reforms and some initial reforms on the expenditure side. The main problem areas are tax evasion and rapidly growing transfer payments. If transfers to cover the cost of growing social welfare benefits and subsidies for public services cannot be financed from taxes, then the income redistribution aims that motivate such expenditures may be thwarted by the unplanned redistribution effects of inflation.

Italy will probably continue to face inflation and balance-of-payments constraints on growth. To domestic inflationary pressure will be added the constant threat of further oil and commodity price increases. If effective fiscal and incomes policies cannot be counted on, then monetary policy will again be employed to force a slowdown in growth in order to obtain some relief from inflation and restore equilibrium in the balance of payments.

On the supply side, Italy still has a potential for moderate growth, based on the entry into the labor force of a growing and better-educated group of workers. Productivity growth, although lower than in earlier years, still offers fairly good potential. The resilience of a large group of small and medium-size businesses is also a positive factor of particular importance for export growth. On the demand side, private consumption growth could rise more rapidly than in recent years (as it did in 1979). Unfortunately, this could be the result of a decline in the high personal savings rate as consumers despair of inflation being brought under control. Public consumption is apt to remain a modest steady support for real growth. Investment in labor-saving machinery and equipment may be sustained by the continued pressure of rising labor costs. The decline in investment in plant expansion after the modest 1973-74 revival may have been arrested in 1978-79. Export demand will depend on the extent to which unit labor costs are contained, the exchange rate is allowed to move, and the world economy grows, in an environment in which problems with energy costs and availability persist.

The most intractable problem is likely to remain inflation, due both to domestic and to international factors. Persistence to a large budget deficit will make it difficult to avoid an accommodating monetary policy.

Despite probable future pressures of the balance of payments, the past record of balance-of-payments adjustment is impressive. At least it appears that periodic economic slowdowns, following a stop-go pattern, do bring about a rather prompt, if unpleasant, restoration of balance-of-payments equilibrium.

In sum, over the medium term, the Italian economy will probably continue to face the same sort of problems that arose in the 1970s. In view of the generally uncertain world economic outlook, at least Italy will not be alone.

TABLE A.1

Treasury Cash Deficit, 1970-78
(billions of lire)

	1970	1971	1972	1973	1974	1975	1976	1977	1978
Receipts	10,596	11,866	12,264	14,263	18,432	23,764	31,975	43,099	53,894
Expenditures	13,055	14,912	15,885	21,565	23,636	34,046	42,381	55,542	87,319
Budget deficit[a]	-2,459	-3,046	-3,621	-7,302	-5,204	-10,282	-10,406	-12,443	-33,425
Minor treasury operations[b]	291	-507	-809	847	-1,936	-4,103	-1,721	36	3,356
Postal Savings Fund	-600	-723	-784	-1,246	-1,881	-2,000	-2,502	-9,625	-3,825
Autonomous entities	-458	-482	-540	-264	59	-135	-108	-382	-43
Total off-budget	-767	-1,712	-2,133	-663	-3,758	-6,238	-4,331	-9,971	-512
Total cash deficit	-3,226	-4,758	-5,754	-7,965	-8,962	-16,520	-14,737	-22,414	-33,937
Less debt consolidation[c]	—	310	155	469	315	2,393	407	5,379	5,211
(Health insurance institutes)	—	—	—	—	—	2,298	407	503	477
(Hospitals)	—	—	—	—	—	—	—	561	2,461
(Provincial/municipal governments)	—	310	155	469	315	95	—	4,315	2,273
Net cash deficit	-3,226	-4,448	-5,599	-7,496	-8,647	-14,127	-14,330	-17,035	-28,726
Current account[a]	-251	-181	-689	-2,313	-624	-3,740	-862	-2,298	-18,249
Capital account	-2,208	-2,865	-2,932	-4,989	-4,580	-6,542	-9,544	-10,145	-15,176
Total	-2,459	-3,046	-3,621	-7,302	-5,204	-10,282	-10,406	-12,443	-33,425

[b] For 1977 and 1978 includes expenditures financed by foreign borrowing of the Cassa per il Mezzogiorno.
[c] Consolidation of health institute and hospital debt is included in budget expenditures; consolidation of local government debt is included in off-budget (Postal Savings Fund) data.
Source: Compiled by the author; Bank of Italy annual reports and appendixes.

TABLE A.2

GDP Sources (Current Lire), 1960–78
(billions)

	Value Added at Market Prices—Goods and Services for Sale						Value Added in Services Not for Sale			Total Value Added at Market Price (Excluding Bank Services)	Indirect Taxes on Imports	GDP at Market Prices
	Primary	Secondary	Tertiary	Total	Less Imputed Bank Services	Net of Bank Services	Public Administration	Other	Total			
1960	2,841	9,577	n.a.	n.a.	-412	n.a.	n.a.	n.a.	n.a.	22,780	427	23,207
1961	3,284	10,606	n.a.	n.a.	-477	n.a.	n.a.	n.a.	n.a.	25,343	467	25,810
1962	3,624	11,975	n.a.	n.a.	-556	n.a.	n.a.	n.a.	n.a.	28,449	549	28,998
1963	3,864	13,758	n.a.	n.a.	-720	n.a.	n.a.	n.a.	n.a.	32,546	669	33,215
1964	4,121	15,023	n.a.	n.a.	-839	n.a.	n.a.	n.a.	n.a.	35,744	616	36,360
1965	4,373	15,888	n.a.	n.a.	-917	n.a.	n.a.	n.a.	n.a.	38,485	639	39,124
1966	4,451	17,188	n.a.	n.a.	-970	n.a.	n.a.	n.a.	n.a.	41,647	744	42,391
1967	4,679	19,256	n.a.	n.a.	-1,067	n.a.	n.a.	n.a.	n.a.	45,847	848	46,695
1968	4,510	20,956	n.a.	n.a.	-1,213	n.a.	n.a.	n.a.	n.a.	49,670	944	50,614
1969	4,978	23,315	n.a.	n.a.	-1,409	n.a.	n.a.	n.a.	n.a.	54,863	1,013	55,876
1970	5,122	26,968	24,204	56,294	-1,646	54,648	6,557	496	7,053	61,701	1,182	62,883
1971	5,299	28,720	26,801	60,820	-1,934	58,886	7,898	558	8,456	67,342	1,168	68,510
1972	5,403	31,214	29,918	66,535	-2,158	64,377	8,980	617	9,597	73,974	1,150	75,124
1973	6,976	37,875	34,398	79,249	-2,763	76,486	10,470	668	11,138	87,624	2,122	89,746
1974	8,096	48,173	42,089	98,358	-4,161	94,197	12,445	792	13,237	107,434	3,285	110,719
1975	9,644	53,205	50,375	113,224	-6,169	107,055	14,215	936	15,151	122,206	3,172	125,378
1976	11,222	68,373	60,853	140,448	-7,126	133,322	17,241	1,128	18,369	151,691	4,966	156,657
1977	13,402	82,354	73,327	169,083	-8,270	160,813	21,535	1,314	22,849	183,662	6,316	189,978
1978	15,729	94,762	84,745	195,236	-9,105	186,131	26,035	1,552	27,587	213,718	7,025	220,743

Note: Total services (including imputed bank services): 1960, 10,774; 1961, 11,930; 1962, 13,406; 1963, 15,644; 1964, 17,439; 1965, 19,141; 1966, 20,978; 1967, 22,979; 1968, 25,417; 1969, 27,979; 1970, 21,257; 1971, 35,257; 1972, 39,515; 1973, 45,536; 1974, 55,326; 1975, 65,526; 1976, 79,222; 1977, 96,176; 1978, 112,332.

Source: Compiled by the author; data from Relazione Generale 1978 and ISTAT, Conti Economici Nazionali 1960–78 (Nuova serie), 1979, pp. 9–10.

TABLE A.3

GDP Sources (1970 Lire), 1960-78
(billions)

| | Value Added at Market Prices—Goods and Services for Sale | | | | | | Value Added in Services Not for Sale | | | Total Value Added at Market Price (Excluding Bank Services) | Indirect Taxes on Imports | GDP at Market Prices |
	Primary	Secondary	Tertiary	Total	Less Imputed Bank Services	Net of Bank Services	Public Administration	Other	Total			
1960	3,969	13,707	13,250	30,926	-720	30,206	n.a.	n.a.	5,475	35,681	412	36,093
1961	4,316	15,114	14,417	33,847	-874	32,973	n.a.	n.a.	5,652	38,625	430	39,055
1962	4,288	16,513	15,333	36,134	-938	35,196	n.a.	n.a.	5,748	40,944	534	41,478
1963	4,388	17,613	16,342	38,343	-1,075	37,268	n.a.	n.a.	5,875	43,143	662	43,805
1964	4,611	17,897	17,040	39,598	-1,183	38,415	n.a.	n.a.	5,995	44,410	620	45,030
1965	4,695	18,383	17,844	40,922	-1,207	39,715	n.a.	n.a.	6,162	45,877	625	46,502
1966	4,828	19,757	18,748	43,333	-1,220	42,113	n.a.	n.a.	6,459	48,572	713	49,285
1967	5,205	21,597	19,919	46,721	-1,308	45,413	n.a.	n.a.	6,601	52,014	809	52,823
1968	5,055	23,643	21,380	50,078	-1,429	48,649	n.a.	n.a.	6,776	55,425	855	56,280
1969	5,138	25,403	22,783	53,324	-1,537	51,787	n.a.	n.a.	6,908	58,695	1,017	59,712
1970	5,122	26,968	24,204	56,294	-1,646	54,648	6,557	496	7,053	61,701	1,182	62,883
1971	5,148	26,920	25,059	57,127	-1,728	55,399	6,817	503	7,320	62,719	1,197	63,916
1972	4,767	27,927	26,180	58,874	-1,821	57,053	7,085	513	7,598	64,651	1,312	65,963
1973	5,101	30,459	27,608	63,168	-1,910	61,258	7,338	525	7,863	69,121	1,480	70,601
1974	5,196	31,870	28,859	65,925	-2,034	63,891	7,573	550	8,123	72,014	1,511	73,525
1975	5,369	29,010	28,854	63,233	-2,085	61,148	7,779	576	8,355	69,503	1,348	70,851
1976	5,149	31,925	29,947	67,021	-2,204	64,817	8,067	563	8,630	73,447	1,564	75,011
1977	5,123	32,404	30,902	68,429	-2,286	66,143	8,279	543	8,822	74,965	1,551	76,516
1978	5,301	33,061	31,838	70,200	-2,370	67,830	8,418	550	8,968	76,798	1,670	78,468

Note: Total services (including imputed bank services): 1960, 18,725; 1961, 20,069; 1962, 21,081; 1963, 22,217; 1964, 23,085; 1965, 24,006; 1966, 25,207; 1967, 26,520; 1968, 28,156; 1969, 29,691; 1970, 31,257; 1971, 32,379; 1972, 33,778; 1973, 35,471; 1974, 36,982; 1975, 37,209; 1976, 38,577; 1977, 39,724; 1978, 40,806.

Source: Compiled by the author; data from ISCO, Relazione Generale 1978 and ISTAT, Conti Economici Nazionali 1960–1978 (Nuova serie), 1979, pp. 9, 11.

TABLE A.4

GDP, Domestic and National Income, 1960–78
(billions of current lire)

	Net Domestic Income at Factor Cost[a]			Net National Income at Factor Cost[a]			Net Indirect Business Taxes	Amortization	Gross Domestic Income—Market Price[b]
	Wages/Salaries	Other	Total	Wages/Salaries	Other	Total			
1960	9,855	8,959	18,814	9,951	8,923	18,874	2,496	1,897	23,207
1961	10,954	9,935	20,889	11,077	9,867	20,944	2,843	2,078	25,810
1962	12,745	10,830	23,575	12,909	10,717	23,626	3,098	2,325	28,998
1963	15,506	11,534	27,040	15,698	11,396	27,094	3,486	2,689	33,215
1964	17,348	12,190	29,538	17,562	12,053	29,615	3,763	3,059	36,360
1965	18,313	13,516	31,829	18,577	13,391	31,968	4,009	3,286	39,124
1966	19,585	15,059	34,644	19,880	14,950	34,830	4,287	3,460	42,391
1967	21,663	16,390	38,053	21,920	16,298	38,218	4,944	3,698	46,695
1968	23,555	17,997	41,552	23,836	17,920	41,756	5,095	3,967	50,614
1969	25,954	20,096	46,050	26,279	20,031	46,310	5,425	4,401	55,876
1970	30,349	21,314	51,663	30,714	21,193	51,907	6,092	5,128	62,883
1971	34,727	21,909	56,636	35,124	21,775	56,899	6,323	5,551	68,510
1972	38,753	24,127	62,880	39,163	23,960	63,123	6,141	6,103	75,124
1973	47,080	27,934	75,014	47,553	27,658	75,211	7,207	7,525	89,746
1974	58,606	32,805	91,411	59,055	32,174	91,229	9,137	10,171	110,719
1975	71,204	33,263	104,467	71,618	32,307	103,925	7,992	12,919	125,378
1976	86,953	42,374	129,327	87,429	41,282	128,711	11,537	15,793	156,657
1977	106,299	49,026	155,325	107,109	47,796	154,905	15,208	19,445	189,978
1978	122,702	58,563	181,265	123,821	57,300	181,121	17,052	22,426	220,743

[a]Difference between net domestic and net national income is net factor income from abroad.

[b]Total Net Domestic Income + Net Indirect Business Taxes + Amortization.

Source: Compiled by the author; data from Relazione Generale (1978), p. 98, and ISTAT, Conti Economici Nazionali 1960–1978 (Nuova serie), 1979, pp. 12, 14–15.

TABLE A.5

GDP Uses (Current Lire), 1960–78
(billions)

	Domestic Consumption			Gross Fixed Investment	Changes in Inventories	Net Foreign Balance	GDP at Market Prices
	Total	Private	Public				
1960	17,898	14,788	3,110	5,240	495	-426	23,207
1961	19,623	16,179	3,444	5,998	588	-399	25,810
1962	22,225	18,243	3,982	6,859	498	-584	28,998
1963	26,112	21,292	4,820	7,975	347	-1,219	33,215
1964	28,530	23,152	5,378	8,075	172	-417	36,360
1965	30,970	24,883	6,087	7,540	276	338	39,124
1966	33,952	27,472	6,480	7,967	356	116	42,391
1967	37,226	30,299	6,927	9,104	491	-126	46,695
1968	39,814	32,273	7,541	10,275	19	506	50,614
1969	43,545	35,366	8,179	11,752	394	185	55,876
1970	48,818	39,840	8,978	13,434	1,077	-446	62,883
1971	54,232	43,249	10,983	13,947	424	-93	68,510
1972	60,084	47,585	12,499	14,842	465	-267	75,124
1973	70,929	56,584	14,345	18,651	3,025	-2,859	89,746
1974	87,474	70,197	17,277	24,775	4,652	-6,182	110,719
1975	101,473	81,446	20,027	25,776	-352	-1,519	125,378
1976	123,553	99,504	24,049	31,396	5,666	-3,958	156,657
1977	150,002	120,329	29,673	37,352	3,515	-891	189,978
1978	175,848	139,545	36,303	41,406	1,854	1,635	220,743

Source: ISTAT, Conti Economici Nazionali 1960–1978 (Nuova serie), 1979, p. 8.

TABLE A.6

GDP Uses (1970 Lire), 1960-78
(billions)

	Domestic Consumption			Gross Fixed Investment	Change in Inventories	Net Foreign Balance	GDP at Market Prices
	Total	Private	Public				
1960	27,563	21,467	6,096	8,206	728	-404	36,093
1961	29,449	23,071	6,378	9,155	843	-392	39,055
1962	31,345	24,719	6,626	10,049	682	-598	41,478
1963	33,833	26,937	6,896	10,861	447	-1,336	43,805
1964	34,995	27,862	7,133	10,229	209	-403	45,030
1965	36,304	28,911	7,393	9,369	323	506	46,502
1966	38,710	31,024	7,686	9,774	408	393	49,285
1967	41,233	33,200	8,033	10,921	551	118	52,823
1968	43,306	34,862	8,444	12,100	21	853	56,280
1969	45,829	37,137	8,692	13,038	421	424	59,712
1970	48,818	39,840	8,978	13,434	1,077	-446	62,883
1971	50,496	41,001	9,495	13,001	398	21	63,916
1972	52,396	42,399	9,997	13,120	413	-34	65,963
1973	55,058	44,848	10,210	14,134	2,169	-760	70,601
1974	56,550	46,020	10,530	15,607	2,186	182	73,525
1975	56,275	45,395	10,880	12,745	-143	1,974	70,851
1976	58,138	46,976	11,162	13,044	1,865	1,964	75,011
1977	59,479	48,071	11,408	13,050	938	3,049	76,516
1978	61,265	49,455	11,810	12,993	465	3,745	78,468

Source: ISTAT, Conti Economici Nazionali 1960-1978 (Nuova serie), 1979, p. 8.

Demographic and Labor Force Trends, 1959-79
(thousands)

	Population (Average Resident)			Labor Force			Participation Rates[a]			Female Share of Labor Force (percent)
	Male	Female	Total	Male	Female	Total	Male	Female	Total	
1959	23,671	24,933	48,604	14,899	6,980	21,879	62.9	28.0	45.0	31.9
1960	23,845	25,122	48,967	14,904	6,641	21,545	62.5	26.4	44.0	30.8
1961	23,871	25,285	49,156	14,825	6,710	21,535	62.1	26.5	43.8	31.2
1962	24,097	25,466	49,563	14,749	6,557	21,306	61.2	25.7	43.0	30.8
1963	24,275	25,661	49,936	14,616	6,236	20,852	60.2	24.3	41.8	29.9
1964	24,549	25,890	50,439	14,786	6,084	20,870	60.2	23.5	41.4	29.2
1965	24,273	26,117	50,840	14,655	5,957	20,612	59.3	22.8	40.5	28.9
1966	24,921	26,306	51,227	14,591	5,776	20,367	58.5	22.0	39.8	28.4
1967	25,176	26,488	51,664	14,719	5,788	20,507	58.5	21.9	39.7	28.2
1968	25,367	26,675	52,042	14,673	5,882	20,555	57.8	22.1	39.5	28.6
1969	25,520	26,856	52,376	14,485	5,884	20,369	56.8	21.9	38.9	28.9
1970	25,704	27,067	52,771	14,547	5,889	20,436	56.6	21.8	38.7	28.8
1971	25,889	27,235	53,124	14,507	5,897	20,404	56.0	21.7	38.4	28.9
1972	26,102	27,446	53,548	14,460	5,833	20,293	55.4	21.3	37.9	28.7
1973	26,304	27,677	53,981	14,443	6,047	20,490	54.9	21.8	38.0	29.5
1974	26,590	27,951	54,541	14,564	6,150	20,714	54.8	22.0	38.0	29.7
1975	26,804	28,163	54,967	14,646	6,300	20,946	54.6	22.4	38.1	30.1
1976	26,992	28,333	55,325	14,698	6,587	21,285	54.5	23.2	38.5	30.9
1977	27,104	28,469	55,573	14,664	6,943	21,607	54.1	24.4	38.9	32.1
1978	27,215	28,591	55,806	14,734	6,996	21,730	54.1	24.5	38.9	32.2
1979*	—	—	—	—	—	22,075	—	—	—	—

*Preliminary.
[a]Labor force divided by population.
Source: Compiled by the author; data from ISTAT, "Note e Relazioni" No. 56 (1979): 26. (New labor survey.)

TABLE A.8

Labor Force, Employment, Unemployment, 1959-79 (thousands)

	Total Employed	Seeking Employment						Total Number	Total Labor Force	Unemployment Rates (percent)		
		Previously Employed		First Job		Marginal[a]				Male	Female	Total
		Number	Percent	Number	Percent	Number	Percent					
1959	20,349	715	46.7	461	30.1	354	23.2	1,530	21,879	6.1	8.8	7.0
1960	20,330	525	43.2	359	29.6	331	27.2	1,215	21,545	4.8	7.4	5.6
1961	20,427	413	37.3	349	31.5	346	31.2	1,108	21,535	4.2	7.3	5.1
1962	20,337	326	33.6	338	34.9	305	31.5	969	21,306	3.5	6.8	4.5
1963	20,045	267	33.1	282	34.9	258	32.0	807	20,852	3.1	5.7	3.9
1964	19,966	312	34.5	304	33.6	288	31.9	904	20,870	3.3	6.8	4.3
1965	19,502	465	41.9	319	28.7	326	29.4	1,110	20,612	4.3	8.1	5.4
1966	19,175	468	39.3	372	31.2	352	29.5	1,192	20,367	4.7	8.9	5.9
1967	19,401	385	34.8	378	34.2	343	31.0	1,106	20,507	4.1	8.7	5.4
1968	19,383	358	30.5	423	36.1	391	33.4	1,172	20,555	4.2	9.5	5.7
1969	19,209	304	26.2	459	39.6	397	34.2	1,160	20,369	4.0	9.9	5.7
1970	19,325	269	24.2	449	40.4	393	35.4	1,111	20,436	3.7	9.6	5.4
1971	19,295	279	25.2	435	39.2	395	35.6	1,109	20,404	3.8	9.5	5.4
1972	18,996	262	20.2	569	43.9	466	35.9	1,297	20,293	4.6	10.9	6.4
1973	19,185	248	19.0	516	39.5	541	41.5	1,305	20,490	4.2	11.6	6.4
1974	19,601	194	17.4	489	44.0	430	38.6	1,113	20,714	3.6	9.6	5.4
1975	19,716	246	20.0	511	41.5	473	38.5	1,230	20,946	3.8	10.7	5.9
1976	19,859	255	17.9	603	42.3	568	39.8	1,426	21,285	4.2	12.2	6.7
1977	20,062	211	13.7	693	44.8	641	41.5	1,545	21,607	4.6	12.5	7.2
1978	20,159	212	13.5	792	50.4	567	36.1	1,571	21,730	4.7	12.6	7.2
1979	20,377	226	13.3	866	51.0	606	35.7	1,698	22,075	n.a.	n.a.	7.7

[a] Consists of workers (for example, students, housewives, retirees) in the surveys who initially claim not to be part of the labor force, but then claim to be seeking employment.

Note: n.a.—not available.

Source: Compiled by the author; data from ISTAT, "Note e Relazioni" No. 56 (1979): 26. (New labor survey.)

TABLE A.9

Total Employment by Sector, 1959–79
(thousands)

	Agriculture	Industry	Services	Total	Dependent[a]	Independent[b] Number	Independent[b] Percent of Total	Percent of Total Agriculture	Percent of Total Industry	Percent of Total Services
1959	6,883	6,651	6,815	20,349	11,345	9,004	44.2	33.8	32.7	33.5
1960	6,611	6,865	6,854	20,330	11,755	8,575	42.2	32.5	33.8	33.7
1961	6,272	7,138	7,017	20,427	12,093	8,334	40.8	30.7	34.9	34.4
1962	5,923	7,341	7,073	20,337	12,463	7,874	38.7	29.1	36.1	34.8
1963	5,436	7,509	7,100	20,045	12,702	7,343	36.6	27.1	37.5	35.4
1964	5,125	7,484	7,357	19,966	12,581	7,385	37.0	25.7	37.5	36.8
1965	5,103	7,183	7,216	19,502	12,214	7,288	37.4	26.2	36.8	37.0
1966	4,810	7,063	7,302	19,175	12,077	7,098	37.0	25.1	36.8	38.1
1967	4,710	7,203	7,488	19,401	12,331	7,070	36.4	24.3	37.1	38.6
1968	4,418	7,292	7,673	19,383	12,467	6,916	35.7	22.8	37.6	39.6
1969	4,204	7,444	7,561	19,209	12,665	6,544	34.1	21.9	38.7	39.4
1970	3,878	7,591	7,856	19,325	12,918	6,407	33.2	20.1	39.3	40.6
1971	3,875	7,617	7,803	19,295	13,078	6,217	32.2	20.1	39.5	40.4
1972	3,593	7,477	7,926	18,996	13,094	5,902	31.1	18.9	39.4	41.7
1973	3,489	7,470	8,226	19,185	13,359	5,826	30.4	18.2	38.9	42.9
1974	3,412	7,639	8,550	19,601	13,745	5,856	29.9	17.4	39.0	43.6
1975	3,274	7,669	8,773	19,716	13,937	5,779	29.3	16.6	38.9	44.5
1976	3,244	7,566	9,049	19,859	14,104	5,755	29.0	16.3	38.1	45.6
1977	3,149	7,666	9,247	20,062	14,360	5,702	28.4	15.7	38.2	46.1
1978	3,090	7,633	9,436	20,159	14,363	5,796	28.8	15.3	37.9	46.8
1979	3,012	7,646	9,719	20,377	n.a.	n.a.	n.a.	14.8	37.5	47.7

[a]Wage and salary workers.
[b]Self-employed.
Note: n.a.—not available.
Source: Compiled by the author; data from ISTAT, "Note e Relazioni" No. 56 (July 1979). (New labor survey.)

TABLE A.10

Prices, 1960–78
(percent annual change; year-over-year unless otherwise indicated)

| December to December | Cost of Living Components | | | | | | Scala Mobile* | Wholesale | | |
	Food	Clothing	Electricity/ Fuel	Housing	Other	Total		Agricultural Products	Nonagricultural Products	Total
1960 1.8	1.0	2.3	-0.3	15.4	3.6	2.7	2.4	1.7	0.7	0.9
1961 3.8	1.6	0.5	-0.5	13.4	3.1	2.9	2.4	1.8	—	0.2
1962 7.3	5.1	4.1	0.7	11.3	3.1	5.1	5.0	8.7	1.5	3.0
1963 8.4	8.0	6.2	3.2	10.1	6.1	7.5	8.4	6.2	4.8	5.2
1964 6.2	5.0	5.6	5.2	7.8	8.0	5.9	7.4	—	4.3	3.4
1965 2.9	4.8	2.3	1.7	4.1	4.7	4.3	5.4	4.0	0.9	1.6
1966 1.8	1.8	1.5	0.6	3.2	2.3	2.1	2.9	1.8	1.5	1.5
1967 1.7	1.1	2.1	1.5	2.9	2.1	2.0	2.1	-0.8	—	-0.2
1968 1.4	0.4	1.9	-0.5	4.8	1.9	1.3	1.7	1.8	—	0.4
1969 4.3	2.7	2.9	—	5.2	2.5	2.8	2.8	5.8	3.5	3.9
1970 5.3	4.5	7.5	6.5	5.5	5.2	5.0	5.0	4.9	7.9	7.3
1971 4.7	3.9	7.3	4.0	2.9	6.5	5.0	4.9	2.2	3.6	3.4
1972 7.4	6.1	6.1	-0.1	2.9	6.4	5.6	6.0	10.2	3.0	4.1
1973 12.3	11.8	12.0	0.9	5.7	9.7	10.4	11.4	27.2	15.2	17.0
1974 25.3	18.3	18.0	41.6	3.8	23.3	19.4	15.2	17.3	45.5	40.7
1975 11.1	18.4	15.3	5.1	13.0	18.2	17.2	18.9	10.8	8.2	8.6
1976 21.8	16.6	16.3	12.9	10.4	17.9	16.5	14.8	23.9	22.7	22.9
1977 14.9	17.6	23.4	29.5	5.8	18.2	18.1	19.5	17.7	16.4	16.6
1978 11.9	13.2	14.7	10.8	8.1	11.8	12.4	12.6	11.2	8.1	8.4

*Calculated from quarterly index.
Source: Compiled by the author; data from ISTAT bulletins and Conti Economici Nazionali 1960–78 (Nuova serie), 1979.

TABLE A.11

GDP Deflators, 1961-78
(percent annual change)

	GDP	Primary*	Secondary*	Services*	Private Domestic Consumption	Public Consumption	Gross Fixed Investments	Exports: Goods and Services	Imports: Goods and Services
1961	2.8	6.3	0.4	3.3	1.7	5.9	2.5	-1.8	-2.3
1962	5.7	11.0	3.3	7.1	5.3	11.3	4.3	0.2	0.2
1963	8.4	4.3	7.7	10.7	7.0	16.3	7.5	2.8	1.7
1964	6.5	1.5	7.4	7.2	5.2	7.9	7.5	3.2	3.5
1965	4.2	4.1	3.0	5.6	3.6	9.2	2.0	-0.9	0.5
1966	2.3	-1.0	0.7	4.4	2.9	2.4	1.2	—	1.7
1967	2.8	-2.5	2.5	4.1	3.0	2.3	2.3	1.2	0.6
1968	1.7	-0.8	-0.7	4.3	1.4	3.6	1.8	0.1	0.5
1969	4.1	8.6	3.6	4.3	2.8	5.4	6.1	2.7	1.3
1970	6.8	3.2	8.9	6.2	5.0	6.3	11.0	6.2	3.5
1971	7.2	2.9	6.7	8.9	5.5	15.7	7.3	4.1	5.2
1972	6.3	10.1	4.8	7.4	6.4	8.0	5.4	2.3	3.7
1973	11.6	21.2	11.2	9.7	12.5	12.4	16.7	15.6	26.2
1974	18.5	13.9	21.6	16.5	20.8	16.8	28.5	36.6	57.2
1975	17.5	15.3	21.3	17.7	17.6	12.2	19.2	10.9	6.0
1976	18.0	21.3	16.8	16.6	18.1	17.0	19.0	20.5	24.0
1977	18.9	20.0	18.6	17.9	18.2	20.7	19.0	19.2	17.0
1978	13.3	13.4	12.8	13.7	12.7	18.2	11.3	7.2	4.5

*Deflators for value added; services include both services for sale and not for sale (including public administration).
Note: GDP series introduced in 1979.
Source: Compiled by the author; data from ISTAT bulletins and Conti Economici Nazionali 1960-78 (Nuova serie), 1979.

TABLE A.12

Summary Balance of Payments, 1960-78
(millions of dollars)

| | Balance of Payments | | | | | | | | Financing | |
| | Trade (f.o.b.) | | | Services and Unilateral Transfers | Current Account | Capital Account | Adjustments | Surplus/ Deficit[a] | Official Position | Commercial Bank Position[a] |
	Exports	Imports	Balance							
1960	3,570	4,204	-634	951	317	167	-41	443	-174	-269
1961	4,103	4,659	-556	1,064	508	202	-133	577	-617	40
1962	4,589	5,469	-880	1,156	276	-309	81	48	-481	433
1963	4,984	6,843	-1,859	1,158	-701	-485	-80	-1,266	602	664
1964	5,863	6,508	-645	1,265	620	110	35	765	-332	-433
1965	7,104	6,458	646	1,563	2,209	-455	-174	1,580	-960	-620
1966	7,929	7,595	334	1,783	2,117	-1,276	-171	670	-288	-382
1967	8,605	8,626	-21	1,620	1,599	-1,023	-284	292	-519	227
1968	10,098	9,050	1,048	1,579	2,627	-1,691	-282	654	61	-715
1969	11,642	11,100	542	1,798	2,340	-3,624	-133	-1,417	705	712
1970b	13,117	13,498	-381	1,513	1,132	-608	-205	319	-375	56
1971b	14,839	14,725	114	1,788	1,902	-931	-223	748	-952	204
1972	18,495	18,441	54	1,955	2,009	-2,701	-561	-1,253	845	408
1973	22,137	26,116	-3,979	1,447	-2,532	2,987	-964	-509	413	96
1974	30,074	38,568	-8,494	475	-8,019	2,399	-101	-5,721	4,853	868
1975	34,553	35,719	-1,166	589	-577	-807	-737	-2,121	2,591	-470
1976	36,997	41,236	-4,239	1,423	-2,816	1,784	-721	-1,753	-970	2,723
1977	44,808	44,942	-134	2,600	2,466	-61	-423	1,982	-6,007	4,025
1978	55,392	52,482	2,910	3,451	6,361	1,536	333	8,230	-7,242	-988

a All data on commercial banks' position (and overall surplus or deficit) have been revised in line with new definitions embodied in 1977 and 1978 published data.

b Published data were adjusted to shift hidden capital flight from services/transfers to capital account. (Published data for 1972-76 already include such an adjustment.)

Note: Through 1970 figures are published dollar data. From 1971 on, data are converted lira data. (lire per dollar): 1971, 625; 1972, 581.5; 1973, 581.5; 1974, 650; 1975, 653; 1976, 832; 1977, 882; 1978, 849.

Source: Compiled by the author; data from Bank of Italy annual reports.

343

TABLE A.13

Creation and Use of Monetary Base, 1960–78
(billions of lire)

		Creation				Use	
	Foreign Sector	Treasury	Credit to Banks	Other	Total	Public	Banks
1960	-38	221	27	18	228	406	-178
1961	390	240	261	-32	859	641	218
1962	607	582	272	-8	1,453	698	755
1963	-718	979	475	-7	729	752	-23
1964	294	795	164	6	931	546	385
1965	627	918	-169	-67	1,309	776	533
1966	234	495	561	-75	1,215	805	410
1967	243	405	627	-59	1,216	1,017	199
1968	123	922	221	-75	1,191	527	664
1969	-648	1,234	707	-105	1,188	1,095	93
1970	319	2,963	-1,276	-74	1,932	763	1,169
1971	478	2,611	90	174	3,353	1,824	1,529
1972	-415	4,171	935	-1,092	3,599	2,407	1,192
1973	-205	7,243	277	-2,229	5,086	3,313	1,773
1974	-3,115	7,671	1,362	-1,812	4,106	2,043	2,063
1975	-1,700	7,780	-389	1,191	6,882	4,124	2,758
1976	1,093	11,745	-1,477	-3,983	7,378	4,080	3,298
1977	5,209	-810	209	4,936	9,544	4,922	4,622
1978	5,820	9,918	-242	-917	14,579	7,614	6,965

Source: Compiled by the author; data from Bank of Italy annual reports.

TABLE A.14

Total Domestic Credit Expansion, 1967–78
(billions of lire)

		Non-Treasury[b]						Percent of Total	
	Treasury[a]	Banks[c]	Special Credit Institutes[d]	Bond Issues[e]	Total	Total	Percent Change	Treasury	Non-Treasury
1967	1,036	2,522	1,384	433	4,339	5,375	11.9	19.3	80.7
1968	1,548	2,012	1,702	571	4,285	5,833	11.6	26.5	73.5
1969	1,386	3,140	1,552	504	5,196	6,582	11.7	21.1	78.9
1970	3,058	3,324	1,654	35	5,013	8,071	12.8	37.9	62.1
1971	4,108	3,821	3,186	519	7,526	11,634	16.4	35.3	64.7
1972	5,415	5,795	3,033	828	9,656	15,071	18.2	35.9	64.1
1973	7,204	7,380	5,473	845	13,698	20,902	21.4	34.5	65.5
1974	8,532	7,789	3,061	69	10,919	19,451	16.4	43.9	56.1
1975	13,619	9,760	5,783	1,705	17,248	30,867	22.4	44.1	55.9
1976	13,593	13,865	4,901	1,017	19,783	33,376	19.8	40.7	59.3
1977	16,857	11,951	5,703	1,283	18,937	35,794	17.7	47.1	52.9
1978	28,202	13,496	6,196	1,125	20,817	49,019	20.6	57.5	42.5

[a]Includes Treasury, Postal Savings Fund, Cassa per il Mezzogiorno, and autonomous entities; excludes contributions from Treasury to special credit institutes.
[b]Credit to rest of economy from banks, special credit institutes, and bond issues.
[c]Domestic credit adjusted to include consolidated debt of health insurance funds.
[d]Domestic credit.
[e]Net issues of local governments, state holding companies, and private companies.
Source: Compiled by the author; data from Bank of Italy Research Office.

TABLE A.15

Money Supply and Income Velocity of Money, 1960-78
(billions of lire)

	M-1		M-3			Velocity	
	Amount	Percent Change	Amount	Percent Change	GDP	M-1[a]	M-3[b]
1960	7,516	13.6	15,147	13.3	23,207	3.09	1.53
1961	8,670	15.4	17,481	15.4	25,810	2.98	1.48
1962	10,174	17.3	20,414	16.8	28,998	2.85	1.42
1963	11,550	13.5	23,025	12.8	33,215	2.88	1.44
1964	12,432	7.6	25,032	8.7	36,360	2.92	1.45
1965	14,435	16.1	28,893	15.4	39,124	2.71	1.35
1966	16,371	13.4	32,879	13.8	42,391	2.59	1.29
1967	18,863	15.2	37,284	13.4	46,695	2.48	1.25
1968	21,127	12.0	41,560	11.5	50,614	2.40	1.22
1969	24,449	15.7	46,315	11.4	55,876	2.29	1.21
1970	31,105	27.2	52,618	13.6	62,883	2.02	1.20
1971	36,956	18.8	61,609	17.1	68,510	1.85	1.11
1972	43,411	17.5	72,855	18.3	75,124	1.73	1.03
1973	53,875	24.1	89,732	23.2	89,746	1.67	1.00
1974	59,498	10.4	103,605	15.5	110,719	1.86	1.07
1975	66,744	12.2	127,914	23.5	125,378	1.88	0.98
1976	79,915	19.7	157,054	22.8	156,657	1.96	1.00
1977	97,189	21.6	194,497	23.8	189,978	1.95	0.98
1978	122,579	26.1	241,233	24.0	220,743	1.80	0.92

[a]GDP ÷ M-1.
[b]GDP ÷ M-3.

Source: Compiled by the author; data from Bank of Italy bulletins (adjusted for revision in net foreign position of commercial banks).

TABLE A.16

Interest Rates, 1970-78
(average for period)

| | Commercial Banks | | | | Special Credit Institutes | | | Securities | | |
| | Borrowing Rates | | | Lending Rate (average)* | Borrowing Rate, Bond Issues (Industrial) | Lending Rates | | Private Bond Yields | Treasury Bills | |
	Interbank (Sight Deposits)	Euromarket (3 months)	Lira Deposits			Subsidized	Ordinary		3 months	12 months
1970	7.57	8.52	4.96	9.15	9.05	4.68	9.78	9.53	—	6.95
1971	5.76	6.58	4.80	9.03	8.17	4.61	9.78	8.61	—	5.93
1972	5.18	5.46	4.39	7.88	7.40	4.56	8.98	7.72	—	4.97
1973	6.93	9.24	4.59	8.31	7.48	4.60	8.71	7.78	—	6.61
1974	14.57	11.01	8.06	14.22	10.20	5.29	12.00	10.85	15.32	15.61
1975	10.64	6.99	7.99	15.08	10.82	6.48	12.00	11.56	12.04	9.23
1976	15.68	5.58	10.95	17.33	13.39	6.58	14.45	14.35	17.81	14.25
1977	14.04	6.00	12.26	18.58	14.56	7.83	15.70	15.41	14.82	15.35
1978	11.50	8.73	10.66	16.00	13.33	7.23	15.45	14.02	11.44	12.51

*Confindustria calculation based on interest rates paid on bank loans, industrial bonds, and special credit institute loans (both ordinary and subsidized), weighted by composition of business liabilities in 1977.

Source: Compiled by the author; Bank of Italy bulletins and Confindustria Research Center Study, Secondo Rapporto CSC sull' Industria Italiana, Vol. 1 (Rome: 1979), p. 22.

BIBLIOGRAPHY

Books

Allen, Kevin, and Andrew A. Stevenson. An Introduction to the Italian Economy. London: Martin Robertson, 1974.

Banco di Roma. The Italian Banking System. Rome, 1974.

Earle, John. Italy in the 1970s. Newton Abbot, England: David and Charles, 1975.

Hildebrand, George H. Growth and Structure in the Economy of Modern Italy. Cambridge, Mass.: Harvard University Press, 1965.

Hughes, H. Stuart. The United States and Italy. 3rd ed. Cambridge, Mass.: Harvard University Press, 1979.

Lutz, Vera. Italy: A Study in Economic Development. Oxford: Oxford University Press, 1962. (Reprinted, Westport, Conn.: Greenwood Press, 1975.)

Podbielski, Gisele. Italy: Development and Crisis in the Postwar Economy. Oxford: Clarendon Press, 1974.

Official Documents

Bank of Italy. Bollettino ("Bulletin"). Various issues, 1960–79. Rome.

Bank of Italy. Modello Econometrico dell' Economia Italiana (II Edizione—M2 BI). Settore Monetario e Finanziario. Rome: 1979.

Bank of Italy. Relazione Annuale ("Annual Report"). Annual issues, 1959–78. Rome.

ISTAT. Annuario di Contabilità Nazionale. Various annual issues, 1970–77.

ISTAT. Bollettino Mensile di Statistica ("Bulletin"). Various monthly issues, 1960–79. Rome.

ISTAT. Compendio Statistico. Annual issues, 1959-78. Rome.

ISTAT. Conti Economici Nazionali 1960-78 (Nuova serie). Rome: 1979.

ISTAT. "Note e Relazioni" No. 56. 1979.

Ministry of Budget and Planning and Ministry of Treasury. Relazione Generale sulla Situazione del Paese ("Relazione Generale"). Annual issues, 1959-78. Rome.

Ministry of Treasury. Conto Riassuntivo del Tesoro (published in Gazzetta Ufficiale). Various monthly issues, 1960-79. Rome.

Journals and Periodicals

Ackley, Gardner. "Outlook for Italy—Down the Drain to Bangladesh." Challenge (March/April 1979): 6-14.

Alessandrini, Pietro. "Lagged Development and Structural Imbalances: the Relative Position of Italy." Banca Nazionale del Lavoro Quarterly Review No. 129 (June 1979): 133-53.

Blancus, Paolo. "The Common Agricultural Policy and Balance of Payments of the EEC Member Countries." Banca Nazionale del Lavoro Quarterly Review No. 127 (December 1978): 355-70.

Cavallari, Francesco, and Gino Faustini. "Labour Costs and Employment in Italy and the EC." Banca Nazionale del Lavoro Quarterly Review No. 126 (September 1978): 251-69.

Ciocca, Pierluigi, Renato Filosa, and Guido Maria Rey. "Integration and Development of the Italian Economy 1951-1971: a Re-evaluation." Banca Nazionale del Lavoro Quarterly Review No. 114 (September 1975): 284-320.

Confindustria. Rassegna di Statistiche del Lavoro. No. 2-3 (1979): 64.

____. Secondo Rapporto CSC sull' Industria Italiana. Rome: 1979.

Contini, Bruno. "The Labour Market in Italy." Banco di Roma, Review of Economic Conditions in Italy 1 (1979): 93-114.

Cotula, Franco, and Paolo Gnes. "L'aggiustamento della bilancia dei pagamenti italiana nel breve periodo." Banca Nazionale del Lavoro, Moneta E Credito Vol. XXVIII No. 107 (September 1974): 231-60.

Dandri, Guido. "The Evolution of the Italian Housing Situation from 1951 to 1978." Banco di Roma, Review of the Economic Conditions in Italy Vol. XXXII No. 2-3 (March-May 1978): 137-52.

European Community. Economia Europea, No. 3 (July 1979).

Falchi, Giannandrea, and Mauro Michelangeli. "IMF Surveillance of Exchange Rates and Problems of the Vicious Circle." Internal Document, Bank of Italy Research Office (April 1974).

Faustini, Gino. "Wage Indexing and Inflation in Italy." Banca Nazionale del Lavoro Quarterly Review No. 119 (December 1976): 364-77.

Fazio, Antonio. "Monetary Policy in Italy from 1970 to 1978." Kredit und Kapital 2 (1979): 145-80.

Filosa, Renato, and Ignazio Visco. "Copertura delle retribuzioni e inflazione a tasso variabile." Banca Nazionale del Lavoro, Moneta e Credito Vol. XXX No. 119 (September 1977): 327-37.

_____. "L'unificazione del valore del punto di contingenza e il grado di indicizzazione delle retribuzioni." Banca Nazionale del Lavoro, Moneta e Credito Vol. XXX No. 117 (March 1977): 55-83.

Fogagnolo, Giorgio. "The Italian Energy Problem: A World View." Banco di Roma, Review of the Economic Conditions in Italy Vol. XXX No. 5 (September 1976): 385-402.

Frey, Luigi. "Il potenziale del lavoro in Italia." Documenti ISVET No. 50 (1975).

Fua, Giorgio. "Employment and Productive Capacity in Italy." Banca Nazionale del Lavoro Quarterly Review No. 122 (September 1977): 215-44.

_____. "Lagged Development and Economic Dualism." Banca Nazionale del Lavoro Quarterly Review No. 125 (June 1978): 123-34.

Gambale, Sergio. "The Crisis in Public Finance in Italy." Banca Nazionale del Lavoro Quarterly Review No. 128 (March 1979): 73-90.

Germozzi, Manlio. "Craft Industry in the Italian Economy Today."
Banco di Roma, Review of the Economic Conditions in Italy
Vol. XXXII No. 4 (July 1978): 201-16.

Girola, Angelo. "Machine Tools: Advanced Technology for Italian
Industry." Banco di Roma, Review of the Economic Conditions in
Italy Vol. XXXI No. 4-5 (July-September 1977): 221-39.

Goldstein, Morris. "Downward Price Inflexibility, Ratchet Effects
and the Inflationary Impact of Import Price Changes: Some Empirical Tests." IMF Staff Papers (November 1977): 569-612.

Gordon, Robert J. "World Inflation and Monetary Accommodation in
Eight Countries." Brookings Papers on Economic Activity II
(1977): 409-77.

Guantario, Luigi. "Tourism in Italy: Its Situation, Problems and
Prospects." Banco di Roma, Review of the Economic Conditions
in Italy Vol. XXXII No. 1 (January 1978): 41-55.

Hill, T. P. Profits and Rates of Return. Paris: OECD, August 1979.

International Monetary Fund. Exchange Arrangements and Exchange
Restrictions. Washington: IMF, 1979.

_____. International Financial Statistics. Various monthly issues,
1969-79. Washington.

ISFOL-Doxa. "Forme e caratteristiche della participazione al lavoro."
Osservatorio ISFOL No. 5 (September 1975).

Izzo, Luigi, and Luigi Spaventa. "Some Internal and External Effects
of the Rise in the Price of Oil." Banca Nazionale del Lavoro Quarterly Review No. 108 (March 1974): 12-27.

Leccisotti, Mario. "Sul problema del risanamento delle imprese."
Bancaria Vol. XXXII No. 1 (January 1977): 28-33.

Lubitz, Raymond. "The Italian Crises of the 1970s." Federal Reserve
Board, International Finance Discussion Papers, No. 120 (1978).

Massacesi, Ettore, and Maria Finzi. "The Labour Market in Italy."
Banco di Roma, Review of the Economic Conditions in Italy
Vol. XXXI No. 3 (May 1977): 117-36.

Mattei, Franco. "Considerazioni ovvie sulla struttura finanziaria delle imprese." Bancaria Vol. XXXII No. 10 (October 1976): 1004-10.

McClam, Warren D. "Targets and Techniques of Monetary Policy in Western Europe." Banca Nazionale del Lavoro Quarterly Review No. 124 (March 1978): 3-27.

Mediobanca. Dati Cumulativi di 856 Società Italiane (1968-1978). Milan: 1979.

Modigliani, Franco, and Tomaso Padoa-Schioppa. "The Management of an Open Economy with '100% Plus' Wage Indexation." Princeton University, Essays in International Finance No. 130. Princeton, N.J.: 1978.

Modigliani, Franco, and Ezio Tarantelli. "Market Forces, Trade Union Action and the Phillips Curve in Italy." Banca Nazionale del Lavoro Quarterly Review No. 120 (March 1977): 3-36.

Monti, Mario. "Transfer Payments to the Business Sector and Crowding Out." Banca Commerciale Italiana, Monetary Trends No. 14 (August 1979): 1-10.

Onofri, Rino. "The Italian Budgetary System." Banco di Roma, Review of Economic Conditions in Italy 2 (1979): 289-306.

Organization for Economic Cooperation and Development. Demand for Money in Major OECD Countries. Economic Outlook Occasional Studies. Paris: OECD, 1979.

_____. Economic Outlook. Paris: July 1979, p. 41.

_____. Monetary Policy in Italy. Monetary Studies Series. Paris: OECD, 1973.

_____. Patterns of Resources Devoted to Research and Experimental Development in the OECD Areas, 1963-71. Paris: OECD, 1975.

Perry, George L. "Determinants of Wage Inflation Around the World." Brookings Papers on Economic Activity II (1975): 403-47.

Quagliariello, Ernesto. "The State of Scientific Research in Italy." Banco di Roma, Review of the Economic Conditions in Italy Vol. XXXI No. 6 (November 1977): 357-73.

Ragone, Gerardo. "Sociological Aspects of the Evolution of Consumption in Italy." Banco di Roma, Review of the Economic Conditions in Italy Vol. XXXII No. 2-3 (March-May 1978): 105-19.

Rossi, Enzo, and Pietro Viola. "'Leads and Lags' della bilancia dei pagamenti dell' Italia negli ultimi anni e fattori che influiscono sul loro andamento." Bancaria Vol. XXXII No. 11 (November 1976): 1102-17.

Sachs, Jeffrey D. "Wages, Profits and Macroeconomic Adjustment: A Comparative Study." Brookings Papers on Economic Activity 2 (1979): 269-332.

Savona, Paolo. "The Italian Industrial Structure: Problems and Prospects." Banco di Roma, Review of Economic Conditions in Italy 1 (1979): 41-63.

Sicca, Lucio. "The Food Industry in Italy and its Growth Prospects." Banco di Roma, Review of the Economic Conditions in Italy Vol. XXXII No. 2-3 (March-May 1978): 121-36.

Spaventa, Luigi. "Ancora sul grado di copertura del salario: un' estensione dell' analisi." Banca Nazionale del Lavoro, Moneta e Credito Vol. XXX No. 118 (June 1977): 217-27.

Troi, Giorgio. "Il rendimento del risparmio finanziaro delle famiglie Italiane dal 1964 al 1976." Banca Nazionale del Lavoro, Moneta e Credito Vol. XXX No. 118 (June 1977): 197-211.

Tullio, Giuseppe. "Le fluttuazioni della bilancia dei pagamenti Italiana: un' analisi empirica della teoria classica." Banca Nazionale del Lavoro, Moneta e Credito Vol. XXXI No. 123 (September 1978): 311-27.

Ulizzi, Adalberto. "Exchange Rate, Relative Inflation and Competitiveness: The Italian Case." Banco di Roma, Review of the Economic Conditions in Italy Vol. XXXI No. 4-5 (July-September 1977): 241-57.

U.S. Department of Labor, Bureau of Labor Statistics. Industrial Disputes, Workers Involved and Worktime Lost, Fourteen Countries, 1955-78. June 1979.

_____. Output per Hour, Hourly Compensation, and Unit Labor Costs in Manufacturing, Eleven Countries, 1950-78. July 1979.

Vaciago, Giacomo. "Monetary Policy in Italy: the Limited Role of Monetarism." Banca Nazionale del Lavoro Quarterly Review No. 123 (December 1977): 333–48.

Valiani, Rolando. "Italian Public Finances." Banco di Roma, Review of Economic Conditions in Italy 1 (1979): 65–92.

Visco, Ignazio. "L'indicizzazione delle retribuzioni in Italia: analysi settoriale e stime per il 1978–79." Rivista di Politica Economica Vol. VII (July 1979): 807–37.

Willett, Thomas D., and Leroy Laney. "Monetarism, Budget Deficits, and Wage Push Inflation: The Cases of Italy and the U.K." Banca Nazionale del Lavoro Quarterly Review No. 127 (December 1978): 315–31.

INDEX

agriculture: credit to, 246, 275–76; economic growth, 94-95, 95-98; food deficit, 95, 96, 176; investment, 96; profit squeeze, 96

autonomous entities: deficits [financing of, 79-81; treasury role, 53]; defined, 52; revenue sources, 54

balance of payments: in 1960s, 6-7; in 1970s, 172-74; capital account, 177, 179, 201-217; current account, 176-77, 214-17; outlook, 330-31; overall balance, 179, 212-16; trade account, 174-76 (see also compensatory borrowing, energy, exchange controls, exchange rate)

bank loans/investments: direct controls, 227-29, 265, 291-94, 302; growth of, 242-44

Bank of Italy (see financial institutions)

banks: net foreign position, 205, 212-16; structure, 220-21, 263-64 (see also exchange controls, monetary base)

"black" labor (see dual labor market)

budget: budget procedures, 59-61; growth of expenditures, 9, 71-74; growth of receipts, 68-71; reform, 60-64; residui attivi and passivi, 60-61; treasury deficit [in 1960s, 8; budget deficit, 68-74; defined, 53-54; effect on public consumption/ investment, 66-67; in 1970s, 64-68; "hot autumn," 16-17; impact on economy, 90; off-budget deficit, 75-84; outlook, 330-31] (see also autonomous entities, fiscal policy, local government, social insurance institutes, tax system, transfers, treasury)

capacity utilization, 156

capital flight, 7, 208-11

capital formation (see investment)

commodity prices (see import prices)

compensatory borrowing: in balance of payments, 16, 176-77, 179-80, 201, 204-5, 212-16; in monetary base, 230-31, 287

competitiveness (see exports)

construction (see industry)

consumption: in 1960s, 5; private, 116-19; public, 118-19, 273-74

credit multiplier, 240-41

credit, total domestic: 219, 232, 242, 294, 295

creditworthiness (see compensatory borrowing)

debt consolidation, health, hospital, local government: background, 72-74, 86-87, 242, 243, 244; of local governments, 81-82; structure of public sector, 52

discount rate: in 1960s, 8-9;

355

basic system, 225-26; use in 1970s, 297-99
dismissals (see job security)
dual labor market ("black" labor), 35-38, 330
dual exchange market (see exchange rate)

EC (see IMF)
economic growth: in 1960s, 3-5; in 1970s, 91-94, 140-42; outlook, 330-31; by sector, 94-102, 140-41; by type of expenditure, 114-30, 141-42 (see also income)
employment: in 1960s, 3-4; in 1970s, 93-94, 140, 142-43; growth by sector, 132-33, 133-36; policy, 320; profitability, 47-50
energy: and balance of payments, 176, 183, 186, 187, 187-92, 216; consumption, 117-18; production, 99; sources and uses, 187-89
Euromarket (see compensatory borrowing, interest rates)
exchange controls: in 1960s, 9; on banks' foreign position, 226-27; basic system, 304; capital outflow deposit, 229-30, 311; foreign finance of export credit, 230, 309, 311; payment terms, 231, 307, 308, 309, 310, 311; prior approval of capital outflow, 230; prior exchange deposit, 229, 269, 291, 309-10, 311; prior import deposit, 229, 289-91, 308; use in 1970s, 307-13, 317 (see also compensatory borrowing, foreign exchange tax)
exchange rate: in 1960s, 9;

and balance of payments adjustment, 203, 216-17; dual market, 307, 308, 313, 315; and inflation, 162, 163, 168; policy approach, 304-5, 306, 317; rate movements, 312-13, 315-16; vicious circle, 317
export credit, 206-207, 244-45, 246, 272, 276-77
export prices, 151, 181-82
exports: in 1960s, 5, 6; in balance of payments, 180-84; in GDP, 129-30 (see also energy, foreign sector)

financial institutions, 218, 219-24, 263-64
financial restructuring: business, 113
fiscal policy: expenditure policy [as a tool, 84, 86-87, 259-70; use of, 272-79]; tax policy [as a tool, 84, 269-70; use of, 270-72, 279]
fiscalization, of social insurance costs of employers, 50, 79, 272, 275
foreign loans/investment (see balance of payments—capital account)
foreign sector: in GDP, 129-30, 142; in monetary base, 238, 265, 282, 301

health insurance (see social insurance)
holding companies (see public enterprise)
"hot autumn," 11-17
housing: construction, 97-99, 275; sources of financing, 251 (see also rent controls)

IMF: credit ceilings, 294; credit

debt consolidation)

monetary base: in 1960s, 8; control of, 282-91; growth by source, 219, 233-40, 265; [central bank credit, 240, 289; foreign sector, 237-38, 282, 287; other, 240, 289, 291; treasury, 238-39, 287-89; growth by uses, 240-41; as target, 231-32, 235-36 (see also exchange controls, monetary tools)

monetary policy: in 1960s, 7-9; basic approach, 232-33, 281-82; "hot autumn," 16-17; use of in 1970s, 281-302

monetary targets, 218-19, 231-33, 265 (see also IMF)

monetary tools, 218, 225-31, 264-65 (see also bank loans/invest., discount rate, exchange controls, open market operations, reserve requirement, securities markets)

money supply: in 1960s, 8; growth in 1970s, 219, 254-58, 295-96; inflation, 160; velocity, 257

oil (see energy, import prices)

open market operations: in 1960s, 8-9; basic system, 226-27; use of, 287-89, 299

overtime: and excess demand, 158; limits on, 40-41

pensions (see social insurance)

population, 131

Postal Savings Fund: revenue source, 54; and structure of public sector, 52 (see also local government)

portfolio investment requirement (see bank loans/

investments)

price controls, 165-67, 171, 320-21, 324-25

prior deposits (see exchange controls)

productivity: in 1960s, 3-5; in 1970s, 38-44, 45-47

profitability: business survey, 125-26; and employment, 47, 50; by sector, 96, 99-100, 101; unit labor costs, 47

public administration: defined, 53; growth of, 102

public enterprise: endowment funds, 74, 272; public sector, 53; treasury financing, 53

public sector: defined, 52-54; revenue sources, 54

public service rates, 81, 83-84, 86, 154-56, 171, 325-26, 327

rent controls, 98-99, 165, 324 (see also housing)

research and development, 39-40

reserve requirement: in 1960s, 8-9; basic system, 225; use of, 291

revenue sharing, 82-84, 85-86 (see also tax reform)

saving: business, 112, 112-13, 126; household, 110-12, 251-52, 252-53; public, 68, 110; share by sector, 108, 110

scala mobile (wage indexation): basic system, 22-27, 322; and indirect taxes, 27-28, 271, 322, 327-28; revisions in, 322-23, 327-28; wage/price spiral, 26-27, 168

securities markets: approval of issues, 228-29; growth of, 246-47, 247-50; structure,

222, 223-24, 263-64

services: in balance of payments [in 1960s, 6-7; in 1970s, 192-201, 207, 217]; in GDP [economic growth, 100-2, 141; profit squeeze, 101]

severance pay (see social insurance)

short-time work: compensation for, 32-33, 321-22; excess demand, 156-58; and productivity, 38-39; use of, 136-37

social insurance: benefit payments, 76-78; contributions/ costs, 28-30, 76-77, 86-87; family allowances, 32; health/ hospital insurance, 31, 55, 73-74, 87; maternity allowances, 32; pension system, 23, 30-31, 78-79, 321-22, 324; redundancy pay, 33; severance pay, 33, 112-13; unemployment pay, 32, 321-22; ten wage supplements, 32-33; workmen's disability, 31 (see also fiscalization)

social insurance institutes: deficits, 28-29, 75-79; revenue sources, 54 (see also debt consolidation)

social reforms, 12, 14, 17

special credit institutes: credit growth, 244, 244-47; structure, 222, 263

state sector (see budget; Treasury deficit)

strikes: in 1970s, 41-44; in "hot autumn," 13-14; regulation of, 43, 44

subsidized credit, 246, 247, 261-63, 301 (see also special credit institutes)

tax elasticity, 68, 70

tax evasion, 58-59, 84-85

tax, foreign exchange, 309-10 310-11

tax reform, 55-56, 58, 84-86

tax system: in 1960s, 9; average tax, 68, 70-71, 112-13; structure, 55-58; tax rates, 56, 58

terms of trade, 168, 190

tourism (see services)

trade credit (see balance of payments; capital account)

transfers: in balance of payments [in 1960s, 6-7; in 1970s, 192-93, 194, 197, 200-1]; in budget [to business, 50, 74, 272-73; to households, 277; to rest of public sector, 72-74, 87-88, 90, 277]

Treasury: borrowing authority, 60-61; minor Treasury operations, 75-79 (see also budget)

Treasury bills (see open market operations)

turnover rate (see job security)

underground economy (see dual labor market)

unemployment: in 1960s, 12, 15-16; in 1970s, 136-40; job security, 47, 137-38; marginal, 138; real wages, 47; youth program, 324

unit labor costs: in 1960s, 6; in 1970s, 44-45; effect on economy, 45-50; inflation, 161-62; outlook, 329-30

"vicious circle" (see exchange rate)

wage contract applicability, 34, 35-36

ABOUT THE AUTHOR

DONALD C. TEMPLEMAN is Director of the Office of Developing Nations Finance in the Office of the Assistant Secretary for International Affairs of the U.S. Treasury Department. While writing this book he was a Federal Executive Fellow at the Brookings Institution in Washington, D.C. Prior to that time he had been Deputy Director of the Office of International Monetary Affairs and Treasury Attaché (1972-77) and Assistant Treasury Attaché (1962-65) at the American Embassy in Rome. He has had other foreign assignments with the U.S. Mission to the OECD and the U.S. Embassy in Bogotá, Colombia, as well as Washington assignments during a career of more than 20 years with the Treasury Department.

Mr. Templeman is the author of "Liberalization of Investments in the OECD" (Journal of World Trade Law, July/August 1972) and has participated in seminars concerning international monetary questions in Italy and the United States.

Mr. Templeman holds a B.S.C. degree in economics from the University of Iowa, an M.A. from the Fletcher School of Law and Diplomacy of Tufts University, and was a candidate for a Ph.D. in economics at George Washington University before his overseas assignments with the Treasury Department.